Victory at Home

Economy and Society in the Modern South

edited by Douglas Flamming and Bryant Simon

During the past half century, the American South has undergone dramatic economic and social transformations. Gone is the South of cotton fields and cotton mills, of monocrop agriculture and rudimentary industries, of desperate poverty and stultifying racial segregation. Gone is the South that Franklin Roosevelt saw as "the Nation's Number One economic problem." But if that South is gone, how can we explain the rise of the "Sunbelt," and what has economic change meant to southerners—their daily lives, their attitudes, their culture? This series aims to answer these critical questions through a multidisciplinary analysis of the region's economic and social development since World War II. It seeks to present the best new research by historians, economists, sociologists, and geographers—fresh scholarship that investigates unexplored topics and boldly reinterprets familiar trends.

The University of Georgia Press   *Athens and London*

Charles D. Chamberlain

VICTORY AT HOME

Manpower and Race in the American South during World War II

© 2003 by the University of Georgia Press
Athens, Georgia 30602

Designed by Louise OFarrell

Set in 10.5/13 Ehrhardt by Graphic Composition, Inc.,
Athens, Georgia
Printed and bound by Maple-Vail
The paper in this book meets the guidelines for permanence
and durability of the Committee on Production Guidelines
for Book Longevity of the Council on Library Resources.

Printed in the United States of America

06 05 04 03 02 C 5 4 3 2 1

06 05 04 03 02 P 5 4 3 2 1

Library of Congress Cataloging-in-Publication Data
Chamberlain, Charles D., 1964–
Victory at home : manpower and race in the American
South during World War II / Charles D. Chamberlain.
p. cm. — (Economy and Society in the Modern South)
Includes bibliographical references and index.
ISBN 0-8203-2429-9 (hardcover : alk. paper) — 0-8203-2443-4
(pbk. : alk. paper)
1. Manpower policy—Southern States—History—20th cen-
tury.   2. World War, 1939–1945—Manpower—Southern
States.   3. Labor supply—Southern States—History—20th
century.   4. African Americans—Employment—Southern
States—History—20th century.   5. Southern States—Rural
conditions.   6. Southern States—Race relations.   I. Title.
II. Series.
HD5725.S85 C48 2003
331.1′0975′09044—dc21   2002004969

British Library Cataloging-in-Publication Data available

To Charley and Nancy,
for living history

Contents

Acknowledgments

I want to acknowledge the many kind persons who provided me with assistance in the completion of this book. First, I thank Larry Powell for taking on the assignment of advising me despite the initial lack of specifics on this project. Many warm thanks go out to Bill Malone for suggesting a study of World War II in the South. Along the way, Marjorie Wheeler, Nan Woodruff, Patricia Sullivan, Michael Honey, Doug Flamming, Walter Hickel, and Jamie Carson all gave me encouragement and some very helpful suggestions.

Throughout my research travels I have felt a special gratitude to the archival staffs that assisted me. The staff at the National Archives in Fort Worth will always hold a special place in my heart, for it was there that the main ideas for this book emerged. Additionally, staff members at the National Archives in College Park, Atlanta, and San Bruno as well as those at the Maryland Room at the University of Maryland and the Special Collections at California State Universities at Long Beach and Northridge all provided invaluable assistance. In San Francisco Gene Vrana and Harvey Schwartz at the International Longshoremen's and Warehousemen's Union Archives guided me to material that filled in some very important human pieces to this story. Thank you all.

Closer to home, I want to express immense gratitude to my wife, Carolyn Thompson, for all her technical and emotional support as well as her love of history. To Carolyn, Josh, pets, and the rest of my extended family, I am eternally grateful for your unconditional love.

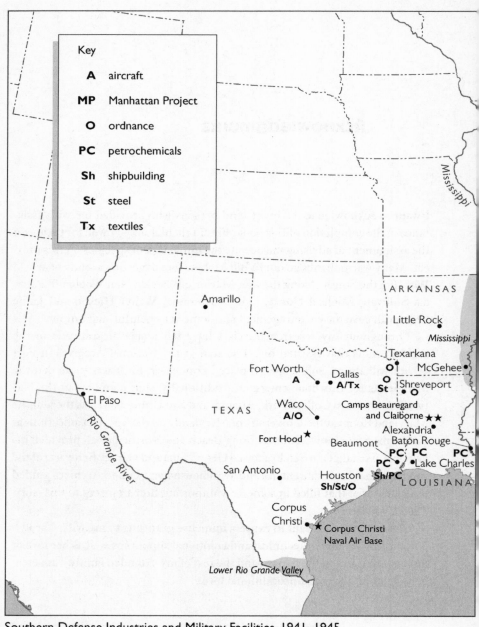

Key

A   aircraft

MP Manhattan Project

O   ordnance

PC petrochemicals

Sh shipbuilding

St steel

Tx textiles

Amarillo

ARKANSAS

Little Rock

Mississippi

Texarkana

Fort Worth **A**   Dallas **A/Tx**   **O**   McGehee

O   Shreveport

St   **O**

El Paso

TEXAS   Waco **A/O**

Camps Beauregard and Claiborne ★★

Rio Grande River

Fort Hood ★

Alexandria

Baton Rouge

Beaumont   **PC**   **PC**   **PC**

PC   Lake Charles

San Antonio

Houston   **Sh/PC**

Sh/St/O   LOUISIANA

Corpus Christi ★ Corpus Christi Naval Air Base

Lower Rio Grande Valley

Mississippi

Southern Defense Industries and Military Facilities, 1941–1945
Source: Information drawn from *Life Magazine* (1941, 1943)

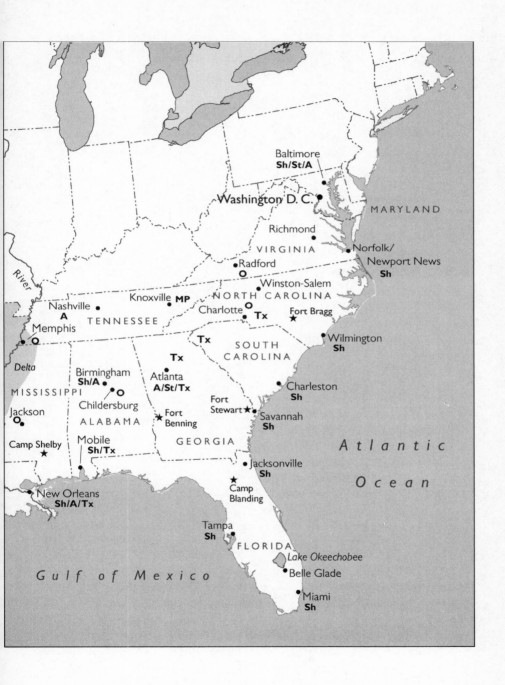

Baltimore
Sh/St/A

Washington D. C.

MARYLAND

Richmond

VIRGINIA

Norfolk/
Newport News
Sh

Radford
○

Winston-Salem

Knoxville **MP**

NORTH CAROLINA

Charlotte
○ **Tx**

Fort Bragg
★

Nashville
A

TENNESSEE

Tx

SOUTH
CAROLINA

Wilmington
Sh

Memphis
○

Tx

Delta

Birmingham
Sh/A ●

Atlanta
A/St/Tx

Charleston
Sh

MISSISSIPPI

○ Childersburg

Fort
Stewart ★

Savannah
Sh

Jackson
○

ALABAMA

★ Fort
Benning

GEORGIA

Camp Shelby
★

Mobile
Sh/Tx

Jacksonville
Sh

New Orleans
Sh/A/Tx

★ Camp
Blanding

A t l a n t i c

O c e a n

Tampa
Sh

FLORIDA

Lake Okeechobee

● Belle Glade

G u l f   o f   M e x i c o

Miami
Sh

Introduction

"Is This America?"

In early 1944 *Washington Post* reporter Agnes Meyer reflected on her yearlong tour of defense industries and communities across the United States. Throughout her journeys from Oregon to Florida and from California to New York, Meyer exposed the specific social welfare problems facing workers on the home front amidst the chaos of mobilization. In the shipyard communities of Mississippi and Alabama, where housing shortages and over-crowding were most extreme, Meyer recalled her shock at seeing "row upon row of tents, trailers and shacks inhabited by families who had emerged from the neglected rural areas of the southern states." As she informed readers, "These people are pitiful. The adults are usually illiterate, the children ragged, undernourished, disease-ridden. Talking to these people was the most difficult assignment I had. They are as shy as wild animals, suspicious and unfriendly even with their neighbors in a trailer or tent six feet away." The journalist then asked, "Is this America?" Answering affirmatively, Meyer warned that "uncivilized as these people may be, they are Americans, toward whom we have an inescapable responsibility. They are, moreover, so numerous that we must in self-defense pull these people up or they will pull the rest of the nation down."[1]

Agnes Meyer's concerns for these "pitiful" and "uncivilized" southerners reflect those of many federal policy makers and reformers during the New Deal and World War II. Prior to Meyer's work, federal art and literature projects such as Dorthea Lange and Paul Taylor's *An American Exodus* (1939) and James Agee and Walker Evans's *Let Us Now Praise Famous Men* (1941) hoped to spark public support for New Deal social welfare and reform programs by presenting southern families as impoverished victims of the region's faltering sharecropping and farm-tenant system. In popular American culture of this period, John Ford's cinematic adaptation of John Steinbeck's *The Grapes of Wrath* in 1940 brought the plight of landless, former sharecropping families in the Southwest (and hence the broader South) to American movie audiences, further enforcing the stereotype of a dignified yet somewhat desperate and primitive white family while advocating the merits of the Farm Security Administration (FSA).[2]

With mobilization for the Second World War, the housing and welfare problems facing war workers replaced New Dealers' concerns for unemployed workers and farmers in the Cotton Belt. And as the Great Depression transformed into the war boom during 1940 and 1941, New Deal programs covering worker housing, welfare, employment services, migrant labor, and health care were directed toward the care of war workers. More so than ever before, the federal government's expanded role during World War II meant that southern families were not autonomous actors in their struggle for economic security and a decent life. During these early war years, FSA photos exposing the welfare and housing problems in southern defense communities represented an important visual and physical link between the federal state and working families in the South.

At this intersection of southern workers' lives and federal agencies, this book explores working families' responses to the opportunities and changes that the war created on the southern home front. Proceeding past the contemporary views of photographers such as Dorthea Lange and journalists such as Agnes Meyer, this book examines the specific ways southern workers and their families utilized the mobilization process and federal programs to gain economic, social, and geographic mobility. For African American and Latino families especially, how did mobilization and federal manpower policies provide the means to overcome the economic, political, and social limitations of Jim Crow?

War workers in the American South were not merely trivial actors on the world stage. On the one hand, the region's workforce provided the foundation of southern elites' economic hegemony. It also held the key to American and Allied productive capabilities in the global conflict. In this context, where "surplus" southern workers emerged as a hot commodity for U.S. war industries, a full-blown political and economic struggle raged between war workers, black leaders, white southern elites, liberal New Dealers, and nonsouthern industrialists to use and shape federal mobilization agencies to meet their own needs. Since World War I and the New Deal, the local administering of federal welfare, housing, and labor agencies served as a basis for controlling workers in the South. This book explores the complex roots of this process during the 1940s as federal mobilization agencies became the battleground over labor control in the South and all of its political, economic, and social ramifications.

World War II in the American South: Old and New Perspectives

In the twenty-five years following World War II, U.S. historians failed to attach much significance to the war's impact on the American South. Federal photographers and some of the region's writers certainly recognized the more profound changes that mobilization wrought on southern society during the conflict. Yet not until the 1960s did scholars really (re)discover the "modern South" and its place in the twentieth century. From the perspective of a quarter century later and more, observers could more readily appreciate the transformation that the war brought about in terms of federal expenditures for military industries and interstate highways as well as the war's effect on race relations. By the late 1960s, the civil rights movement, led in part by many veterans, partially dismantled segregation and disfranchisement, causing a reordering of the modern South's social, political, and economic fabric.[3]

Gradually since the 1960s, the parameters of an emerging debate over the Second World War's effect on the South began to take shape. In 1982 Morton Sosna posited that the war may have had a greater impact on the region than even the Civil War.[4] A few years thereafter, James Cobb emphasized the region's more enduring economic characteristics when he argued that despite the war's modernizing effects, the southern economy still rested on its ability to sell a business friendly image of antiunion practices and low wages.[5] Between Sosna and Cobb, historians began to recognize how, in fact, the southern experience conveyed an intricate mix of change and continuity, action and reaction, progress and retraction between the depression and the cold war.

As an extension of the New Deal, war mobilization centered to a large degree on the federal presence in the South. This continued and expanded federal presence has led some historians to characterize the war as a second New Deal. Whereas historian Pete Daniel describes the New Deal in the South as "complex, contradictory, and revolutionary," this work examines the war's ambiguous and far-reaching consequences in the region. Since the 1980s historians have explored federal war mobilization policies as they extended from New Deal programs, and many, like Daniel, emphasize the paradoxical nature of federal policy as it was administered in the South during this period. Foremost among recent works is Bruce Schulman's study of the South's transformation from the nation's number one economic problem, according to FDR, to the modern Sunbelt. As Schulman contends, federal New Deal laws and war policies certainly pulled the suburban South into the American economic mainstream, even as southern states maintained economic and social segregation and employers excluded African Americans from the new, high-wage, federally financed military and aerospace industries during the 1950s and 1960s.[6]

In searching for the origins of the modern South and Southwest, new labor and civil rights historians have illuminated the lives of workers as they were affected by federal mobilization and labor policies during the war. Drawing from and moving beyond the limited perspectives of Works Progress Administration (WPA) artists and liberal writers from the 1940s, many new historians illustrate how southern families' own outlook toward the depression and war mobilization was in fact very complex and shaped by a great variety of circumstances. No longer the stereotypical white migrant family documented by Dorthea Lange and Agnes Meyer, southern workers and their families have emerged as diverse, active agents of their own destinies during the war as they utilized a variety of strategies, including migration, institution building, and labor organizing to improve their lives and gain economic security.[7]

Given the increasingly sophisticated analysis of World War II's effect on the South, this book examines the nuances of mobilization at the local and regional levels and how southern workers emerged at the center of a political and economic struggle over the future of the region and the United States. The war provides an excellent context for studying the intersection of working families and the federal state in the South, because the rapid economic development and augmented federal presence signaled a meaningful transformation in the lives of most southerners. Moreover, the war's large-scale and almost overnight industrialization offers a rich historical backdrop for examining struggles within and outside of the South over the recruitment and organizing of southern workers for defense industries.

Because the workplace was the center of African American demands for civil rights during the war, black workers and labor activists emerge as important leaders in the regional and national struggle for democracy in the United States. At a time when the slogan "Victory at Home and Abroad" symbolized the black struggle for civil rights, African Americans used jobs and fair employment to force the federal government into acting on the promise of equality.[8] In the South, where the question of racial equality held profound implications for American society, black workers' crusade for economic equality and a "victory at home" presented a crucial test of American democracy. Importantly, this struggle over jobs reveals a great deal about African American goals and strategies during the war as well as those of white workers, New Deal liberals, southern elites, and defense industrialists, all of whom hoped to gain from mobilization.

In many respects, the fair employment question during the war would serve as a harbinger of battles over civil and states' rights after the war. As historian Merl Reed contends, the 1940s were a "seedtime" of the modern civil rights movement. Since the 1970s Reed and other historians have explored the wartime battle over jobs and civil rights through the activities of the Fair Employment Practices Commission (FEPC), the federal agency President Roosevelt created to fight discrimination in America's defense industries. Yet, whereas Reed has focused largely on the administrative aspects of the agency in Washington, scholars have more recently begun to uncover the stories of the FEPC at the local and state levels in the South. Among these new labor and civil rights studies, a few have focused on grassroots labor movements in which workers and civil rights leaders, in conjunction with the FEPC at the local level, mobilized for fair employment, with mixed results. As historians gain a greater understanding of the intersection of workers and the state in the workplace, this book seeks to provide a regional synthesis of this struggle for equality and, specifically, the ways in which local African American civil rights and labor activists initiated an indigenous jobs movement with support from liberal allies in the FEPC and the War Manpower Commission (WMC) across the South and Southwest.[9]

The networks that developed over the manpower issue are important because they reflect the growing political sophistication of black leadership during the war. Recently, political scientist Daniel Kryder has provided an advanced analysis of African American strategies for gaining economic concessions from the Roosevelt administration and the role that the national labor shortage played in providing African Americans with political leverage on the home front.[10] This book adds to this growing body of work by looking at this power struggle in the South and the ways that labor mobilization brought southern workers to the forefront of regional and national debates over the future of the South in terms of economic and social equality. Even as African Americans and Latinos sought to use the war and the expanded federal presence to their advantage, white workers and employers resisted this movement for fair employment in the South and all it represented. In this battle, the effort of both white workers and management to preserve racial inequality in the workplace foretold the rise of massive resistance ten and fifteen years later.

The Cotton Belt at the Crossroads, 1939

During the 1930s, as white southern leaders began to realize that the era of economic isolation and the undisputed reign of cotton were coming to an end, they nonetheless tried to preserve their control over the region's labor force as a means of maintaining their social, political, and economic hegemony. It is this fundamentally conservative movement that stood at the center of conflict within the American South as it groped its way toward economic recovery and modernization. In their quest to maintain political and economic control, white conservatives largely sought to direct the administration of federal farming, industry, labor, and welfare programs in the region to their benefit.

By 1939 New Deal policies along with the decline of cotton culture transformed the South's social, economic, and political order in both subtle and dramatic ways. Because the region's social and political order rested on poverty, dependence, and racial segregation among the region's workers, New Deal programs and farming trends that affected the status of workers therefore threatened the existing racial and social hierarchy. Under Agriculture Adjustment Administration (AAA) acreage reduction programs, rural labor relations shifted abruptly from the sharecropping system to a wage labor system. Over the decade, close to a million southern families found themselves forced off the land and facing economic insecurity. Like other enclosure movements around the world, the process of displacement in the South was quite uneven and fraught with ambivalence among both the region's economic elite and the working families affected directly.[11]

New Deal policies affecting the region's manufacturing industries also had a tremendous impact on the South's social and economic order. Under the National Industrial Recovery Act (NIRA), southern industries grudgingly acquiesced to national labor standards, while employers also displaced low-wage, unskilled workers, many of whom were African American. After 1935 other important New Deal acts ushered in more challenges to southern labor relations. With the passage of the Social Security Act in 1935, many southern workers gained new ties to the federal welfare state and loosened the bonds of

6

dependence to local institutions. With the National Labor Relations Act (Wagner Act) passed that same year, southern workers gained the right to bargain collectively for the first time. The act precipitated the emergence of interracial organizing of industrial workers by the newly formed Congress of Industrial Organizations (CIO) throughout the South, a symbolic threat to segregation in the workplace. In the following years, the Bankhead-Jones Farm Tenant Act of 1937 and the Fair Labor Standards Act of 1938 further challenged the status quo of labor and race relations in the South by addressing the low wages and exploitative conditions within southern industries, including agriculture.[12]

The economic changes initiated through New Deal laws and federal programs did represent symbolic challenges to the region's status quo. Yet because poverty and dependence were the economic underpinnings to the region's labor system, white southern elites often co-opted or evaded any federal programs that threatened their dominance through the reforming of working conditions and wages. Hence, during the Great Depression, southern industrial and agricultural economies underwent profound structural changes, and employers generally preserved the region's social and racial hierarchy. While southern conservatives made every attempt to preserve their economic hegemony, Franklin Roosevelt, along with liberal New Dealers and social reformers, continued to seek solutions to the region's economic underdevelopment.

On the verge of World War II, southern poverty had emerged as a national issue not only through New Deal programs directed at economic recovery but also through the popular media's coverage of migrants and evicted sharecroppers. Yet no national or regional consensus existed regarding the strategies that would be best suited for lifting the region out of its economic depression. In many respects, southern workers stood at the center of the debate between liberals and conservatives over the South's recovery. On the one hand, the New Deal policy makers and social reformers emphasized the impoverished conditions of the region's working families and advocated increased federal involvement. On the other hand, southern economic boosters underscored the region's potential for industrial manufacturing, promoting the South's low wages and "docile" workforce as the basis for successful economic expansion.[13]

Overcoming their different concerns over the reform and exploitation of southern workers, by 1940 both conservative boosters and liberal reformers embraced visionary schemes, such as that promoted by the *Dallas Morning News*, that described farming regions "dotted with large and small factories making plastics, starch, synthetic fibers, paper, rapid drying oils, serving food and other technical industries." Beginning in 1937, a new crusade for economic development under the banner "Balance Agriculture with Industry" (BAWI) began in Mississippi as an effort to raise economic standards within the region. By late 1939 and 1940, the BAWI movement became *the* regional slogan for progress among prodevelopment southern leaders and especially the Southern Governors Conference. In 1940 national economic boosters hailed the region's first newsprint mill at the Southland Paper Mills in Lufkin, Texas, as an indicator of industrial trends and a symbol of southern economic balance. That same year, a new United States Department of Agriculture (USDA) Regional Research Laboratory in New Orleans also symbolized the integration of agriculture and manufacturing in the South.[14]

Conservatives largely drove the BAWI movement within the South, yet, increasingly, more persons within and outside of the region viewed the possibility of new industries as a solution to underemployment and the rural crisis. In 1939, W. C. Lassetter, editor of *Progressive Farmer,* told national agronomists that "the South has need of increased industry to provide employment for labor displaced by the greater use of machinery on the farms." Likewise, noteworthy southern liberals such as Howard Odum, Rupert Vance, and members of the Southern Conference of Human Welfare also began openly to support the use of manufacturing to employ surplus farm labor. With war approaching and southerners looking to the federal government for defense projects, those persons concerned with the depressed state of agriculture hoped prospective defense industries would relieve a situation the *New Orleans Times-Picayune* described as "temporary distress" in the cotton and cane areas.[15]

Despite the rosy vision of southern boosters promoting new industries in the South, their plan faced some serious contradictions. To start, the displacement of sharecroppers and tenants throughout the cotton and cane regions would outpace USDA research and the building of new rural industries in the South. As Pete Daniel suggests, southern cotton displacement was one aspect of the ongoing capitalization of agriculture, well out of the hands of small farmers. Under USDA policies, commercial farmers increasingly sought to build a capitalist structure more like that of the business world. Despite small farmers' hopes, chemurgic research emerged from the scientific farming movement promoted by the USDA and the department's alliance with southern politicians, the Extension Service, land-grant universities, and the Farm Bureau, all of which encouraged commercial farmers at the expense of the tenant class.[16]

Second, the exclusion of African Americans from many new southern industries meant that a large percentage of displaced rural southerners could not benefit directly from the industry campaign. As industrialists discovered with the wave of new war industries in 1940 and 1941, black workers and community labor leaders largely resented white expectations that African Americans would return to the farms, while displaced white families from rural areas got war jobs easily. The new industries actively maintained the regional system of economic segregation in the workplace.

Despite the prevalent rhetoric of patriotism and duty through war work, African Americans found themselves excluded from new industries in the same manner they had been initially barred from New Deal public works projects and welfare programs. Black and Latino employees who did get industry jobs were relegated to unskilled jobs, unequal pay, and often a Jim Crow working environment. Ultimately, this labor policy encouraged black underemployment and poverty as a means of maintaining racial hierarchy and dependence. African Americans in the South were keenly aware of this reality and used a variety of means, including migration and active protest, to overcome these economic limitations and the false rhetoric of boosters.

Race and Worker Mobility in the American South

By 1939 the American South stood at a crossroad between its agricultural past and an uncertain industrial future. Even with the promise of industry raising economic standards within the region, southern boosters were often ambivalent about the actual effect of industry on the region's labor force. In many respects, southern businessmen benefited greatly from the region's surplus labor pool during the Great Depression. Thus, as the process of displacement severed the bonds of dependency between growers and rural workers, many employers insisted on maintaining some economic and social control over their workers. While the initial growth of war industries in 1940 fulfilled the vision of a region dotted with manufacturing plants, the region's employers in traditional, low-wage industries faced new challenges when workers left to seek federal defense dollars and African American workers demanded access to training and employment opportunities. Mobilization thus enabled the region's working families to gain unprecedented geographic and economic mobility and in the process threatened the South's culture of poverty and dependence.

As the war intensified during 1940, southern labor became a valuable commodity for American production. The federal government, southern employers, and nonsouthern industries battled over the allocation of the region's surplus labor force. In this struggle, control of southern labor emerged as a central concern for these powerful interests as well as for the workers themselves, who for their part sought to use mobilization to gain economic mobility and a possible ticket out of the low-wage South. In this context, workers' physical mobility became a powerful symbol of freedom and economic democracy for southerners and especially African Americans.

Since Reconstruction, worker mobility had characterized southern employment and the region's sharecropping system. Throughout the Cotton Belt, many sharecropper and tenant families moved about in search of a better deal on housing or crop shares. As rural areas of the South and Southwest industrialized during the Gilded Age, farming families also sought to supplement their incomes with work in textiles, mining, tobacco, and food processing. Such seasonal work initially involved moving short distances between farms, mills, mines, or camps, yet by the early twentieth century, workers found themselves annually migrating between rural areas, small towns, and cities to work these seasonal industries.

The ranks of migrant and seasonal industry workers expanded dramatically during the 1920s and 1930s as farming operations became more mechanized and capitalized and New Deal farm policies released rural families from the land throughout the Cotton Belt. Dorthea Lange and Paul Taylor, along with other federal WPA artists, took particular notice of the thousands of displaced rural persons and seasonal workers. Many of the families documented by the artists were former tenants and sharecroppers who found themselves "tractored off" the land into the new role of day-wage farmworkers. Other small farming families found themselves foreclosed because of environmental problems (such as the dust bowl and erosion) or a general inability to compete in the depressed cotton market. With the growing displacement of this rural peasant and laborer class from the land and the return of urban workers to rural areas, migrant farm labor ranks swelled close to a million persons during the 1930s.[17]

Hence, on the eve of World War II, the regional labor force was largely seasonal and migratory, and worker mobility remained an integral component of both rural and urban economies. In the urban South and Southwest, industries such as textiles and garments, tobacco and food processing, railroads, steel, and woodworking employed workers on a seasonal basis and resisted new attempts to organize workers. In the rural areas, the large, mechanized, and absentee-owned farming operations also depended on migrant laborers at peak harvest and planting seasons. From California to Mississippi, large-scale cotton and vegetable farms employed Mexican immigrants as well as former cotton tenants. In the southeastern states, cotton, vegetable, and fruit growers depended on tens of thousands of white and African American migrant families, many recently expelled from the land.[18]

As New Dealers promoted federal programs to reform the lives of rural families and economic refugees in the cities, southern business and especially agricultural interests used these same federal programs to immobilize workers and drive wages downward. Beginning with the initial federal relief projects in the South under the Civilian Works Administration in 1933, local southern elites who had interests in large farming operations manipulated state and county welfare offices to insure that farmworkers would work for low wages during harvest and that the workers did not become economically independent enough to forgo farm labor jobs. In southern Louisiana, for example, during the autumn of 1937 state relief administrators removed African Americans from the local WPA relief rolls and Civilian Conservation Corps (CCC) camps until the sugarcane harvest concluded. Continuously through the 1930s in Louisiana, Mississippi, Alabama, and Georgia, state and local relief officials within state Unemployment Compensation (UC) offices removed rural families from the welfare rolls and federal works projects during harvesttime. To the West, growers and relief officials from Texas to California also reduced state welfare rolls to create surplus labor pools and thereby drive wages down during the depression.[19]

Farming and seasonal industries also influenced other federal agencies that controlled labor in the South and Southwest. After 1935, federally affiliated State Employment Service (SES) offices provided free public employment placement services that served both workers and businesses. In the South, the majority of SES offices in the region supplied mostly unskilled and nonwhite workers to a variety of low-wage industries, including domestic service, construction, and especially agriculture. Hence, local elites used state employment offices as a means of contracting low-wage, unskilled labor. Under the Social Security Act of 1935, state UC and SES offices united under one department within all states, and they were administered out of one office at the local level. The more centralized local office arrangement allowed local elites to recruit low-wage workers directly from welfare rolls for farming and domestic service jobs. This consolidated system thus enabled local industrial and farming interests to essentially control welfare and job placement services at the local level.

After 1935, the Resettlement Administration (RA) and its successor, the Farm Security Administration (FSA), emerged as the major political battleground over the issue of labor control and worker mobility in the South and Southwest. To the consternation of rural capitalists in the South, the FSA promoted the yeoman ideal through various "back to the land" programs such as homesteading, loans for buying farms, and even experimental farming settlements. The FSA's agenda reflected the New Deal impulse toward economic recovery and social reform, and the agency did provide aid to a considerable number of farmers. While the economic reality of depressed agricultural markets made any FSA homestead and loan programs ineffective, conservatives throughout the Cotton Belt resented the federal effort to help low-income rural persons become economically independent.[20]

The FSA's other major program, that of reforming the migrant labor system throughout the South and Southwest, also illustrated the complex role that federal agencies maintained with small farmers and industrial growers in the region. In its migrant labor program, the FSA hoped to reform the exploitative system of labor contracting and poor migrant worker housing, health, and working conditions. From California to Florida, local growers resisted such efforts to give farmworkers any leverage in the labor market. As part of its agenda to reform the migrant labor system, the FSA worked hand in hand with SES offices to provide labor for industrial growers in Florida, Louisiana, Texas, and the western Cotton Belt. But because the FSA's agenda stressed reform and encouraged mobility, most growers avoided it or openly opposed its presence in rural areas.

Hence by 1939, close to a million landless families in the South sought economic security in a region where labor control stood at the center of the region's changing society and economy. The fact that a large majority of these families were African American and Mexican American was of no small significance in a region where labor and race relations were often inseparable. Whiteness in the South and Southwest gave the celebrated landless white farming families the ability to gain economic mobility without many social limitations and often plenty of state support through federal vocational training and job placement. For the region's nonwhite families, who were largely ignored by the media, the mobilization process often challenged regional labor and race traditions that encouraged economic insecurity and hence dependence on local white patrons and economic elites. As black and Latino families overcame the control of southern employers and the limitations of segregation in both small and large ways and through both passive and active means, their efforts represented a significant shift in southern race relations and, hence, within American society.

Mobilizing Southern Workers for American Industry

As white, African American, and Latino families sought economic and social mobility outside of the Cotton Belt, their migration to and settlement in the North and the West left an indelible mark on American society. Communities outside the South reacted in a variety of ways to southern migrants, but, most often, southern families' presence in these nonsouthern communities challenged American society's own views about national identity and the meaning of equality. As northern and western cities found themselves experiencing racial problems long attributed to peculiar southern racial conservatism, their responses revealed much about white attitudes toward culture and race throughout the United States.

This book tells the story of national mobilization and the strategies that working people in the American South utilized to improve their own lives. Thus, while the focus is on southern workers and their families, the story itself is one that involves the entire United States. If one subscribes to the argument that U.S. production capacity won the war, then one has to acknowledge how southern families were absolutely integral to an Allied victory. Ironically, as southern employers valued the region's labor surplus and the economic desperation of its workers, so too did defense contractors and federal labor recruiters throughout the West and North look on the South's workforce as the key to providing labor for their expanding war industries. By recruiting "help from the hinterland," as one Ohio industry referred to southern workers, northern and western industries changed the social fabric of the United States forever.[21]

The mobilization of southern workers was a process that changed and challenged the national identity of the United States as a multiracial society. As southerners moved into nonsouthern cities, their racial and cultural baggage affected working communities everywhere. In this context of national mobilization, this study examines workers' ability to achieve economic security as well as geographic and social mobility. Workers throughout the South sought to negotiate the complex world of both southern and national labor relations during the war in an attempt to improve their own lives. In essence, families and workers utilized a wide variety of strategies, including union organizing, direct action protest over discrimination, job shopping, migration, and federal labor recruitment to make their lives more secure. Whereas many families throughout the United States also used these same actions to climb the nation's economic ladder, southern families' ability to gain economic and social mobility symbolized the crossing of a new threshold of economic and social change for themselves, the South, and the nation at large. For African American and Latino families from the Cotton Belt, mobilization engendered a new commitment to realizing economic and social equality in a war for democracy at home.

1. Tents, Trailers, and Shack Towns

Mobilizing the Southern Home Front, 1939–1942

In January 1941, *Life* magazine reported on the progress of military construction projects throughout the United States. While painting a flattering portrait of a new Du Pont ordnance plant in Charlestown, Indiana, the popular journal also focused on the housing problems at Camp Blanding, a new military base outside Starke, Florida. One photograph in particular displayed what *Life* described as a camp of "penniless migrant workers and their families" that had sprung up "along roadsides and in vacant lots" near the base. "Hoping to get a job," the caption explained, families "threw up flimsy shelters, lived shivering and starving amidst hogs and mangy dogs." And as construction neared completion, the magazine assured readers, "most of these vagrants wandered away" and "looked for jobs further South."[1]

That winter, Camp Blanding represented the extreme example of a booming construction economy on the southern home front. When the building first began near Starke, some 32,000 persons showed up at Florida SES offices to apply for some 22,000 jobs.[2] Like many construction boomtowns throughout the United States, Starke, Florida, found itself overrun with migrant workers and their families living out in the open. In this context, *Life* chose to focus on the extremes of worker poverty and housing conditions in the South. Of course, not all migrant workers and their families lived with mangy dogs and swine in southern defense boomtowns. Such projects attracted a great variety of classes and Americans from every state. However, the specter of so many low-income migrant families from the South living in rather desperate housing and sanitation conditions undoubtedly appalled more sheltered Americans during a time when *The Grapes of Wrath*—through both John Steinbeck's novel and John Ford's movie—had illustrated the tragic plight of displaced rural families.

Across much of the American South during the Second World War, tent communities, trailer camps, and shack towns sprang up on the outskirts of developing towns. With the rapid expansion of war industries, workers seeking better wages flocked to defense industry boomtowns in the South. Some of these workers earned in one hour what some farmworkers made in a single day.[3] On the threshold of war, the uncontrolled movement of workers within the South resulted largely from New Deal agricultural policies and technological changes in cotton production. A declining sharecropping and tenant system forced many farmworkers onto seasonal migrant worker trails. As the region's surplus manpower attracted new industries and defense contractors, competition between white and black workers for war jobs as well as increased efforts to organize unions in southern industries made the process of economic development in the depressed region both complex and profoundly disruptive. With the war's abrupt infusion of government capital and, hence, greater federal control, the South faced complex questions over states' rights, the increased presence of organized labor, and the role of African American workers in a new industrial era.

World War II hit the American South at a time when southern economic boosters hoped to "balance agriculture with industry," a slogan that symbolically promoted economic diversification while acquiescing to the needs of agriculture. For the region's labor force, balancing agricultural and industrial needs meant ideally that industrial employers maintained de facto employment policies that gave all new industrial jobs to white workers to avoid any competition with growers over the region's predominantly African American and Latino rural labor force. Despite this ideal, the mobilization process threatened to upset this "balance" and with it the traditional class and race relations that undergirded white political and economic control in the South. Hence, employers in these low-wage industries used both legal and extra-legal means to hinder the exodus of their workers to defense industries.

In the initial stages of worker mobilization and contract procurement, alliances between the American Federation of Labor (AFL) and federal production and manpower agencies, particularly, the Office of Production Management (OPM) and the Bureau of Employment Security (BES), sustained this labor caste system under the pretext of preserving racial harmony. Thus, in defense industries, wage scales and job classification reflected the greater racial hierarchy that favored white workers. In this context, management and more conservative organized labor leaders reserved skilled trades and most jobs generally for rural white in-migrants and thereby limited nonwhites to unskilled positions or declined to hire them at all. However, in coastal cities with large African American populations, such as Charleston, Mobile, Tampa, New Orleans, and Beaumont, the continued employment of rural white in-migrants at the expense of local nonwhite labor exacerbated community tensions, overcrowding and overburdening local government services. In coastal cities that encouraged white in-migration, the proliferation of tent cities and shack towns symbolized the social chaos endemic to the southern home front.

A Southern Dilemma: War Mobilization and Federal Planning

Beginning in 1940, defense contractor money transformed rural communities into boomtowns overnight, and the subsequent housing problems attracted national media attention.[4] Migrant tent and trailer settlements encircled Fort Bragg near Fayetteville, North Carolina; as noted earlier, similar growth occurred around Camp Blanding outside of Starke, Florida. The same conditions existed at Fort Stewart near Savannah and at Fort Benning east of Columbus, Georgia; at Craig Air Force Base on the outskirts of Selma, Alabama; at Camp Shelby outside of Hattiesburg, Mississippi; at Camps Beauregard and Claiborne near Alexandria, Louisiana; and at Corpus Christi Naval Air Base near Corpus Christi, Texas. For many such communities, the militarization at the beginning of the Second World War led to a new economic boon for local services and housing industries well into the cold war era. At the same time, however, New Deal liberals and southern conservatives failed initially to see eye to eye on the federal government's expanded role in providing welfare, housing, and overall planning for defense communities.[5]

With the first wave of ordnance and chemical plant construction in 1940–41, severe lack of housing for migrant war workers created considerable challenges to federal housing and planning administrators in such Cotton Belt towns as Texarkana and Karnac, Texas; Childersburg, Alabama; Millington, Tennessee; Flora, Mississippi; and Radford, Virginia. In Texarkana, for instance, the construction of the Red River and Lone Star ordnance plant reservations in 1941–42 spurred the growth of over thirteen hundred new shacks set up in temporary communities named "Victory City" and "Defense

City." And as housing needs for migrants overwhelmed communities such as Radford, federal housing agencies, including the FSA, struggled to provide even basic accommodations for war workers and displaced farmworkers.[6]

Shipbuilding cities along the Gulf and southern Atlantic Coasts attracted the greatest number of defense migrants from all over the United States. On the western Gulf Coast especially, shipyard work amidst the massive plant construction program for the nation's new synthetic rubber industry over-whelmed the neighboring cities of Lake Charles, Louisiana, and Beaumont-Orange, Texas. In the Lone Star State, the sleepy fishing village of Freeport, south of Houston, stood out as an extreme example of inadequate worker housing. In 1940 the Texas SES attempted to induce over seventeen thousand workers to migrate for the construction of a new Dow styrene plant. At its peak in 1941, Dow's plant construction in Freeport required eight thousand migrant workers at one time, as much as five times the population of the pre-vious year.

The lack of housing and federal oversight led many migrants to make do with the resources at hand in Freeport. As one federal welfare official ob-served in February 1942, shacks and cabins were "constructed of old lumber, tin and other scrap material" in an area with "twenty-five white families liv-ing in the same houses with Negroes and Mexican families." While the com-forts of migrant communities were few, workers and their families persist-ently sought the government-contract wages paid in war jobs, such as those provided at the Dow plant. Many of the migrants failed to obtain housing in Freeport; over one hundred people slept on the nearby beach, while some two thousand new shacks, trailers, and tents appeared in the area. According to federal health officials, fifty of the poorer of these migrants congregated in a trailer camp "directly on the shores of a reeking, weedy swamp."[7]

Housing conditions like those found in Freeport and other southern boomtowns shocked outsiders, such as *Washington Post* reporter Agnes Meyer, who toured the Gulf Coast in 1943. Meyer described how in Pascagoula and Mobile she observed the rows of tents, trailers, and shacks inhabited by mi-grant families from the hinterland. In Orange, Texas, in the heart of a ship-building and petrochemical construction area, Meyer visited an African American migrant community and reported that "in one shack where the floor sank dangerously beneath my feet, and my heels caught in the chinks be-tween the slats, I found two families with eight children each in three crowded rooms, while two night-shift workers were sleeping in box-like ex-tensions off the middle portion."[8]

Meyer's focus on the problems of defense communities reflected an overall concern among New Deal planning advocates toward the housing and social welfare of war workers. Such problems were by no means unique to the southern states. However, Meyer and other outsiders consistently dramatized the existence of migrant families in the South. In 1941 and 1942, FSA photographers working under the newly created Office of War Information focused their cameras on the trailer towns and tent cities of the South more so than other regions. Meyer and federal photographers used southern migrant communities to support the federal agenda, under Roosevelt's National Resources Planning Board (NRPB), for migrant defense worker housing and reform measures.[9]

As NRPB officials discovered in 1941 and 1942, southern communities were generally unprepared for and unwilling to deal with the chaos of wartime migration. Generally, overnight boomtowns confounded problems by failing to plan for in-migration and welfare services. Planning in general remained an elusive concept for more laissez-faire local and state administrators. During the New Deal dam-building projects in the western states and in the Tennessee Valley, the federal government had become familiar with the housing and transportation problems that surrounded large-scale federal public works projects. Since the mid-1930s, liberal planners in federal agencies such as the FSA and the Tennessee Valley Authority (TVA) used housing and welfare services for migrants and federal workers as the basis for community planning in the South. By 1940 E. S. Draper, a federal housing administrator under the TVA, observed "an increasing awareness in many local communities in the South" in regard to "their need and responsibility for local planning." Drawing his ideal of planning from the TVA model, Draper advocated that southern towns receive greater technical guidance from federal agencies such as the WPA and the United States Housing Authority (USHA).[10]

The federal dam-building projects of the 1930s offered valuable experience to federal officials in the logistical problems of worker mobilization for wartime defense projects.[11] Yet in the South, many communities resisted any planning efforts to facilitate the process. The problems in the initial stages of mobilization in Texas illustrate well how conservative state administrations resisted attempts to create powerful state planning agencies and how the state maintained a hands-off approach to local assistance even under the increased needs of war migration. As federal public health officials complained, Texas counties did not have the power to pass or reinforce ordinances that regulated sanitation and development. While boomtown residents reacted adversely to prostitution and hard drinking, they often remained reluctant to regulate the behavior of migrants through legal means.[12]

Some Texas cities, such as Amarillo and Port Neches, did enact housing and trailer zoning ordinances. Yet most cities resisted federal attempts to promote zoning and planning efforts. In the more extreme case of Killeen, the boomtown outside of Camp Hood in central Texas, city officials claimed they lacked community facilities, money, and experience to deal adequately with mobilization problems. According to federal investigators, Killeen's city officials expected federal agencies to shoulder the full responsibility of welfare, health, and housing inadequacies.[13]

In the emerging Sunbelt generally, no consensus existed regarding state responsibility for war planning and mobilization. However, the growing federal presence in southern towns during the war emergency signaled a change for local politics and at times a challenge to local sovereignty. Under the strains of war mobilization, an area's ability to provide some planning for housing and welfare services often determined circumstances of either chaos or stability. Agnes Meyer revealed how southern cities responded differently to wartime migration and overcrowding. On the one hand, Meyer declared that Mobile, Alabama, was "the extreme example of what happens in a large but poorly organized community when it is overrun by war workers." In contrast, Meyer praised nearby Pascagoula, Mississippi, as "the only city, North or South, in which I found the civic leaders, the social workers, and the private citizens cooperating, not only to meet, but to anticipate the needs of the Negro population." As Meyer indicated, local agencies' ability to cooperate during wartime helped to provide some sense of social stability.[14]

A Southern Dilemma: Controlling War Workers

Throughout the South in 1942, the federal government focused on public health as a means of bringing some sense of order out of the demographic chaos at the local level. As wartime mobilization commenced, the NRPB hoped to provide stable work communities for defense production by expanding planning, public health, and welfare services. Thus, with the chaos of mobilization, the federal presence expanded services in the United States Public Health Service for health care, the United States Public Housing Administration and the FSA for shelter, the BES for employment services and unemployment compensation, the WPA and the National Youth Administration (NYA) for technical training. Like the New Deal and the First World War before it, the Second World War increased dramatically the ties between southern people and the federal government.[15] As the growth of federal social welfare programs gave workers greater economic leverage in 1940 and 1941, employers in the South resented this aspect of mobilization.

Generally, military and industrial construction projects required the greatest need for expanded federal planning and social welfare programs. In Childersburg, Alabama, for instance, the construction of a Du Pont ordnance plant drew close to twenty thousand workers and their families while displacing longtime rural residents at the same time. On the plant reservation site, the military expropriated a thirteen-hundred-acre plantation owned by the Keith family for four generations. In March 1941, owner Alston Keith complained in letters to state congressmen, Alabama governor Frank Dixon, and President Roosevelt that "my tenants are in a pitiful situation." Keith observed, "They haven't planted a spring garden and without reimbursement for the value of their leases, will have no money to make a new crop." Even while the new industry created some economic opportunities for tenants, Keith observed that "a large number of them are not physically able or desire to work at the powder plant."[16]

At the beginning of the war, the FSA took responsibility for assisting families displaced from military reservations. However, the experiences of migrant defense families in Louisiana and Texas indicate that federal assistance did not extend to all migrant and landless families. In Alexandria, Louisiana, for instance, migrants seeking employment in the nearby area did not want to go back to their old homes because, as one man stated, "they ha[d] nothing for which to return." Many families evicted from their land when the military reserves were built failed to receive settlement cash grants and were "homeless and without resources" to purchase or build new homes.[17]

In the cotton, oil, and lumber region between Shreveport, Louisiana, and Texarkana, Texas, the experiences of hundreds of families suggest how rural persons reacted in a variety of ways to federal displacement. Near Shreveport more than three hundred families were forced off their land to make way for the Cedar Grove and Louisiana ordnance plants. The FSA provided fifteen- to thirty-dollar cash grants to pay for resettlement. Officials noted that the majority of displaced families reinvested in homes. However, some families were so heavily in debt that, after settlement of back debts, they were unable to buy homes.[18] Outside of Texarkana, the Lone Star and Red River ordnance plant sites uprooted at least 370 farming families. The FSA created a temporary housing colony for 175 of the displaced families near the plant and reported that men in these families secured work at the plants. Nevertheless, federal authorities indicated that numerous homeless families "had no plans at all for the future," while "all were perplexed and inclined to be somewhat resentful at this break in their pattern of their lives."[19]

Southern communities and employers had long dealt with seasonal migrant workers in local industries, yet the large scale of industrial and military mobilization led to an unprecedented number of homeless families seeking economic opportunity in urban areas. Defense opportunities and displacement tended to stimulate migration among low-income groups especially. In Louisiana local and federal officials felt helpless to regulate what one man described as the statewide migration of "workers and their families moving from one defense project to another in search of employment, families of soldiers moving into the communities from other camps, families displaced from the plant sites and artillery ranges."[20]

Because defense wages attracted part-time and seasonal workers, the construction boom in the South strained labor relations between rural workers and their employers. Low-wage rural industries, farming, lumber, mining, and textiles faced increasing competition for labor with the construction of cost-plus, fixed-fee defense projects in nearby towns or cities. For example, when the military camps were first built near Alexandria, Louisiana, in May 1941, local sugarcane planters protested how 75 percent of the labor force migrated to nearby construction projects following the harvest season of 1940. The sugarcane planters complained they could not obtain the usual cheap farm labor to plant their crops. As the harvest season began in the fall of 1941, Louisiana SES officials found that agricultural workers who entered the construction field as unskilled laborers made recruitment of harvest hands increasingly difficult for northern Louisiana cotton producers. By 1941 the Alabama SES noticed that industries such as lumber and mining were tightening.[21] This flight of workers from the traditional low-wage jobs to defense industries illustrated how southern families were eager to gain economic mobility. For employers this increased worker mobility reflected the growing and profound political, economic, and social conflict over control of manpower resources in the American South.

In theory, state and federal manpower agencies, such as the BES and its 1942 successor, the War Manpower Commission (WMC), were to stabilize local labor markets and thus insure production for both agriculture and manufacturing during the war effort. In states such as Alabama, the SES boasted of its ability to balance the seasonal needs of large-scale cotton planters with the labor requirements of the heavy industries in Birmingham by working "hand in glove with the employer and worker . . . to render a full time placement service." Indeed, industrial farming and manufacturing interests comprised

Chapter One

the main clients of most southern SES offices. Prior to the war, in states like Alabama, the largest industrial steel and manufacturing corporations in Birmingham as well as rural industries and planters in need of seasonal workers utilized the state SES.[22]

Throughout the nation, federally affiliated SES offices provided free public employment services that served both workers and businesses. In the South, the majority of SES offices in the region placed mostly unskilled and minority workers (hence, low-wage workers) with a variety of employers. In Georgia in 1939, for instance, most of the job placements (20 percent) were in "personal services," supplying domestic servants, the majority of whom were black women. The next largest categories included private construction (14 percent) and farming (12 percent), where unskilled African American workers were needed.[23] The Georgia SES farm placement program, however, paled in comparison to other states' programs.

Since the First World War, farm labor programs had become the center of SES activities in the cotton and sugarcane regions. By the late 1930s, federal planners in the FSA worked cooperatively with SES Farm Placement Divisions to bring some order to seasonal migrant worker labor markets throughout the Southeast and Southwest. In 1940 the Louisiana SES Farm Placement Division placed some forty thousand agricultural workers, and the FSA administered housing needs for migrants. In Texas and Florida especially, FSA and SES Farm Placement Division administrators largely coordinated the seasonal migrant farming stream to serve industrial growers. Astonishingly, during this period, the Texas SES Farm Placement Division program for cotton growers placed over 400,000 workers in 1938 and over 593,000 workers in 1940.[24]

By the late 1930s, acreage reduction and mechanization both contributed to an abundance of seasonal and part-time workers. Beginning in 1933, large surplus commodities such as cotton and sugarcane underwent severe acreage cutbacks, to the apparent concern of many conservative industry spokesmen. In the spring of 1940, for instance, Charles Farwell, chairman of the American Sugar Cane League Education Committee in Louisiana, warned that twenty thousand workers would lose their jobs if fifty thousand acres were plowed under according to AAA sugar quotas. For the 1940 season, Farwell claimed, sugar planters in Louisiana foresaw no need for 6,757 "regular" farmworkers, 3,268 part-time workers employed during cultivation, and 10,000 more during harvest season.[25]

Rural industries in the South generally benefited from the surplus labor created from displacement. Realizing this fact, farmworkers throughout the

Cotton Belt and especially the Southern Tenant Farmers Union (STFU) dramatized the problems of displaced farmworkers as they were evicted from plantations and suffered violence from growers. In January 1940, African American tenant farmers organized by United Cannery, Agricultural, Packing and Allied Workers of America (UCAPAWA) with the CIO and the STFU visited Washington to lobby for greater protection from displacement under crop reduction programs in the South. Increasingly, the plight of homeless rural families took on national political importance and symbolized the deep ideological divisions between liberals and conservatives over the interference of the federal government in rural labor relations.[26]

Despite the economic realities of the cotton market, agricultural experts in states like Texas, where mechanization and AAA plow ups proceeded rapidly, continued to promote the ideal that farming families could earn a decent living on the land. For example, T. O. Walton, president of Texas A&M, advocated greater landownership as a solution to the problems of small farmers, proclaiming that the Texas farm was "still a good place on which to live and be happy." "There is no reason," Walton argued, "why a living on the farm cannot be maintained at an acceptable standard." Likewise, Victor Schoffelmeyer, agriculture editor of the *Dallas Morning News*, preached similar platitudes for black farmers. While urging greater Negro landownership, Schoffelmeyer proclaimed that "the farm [was] not a place to get rich" but was a place to make a stable living. Such ideals stood at the heart of FSA policies, which maintained the belief that poor farmers, tenants, and sharecroppers were best off by staying on the land. As R. W. Hudgens, FSA administrator, told a regional FSA meeting in Dallas, "Industry and the city can't absorb these people forced from the land." Hudgens then urged, "We must give the poor farmer security of land tenure, teach him what to do with his land and help him live on it."[27]

As FSA officials and farmworkers unions expressed concern over the regional "farm problem," agricultural employers in the spring of 1941 complained of alleged labor shortages due to nearby war industries. In March, Louisiana strawberry growers claimed harvest hands had migrated to nearby defense industries, especially to New Orleans. That same spring, the Alexandria area sugarcane planters complained to Louisiana SES officials about the loss of hands to nearby defense construction sites and the labor shortage for cultivation and harvest. For rural employers dependent largely on African American seasonal harvest labor, the initial defense projects in the South presented a threat to control of their surplus labor supply. As this transformation occurred, planters, industrialists, and federal manpower administrators throughout the South sought greater controls to insure that the war would not endanger rural labor supplies.[28]

Southern Labor and Allied Victory

By 1941 southern manpower had become a valuable commodity to insure not only an Allied victory but America's economic dominance internationally and southern elites' political and economic power locally. In plantation regions where farmworkers' dependency undergirded local economic and social power, the flight of farmworkers to defense industries indicated an unorganized strike against depression era farm wages and a challenge to local elites' economic control over seasonal workers. The region's employers had long enjoyed the low wages associated with surplus labor markets. President Roosevelt sought also to capitalize on the South's labor surplus in the placement of defense industries throughout the region.

Under Roosevelt's urgings and over the dissent among the old-line East Coast industrial interests, the Plant Site Board Committee of the OPM consciously located new industries south of the Potomac and west of the Mississippi throughout 1940 and 1941. The administration intended to use the war emergency, as it had the New Deal, to foster economic development in the South and West. Indeed, both the TVA and Columbia River dams laid the foundations for defense industries' electrical power needs in these two regions. As the OPM proceeded with defense plant funding in the South, the issue of adequate and even surplus manpower within local communities took on new significance in regional race relations and politics. According to Bruce Schulman, federal war production officials hoped to exploit reservoirs of "ineffectively used labor" in the South and planned to ensure that "every possible preference be given to locations where large reserves of unemployed or poorly employed people are available."[29]

As defense contractors began using SES offices to obtain workers, those offices working with state Unemployment Compensation (UC) offices drew from persons registered for state welfare benefits. Such a practical recruitment and placement system developed from the New Deal's expansion of welfare and employment services. The Social Security Act of 1935 created the BES, which then gave states grants to administer unemployment and employment service agencies. Consequently, after 1935, SES offices and UC divisions became two cooperating agencies under state departments of labor and industry.[30] As UC divisions and SES offices recruited workers from welfare rolls, the system enabled state administrators to coordinate the reduction of welfare rolls and the mobilization of defense workers.

In the South, however, the merging of welfare and employment services also provided the means for state administrators to control wages and labor markets to the benefit of business interests. Throughout the southern states in 1940, the number of unemployment benefit claims began to diminish when defense projects began to provide jobs. In Alabama in that year, SES director C. F. Anderson celebrated the fact that only 104,312 persons were "actively seeking work," a great improvement over the 275,000 unemployed workers in Alabama at the peak of the Great Depression in 1933. Similarly, in neighboring states in 1940, the Louisiana SES reported some 160,000 benefit claimants, while Georgia had some 150,000 claimants.[31] Yet until defense industry employment opportunities arrived, southern politicians lobbied for the continuation of WPA projects in areas with high numbers of registered welfare recipients. In Louisiana, the fact that some 28,000 families depended on the WPA as late as November 1940 prompted Governor Sam Jones to push hard for the continuation of WPA funds to his state.[32]

The mobilization effort continued patterns of racial exclusion inherent in many New Deal welfare and training programs within the South. Throughout 1940 and 1941, white workers found ample training and employment opportunities in defense. However, the exclusion of black workers from defense industries combined with canceled welfare benefits embittered many African Americans in urban areas. In New Orleans in July 1941, black community leaders declared that welfare roll reductions for over four thousand members combined with the lack of defense opportunities contributed to a critical unemployment situation. Likewise, Dallas NAACP officials also protested the dropping of black trainees from NYA rolls to make way for white boys in defense centers.[33] In Mississippi, leaders in the Jackson NAACP complained to President Roosevelt that the WPA office reserved all WPA defense jobs for white women. According to the men, the federal government maintained "scores of WPA Sewing Room Projects all over Mississippi for white women," while the black women failed to "receive one dollar from such projects, nor from any other Federal Project in this State."[34]

Throughout the South and Southwest, state labor and industry departments commonly denied unemployment compensation to part-time and seasonal workers, most of whom were either black or Hispanic by 1940. As the Florida SES argued, denying benefits to seasonal workers was needed to "protect the solvency of the unemployment compensation fund." Clearly, however, the denial of welfare benefits to part-time farmworkers served the interests of state growers and employers in need of cheap, unskilled labor. Thus, racial ideology and southern business needs largely shaped the initial distribution of training and defense opportunities.[35]

In the summer of 1941, unemployment problems plagued urban African Americans, while southern employers in both agriculture and industrial manufacturing sectors complained of labor shortages. Management was undoubtedly adjusting to the decline of a surplus labor market, especially in rural areas. Yet the South's belated entry into national defense programs had also depleted its industrial labor resources as southern tradesmen migrated to defense projects already begun elsewhere. In August, New Orleans experienced its first labor pinch since 1928 as workers moved away to take jobs in the industrial Northeast and Midwest, the aircraft industry in Texas and Oklahoma, and military construction jobs in British Guyana and Trinidad.[36]

Southern industrialists and boosters were well aware that local labor resources could ultimately determine success in gaining defense projects. In the summer of 1941, OPM Plant Site Board Committee allocations in the South represented the key opportunity for communities to gain permanent industries. Throughout the 1930s, economic boosters such as the *Manufacturers' Record* boasted of the South's "abundance of manpower" as "industry's greatest asset."[37] In spite of such claims and in spite of the preponderance of persons on relief, by the summer of 1941 the alleged southern labor shortage in both skilled and unskilled work suggested that industries and state manpower officials faced a complex and daunting task for supplying southern defense industries with skilled workers.

Initially, southern SES offices assumed that the local labor resources and training facilities would be adequate to meet the manpower needs of new defense industries. Generally, upland cities attracting the aircraft industry did not have to import white workers, unlike coastal cities in the South. For example, in Dallas in October 1940, civic planners greeted the arrival of the aircraft industry in the Southwest with confidence that the city and nearby suburbs could provide all the plant's labor. North American Aviation, Inc. (NAA), building a seven-million-dollar bomber plant in the suburb of Grand Prairie, had in fact chosen the Dallas area for expansion because of its ample labor supply. In Atlanta also in 1941, local Chamber of Commerce official Frank Shaw believed that the 25,000 persons registered for unemployment compensation in the Atlanta area would provide an excellent source of labor for the new Bell bomber plant under development.[38]

In the region known for its surplus labor force, federal procurement and state manpower officials debated the adequacy of local labor resources for the emerging shipbuilding industry. The rapid expansion of shipbuilding in cities such as New Orleans injected a sense of urgency for state officials involved in defense preparation. In the spring and summer of 1941, the Louisiana Department of Labor and the Louisiana SES, Delta Shipbuilding Company, the AFL Metal Trades Council, and the OPM struggled to coordinate New Orleans's shipbuilding manpower and training needs. The presence of Delta in the city along with the booming Higgins Industries presented tremendous industrial employment opportunities to residents of this southern city, which had the highest poverty rate in the nation. Yet like many other cities in the South in 1940, New Orleans's labor force remained largely unskilled. This lack of skilled workers raised doubts among some federal procurement officials about the South's ability to provide adequate training programs for the large-scale aircraft and shipbuilding plants, "war babies" employing up to twenty thousand persons per plant.[39]

As rapid industrial development came to New Orleans in 1941, local workers found themselves excluded from defense projects by hiring policies that favored skilled outsiders. Sensing a political opportunity, freshman congressman F. Edward Hebert from New Orleans proclaimed on a local radio station how "an out of town bunch" controlled Delta shipyards in New Orleans "lock, stock and barrel" while "our people" were "crying for work." Citing the large number of out-of-state cars in the plant's parking lot, Hebert charged the American Shipbuilding Corporation, Delta's parent company in Cleveland, with "taking the whole hog and not giving our own people anything but the crumbs." Such concerns reflected the expectation among southern economic boosters that federally financed war plants in the South would provide immediate relief for depressed cities like New Orleans. With surplus southern labor and underemployment, nonsouthern migrants symbolized continued economic injustice and discrimination to unemployed workers and southern politicians eager to reduce welfare rolls and insure permanent industries.[40]

In rural areas such as Talladega County, Alabama, the construction of the new Du Pont powder plant near Childersburg exhibited the same hiring and exclusion problems as in New Orleans's shipbuilding industry. In the summer and fall of 1941, Governor Frank Dixon received countless letters from Alabama men begging for defense jobs at the central Alabama plant. Yet, as the Alabama SES attempted to give priority placement to residents of Talladega County and Alabama generally, local and state residents found themselves shut out of such defense jobs because outside contractors brought in their own construction labor crews.

In the Childersburg case, migrant construction workers claimed local residency in order to receive job placement preference from the local SES offices. Because understaffed SES offices lacked the administrative capacity and facilities to validate the workers' claims, local administrators were forced to take the word of each applicant. Under the increased burden of wartime mobilization, the local BES offices for welfare and employment services were largely unable to effect a smooth transition from the depression to the war's economic boom.[41]

In reality, all industrializing areas in the South depended on the in-migration of skilled labor for construction and new defense training programs. Interstate migration occurred commonly along the farmworker trails of the 1930s. As Dorthea Lange and Paul Taylor observed, the cars at migrant cotton-picker camps in the West often had license plates from all over the United States. Highly mobile and migratory workers followed defense project migrant trails into southern communities that were experiencing the social chaos of economic boom and bust.[42]

In the construction industry, with few exceptions, contractors' use of migrant crews often necessitated only minimum employment of local unskilled workers. At Camp Blanding, for instance, Florida state labor officials observed that license plates on automobiles, trucks, and trailers in the Starke area came from almost every county in Florida and almost every state.[43] The use of mobile construction crews also occurred with the building of Camp Shelby near Hattiesburg, Mississippi, where the contractor, J. A. Jones Company, recruited only five thousand local workers in addition to a company crew of twelve thousand. Outside of Texarkana, Texas, the contractors for the Red River and Lone Star ordnance plants used roughly three thousand white and two thousand African American local workers while employing a migrant crew of some thirteen thousand persons.[44]

On construction defense jobs with AFL contracts, union members were often professional skilled migrants. At the construction of Camp Bowie near Brownwood, Texas, for instance, the carpenters union claimed that its members, composing 75 percent of the labor force, came originally from West Texas, Mississippi, Louisiana, New Mexico, Arizona, and Missouri. According to the union secretary, once the work was completed at Camp Bowie, these workers planned to move on to other defense jobs in Texas such as Camp Hitchcock, Corpus Christi Naval Air Base, the shipbuilding yards at Beaumont-Orange, and the Consolidated-Vultee (Convair) aircraft plant in Fort Worth.[45]

The Southern Governors' Dilemma

As worker mobilization proceeded across the South in 1941, southern states sensed the inevitability of increased federal control of labor markets. However, no consensus existed among the states regarding the federal role in mobilizing southern workers for the national defense program. As they had during the First World War, political leaders questioned the extent of centralized federal control of labor markets in 1941.[46] Conservative politicians, state manpower administrators, and industrialists especially feared increasing federal power over the SES and UC divisions.

In October 1941, the SES Interstate Conference declared officially its opposition to "federalization of any part of the Employment Security Program." In their protests, conservative state administrators anticipated a federal challenge to local control and state sovereignty. As one antifederal newsletter, the *Advisor*, declared, the majority of state administrators were fundamentally opposed to increased federal domination of state programs, as they "must bear the brunt of the Social Security Boards' attempts at domination."[47]

While state officials throughout the nation defended the autonomy of their agencies, the states' rights tradition in southern politics created an especially vigorous rhetorical defense among southern governors. Alabama governor Frank Dixon emerged as the most outspoken advocate of southern states' rights and the need to maintain state control of SES offices and UC divisions. The opposition of many conservatives extended from their antagonism toward the National Labor Relations Act of 1935 and the Fair Labor Standards Act of 1938. Naturally, business interests such as the Birmingham Chamber of Commerce and numerous other southern chambers supported Frank Dixon in his efforts to prevent increased federal authority over labor and welfare services in the South.[48]

Beginning in December 1941, conservatives' fears were realized when Roosevelt federalized the State Employment Services. By April 1942, complaints over chronic manpower problems throughout the United States led President Roosevelt to create the WMC.[49] Roosevelt hoped to provide a more centralized wartime agency that would mobilize U.S. workers more efficiently. The WMC, in effect, emerged directly out of the BES and its employment division, the United States Employment Service (USES). Quite logically, Roosevelt appointed BES director Paul McNutt as the chairman of the new agency, while the WMC assumed jurisdiction over existing BES facilities and its national bureaucratic structure. In doing so, the WMC oversaw twelve manpower regions covering various parts of the United States. In the South, the WMC oversaw four subregions that roughly covered the Mid-Atlantic, the Southeast, the Southwest, and the Ozarks. To streamline and centralize all federal mobilization agencies, regional manpower offices shifted from Birmingham to Atlanta for the Southeast and from San Antonio to Dallas for the Southwest.

In the year leading up to the WMC's creation, the mobilization effort revealed southern governors' ambivalence toward increased federal control of the region's workers, especially its migrant workers. State Employment Security administrators in the South found themselves coming to terms with the housing and welfare problems of migrant workers for the first time. In 1940, California congressman John H. Tolan, as chairman of the Special Committee Investigating the Interstate Migration of Destitute Citizens (the Tolan Committee), brought about a greater awareness of migrant workers not only in the West but throughout all regions. During the summer, the Tolan Committee sponsored a national tour to examine the issue of destitute migrant workers in six U.S. regions. At its Montgomery, Alabama, hearings, migrant workers from the southern states testified about the national scope of their travels and hence the national scope of the migrant housing and welfare problem.[50]

The Tolan Committee's promotion of federal regulation of migrant labor provoked the ire of southern conservatives and SES administrators who questioned the existence of a migrant labor welfare problem in the South.[51] In particular, the Southern Governors Conference chose to ignore the fact that Florida was home to some thirty thousand seasonal migrants who lived and traveled the Atlantic seaboard annually in search of harvest jobs that paid meager wages and offered squalid accommodations.[52] In large part, such resistance to greater federal control among conservative southern capitalists reflected their desires to minimize labor regulation and thereby maintain the low wages that made southern industry (including agriculture) competitive in the national and global markets. In denying a problem existed for southern migrant workers, the Southern Governors Conference's laissez-faire attitude foreshadowed southern states' unwillingness to plan for social welfare problems exacerbated by the large-scale mobilization of migrant southern workers to defense-related construction projects.

Despite the southern governors' hands-off attitude toward the welfare of migrants, the mobilization of workers for southern defense projects prompted state administrators to address the welfare and housing issue more seriously. In December 1940, state administrators in a variety of state welfare and employment agencies met in Atlanta for the Interstate Conference on Migratory Labor. The conference continued efforts begun during the Tolan Committee hearings to bring together southern representatives from organized labor and state and federal offices of labor, employment services, agriculture, health, public welfare, and education. And, as it had during the August hearings, testimony addressed the problems faced by both agricultural and industrial workers with the decline of the sharecropping system and the increase in mechanization. Most significantly, the conference members acknowledged the growing problems associated with migration to new defense projects such as Camp Blanding, Florida, and Fort Bragg, North Carolina. Gradually, southern and federal administrators admitted that some manpower controls would be needed in order to mobilize defense workers efficiently and also to protect the South's labor reserves.[53]

In the overall context of providing "controlled migration," the conference recommended the full participation of the SES, organized labor, and industry in placing workers in defense-related jobs. It also promoted the strict regulation and control of interstate contractors and private employment services. Drawing on concerns dating back to the First World War, conservative manpower administrators, representing the interests of southern capitalists, hoped to prevent the uncontrolled recruitment of southern workers for northern industries. At the same time, more liberal participants recommended extending the coverage of labor and social security laws to all workers then excluded, such as those in "industrialized agriculture" and food-processing industries. Liberal conference members also supported upgrading present welfare and resettlement services to assist not only defense migrant workers but also those persons displaced by the creation of new military facilities. Although such policies ensured growth of the federal government, southern state administrators supported this theoretical improvement in state planning and welfare to prove to Washington that the South was capable of meeting the demands of mobilization.[54]

In their efforts to streamline worker recruitment, southern governors increasingly relied on closed-shop agreements with the AFL building and metal trades, which dominated construction and shipbuilding across the South. From its inception, the WMC under Chairman Paul McNutt continued USES mobilization practices by working closely with the AFL in the placement of workers in defense contract jobs. As part of the wartime organizational structure, the WMC established a Management-Labor Policy Committee (MLPC) that consisted of representatives from private industry and agriculture along with those from the AFL and the CIO to further advise McNutt on manpower policy formulation. In this capacity, the WMC, along with the War Labor Board and the United States Maritime Commission, served an important role in fostering more intimate ties between organized labor and the state. Even locally, the establishment of management-labor committees ensured that at the metropolitan level, industry and labor would make greater efforts to coordinate production, manpower, and housing problems.[55]

Arrangements between defense contractors, the USES, and the AFL theoretically facilitated a more systematic placement effort. And for some state political machines the arrangement also helped exclude the more leftist CIO from gaining a foothold in emerging southern defense industries. For example, during the spring of 1941, the Alabama SES entered into agreements with the AFL Building and Construction Trades Council of Jefferson County and with other area councils in Alabama over the complaints of the United Construction Workers of Birmingham (CIO).[56] Such agreements between SES offices and the AFL were also made in shipbuilding establishments along the Gulf Coast under the Gulf Zone Stabilization Agreement of 1941, causing the CIO often to accuse the AFL and OPM (and eventually the War Production Board) of establishing labor rackets within the industry. In New Orleans, for instance, the CIO suspected during 1942 that the War Production Board and Louisiana SES had arranged a "back-door" deal with the local AFL Metal Trades Council in the organizing of Delta shipyards.[57]

As the National Labor Relations Board (NLRB) and eventually the War Labor Board sanctioned the closed shop in southern defense industries, the CIO and AFL undertook campaigns to organize the largest number of southern workers in the region's history. Given that AFL metal and building trades represented from fifteen to thirty thousand defense workers in some southern cities, AFL leaders' political clout increased dramatically with mobilization. And in states such as Alabama, Maryland, and Texas, where CIO steel, oil, and shipbuilding unions represented similar numbers of workers in 1942, conservative CIO leaders also gained some political leverage. With this rapid and large-scale organization of southern defense workers, state administrations and southern business elites wanted to ensure that defense workers came under the control of the AFL and not the CIO. Hence, most major shipyards with closed-shop agreements along the Gulf Coast signed with the AFL metal trades, while construction projects throughout the South relied on contracts with AFL building trades. Throughout 1942 and 1943, the AFL continued to cement political ties to state administrations as it continued to make organizing gains in the shipbuilding and construction industries throughout the South.[58]

Despite these coordinated attempts to solve the region's manpower problems in 1942, by the end of that year, southern industries encountered increasing shortages of white males. As these labor resources tightened in southern cities and the need for in-migrant skilled trainees increased, the hiring of local women and African Americans and Latinos became integral to insuring local production. Given the choice of hiring local white women or utilizing African Americans or Latino workers, many southern communities saw less of a threat to southern traditions with the former. By hiring what the WMC called "idle" white women, southern industrialists could expand the region's workforce without compromising the privilege of whiteness in the job market. In recruiting women, federal manpower officials stressed the temporary nature of their role in war work. And, outside of the CIO, working women and housewives in the South generally lacked any organized voice or feminist institutions that advocated for women's and workers' rights. These factors certainly appealed to conservative southern employers who hoped to avoid any major challenges to southern labor and racial customs during mobilization.[59]

The decision to recruit women for defense work in the South signaled a new effort to hire local labor resources and avoid the constant in-migration of white male workers and their families into southern communities. Nevertheless, as long as black workers continued to be excluded, African American labor leaders, federal planning advocates, and white liberal labor leaders consistently demanded equal employment opportunities for black defense workers. The creation of the Fair Employment Practices Committee (FEPC) in the summer of 1941, along with increasing demands for jobs among southern African Americans, placed pressure on OPM, WMC, and USES officials to utilize nonwhite labor more effectively in emerging industrial areas throughout the South. In theory, local southern industries could utilize local trained women, African Americans, and Latinos to avoid the necessary in-migration of rural whites that would only tax local services and housing resources. Manpower officials dubbed this policy "full utilization." In reality, however, southern manpower administrators proved reluctant to realize the policy for fear of challenging the segregated southern labor market and hence the region's labor caste system.

Chaos and Worker Mobility on the Southern Home Front

In 1941 and 1942, the failure to implement the full utilization policy in both Baltimore and Charleston led to some questions about the South's ability to meet the war's manpower needs. Beginning in the summer of 1941, Baltimore faced a serious manpower shortage with the expansion of Bethlehem Steel and Shipyards and Martin Aircraft facilities. As Charm City's manpower problems continued into the summer and fall of 1942, the *Baltimore Sun* and the *New York Times* remained critical of Baltimore's inability to avoid further in-migration. Already, some 20,000 white migrants had arrived from North Carolina and West Virginia at the rate of 3,500 per month. Likewise, in Charleston in September 1942, local industries and the USES planned to import some nine thousand white workers even though four thousand black workers were registered at the local office. Even as the city faced a housing shortage crisis due to an influx of some 100,000 migrants, it continued to recruit white workers from the hinterland as local African Americans were relegated to nonessential jobs or remained unemployed. As southern industrialists and manpower officials were to discover through high turnover rates at defense plants, both black and white workers would resent the social chaos endemic to this policy.

The initial failure to execute full utilization in southern industrial areas resulted from a variety of factors. In Baltimore, the *New York Times* reported that some local women resisted leaving their role of homemaker, while others feared that employment might jeopardize their status as dependents, causing their husbands to be drafted.[60] Most commonly, however, the failure to implement full utilization stemmed from the hiring and placement system policies practiced by industrial personnel directors in cooperation with organized labor representatives and WMC and USES administrators. And, since WMC policies were only voluntary, the agency remained unable to enforce programs to improve local or area manpower problems. At most, the WMC only recommended to the WPB that noncompliant industrial areas or plants should not receive further war contracts or matériel.[61]

In 1942, Mobile, Alabama, emerged as one of the more extreme examples of a southern coastal city experiencing the severe stresses of uncontrolled wartime in-migration. City residents saw over 55,000 workers move in to meet the demand for 40,000 workers at the shipyards. By April 1942, the city's housing clearly was unable to meet the needs of its migrant workers. As Alabama SES officials observed, "almost every conceivable housing facility" was taken, and trailer camps were "cropping up outside the city limits without any visible sanitary arrangements."[62] In both the national and local press, reporters expressed shock at the living conditions of defense workers. As the *Mobile Register* noted, "Casual observers, driving through the outskirts of the city" during the summer of 1942, "expressed deep concern and at times, horror at the crowded conditions in trailer camps, the sudden appearance of tent cities," and "one or two cases of families living out in the open."[63]

Federal housing agencies did eventually build thousands of new permanent houses and temporary dormitories for workers. Nonetheless, the media's and the government's reporting of Mobile's wartime experiences provides insight into the ways that southern defense workers viewed the economic opportunity engendered by mobilization. Migrant families' responses to the chaos of wartime conditions reveal much about their priorities and goals. Yet one must first understand how outsiders presented only limited views of southern migrant defense workers.

Farm Security Administration photographers documented southern defense worker communities fairly extensively. Some photographers such as Russell Lee observed a great variety of classes and housing conditions in Texas. Other photographers, such as Marion Post Walcott, focused largely on the workers' squalid trailer camps in Louisiana and Georgia, just as FSA photographers had aimed their cameras at "Okie" tent and trailer camps in California during the late depression. Journalists like Agnes Meyer often assumed that southern defense workers were ignorant, uneducated, and unsophisticated—also like the portrayal of southwestern migrants in the West three years earlier.[64]

As with the Okies in California, rarely does one hear the southern migrant workers' point of view about the welfare, manpower, and housing problems they faced in the South. Yet if one probes the lives of southern defense workers beyond the limited lenses and pens of outsiders, there emerges a diverse and complex workforce in southern defense communities. Migrant families were by no means one-dimensional or passive, nor were they all white or rural in origin. At different times within defense communities, migrant families and individual workers employed a variety of strategies to achieve their goals of survival, economic stability, and eventually economic gain.

Southern defense workers were a more diverse lot than most contemporary observers believed or understood. Certainly, in the shipyards, many workers were young rural male migrants from the southern hinterland. The stereotypical shipyard worker was, as *Life* reported, "an 18 year old fresh off of his daddy's cotton farm" who could become a "tacker" welder after four weeks' training. Southern defense communities also contained a mixture of single men, families, veteran skilled workers, local urban residents, and commuters who relinquished their peacetime jobs for defense wages. For example, *Life* observed three men in Tampa who left jobs in cigar rolling, railroad, and oil field work to come work in the shipyards. One of the men, thirty-year-old Joe Diaz, originally worked in a "Spanish cigar factory," and by May 1942 he "bucked" rivets with "a Georgia farm boy." Southern defense projects also attracted black workers like Ernest "Bear" Lewis of New Orleans who obtained employment as common laborers and truck drivers.[65]

For young white men, defense jobs as helpers under welders, electricians, and riveters provided valuable and free on-the-job training and, hence, offered upward mobility. For white women and African Americans, however, these same opportunities were not available initially. In southern shipyards prior to 1943, women found little or no training and employment opportunities. Among the region's new defense industries, rural ordnance plants offered the least resistance to the hiring of white women in large numbers. Surprisingly, scholars have not acknowledged the significance of the southern munitions industry in regard to both women's employment opportunities and job segregation by gender. In many respects, the hiring of white women in ordnance plants represented an important extension of women's employment in textiles and garments prior to the war.[66]

Class and ethnic diversity in defense communities and on the shop floor complicated the mobilization process in the South. At the community level, older community residents often viewed migrants as unsanitary as well as a threat to the moral fiber and social order of their communities. In many respects, the war exposed class tensions between workers and middle-class residents.[67] On the shop floors, and especially in the shipyards, conflicts existed between labor and management, skilled veteran workers and raw trained recruits, male and female workers, ethnic groups, and rival unions. At times, older veteran workers resented the threat to craft superiority that the war brought about with federal training of younger men. Older workers also viewed women and nonwhites as economic competitors. Some of these conflicts manifested themselves in organizing efforts, during which white tradesmen embraced the AFL craft ideology and unskilled workers supported the CIO's industrial organization.[68] Indeed, the diverse results of CIO and AFL elections under the War Labor Board illustrate the great variety of organizing strategies among the unions as well as the diverse priorities that workers themselves maintained.[69]

Despite their differences, workers in southern defense industries also shared many of the same basic concerns. The increasing cooperation between the AFL and the CIO during the war underscored the common ground on which many workers stood. More specifically, common goals among workers (as well as between the AFL and the CIO) included opposition to "job freezes," regional wage disparities, and closed-shop bans as well as the support of wage increases, price ceilings, and a living wage for working families.[70]

Workers' actions illustrate best how they valued geographic and economic mobility during the war. More specifically, the rapid turnover in southern defense labor markets suggests that defense workers valued their ability to migrate as a key survival strategy and eventually as a means of economic and even social mobility. Both black and white defense workers especially resented work-or-fight laws and job freezes that employers and state labor officials used to immobilize those employed in essential war jobs. As welder Sam Marino of Mobile complained to the CIO, draft boards threatened many southern defense workers with military service if they changed jobs in order to survive or move up the economic ladder.[71]

As southern industries hoped to immobilize workers through greater federal manpower controls, workers protested these policies and continued moving on to jobs that paid higher wages. Reports of Mobile's workers during the early years of the war illustrate how workers consistently migrated out of the area rather than face the lower wages of southern shipyards and the lack of decent housing. In April 1942, one hundred workers quit the shipyards in one day because of inadequate housing. That same month, a representative from the Industrial Union of Marine and Shipbuilding Workers Association (IUMSWA) Local 18 reported that fifty-one skilled mechanics left Mobile after working two or three days because of the poor housing situation. The same scenario occurred in coastal shipbuilding cities throughout the South, where workers, especially poorer upland whites, had flocked seeking new job opportunities.[72]

Defense workers in Mobile also fought local attempts to curb their ability to park their trailers and set up camp where they chose. When Mobile's city council proposed an ordinance zoning the areas where trailers could not park throughout the city, residents of the trailer communities petitioned against the law with support from IUMSWA Local 18.[73] For workers who sought economic stability and advancement, the issue of mobility assumed primary importance at the time. *Fortune* magazine declared that worker absenteeism in Mobile was "no strike."[74] However, one cannot deny that as families moved out of the more chaotic wartime communities, the act of migrating took on a significance of its own. Workers were not mere pawns, and they valued their ability to move and seek new economic opportunities. Thus, job shopping was a right that many southern workers valued in their quest for economic mobility.

The chaos of southern wartime communities reflected several factors endemic to the South. Certainly, the large number of defense workers crowding these defense centers illustrated the desperate state of agriculture and employment and the great number of young men and women, both rural and urban residents, who sought the economic opportunity of defense jobs. Coming out of the economic downturn of the 1930s, southern defense jobs served as a magnet to families seeking a way up and out of the South's depressed condition.

Many southern communities' resistance to planning and regulation also had an effect on labor market conditions and high turnover rates in southern defense communities. Even when towns such as Mobile began expanding their permanent and temporary housing stock with help from the federal National Housing Authority, the low level of southern wages at the national level often drove out workers who sought greater economic mobility. For the enterprising family, the southern shipyard jobs served as stepping stones to defense jobs in the West and the North. As long as southern industries and state officials perpetuated wage and hiring policies that produced dissatisfied workers, management would pay the price of high turnover rates and labor instability.

As mobilization transformed the southern economy from depression to boom time, southern workers shifted their priorities and strategies that focused on survival to those that focused on economic mobility. Within southern society, the caste divisions on the shop floor severely limited such strategies for African Americans and in turn limited the ability of southern defense industries to mobilize efficiently. Granted, southern industries did ultimately meet production quotas under the segregated labor market. Yet as black labor leaders and the workers themselves demanded the same economic opportunities as their white colleagues, southern communities, employers, and labor unions faced a dilemma in which the issues of economic opportunity and equality came to the forefront of mobilization. The merging of equal opportunity and equal rights during the war signaled that the war would challenge symbolically the power of Jim Crow and the limits of opportunity for nonwhites in the South.

2. "Empty Sermons"

Race and Economic Mobility on the
Southern Home Front, 1940–1942

Manpower problems plagued shipyards across the American South during the fall of 1942. That year, employers complained of skilled white labor shortages, while African American workers continued to find themselves excluded from the yards in skilled and unskilled positions. As the national movement for fair employment tested the integrity of American democratic ideals at home, New Orleans's local black newspaper, the *Louisiana Weekly,* chastised the War Manpower Commission (WMC) and defense industry hiring policies, which they believed were at the heart of the job dilemma. "White farmers and common laborers from adjacent territories have been brought in to fill the labor need," the *Weekly* complained, and "because of the failure to use local Negro labor before bringing in outside labor, the morale of the colored has been impaired to no small degree."[1]

Since 1940, African American labor leaders and community activists in cities throughout the South had experienced frustration in their efforts to overcome racial barriers to defense jobs. Black workers in the South applied for jobs in war industries through the United States Employment Service (USES), the field arm of the WMC, which continued to place them in farm jobs and other menial positions not associated directly with the defense effort. In November 1942, Paul Dixon, a black labor leader and civic activist in New Orleans, wrote to WMC chairman Paul

McNutt complaining of the USES's racial exclusion policy in the Crescent City. Throughout that year, Dixon had assisted the New Orleans USES as a de facto labor contractor in finding workers for the plantations and farms near the city. Beginning in the fall, the New Orleans SES had sought Dixon's assistance in recruiting skilled black workers for defense industry jobs in Hawthorne, Nevada, and Salt Lake City, Utah, as well as in the shipyards of Portland, Oregon, and the San Francisco Bay Area. In this context of limited economic opportunities within the urban South, Dixon informed McNutt that he had "cheerfully given [the WMC] assistance" in recruiting workers and that recently "many men have been placed at these yards from this area."[2]

Paul Dixon's actions in the early 1940s illustrate the complex environment within which some southern black leaders sought economic gains for workers at the beginning of the war. In 1942, Dixon worked with the New Orleans SES to secure farm labor, represented skilled black workers at the local Jim Crow union of the Boilermakers AFL Local 37-A, and served as president of the Shakespeare Civic League, a local organization. In this segregated labor market and society, Dixon cautiously pushed his agenda of gaining access to defense jobs. As John Beecher, a staff member of the Fair Employment Practices Committee (FEPC) field office, reported in the spring of 1942, Paul Dixon displayed the "deference and religiosity of the typical 'white man's Negro,'" yet beneath the facade, Beecher observed within Dixon a "great shrewdness."[3]

Across the South, leaders like Dixon represented the emergence of a distinct movement to gain economic opportunity and defense jobs for black workers after 1939. Labor leaders and fair employment activists like Dixon increasingly sought the assistance of the federal government in their quest for defense jobs. Under the evolving southern WMC policy in 1942, USES offices stepped up the recruiting of skilled and unskilled African American men and women throughout the South for defense projects and industries in the North and West. This regional policy opened up new job opportunities to both skilled and unskilled southern black workers. And in doing so, the policy illustrated the ways in which the federal government, through mobilization agencies such as the War Manpower Commission, played an increasingly important role in helping black southerners find economic security and mobility in the 1940s.[4]

The Jobs Movement in the South

Paul Dixon's cooperation with the New Orleans USES in recruiting local black trainees for western industries followed three years of frustrated attempts among African Americans to secure both industrial training and employment. Beginning in 1940, southern black activists in trade unions and civic organizations, National Urban League (NUL) affiliates, and National Association for the Advancement of Colored People (NAACP) chapters comprised a national effort to give African Americans jobs in war projects. This jobs movement called into question the federal government's role in thwarting or nurturing equal rights, as the wartime rhetoric of democratic ideals heightened concerns with civic equality. In the South, however, while some idealistic black leaders supported the jobs movement in the cause of equality, many black workers sought simply the economic opportunities that defense jobs provided.

The recruiting of southern black workers for western and northern industries reflected the WMC's effort to meet war production needs rather than civil rights demands. At times, federal manpower officials acknowledged the issue of equal employment. With the creation of the Negro Manpower Division of the WMC in 1942, for instance, WMC chairman Paul McNutt claimed that the full integration of "Negroes and other minority groups" into war production was "one" of the commission's "primary objectives." More realistically, however, McNutt also claimed later that the WMC's mission was to find jobs for people, unlike the FEPC, whose job was to remove barriers to fair employment. Although McNutt and some WMC officials were generally liberal on racial issues, military production and local racial customs took precedence over fair employment practices. And because the FEPC lacked any enforcement powers and the WMC programs were strictly voluntary, WMC administrators remained unable to force industries to integrate.[5]

The conservatism of WMC and War Production Board (WPB) leadership also hindered liberals' efforts to fight job discrimination under the cause of equal rights. Generally, the WMC and WPB were comprised of military procurement agency representatives, local industrialists, and AFL and CIO representatives at the national and regional levels. Naturally, such men prioritized war production needs. They often identified with the economic and social status quo and opposed any use of the war effort to further liberal social reforms. In the South especially, conservatives on WMC regional boards were often the greatest source of resistance to FEPC efforts.[6]

Locally, businessmen and industrialists in the South either offered passive resistance or stressed a gradualist approach to fair employment. In general, conservative opposition to African American industrial integration remained both virulent and passive in public and private sectors. As one businessman described the effort to break down racial barriers in New Orleans's industries,

"It's like you were sewed up inside of a feather bed, you can't get your hands on anything and rip it open." Likewise, FEPC investigator John Beecher characterized New Orleans as "paradoxically most urbane and most provincial," knowing how to "proceed on its way with little regard to laws and regulations imposed from the outside, while putting up no undue show of rebellion."[7]

During the initial period when new defense contracts held promise for the depressed southern economy, the Atlanta and New Orleans Urban Leagues along with the Dallas Negro Chamber of Commerce emerged as the preeminent local black institutions in the regional defense jobs movement. Certainly, these groups' experience with job placement and industrial relations after World War I positioned them well for mobilization. Moreover, both the National Urban League and the Negro Chamber of Commerce were products of Booker T. Washington's conservative social philosophy, which supported economic advancement for African Americans and avoided direct action tactics for civil rights and social equality. In the South, their moderate race relations strategy with an emphasis on economics was integral to avoiding the ire of reactionary white conservatives.[8]

Prior to the war, these organizations focused on job placement, social welfare, and business development. The Atlanta Urban League (AUL), founded in 1919, was by 1940 the oldest continuously operating Urban League affiliate in the South. Under Executive Secretary William Y. Bell, the AUL began in the early 1940s to focus on the issue of defense job opportunities. The New Orleans Urban League (NOUL), established in 1938, was a much newer affiliate. Under the direction of Industrial Secretary Clarence Laws, a native New Orleanian and social worker, the NOUL in 1940 quickly embraced the jobs movement. The Dallas Negro Chamber of Commerce (DNCC) was founded in 1926 as an offshoot of the National Negro Business League. During the 1930s the DNCC, under the strong leadership of A. Maceo Smith, Maynard Jackson Sr., and Virgil Williams, emerged as the most organized and dynamic Negro Chamber in the South. Initially, the DNCC concerned itself with improving black economic opportunities, educational facilities, and housing in Dallas, but by 1940 it naturally saw war mobilization as a means of improving economic standards for African Americans.[9]

The defense jobs movement that began in 1940 built on the efforts of leftists, liberals, labor leaders, and black activists who, after 1933, demanded fair wages and racial job quotas on federal relief work programs. At the top levels in Washington, New Deal liberals such as New York senator Robert Wagner, Secretary of Interior Harold Ickes, and his assistant, Clark Foreman, made a special point of challenging racial discrimination in federal job programs and relief agencies.[10] During this period, nationally respected labor leaders A. P. Randolph, a native of Jacksonville, Florida, and head of the Sleeping Car Porters, and Sidney Hillman of the Amalgamated Clothing Workers emerged as key allies of New Deal liberals in battling for job equality in the public and private sectors. In many respects, these national leaders' concerns emerged from American workers' demands for greater access to federal relief jobs and fair wages.[11]

In industrialized southern cities, a number of local African American organizations mobilized support for fair wages and inclusion in federal relief projects as part of the larger movement for civic equality and labor rights. In Dallas, for instance, middle-class women in the Negro Women's Club successfully prevented the exclusion of local African Americans from local New Deal programs. In New Orleans, working-class church and labor alliances battled for inclusion in new federal relief projects. In the urban South generally, black workers in industries with some of the lowest wages in the nation felt especially motivated to fight for National Recovery Administration (NRA) wage and hour codes. Hence, working-class women organized in laundry and domestic service unions, while men organized in railway and transportation industries and dock and warehouse unions that articulated these black workers' goals.[12]

With the onset of vigorous grassroots labor activity during the 1930s, the AFL began using black organizers in the South for the first time to recruit workers in longshoring and railway work. In the process, the AFL consolidated political and economic ties to the black working class, especially in coastal cities, where the International Longshoremen's Association (ILA) emerged as a powerful union. After 1935, the newly formed CIO, with its leftist organizers and support of interracialism, also sought to use black organizers in the shipyards, steel mills, docks and warehouses, cotton mills, and low-wage plants where African Americans worked in large numbers. In doing so, the CIO also vied for the political loyalty of the black working class, and it gave increasing leverage to those labor leaders who could mobilize large political blocks of potential black workers.[13]

Both the NAACP and the Urban League responded to this heightened labor activism by actively supporting workers' concerns. In the process, they forged new ties to black working-class men and women through coalitions with black churches and labor unions.[14] By the early 1930s, the NAACP displayed a new and invigorated interest in challenging discrimination in the southern labor market. In 1933, NAACP president Walter White exposed the working conditions for black workers in the Army Corps of Engineers levee camps in the Mississippi Delta. The NAACP alleged that the workers were held in peonage, and it demanded a federal investigation. The NAACP also focused on securing greater inclusion for black workers in the New Deal work projects under the Federal Emergency Relief Act (FERA) and fair wages under NRA codes throughout southern industries such as lumber, textiles, coal, and laundry.[15]

After the First World War, the NUL as a rule avoided overt political activism. Yet with the "new radicalism" of the 1930s, the New Orleans and Atlanta affiliates cultivated greater political ties with segregated black AFL labor unions.[16] In 1940, Clarence Laws organized the Committee on Trade and Industrial Relations to promote unionism and to keep black workers informed of key labor issues and legislation. Beginning in 1934, the AUL formed the Negro Workers Councils to promote and support local black labor unions such as the AFL painters and laborers unions well into the 1940s. Such ties had their price for the AUL, however. One October night in 1934, Atlanta police raided the AUL office and an AFL painters union meeting under the pretense of looking for Communist literature. While they failed to find any subversive material, such a show of force suggests that white businesses feared that the AUL's support of even AFL unions threatened the economic and social status quo in the Gate City.[17]

This closer relationship between local affiliates and labor unions grew out of the Negro Workers Councils created by the Urban League in 1934. The councils, originally headed by Lester Granger, promoted interracial worker solidarity and self-determination of black workers. Under the young leader, they also challenged discriminatory barriers that prevented equal opportunity for black men and women in manufacturing industries. Thus, during the 1930s the NUL expanded its role from social work to labor activism and the fight for equal economic opportunity through the integration of industries. With the passage of the Social Security Act in 1935, the NUL requested the USES to insure fair job placement of black workers. When Granger was appointed executive director of the NUL in 1941, his experience in reforming the USES prepared the organization well for its role in fighting for defense jobs.[18]

With the explosion of labor union activity in black communities throughout the South during the 1930s, New Orleans's black working class provided fertile ground for grassroots labor activism. In this southern city, which had the largest urban black population in the South and was also one of the most industrialized urban centers of the region, there emerged a unique coalition of labor union members and church congregations to protest discrimination and support greater economic opportunities for African Americans.[19] By

1941, the jobs issue and the heightened concern with equality brought together black CIO and AFL unions, ministerial alliances, the NOUL, and the local NAACP chapter to demand training for African Americans in New Orleans
shipyards. That fall, Ernest J. Wright, the outspoken organizer for the local
United Garment Workers Association (CIO), along with Rev. A. L. Davis,
founded the People's Defense League, a broad church and labor coalition, to
mobilize against defense discrimination and disfranchisement. In a striking
display of militancy, the People's Defense League consistently held large
public meetings in Shakespeare Park throughout the early war years to protest discrimination and civic inequality.[20]

Similar coalitions between churches, unions, and institutions such as the
Urban League and the NAACP had flowered nationally prior to 1941. Yet in
the South, the People's Defense League's protest tactics and ties to the CIO
during the war made it appear more radical than most other civil rights organizations in the region. In comparison, the League for Civil Rights and Justice, a local organization headed by A. P. Tureaud and other middle-class
reformers in New Orleans, also sought links to the working class. However,
the League for Civil Rights and Justice was, like the NAACP, largely committed to battling discrimination through legal means and not direct action.[21] In
Dallas and Houston, black leaders in the jobs movement failed to connect
with working-class communities. In Houston, black workers in steel and railway industries rejected the strategies of media mogul Carter Wesley and local
labor contractor C. W. Rice.[22] In Dallas, black middle-class leaders remained
neutral toward maintaining open ties to organized labor. To be sure, the Dallas NAACP chapter and the DNCC worked with the AFL carpenters Local 774
to challenge their exclusion from the federal defense housing project in
Grand Prairie. Yet, generally, during this period Dallas's black civic leaders
distanced themselves from organized labor and especially the CIO. This
general reluctance or low profile may have been a reaction to the brutality
suffered by garment and auto workers who established CIO unions in Dallas
in 1937 and 1938.[23]

The Jobs Movement Goes to War

The national fair employment movement had by 1941 linked A. Philip Randolph; Lester Granger, newly appointed executive director of the National
Urban League; and Walter White, president of the NAACP. Drawing from the
demands for fair wages and job quotas made during the 1930s, the March
on Washington movement insisted on a broad dismantling of discrimination

in all federal projects and agencies and, more specifically, in the national defense program. In its demands, the movement's stance was both militant and brash.[24]

Behind the scenes, southern Urban League affiliates had been making discreet efforts to secure defense training and employment of black workers. Beginning in May 1940, the NUL notified all branch secretaries of the campaign to include African Americans in national defense programs. In New Orleans, for instance, Clarence Laws enthusiastically supported the idea proposing that advocates of defense integration should emphasize the patriotism and loyalty of African Americans as well as the potential benefits of black defense wages for the national economy. Laws's strategies stressed the moderate and even conservative rhetoric of Urban League race relations philosophy in the struggle for industrial integration, a potentially volatile issue in the South.[25]

In several southern cities, Urban League secretaries negotiated for greater black inclusion in defense construction projects with some success. Beginning in the summer of 1940, Clarence Laws applied political pressure to get black tradesmen hired for the construction of the La Garde Army Hospital in New Orleans. He eventually obtained employment for three hundred carpenters with the local black AFL carpenters union. After gaining this concession, the NOUL industrial secretary turned to securing training and employment for African Americans in the city's burgeoning shipbuilding industry.[26] The following year, William Bell of the AUL helped broker the hiring of forty black carpenters and fifteen painters at Camp Gordon outside of the city, while the Little Rock Urban League also secured employment for black workers at Camp Robinson.[27]

In these cities, Urban League success with the AFL building trades set a precedent for other southern affiliates in the succeeding years. In Virginia during 1942, the Richmond Urban League (RUL) negotiated with the newly formed Office of Production Management (OPM) and the AFL to get thirty-six workers placed at the Gilpin Court Housing Project and the Bellwood Army Depot and as many as 218 workers placed at the construction of Camp Picket at Blackstone, Virginia. The RUL also gained training opportunities in the shipbuilding trades for local African Americans in 1942.[28] The following year in Arkansas, the Little Rock Urban League again arranged meetings with the white carpenters Local 690, contractors, and federal representatives of the Public Housing Authority to secure work for black carpenters at the Bauxite defense housing project. In these cities, NUL industrial relations departments provided vital assistance to southern black tradesmen who hoped to gain economic mobility.[29]

Outside of construction trades, however, efforts to gain training and employment in aircraft and shipbuilding industries remained elusive for black men and women throughout the South. Dallas's jobs movement, which began in 1940, characterizes the nature of passive resistance among white leaders over war training and employment in the city's aircraft industry. For over three years, the DNCC and the Dallas chapter of the NAACP waged a local movement for industrial training and integration by seeking assistance from the federal government at the local, state, and national levels. From the beginning, black leaders in Dallas hoped to build personal ties to the city's white elites in local business and government. DNCC executive secretary Maynard Jackson Sr. also sought to use contacts with black officials at the state National Youth Administration (NYA) office in Austin and, after 1941, within the OPM. Despite their efforts, however, in 1941 and 1942 Maceo Smith and the DNCC encountered continuous delays from local USES and city administrators in the effort to gain training facilities for the new aircraft industry and defense jobs in general.[30]

Since 1933, black industrial relations leaders had sought federal support on the jobs issue from liberal allies in the federal government. After June 1941, they hoped to enforce Roosevelt's Executive Order 8802, which prohibited discrimination on government contract jobs. Throughout the war, local leaders established and consolidated regional political networks through federally appointed "black cabinet" officials. As part of his race management strategy, Roosevelt appointed African Americans, including Mary McLeod Bethune, Robert Weaver, and Lawrence Oxley, to oversee minority divisions of New Deal programs and federal labor departments. With the heightened manpower needs of the defense program, liberal federal administrators active in the South from the OPM and the FEPC provided the political foundations for a more coordinated regional fair employment movement.[31]

In the years prior to Pearl Harbor, black labor and political networks in the South and Southwest were bolstered by state-, regional-, and national-level patronage appointments in the Democratic Party. On the labor front, New Deal liberals made a special point of challenging racial discrimination in federal job programs and relief agencies. After 1933, Lawrence Oxley, head of Negro Services in the United States Department of Labor, served as an important liaison, advocate, and arbitrator of black labor concerns throughout the United States, including Louisiana.[32] In this developing network of federal labor advisors and labor leaders, older black institutions such as the Knights of Pythias facilitated federal labor relations for black workers. In New Orleans, for example, Pythian chancellor S. W. Green successfully negotiated for the hiring of skilled black workers for the federal Hoover Dam and All American Canal projects out west.[33] In Dallas, the Colored Knights of Pythias actually pioneered the placement of black workers on federal projects, so that by the fall of 1933, black-operated FERA job centers existed in New Orleans, Atlanta, and Jacksonville.[34] Locally, these institutional and church leaders, who served as de facto labor contractors for federal public works programs, became essential to maintaining black political and economic leverage within the Democratic Party.[35]

With war mobilization, Roosevelt continued to rely on white and black advisors to manage race and manpower problems. When the president formed the OPM early in 1941, new director Sidney Hillman appointed Robert Weaver head of the new Negro Employment and Training Division and Will Alexander, a southern liberal, as director of the Minority Group Services. Naturally, black leaders in the Southwest sought to use these new appointments for influence in the jobs movement stand-off. On the eve of the threatened March on Washington, Maynard Jackson in Dallas notified Robert Weaver of the discriminatory practices of North American Aviation (NAA) in nearby Grand Prairie, Texas.[36] Clarence Laws also sought the OPM's influence in fighting Delta Shipyards in New Orleans by requesting assistance from Weaver and George Streator of the OPM's Negro Employment and Training Division. By early 1942, both Streator and Weaver, now under the newly formed War Production Board (WPB), made trips to the South, stopping in New Orleans, Houston, and Dallas to negotiate with the AFL Trades Councils and local industries on the integration issue. In Dallas, the DNCC and the NAACP sought the assistance of the FEPC and Streator to investigate the exclusion of AFL carpenters Local 774 from Dallas area housing projects. In New Orleans, the NOUL and Clarence Laws wanted assurances that black New Orleanians would not be relegated only to farmwork during the war. As federal liaison to the black community, Streator in fact had little influence within the conservative OPM. While labor officials like Streator, Weaver, and Oxley understood their limits in shaping production policy, they nonetheless integrated specific defense projects when they could on a case-by-case basis. More importantly, their presence helped consolidate new political networks among black Democrats in the South.[37]

The OPM's and eventually the WPB's seemingly paradoxical stance on equal employment reflected not only the exigencies of war but also the factions of civil rights supporters and extreme conservatives within the agencies. While the FEPC remained under control of the OPM and later the WPB, the conservatism within these two production and procurement agencies contrasted greatly with the more liberal goals of the FEPC. WPB leadership at the regional level certainly set the tone for maintaining the racial status quo. Frank Neely, the southern regional director of the WPB and chairman of the Federal Reserve Bank in Atlanta, openly voiced his displeasure with any FEPC goals. As John Beecher discovered in the spring of 1942 on a visit with Neely, the WPB director opposed any FEPC activities in the South. In reference to the AUL's drive for jobs at the Bell bomber plant, Neely labeled the effort as an Axis conspiracy and an example of "agitation" to "create dissension and to impede the war effort." In a rather heated exchange with Beecher, Neely argued that the only discrimination that concerned him was that against southern industries.[38]

The FEPC Comes South

Despite such white intransigence, the fight against discrimination in defense industries stimulated black activists in the South. The founding of the FEPC as a division of the OPM in June 1941 bolstered the political alliances gained within Negro Divisions of the OPM and WPB. One month after the creation of the FEPC, Carter Wesley in Houston used the committee's West Coast Aircraft Hearings in Los Angeles to publicize discriminatory employment practices by NAA in Dallas and Convair in Fort Worth. Up to that point, NAA in Dallas had employed only forty-two black workers under a 123-million-dollar contract. Hence, Wesley asked the FEPC's Ernest Dickerson to include NAA's plant near Dallas in the government investigation of discrimination at the NAA plant in Inglewood, California. As state director of the Allied for Defense Council in Texas, Wesley also organized local Defense Councils in black communities throughout the state. By using his own newspapers in Texas and Louisiana to focus on the jobs movement, Wesley exemplified the growing effort to publicize the FEPC's agenda to workers and to report job discrimination where it existed throughout the South and Southwest.[39]

The southern jobs movement received a symbolic boost in February 1942 when the FEPC scheduled the committee's fourth regional hearings for Birmingham, Alabama, the industrial heart of Dixie. During the four months preceding the June hearings, FEPC field examiners traveled throughout Louisiana, Mississippi, Tennessee, Alabama, and Georgia and made their first real forays into the Deep South. In the process, the FEPC field staff established and strengthened contacts with local liberal, labor, and black organizations that hoped to press forward on the jobs issue. In Georgia especially, the FEPC made new contacts with the Savannah NAACP, the Macon Citizens Committee, as well as Atlanta's Negro Committee for Defense Training (NCDT), an organization formed with the help of William Bell and the AUL.[40]

Prior to February 1942, the FEPC garnered slow support from southern workers locked out of war industries. That winter, reports of discrimination in southern defense industries from the national office of the NAACP arrived gradually at FEPC field offices. Throughout 1941 and early 1942, the NAACP headquarters in New York received letters from a couple of local chapter leaders in Virginia as well as some African American workers in Pensacola and Cherry Point, North Carolina, seeking justice in defense employment. With the arrival of the FEPC investigators in the South beginning in February 1942, the trickle of letters seeking help from the NAACP and the FEPC turned into a flow. By April and continuing through November, the NAACP headquarters obtained letters protesting job discrimination from local chapters, church leaders, and workers in smaller towns such as Roanoke, Portsmouth, and Gloucester County, Virginia, as well as larger city chapters in Tampa, Mobile, Jackson, Charlotte, Savannah, and Atlanta. With its growing commitment to labor relations, the NAACP represented a key institution for local workers in the fight for fair employment.[41]

During the spring and summer of 1942 the FEPC's regional presence galvanized leaders and workers in black communities throughout the South. In McGehee, Arkansas, Ennis Crawford sought help from the NAACP because black carpenters received forty cents per hour while white workers made one dollar per hour in the construction of a Japanese intern camp. In Charlotte, North Carolina, local secretary Kelly Alexander wrote the NAACP in New York for help in securing construction jobs at a nearby naval ordnance plant. Likewise, local elites in the Jackson, Mississippi, NAACP chapter sent a long, eloquent resolution to the NAACP, President Roosevelt, Congress, the OPM, and the FEPC demanding work for black women at a new ordnance plant in nearby Flora. The leaders emphasized how in Jackson "the biggest crowd of Colored people in this City for many years" had gathered to protest the all-white hiring policy at the plant. The group cited the fact that "much suffering" existed in Mississippi among African Americans "for want of work" and that large numbers had been "forced off the farms, due to this great curtailment of agriculture and the closing down of non-defense industry."[42] In states like Mississippi, where agricultural displacement and denial of WPA funds to African Americans were severe, the need for defense opportunities created a special urgency.

As the FEPC began to assess industrial discrimination across the South, African American leadership in New Orleans and Atlanta stood out as the most advanced and well organized in the region. Black advancement in these two cities stemmed in large part from the presence of several historically black universities and dedicated social workers, such as Ernest Wright and Clarence Laws in New Orleans and William Bell in Atlanta. The respected sociologist Ira De A. Reid at Atlanta University was another key black activist committed to labor reform and fair employment in the South.[43] Hence, the tight networks between social workers and the NUL affiliates accounted for the high level of organization in the struggle for job opportunities in both New Orleans and Atlanta. In contrast, the accomplishments of NUL affiliates in other southern cities, such as Memphis, Little Rock, Tampa, and Richmond, never matched those in New Orleans and Atlanta. In Memphis, especially, the state political machine under Edward H. Crump allied with the AFL to curtail the local affiliate's industrial relations agenda.[44]

Atlanta, as the headquarters for the entire NUL southern regional office, received a large share of attention and funding from the national office. William Bell, as both the executive secretary of the AUL and the head of the NUL southern regional office, focused much of his energies in 1941 and 1942 on the defense jobs issue in Atlanta. In the region overall, Clarence Laws remained the most militant and outspoken proponent of economic justice from 1940 until he was drafted in the winter of 1943.[45] As part of the Urban League's southern strategy, these local affiliates initiated well-organized campaigns for jobs in new defense industries. At one point, Clarence Laws gathered seven thousand applications for Delta Shipyards in New Orleans, while in Atlanta William Bell presented Bell Aircraft and local officials with eight thousand applications for training and employment. Robert Weaver recognized such hard work in May 1942 when he lauded both Laws and Bell specifically for their efforts to negotiate and cooperate with organized labor and the federal government. However, their efforts remained severely limited by local forces.[46]

The Limits of the Jobs Movement in the South, 1941–1942

Generally, the question of jobs boiled down to AFL local unions' commitment to discrimination. AFL trade unions succeeded by guaranteeing jobs to white workers based on the ideal of white privilege. Because most government jobs maintained contracts with the AFL, the conservative union's exclusion of black labor in the construction and shipbuilding trades helped maintain and consolidate white dominance in those fields. In some cases, building contractors even replaced all-black AFL painters and masons with white AFL crews.

This extreme but not uncommon practice was noted by William Moses, secretary of AFL painters Local 805 at the Pensacola Naval Air Station in December 1940 and even later at the Ingalls Shipyard in Pascagoula, Mississippi, and at Fort McPherson, Georgia.[47] Despite such discrimination, the AFL maintained a significant presence in southern black communities largely because of local and regional labor politics. In the 1930s, local machines in cities like Dallas, New Orleans, and Memphis allied with the AFL to limit the influence of more leftist CIO organizers. With the initial defense mobilization in the South, this political labor alliance continued under OPM and AFL agreements to serve the same purpose.[48]

Faced with few options, African American AFL representatives attempted to work within the AFL's Jim Crow confines and utilize any political leverage within the unions to gain jobs for black tradesmen. In New Orleans in 1942, A. J. Perrault, AFL bricklayers business agent, and Charles Lowe, business agent for AFL painters, along with Paul Dixon, agent of the shipbuilders segregated auxiliary, allied closely with Clarence Laws and the NOUL in pressuring the WPB for greater job opportunities. Likewise in Mobile, local NAACP leader and civil rights activist J. L. LeFlore initially supported the AFL in an effort to secure jobs for African Americans in defense-related construction projects and the local shipbuilding industry.[49]

For many working Americans generally, shipbuilding jobs were attractive because workers visibly supported the war effort by holding a vital war job and the wages were high. For southerners specifically, the burgeoning industry represented a dramatic shift toward a new industrial economy while offering unprecedented wages in a depressed region. In the South, however, shipyards remained bastions of white power and manhood and an environment where women and nonwhites were to know their limited place in the social and economic order. Among all defense industries, shipbuilding, because of its craft-based classification system, was the most conservative in its hiring policies. The domination of shipyards by the AFL metal trades in the South almost guaranteed black exclusion from the yards in specific crafts.

Facing continued exclusion into 1942, African American industrial integrationists in Louisiana and Alabama observed how their present exclusion in defense industries contrasted to the greater job opportunities available during the First World War. According to Paul Dixon, black workers in New Orleans during World War I entirely manned one of the two shipways at the Donulut and Williams Shipbuilding Company and constituted 75 percent of the workforce at the Jahncke Dry Docks. John Beecher heard from veteran black workers in Mobile that during the Great War the old Chickasaw Shipbuilding Company yard employed a high proportion of black workers, with some in such skilled occupations as riveting.[50] In fact, by 1942, the fifty-year-old Newport News Shipbuilding Company in Virginia represented the only major yard in the South to employ numbers of African Americans as skilled riveters.[51]

The exclusion of black men from southern shipyards during the early 1940s reflected the continued trend of laying off African Americans under the NRA wage codes of the 1930s.[52] Not only were skilled black workers excluded in the South during the Second World War, but shipyards such as Gulf in Mobile (the site of the Chickasaw yard) and Levingston in Orange, Texas, refused to hire black workers in even unskilled capacities. In 1944 economist Herbert Northrup argued that the disparity in opportunities for skilled black workers between the First and Second World Wars in southern shipyards stemmed from stricter enforcement of Boilermakers' (IBB) discriminatory policies. Robert Weaver, former head of the WMC Minority Group Services, attributed the exclusion of black welders to the symbolic role that welding held in the segregated southern labor market. According to Weaver, welding was first introduced to electricians during the 1930s. Because the AFL electricians' trade excluded African Americans, by 1940 and 1941, the welding trade in all southern shipyards was solely a white privilege. Under the southern labor caste system, the training of black workers in welding represented not only a potential threat to white job opportunities but a challenge to the labor hierarchy.[53]

The persistence of AFL contracts in the southern shipyards made it nearly impossible for black workers to find employment in their crafts in the yards. The AFL organized the majority of yards in the Gulf, as it held contracts with shipbuilding concerns in Galveston, Beaumont, New Orleans, Pascagoula, Mobile, and Tampa. In yards that remained open shop or with company unions, hiring policies also excluded black workers from skilled positions and maintained racial caste barriers on the shop floor.[54] In this regional labor battle for shipyard workers during the war, plants with Industrial Union of Marine and Shipbuilding Workers (IUMSWA-CIO) representation did offer some potential hope for black workers seeking some industrial democracy.

As the CIO's shipbuilding union based out of Patterson, New Jersey, IUMSWA had been organizing southern shipyards since the late 1930s. By 1941, IUMSWA had secured contracts at the majority of yards in the Northeast but faced greater obstruction in the Great Lakes region, the West Coast, and the South. In the southern yards along the Gulf and Atlantic Coasts especially, union organizers often faced resistance from conservative workers and local machines allied with local law enforcement, the AFL, and most shipyard management. The CIO in principle committed itself to mobilizing all industrial workers and supporting a "culture of unity" among different ethnic groups on the shop floor. This organizing strategy together with the union's leftist ties made southern elites particularly resistant to IUMSWA after 1937.[55]

Remarkably, by 1939 IUMSWA held two large yards in the Gulf South. New Orleans workers at the Todd-Johnson Dry Docks voted IUMSWA as their bargaining agent, and throughout the 1940s IUMSWA Local 29 maintained a loose hold on the Todd-Johnson yard. In Mobile, IUMSWA Local 18 organized the Alabama Dry Dock and Shipbuilding Company (ADDSCO) yard in 1938. Together, these two yards represented the two major CIO shipyards on the Gulf Coast. In the South Atlantic, IUMSWA Local 59 at the Miami Shipbuilding Company represented a small but important gain for the CIO in Florida. IUMSWA's rhetorical support of employing semiskilled and skilled black workers often served as a key to organizing black workers. Yet union organizers at IUMSWA, as with most other CIO unions with white majorities throughout the South, often hesitated to openly embrace a civil rights platform for fear of alienating the more conservative white workers.[56]

Nationally, the IBB AFL maintained all-black auxiliaries in cities with large numbers of black workers in the West and the Great Lakes region. In the South, black auxiliaries existed in Tampa and New Orleans.[57] Paul Dixon, as the new business agent in New Orleans, urged all black men interested in registering for shipyard jobs to visit the IBB Local 37-A office on LaSalle Street near the NAACP chapter office and Shakespeare Park, where the People's Defense League held public protest meetings. Since the AFL building and metal trades controlled the yards at both Higgins Industries and Delta, black workers' only chance at finding employment in these yards lay with the IBB and other AFL trade unions. As with all other AFL auxiliaries in the nation, the IBB Local 37-A in New Orleans maintained little power under the Jim Crow setup, in which black members had no vote, only half benefits and insurance, and no real grievance procedure in place. Despite such barriers, Paul Dixon, through his alliance with the NOUL, worked diligently to procure jobs for local African Americans. By late 1942, however, Dixon's persistent attempts to secure employment of skilled black workers at Delta resulted in his discharge from the IBB.[58]

The experiences of black AFL labor leaders in New Orleans illustrate the extreme limits of black power within unions dominated by conservative white craftsmen. During the spring of 1942, John Beecher found that Ernest Delpit, the AFL carpenters representative, and A. J. Perrault of the bricklayers union both considered William Donnell, white AFL organizer, to be the person principally responsible for their exclusion from defense-related job opportunities. Likewise, when Paul Dixon began to form his IBB auxiliary in February 1942, he received resistance and veiled threats from local representative J. McCollum and other white members of Local 37. Once Dixon formed 37-A, the auxiliary, he claimed that the white representatives physically and verbally abused him whenever he visited the IBB Local 37 office.[59]

By the summer of 1942, the jobs issue had polarized many southern communities along racial lines. Most often, black fair employment leaders found themselves allied against white labor leaders and education officials intent on preserving the status quo. In Atlanta, the AUL and the Negro Committee for Defense Training (NCDT) lined up against the Georgia Department of Vocational Education and the Georgia SES office to secure training as well as the AFL's International Association of Machinists (IAM) for proposed jobs at the new Bell bomber plant. In Dallas, the DNCC pushed hard for training for the new aircraft plants in Dallas and Fort Worth, only to receive token training opportunities from the local school board and NAA personnel. In New Orleans, the NOUL's Clarence Laws along with more militant leaders of the People's Defense League, A. L. Davis and Ernest Wright, led the fight for skilled training in that city against the local school board and the AFL Metal Trades Council throughout 1941. Likewise in Mobile, local NAACP president J. L. LeFlore experienced tremendous resistance to training and employment of black workers from the local AFL Metal Trades Council in alliance with local and state training officials.[60]

Two weeks after the U.S. military victory at Midway in the Pacific, the FEPC's Birmingham hearings brought this domestic conflict to the national political arena. Urban League secretaries Clarence Laws and William Bell featured prominently in the testimonies against the lack of training and employment opportunities for southern African Americans. In addition, the FEPC heard testimony from New Orleans's Paul Dixon as he recounted failed attempts to gain referrals for skilled black shipyard workers at Delta in New Orleans. In opposition to these more progressive factions, representatives testified in behalf of the AFL Metal Trades Councils of New Orleans and Mobile as well as private corporations, including Delta Shipyards in New Orleans, ADDSCO in Mobile, and the Bell bomber plant in Atlanta, most of whom blamed the AFL for the employment policies.[61]

FEPC strategists sought to avoid ideological divisiveness by focusing on the war production problems caused by southern defense industries' reluctance to utilize skilled black workers. As John Beecher observed to the FEPC's Will

Alexander, agitation would "do far more harm than good, and result in excluding Negroes from the few opportunities which remained open to them in the South." Furthermore, as Beecher noted, "there was no real demand on the part of Negro workers to back this agitation carried on by a few self-styled leaders like LeFlore in Mobile." Beecher's observations suggest that black workers themselves avoided direct action as a strategy. By emphasizing the production angle, the FEPC hoped to gain the backing of the War and Navy Departments and thereby steer clear of what FEPC executive secretary Lawrence Cramer called "vague generalizations about democracy or constitutional rights."[62]

White conservatives still resented what they saw at the Birmingham hearings as a federal challenge to southern social customs and states' rights under the guise of maintaining war production schedules. As Alabama governor Frank Dixon declared in July 1942, "the present emergency should not be used as a pretext to bring about the abolition of the color lines in the South."[63] During that month, in a highly publicized speech to Alabama Kiwanis members, Dixon declared his refusal to sign an agreement with the Defense Supplies Corporation for cloth made in Alabama, because the contract contained a nondiscrimination clause. Throughout the South during that summer and fall, thousands of white conservative businessmen and workers as well as over forty-two newspaper editorials supported Dixon's symbolic declaration. This broad support illustrates the degree to which the race issue excited white conservatives.[64]

Ultimately, however, Frank Dixon acquiesced on the issue of employing black workers in defense industries.[65] By September, he supported black training and employment in war industries with the guarantee that "any such training and use" would have to be "within the bounds of the segregation system established by law and social custom in the southern states."[66] As the governor began to compromise on the issue of mobilizing black workers, he revealed an understanding among some southern capitalists and conservative black leaders that expanding black employment would not compromise segregation.

Among southern industrialists, New Orleans shipbuilder Andrew Jackson Higgins became the most outspoken on the full utilization of black workers under segregation. In the spring of 1942, Higgins received a thirty-million-dollar United States Maritime Commission (USMC) contract for an all-welded, assembly line Liberty shipyard outside of New Orleans near the village of Michoud. The largest contract in USMC history, the Michoud facility plans initially called for anywhere from 40,000 to 100,000 workers to migrate to New Orleans, a prospect that raised questions about the city's ability to accommodate such a large influx of workers. In response to the question of labor, Higgins openly supported the utilization of African American skilled workers on a large scale. In April 1942, Eleanor Roosevelt, in her nationally syndicated "My Day" column, lauded Higgins's recent speech to the Southern Conference on Human Welfare in Nashville, where he outlined plans to train black and white workers on a fifty-fifty basis in New Orleans.[67]

Generally, the majority of southern employers refrained from such liberal training and employment policies. However, Higgins presented the plan as a way to utilize local labor and avoid problems associated with uncontrolled white migration into the city. As Higgins informed the FEPC's Ernest Trimble, "In a nutshell, we are going to use plain common sense and there is going to be no prejudice." At the same time, such a standpoint represented far more than practical policy to African Americans in New Orleans. The employment of approximately twenty thousand black workers in a large southern industry with potential industrial permanency would represent a dramatic shift in southern and national employment practices. As Clarence Laws hoped, the Higgins policy "would improve the morale of local Negroes and give new training and employment patterns for industrialists throughout the nation."[68]

That spring, the New Orleans AFL Metal Trades Council allegedly agreed to utilize black labor at Higgins's Michoud plant. Despite their claims in the summer of 1941 that "boilermakers at Higgins are white only," by April 1942, the *Louisiana Weekly* announced that the local IBB representatives at Higgins had agreed to work with skilled African American labor. Throughout the spring, Higgins continued to support the training and employment of southern African Americans. In April, Higgins spoke to the Louisiana State Federation of Labor regarding the possibilities of "tapping" black labor in the South. And in a response to the *Weekly*'s skepticism about his company employing skilled black workers, Higgins continued to promote his liberal hiring policy by arguing that "our company may be the means of showing that the two races can get along well together with equal respect for the other and equal rates for the same work."[69]

In his spring tour of the South, FEPC investigator John Beecher discovered that some southern industrialists in Birmingham, the South's most industrial city, nominally approved of training and utilizing black industrial labor when pressed on the issue. Tennessee Coal and Iron's personnel director, Robert Vance, advocated the need for black training while emphasizing the necessity of keeping "racial equality" out of the training and employment program. According to Vance, an insistence on "social equality of the Negro with the whites would do damage to help the Negro from an economic viewpoint." Likewise, Donald Cramer of Avondale Mills in Birmingham also favored "giving Negroes in Birmingham the training necessary to raise their income status," yet he quickly added that "the question of social equality with the whites need not be raised at this time."[70]

Mirroring industrialists' views on segregation, African American jobs movement leaders in these southern cities also consciously advocated segregated training and employment and deferred the social equality issue in order to gain even basic economic concessions. For instance, John Beecher found that Emory Jackson, African American editor of the *Birmingham World*, advocated black training while demurring that "we have never agitated for social equality." On the employment front, leaders such as Clarence Laws and DNCC executive secretary Virgil Williams supported segregated working conditions. Laws wrote to Jesse Thomas, field director of the NUL, regarding the possibility of a segregated shop at Delta Shipyards in October 1941. While he did not favor "this discrimination," Laws felt that if they could get "one shop which will give employment to between 800 to 1,000 men," then they might be able to use it "as an opening wedge to get into other shops." In Dallas, the Negro Chamber of Commerce, frustrated by exclusion at North American, also sought segregated facilities as an accommodation. In 1942, Virgil Williams informed the FEPC how the chamber intended to employ "large numbers" of workers "so that complete departments" would be "manned by Negroes rather than mixing white and Negro workers together." In utilizing such conservative strategies, these men reluctantly prioritized economic gains for workers over the ideals of social equality.[71] Yet, by doing so, their strategy reflected the pragmatic goals of most workers who resented segregation but were eager to gain economic mobility.

WMC Recruitment and African American Mobility

In the months following the Birmingham hearings, black leaders in the South remained both accommodating and impatient on the jobs issue. Yet in early August 1942, their hope turned to bitterness when Roosevelt neutralized the FEPC's power completely by transferring it from the War Production Board to the War Manpower Commission. While the specific causes of the FEPC's disruptive move may be difficult to pinpoint, certainly Roosevelt's need to accommodate southern critics of the FEPC in an election year provided the greatest motive. Other reasons for the change involved internal politics within the FEPC and WPB as well as conservative reaction to the proposed

Southwest hearings in El Paso. In any case, the transfer dealt a psychological blow to the jobs movement by eliminating the field staff that solidified liberal labor and civil rights networks and by canceling the forthcoming El Paso hearings. Importantly also, the agency's decline from August 1942 to the summer of 1943 forced black leaders in the South to bargain solely with the War Manpower Commission in the struggle for jobs.[72]

In New Orleans, job prospects for skilled black workers appeared even dimmer in the weeks preceding the FEPC transfer, when the USMC suddenly canceled the thirty-million-dollar Liberty ship contract for Higgins Industries. Immediately, Andrew Jackson Higgins, along with Congressman F. Edward Hebert, AFL Metal Trades Council leaders, and African American leaders all expressed tremendous contempt and outrage at the USMC's news. Hebert and New Orleans AFL Metal Trades Council representatives demanded an investigation into the affair. Higgins and Hebert both charged that the USMC canceled the contract under pressure from old-line eastern shipbuilders within the commission who feared increased competition from Higgins. In response, the USMC and the WPB blamed a nationwide shortage of steel. Although the incident illustrated the antagonism between southern and eastern industrial interests, the city of New Orleans, in all likelihood, would not have been able to accommodate the shipyard's manpower needs and an influx of up to 100,000 persons in 1942. At that time, the city was already experiencing a housing shortage, and the plans for producing forty thousand new houses were not likely to mature with the WPB's restrictive priorities on building materials. In fact, after brief negotiations, Roosevelt approved utilizing the Michoud facility for aircraft manufacturing, a project much more manageable for New Orleans than the giant Liberty shipbuilding plant.[73]

African Americans in New Orleans reacted even more bitterly to the Michoud contract cancellation than did white conservatives. But whereas local white boosters pointed to East Coast interests in the motives of the USMC, local black leaders chastised local conservatives themselves for their complacency on the matter. As the *Louisiana Weekly* wrote, "The greatest mystery of this whole incident will remain the lack of interest by white civic and business organizations of New Orleans." In its questioning of the affair, the *Weekly* singled out the New Orleans Association of Commerce, the Kiwanis, and the Young Men's Business Club specifically for criticism while giving credit to the local AFL Metal Trades Council for demanding an answer to the contract cancellation. As the *Weekly* declared, "Some hint that business heads were envious of the wages which labor would have received at Higgins Industries, particularly Negro labor." Further questioning the motives of

Chapter Two

civic leaders, the *Weekly* continued, "We know that to some people of questioned democratic loyalty, keeping certain economic and racial patterns intact is more important than winning the war itself." While black New Orleanians had their own suspicions, Higgins also acknowledged the potential effect of the plant on local wages and labor relations. As Higgins stated in October 1942, while he could not prove that local powers scuttled the plan, he understood that many of the shipyard's opponents in New Orleans "were afraid they might lose their chauffeur, or have to pay their servants more."[74]

In this pattern of resistance, black southerners felt tremendous acrimony toward the lack of employment opportunities during the war boom in 1942. John Beecher reported in the spring of 1942, "Wherever I have gone I have found Negroes deeply resentful over their exclusion from defense training opportunities and consequently defense jobs." Moreover, Beecher observed, "This resentment is by no means confined to the Negro leadership in various communities, but it is widespread amongst the less articulate." In October 1942, E. J. Wright, CIO organizer and civil rights activist in New Orleans, observed a great indifference toward the war among many underemployed black New Orleanians along Rampart Street, one of the city's main black business thoroughfares. The street symbolized "the action and frame of mind of a certain strata of our group," Wright noticed. Claiming that the "Rampart Street syndrome" was common throughout the South and the United States, Wright announced that "empty sermons about freedom and democracy and what the war is all about fall upon the ears of persons so blinded by the limitations of their own individual lives" that they were "unable to grasp the full meaning of the war."[75]

African Americans in the South resented the continuation of employment discrimination while they were asked to support the fight against fascism. In 1941 and 1942, the black masses throughout the United States expressed tremendous frustration and ill will toward the continued denial of civil rights during wartime. Starting in early 1942, black media embraced the "Double V" slogan in an effort to temper this anger. Publicizing both the fight abroad and at home allowed the black media in the South to openly address the exclusion of African Americans from defense industries and the attempts to force them into agricultural labor.[76] In New Orleans, Clarence Laws continued the fight for fair employment by repeatedly challenging Delta Shipyards, the local USES office, and the AFL in his own column, "Headline Highlights," and through Urban League press releases. Laws questioned white patriotism when he wrote, "Negroes can ill afford to forget" that although the Allies had not begun to win the war, "reactionary forces" worked continually "to retard the progress of the Negro." In another column, Laws further charged that white conservatives were "more concerned with preserving the economic and intellectual status quo than they are winning the war itself."[77]

Black workers demanding defense jobs in turn reacted indignantly to attempts by the USES to recruit them solely for the 1942 fall harvest. As the FEPC's field staff discovered in the spring and as the *Louisiana Weekly* publicized in the fall of 1942, African Americans in New Orleans feared that they were to be forced on to farms as they had in the past.[78] The *Louisiana Weekly* became openly incensed during the harvest season in 1942 as southern agricultural employers increased efforts to maintain control over the black rural labor force. With increasing enforcement of work-or-fight laws throughout the South, more moderate papers such as Carter Wesley's *Dallas Express* argued that farmwork for black Dallasites could provide "wholesome fresh air and food of the country." In contrast, the *Louisiana Weekly* spoke more forcefully against the issue throughout the fall of 1942. In an editorial entitled "Slavery 1942," the paper criticized the "work or jail" orders and antimigratory laws designed to "maintain control of the vast Southern reservoir of cheap labor." As the editorial charged, southern states "don't want to lose their black labor." As they had during World War I, rural black families in the South encountered severe resistance in their efforts to leave farm and domestic work for higher wages elsewhere.[79]

That previous spring, Clarence Laws had hoped to use black participation in southern agricultural production as a means of winning economic concessions for the black community. Specifically, the Urban League director demanded assurances that black New Orleanians would be offered war industry jobs if they were going to cooperate with the WPB and the USDA in the "Food for Victory" program. In a conference with George Streator, Louisiana SES director Henry LeBlanc, and black AFL painters and bricklayers representatives, Clarence Laws declared that until the WPB assured him such demands were met, black workers would not participate voluntarily in the farm program or any other program. While the USES and Delta Shipyards continued to stall on Laws's demands during the summer and fall of 1942, Paul Dixon's cooperation with the USES in recruiting farmworkers may have certainly facilitated the eventual WMC placement of black workers in New Orleans for defense jobs out west.[80]

In a belated but symbolic concession to the southern jobs movement, the WPA, NYA, and United States Office of Education in the South finally began sponsoring token segregated training programs for African Americans in 1942. Initially, southern states established their first black defense job-training programs at land grant colleges and technical schools, such as Tuskegee Institute, Louisiana's Southern University, and Texas's Prairie View A&M. City leaders also slowly acquiesced to black demands for training facilities. The WPA established shipbuilding training programs at Xavier University in New Orleans and at a center in Houston late in 1941. In Atlanta, the first black segregated training facilities for the Bell bomber plant at the Booker T. Washington Aircraft School did not begin until November 1942, the same month that Dallas received its first training classes for black workers in the aircraft industry.[81]

These federally sponsored programs trained African American men and women from the South for jobs in welding, sheet metal, electrical, and mechanical work. NYA defense programs, which ran from 1942 to 1943, offered several thousand young black men and women new economic opportunities otherwise not available to them. At one center in Dallas, women even comprised 80 percent of the graduates.[82] Theoretically, federal manpower administrators in the South were to find defense jobs for these hundreds of students. However, in the Jim Crow job placement system, African Americans had little chance for advancement in the South. Under the WMC, as a more sophisticated interstate and interregional USES recruitment and placement manpower program developed, the WMC's ability to recruit skilled white trainees throughout the South for southern industries perpetuated the exclusion of African Americans from local defense industries. For the Gulf Coast shipyards especially, the USES established a more efficient recruitment network between federal and private white training centers and defense plants throughout the region and the nation.[83]

As black trainees began graduating from training programs in Texas and Louisiana during the spring and summer of 1942, the WMC regional office in Dallas expanded the recruiting of southern black graduates in these states for shipyards in the North and the West. Thus, the WMC developed a practice of exporting locally trained black workers for defense jobs outside of the South while it imported trained white workers from all over the nation for southern industries. This policy contradicted the WMC's standard employment stabilization policy of utilizing local labor to avoid unnecessary in-migration.

In Houston the establishment of an African American training facility in November 1941 presented a test case for the employment of locally trained black workers in the Southwest. As graduates sought employment in local industries that spring, S. B. Byars, director of the Houston Negro Training School, talked with the personnel directors in Houston's two shipyards, which employed over fifteen thousand workers each. At the locally owned

Brown Shipyards, the director told Byars that "the time was not ripe" for integration due to friction with first-class welders. Likewise, the personnel director of Houston Shipyards, a subsidiary of the Todd Corporation in New York, informed Byars that trainees would not be safe due to "general unrest in the shipyards." After these unofficial visits, Byars never followed up with Brown or Houston on the possibility of employing trained black workers. Instead, he initiated talks with the Houston USES about the possibility of gaining referrals to shipyards for the graduates. According to Byars, the USES told him that "the boys completing our training would be listed and referred to the shipyards along with others." When no placements or calls from the USES came in Houston, Byars then contacted the Houston area WMC, which arranged to have Byars's students get releases for other areas. By September 1942, Byars's graduates had found work at Higgins in New Orleans as well as shipyards in Massachusetts and California.[84]

In the spring of 1942, the New Orleans WMC and USES offices began placing skilled graduates from Xavier University's welding program in shipyards outside Louisiana. To publicize this new policy, the *Louisiana Weekly* ran a front-page photo that featured three local welders who had left New Orleans to work in Virginia shipyards. As the newly formed WMC began organizing interregional recruitment and placement networks, USES offices, as the field arm of the WMC, commonly sought key persons in the black community to assist in the recruitment of black labor. Up to the summer of 1942, USES administrators in New Orleans had requested Paul Dixon's assistance in securing agricultural workers for the Farm Placement Division in the office. Yet whenever Dixon pressed the New Orleans USES to place skilled workers at Delta Shipyards, he was repeatedly denied any openings for skilled workers.[85] James H. Bond, the WMC Region X director in Dallas, responded to Dixon's persistent requests by arguing quite sincerely that "the problem" of utilizing black workers in the South had "numerous ramifications" and would "require a little more time to overcome than in other sections of this region." Thus, to avoid local industrial integration, the New Orleans USES requested Dixon's assistance in securing black workers for the shipyards in California and Oregon as well as plants in Utah and Nevada during the summer of 1942.[86]

The development of the WMC's recruitment policy, placing skilled southern black workers in East and West Coast shipyards, represented a distinct departure from the southern practice of placing skilled black workers only in agricultural and unskilled labor jobs. The WMC's national interregional recruitment network in fact provided skilled employment for a fair number of

African Americans trained in the South under the WPA and NYA in 1942 and 1943. According to the *Dallas Express,* the NYA at Prairie View, Texas, trained close to 241 workers from July 1942 to April 1943. The WMC placed the majority of those workers in California, Oregon, and Washington shipyards. According to S. B. Byars, by May 1944 Houston's WPA training had produced close to seven or eight hundred graduates who found work in the yards of Higgins in New Orleans, Cal Ship and Consolidated Shipyards in Los Angeles, Pacific Bridge in San Francisco, Moore Dry Docks and Bethlehem Steel in Oakland, Mare Island Shipyards in Vallejo, California, the Kaiser yards in Richmond, California, Portland, Vancouver, and Seattle, as well as the Sun Shipyard in Chester, Pennsylvania.[87]

In WMC Region VII, which covered the Southeast, administrators also began recruiting southern-trained black workers for East and West Coast defense industries in 1942. In May, the WMC was rapidly placing graduates of the Florida Normal War Training Center in Jacksonville in shipyards and airports in places such as Chester, Pennsylvania, Brunswick, Georgia, Bridgeport, Connecticut, and other cities, including Charleston, Norfolk, Los Angeles, and Chicago. During that month, the WMC began openly recruiting trained workers in Atlanta for West Coast shipyards in Puget Sound and the San Francisco Bay Area. By July, the Atlanta NYA announced that some 693 out of 1,315 youth graduates had been placed in skilled jobs throughout the nation where they were earning as much as $9.38 per day.

As the Booker T. Washington Aircraft School in Atlanta began producing some fifteen to twenty-five workers every two weeks, many graduates failed to find skilled work at the Bell bomber plant. Hence, the WMC and AUL began placing the workers in aircraft plants in California, Connecticut, Pennsylvania, New York, Ohio, Alabama, and Maryland. Beginning in July 1942, the WMC recruited some thirty-one black women trained by the Fayetteville, North Carolina, NYA for General Electric and the Fort Mammoth Signal Corporation in New Jersey. This placement process is significant, because for many female workers, training and employment opportunities in the electrical and aircraft industries represented important means of gaining economic independence for the first time.[88]

The continued exclusion of local workers from local shipyards and aircraft plants in the South in 1942 symbolized WMC and USES ineffectiveness in implementing manpower stabilization plans. When Paul Dixon complained to Paul McNutt in November 1942, Dixon exposed the regional WMC's exporting of trained black workers. In response, the WMC director of operations in Washington politely reprimanded WMC Region X officials for their failure to push for the employment of qualified labor in the local shipyards.[89] Despite such pressure from Washington, the regional WMC and local USES offices failed to enforce the Washington office's suggestions.

Throughout 1942 and 1943 the Dallas area WMC continuously recruited trained black workers from Texas NYA training centers for West Coast industries, placing 50 of 241 NYA graduates up to April 1943. The WMC sent trainees not only from Dallas but also from nearby smaller towns such as McKinney and Denison, where employers refused to hire them. Despite assurances that local WMC officials were interested in "proper training programs for Negro people of Dallas," the city's black defense job-training center closed in September 1943 due to low attendance. In response, *Dallas Express* reporter J. Clarence Davis criticized white authorities' lack of support for the center. Accusing city leaders of establishing the training center "under a death plan," Davis lamented that of the 225 graduates, "the majority . . . who got jobs were forced to go to other states."[90]

The WMC's recruitment policy raises questions about the agency's (and hence the federal government's) role in preserving the economic status quo in the region while also providing economic mobility for black southerners.[91] Southern conservatives often spoke out vehemently against the FEPC and its symbolic challenge to southern traditions despite its lack of enforcement capabilities. Perhaps because the WMC avoided enforcing fair employment practices, conservatives initially overlooked its role in actively recruiting African Americans for work outside of the South. Such a policy reduced regional surplus labor market resources and challenged local employers' control of labor markets. Eventually, however, the federally sponsored recruitment program did not go unnoticed by southern conservatives.

The WMC discovered throughout 1942 that rural employers in particular resisted the war's drain on local labor supplies. As WMC recruiting networks became more sophisticated throughout 1942, southern rural employers began to maintain control over their local labor resources by resisting federal regulation of local labor markets. Rural employers, like urban industrialists and African American integrationists, attempted to maintain relations with local USES offices and to influence decisions that affected local labor policies. Relations between the southern WMC and rural conservatives at the beginning of the war, however, were not always cordial. With the increased demands from conservative rural elites and African American fair employment advocates, the WMC in the South became mired in a debate over manpower that reflected the transformation of national labor needs.

During the latter part of 1942, the WMC's focus on equal access to defense work in the South reflected federal concerns over African American wartime morale as well as manpower efficiency. As WMC administrators in Washington informed regional representatives in Dallas, the USES must "improve the quality and significance of our work in the South and with the Negro community." Throughout the fall of 1942, WMC's Frank McSherry existed as the sole staff member in Washington who dealt directly with discrimination complaints in Texas and Georgia. By December 1942, however, McSherry was called for active duty, and no successor followed up on his interest in the discrimination cases. With such inattention and apathy toward these complaints, the WMC generally failed to gain the trust of black leaders in the jobs movement.[92]

As white male labor resources dwindled and local manpower needs increased in 1943, African American industrial integrationists in the South and Southwest continued to challenge employment discrimination with mixed results. The futile experiences of these activists in 1942 illustrate the arbitrary conditions within local labor markets, which had little bearing on when and to what degree black workers found employment in southern defense industries. Nevertheless, the emergence of a distinct but fragmented integration movement in the South represented the growth of political alliances among black leaders concerned specifically with the struggle for labor and civil rights. This evolving union of local southern activists, black cabinet members, and the field staff of the FEPC in the spring of 1942 illustrated the potential role of the federal government in providing wartime economic opportunities for black southerners. While the integration movement remained somewhat fragmented and locally centered, the increased federal presence on the southern home front nonetheless helped consolidate black political networks in the South.

For African American workers in search of defense industry wages, the growing sophistication of the WMC interregional recruitment and placement system provided a measure of economic and geographic mobility. As the FEPC retreated from the South after the Birmingham hearings, southern African Americans continued to push for job equality with limited assistance from the NYA, WMC, and USES offices in the region. For many black men and women seeking economic mobility, migration to the West and the North often proved to be the most logical strategy for achieving their goals during the war. As the WMC interregional recruitment program for national defense industries bloomed in 1942, black workers excluded from southern industries naturally served as prime targets for the national job recruitment program. By providing black men and women in the South with access to defense jobs with higher wages and the potential for upward mobility, the WMC emerged as an important but historically overlooked federal agency in New Dealers' efforts to battle southern poverty and black economic exclusion.

Through the WMC recruitment networks black families in the South established both temporary and permanent homes in urban defense centers outside of the South, such as Los Angeles and Detroit. As the WMC recruited hundreds of trained black workers, the agency's recruitment of thousands of unskilled southern workers for common labor defense jobs in the West touched the lives of more and more black families. Continued exclusion from high-wage and skilled jobs within the South and the higher wages of jobs outside it pushed and pulled black families far from their native homes. By migrating, black workers, like their white and Hispanic working counterparts, used their mobility and independence to gain economic opportunity. As the federal defense contractors began to cover transportation costs, black families took advantage of the mobilization process to gain a new sense of freedom.

3. "On the Train and Gone"

Worker Mobility in the Cotton Belt, 1941–1945

In June 1944, lumberman George Franklin of Holly Ridge, Louisiana, complained to the War Production Board that he was "losing men everyday" to E. I. Du Pont and Kaiser Industries in the northwestern United States and Western Moulded Products in Los Angeles. According to Franklin, the company statements that farm and lumber workers "need not apply" did not "mean a thing" as the western companies hired "anyone who [went] to them." Most frustrating to Franklin was when companies such as Du Pont gave "Negroes money or tickets to send back home for someone [else] to come out there." Franklin worked closely with the nearby Monroe, Louisiana, United States Employment Service to prevent "frozen" workers from leaving. Nevertheless, the lumberman still lost two hundred black employees without government clearance. As Franklin lamented, "The Negro [was] on the train and gone."[1]

The flight of unskilled workers from farms and low-wage industries in the South and Southwest during World War II created tremendous unease among farm and lumber operators. Beginning with the initial construction of defense facilities throughout the Cotton Belt in 1941, inflated wages in new industries attracted rural workers, many of whom at the start of the war earned some of the lowest wages in the nation.[2] As defense mobilization unleashed a dramatic shift in rural labor relations, employers in low-wage rural industries demanded greater control of local labor markets. In farming and lumber, both of which relied largely on unskilled Mexican American and African American labor, the wartime mobility of workers challenged employers' authority over local workforces and hence regional labor customs. Paradoxically, even as rural employers and southern states sought to restrict the movement of unskilled workers, federal manpower recruitment networks and illicit labor piracy enabled farm and lumber workers to achieve greater social and economic independence during the war.[3]

During the late 1930s, migrant farmworkers moved in and out of the South annually on migrant trails leading up the Atlantic Coast and over to the Great Lakes, the Plains states, and out west. Gradually after 1935, these farmworkers became the focus of administrators in State Employment Service (SES) offices and the federal Farm Security Administration (FSA), which sought to reform the chaotic and exploitative labor market in the rural South and Southwest. Together, the two agencies assumed responsibility for housing, transportation, and job placement for migrant farmworkers.[4] They also protected state and regional farm interests by controlling "disorderly" recruiting, or the "pirating" of farmworkers, by unlicensed labor contractors for out-of-state industries. Yet whereas many rural employers hoped to prevent the pirating of local workers, they nevertheless viewed state and federal farm placement programs as a direct threat to their own local control over workers and, hence, their political and economic status quo.

As national war production expanded in 1942, federal manpower administrators in the newly created War Manpower Commission (WMC) and the United States Employment Service (USES) stepped up labor recruitment for important defense industry labor markets throughout the states. Building on preexisting FSA farmworker placement networks, the WMC implemented a nationwide interregional labor recruitment program. This program in effect gave the West Coast, as a regional labor market, the highest national priority for U.S. manpower needs, while the industrial Midwest served as the second largest labor import market. By 1943, the WMC had mandated that regions with traditional surplus labor resources, such as the South and the Great Plains, were to release surplus manpower to areas with shortages, such as the West Coast and Midwest.[5] This federal policy exacerbated tensions between rural employers and the state because it encouraged the flight of rural workers from farms and lumber mills by means of labor piracy and individual outmigration.

Under the war emergency, national military mandates instigating the export of workers from the Cotton Belt ultimately revealed the limits of rural

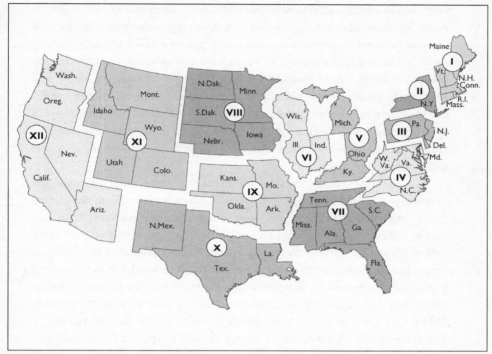

War Manpower Commission Regions of the United States, 1942–1945

elites' power in these regions. Employers attempted to immobilize workers through the enforcement of old and new labor laws. Yet African American and Mexican American workers exercised their legal right to move. During the war, defense industries and federal labor networks extended economic and social opportunities to unskilled workers. In the rural South, white, black, and Latino families used these formal and informal networks to sever the bonds of dependence with their employers. For Mexican Americans and African Americans especially, the war fused the concepts of mobility and freedom.[6]

Worker Mobility in the Cotton Belt

As the South stood on the threshold of war in 1939, the region's economy was largely dependent on a migrant workforce that moved in and out of the region with the seasons. Since the Gilded Age, many farmworkers and underemployed city dwellers had found part-time and seasonal employment in mining, tobacco processing, lumber, and textile mills. By the early 1940s, large, mechanized, and absentee-owned farming operations throughout the emerging Sunbelt depended on migrant labor at peak harvest and planting seasons. In Florida, produce and sugarcane growers relied on some forty to sixty thousand migrants, many of whom were cotton refugees from Georgia and other southeastern states. All across the lower Mississippi Valley and southern Louisiana, cotton and sugarcane operations employed migrant workers, many of whom were upland farmers or former tenants and sharecroppers from the immediate region.[7] In Louisiana alone, cotton harvests required close to 200,000 persons, while sugarcane and rice harvests required 55,000 and 34,000, respectively.[8]

With the shift of national cotton culture to the West during the 1930s, the Southwest emerged as a migrant crossroad, where workers from the United States and Mexico competed for work in seasonal industries and especially cotton. Despite wages as low as seventy-five cents per hundred pounds of cotton offered by Texas growers, state farm officials estimated that by 1940 from 350,000 to 600,000 migratory farmworkers wandered across the state to work cotton and produce farms at peak harvest seasons.[9] In the southwestern cotton migrant stream, Mexicans formed the majority of workers, particularly within the annual trek from South Texas in July to harvest seasons in North Texas and adjoining states during the fall. Displaced white and black families also worked the state's cotton and produce harvests but in fewer numbers than their Hispanic colleagues.[10] From Central and North Texas eastward through the old Cotton Belt, black, Mexican, and white families faced a bare existence on monthly WPA payments ranging from five to twenty-five dollars per family or opted for wages in the western migrant streams that paid as high as one to two dollars a day. As Dorthea Lange and other FSA photographers emphasized through their images, the promise of western wages and higher relief benefits in California attracted thousands of farming families barely able to subsist on living wages or relief in Texas and adjoining states.[11]

Socially and economically, one's status on the metaphorical migrant ladder was often determined by one's relative mobility and accommodations. Certainly, having an automobile and a house trailer provided a means of economic and social independence. Hence, many displaced farming families and single migrant men constructed homemade trailers for shelter to tow behind their autos or trucks. Federal rural housing reforms after 1937 enabled thousands of families to apply for residence in both permanent and temporary FSA camps, where social workers sponsored educational, religious, and recreational programs for families. Even with such New Deal reforms, however,

Chapter Three

the majority of families traveled the region's highways in between squatters' camps in the brush or labor contractors' camps, where working and living conditions were often hazardous and unsanitary.[12]

After the First World War, the greater availability of automobiles enabled migrant families to move farther afield from their homes with greater ease. At the same time, employers in the North and the Far West increasingly encouraged the immigration of former farming families from the Cotton Belt who relied on migrant farmwork for their survival. In 1938 and 1939, for example, southern migrants flooded rural labor markets in California with encouragement from growers, Chambers of Commerce, and newspapers in the Golden State that eagerly used the newcomers to break organizing efforts among Mexican migrant pickers in the cotton and produce fields.[13] In the sugar beet fields of the Great Lakes region, employers imported Mexicans from Texas to break organizing attempts among European immigrant workers. Initially, labor contracting in South Texas remained unsophisticated, unregulated, and chaotic and included Mexican truck drivers smuggling Mexican workers out of South Texas under cover of darkness and the back roads. Yet after European sugar beet workers struck in the Great Lakes in 1938, northern growers developed a streamlined recruiting network that linked the Beet Growers Employment Committee and specific Mexican labor contractors in Texas.[14]

This annual sugar beet and western cotton migration naturally concerned Texas farm labor interests and state labor officials who sought, with the help of the Texas Highway Patrol, to curb the numbers of workers leaving the state. With the increase in sugar beet recruiting efforts, labor officials enforced the state's emigrant agent law passed in 1929 to regulate and discourage out-of-state labor contracting. Because licensing fees were high, at over one thousand dollars, a "bootleg" market in Mexican workers heading north continued to exist. Even with the high fees, the regulated contracting business grew quite rapidly as it became lucrative for numerous Mexican American entrepreneurs in South Texas. By 1940, the Texas Bureau of Labor Statistics had granted licenses to over fifty employment agencies, with many of these licenses renewed from the previous year.[15]

During the depression, San Antonio emerged as the center of sugar beet recruitment. Carey McWilliams, the California farm labor activist and attorney, visited the Alamo City and found a thriving business for labor contractors, who operated under the watchful eye of the Texas Bureau of Labor Statistics. According to Williams, the northern beet growers requested that labor contractors avoid recruiting San Antonio's "urbanized proletariat," consisting of pecan shellers, street cleaners, dishwashers, and common laborers. The northern growers, like their counterparts in Texas and California, preferred rural Mexican families from the farming areas outside of El Paso, Brownsville, Corpus Christi, and Crystal City.[16]

Thousands of rural families took the economic risk of migrating north. In the spring of 1940, McWilliams described scenes at labor contractor Frank Cortez's funeral home on San Antonio's West Side, where families "from all over Texas" arrived in "trucks and jalopies heavily laden with women, youngsters, dogs and chickens." On arrival, migrant families waited for days in lines outside the funeral home and stayed with friends, slept in their cars, and socialized. Once the hiring process was completed, the fifteen-hundred-mile journey began. At times, men were packed up to sixty deep in open trucks or boarded onto special trains with no scheduled stops from San Antonio to the Great Lakes farms. Other families traveled the route in their own car or truck, with no guarantee of arrival. Workers' willingness to tolerate such difficulties illustrates how economic conditions pushed and pulled many out of Texas.[17]

As the northern beet fields lured over fifteen thousand migrants annually, South Texas growers noticed that migrants were also traveling to Louisiana, Arkansas, and Mississippi for higher wages.[18] Mississippi valley cotton planters, like farm managers in California and the Great Lakes, began importing Mexicans from Texas in order to lower production expenses and avoid the economic burdens of the southern sharecropping system. As southern sociologists Arthur Raper and Ira De A. Reid noted in 1941, Delta planters found it "cheaper to use long-distance telephone and send a truck from Greenville, Mississippi to San Antonio, Texas, for choppers to pick cotton, than to house and furnish families on a plantation."[19] For southern workers, the importation of Mexican workers often provided incentive for their own out-migration.

The Workers' War in the Cotton Belt

Worker mobility increasingly concerned rural employers throughout the Cotton Belt who feared the social and economic costs of an exodus to farming and industry jobs outside of the region. During the war emergency, their concerns multiplied dramatically. In response to the flight of rural workers to war industries, capitalists and local manpower administrators throughout the Cotton Belt sought to immobilize workers in low-wage industries through a variety of means.

Like most cotton states in 1942, Texas lost thousands of seasonal cotton pickers to employers in the West and North. At the end of the farming season, James Bond, director of War Manpower Commission Region X, which covered Texas, Louisiana, and New Mexico, complained to manpower officials in Washington about the matter. According to Bond, Texas growers suffered a net loss of 100,000 workers in 1942 alone, which came on the heels of losing close to 34,000 farmworkers in 1940 and 1941. Most disturbing of all, "younger and huskier boys" either remained in the North as casual agricultural workers or "drifted to the larger industrial cities," where they were "permanently lost to agriculture."[20]

Beginning in 1942, the depression era labor surplus came to an abrupt end as southern migrants tapped into new industrial opportunities that provided high wages to unskilled workers. This wartime economic boom altered rural industrial labor relations dramatically when defense construction wages allowed workers to forgo the low wages offered in farming, lumber, mining, and other extractive industries. In Florida the number of Atlantic Coast migrants had by 1943 dropped from a depression era high of thirty thousand to ten thousand. In Texas, the general supply of farmworkers decreased by 200,000 between 1941 and 1943, while the lumber workforce declined by 22,000 from 1940 to 1945. Throughout the entire nation the war affected not only migrant workers but also full-time resident farmworkers. In 1943, the Bureau of Agricultural Economics reported that some 2.8 million farmworkers in the United States were in either the military or war industries. And within the migrant labor stream, the labor surplus declined throughout the nation from 1 million to 600,000 during the war.[21]

With the establishment of the War Manpower Commission in April 1942, regional directors James Bond (Region X—the Southwest) and B. F. Ashe (Region VII—the Southeast) pursued policies that protected state and regional labor resources from recruitment to the North and the West. In the southern states east of the Mississippi River, Region VII director B. F. Ashe, a former professor, worked under the influence of powerful growers in the "black belts" and the Everglades to supply adequate and perhaps surplus labor to rural industries. Southeastern farming interests also had a powerful voice in southern manpower policy when Oscar Johnston, president of the 38,000-acre Delta Pine and Land Company and of the National Cotton Council, was appointed to the regional WMC Labor Management Committee to stabilize labor relations.[22]

In the Southwest, James Bond's promotion from Texas SES director to WMC regional director in 1942 also gave the South's powerful agricultural interests an ally in the protection of rural labor resources.[23] Under Bond's tenure as Texas SES director from 1935 to 1942, state officials developed a sophisticated farm placement system that controlled the annual movement of migrant cotton pickers during the harvest season. The Texas SES's farm placement service under Bond established a model for managing rural labor markets efficiently.[24] By January 1943, Bond's proven experience served him well when he was promoted to WMC deputy executive director in Washington, D.C., a post he held until March 1944. Under his tenure in Washington, WMC and USES offices in the Cotton Belt pursued policies that protected state and regional labor resources from recruitment to the North and the West. Despite a general sympathy for farm interests' labor needs during the war, however, Bond and southern manpower administrators found themselves enforcing national defense interests at odds with regional labor customs.

In many respects, the control over rural labor in the Cotton Belt reflected larger political battles over the role of the federal government in regulating industrial farmworkers and the meaning of democracy for these workers under the New Deal. To the dismay of conservative employers who resented federal intrusion, the FSA hoped to eliminate worker exploitation by regulating the migrant labor contract system.[25] In Texas, a cooperative system developed in which the Texas SES served as a state labor agent and the FSA oversaw the transporting, housing, health, and recreation of migrant workers. Texas growers, like those elsewhere in the region, resented the FSA's liberal leanings and suspected the agency of fomenting labor organizing and worker education. Large growers, many of whom were out-of-state investors, purposefully avoided the FSA and the Texas SES while they encouraged private labor contractors to drive wages down through the importation of surplus labor.[26] Even when operators cooperated with the Texas SES, officials noted that the largest cotton growers in South Texas and the Panhandle were most likely to request surplus labor from the Texas SES in order to depress wages. In the border region especially, growers' easy access to Mexican labor influenced labor market customs and often inhibited the efforts of state and federal manpower administrators to regulate labor resources efficiently.[27]

For Texas's native workers, the influx of Mexican immigrant workers naturally reduced any leverage in bargaining for decent pay. Yet higher wages outside of the state provided migrant workers with the economic incentive to bypass Texas's low farm wages. As Texas SES officials reported in 1941, cotton pickers in Nueces and San Patricio Counties, the heart of the Coastal Bend cotton district, moved on before the fall cotton harvest was ready. Because South Texas farmers would only pay sixty cents per hundred pounds of cotton, migrant families in South Texas departed for the cotton fields of

Mississippi or Arizona, where operators offered one dollar per hundred pounds.[28]

By the summer of 1943, the reduced labor supply and rising wages within South Texas gave Mexican families new bargaining power and a new sense of economic independence. At the time, manpower officials noticed how the tighter labor market allowed farmworker families to shop around, implement work slowdowns, and hold out for higher wages within the valley. In addition, the increase in daily farmworker wages from one dollar in 1941 to as high as three dollars in 1943 allowed Mexican families to send their men into the fields and canneries while the women and children remained at home. According to Texas officials, most male household heads preferred this arrangement because they disliked sending "their women folk into the fields without protection."[29]

In Florida in 1943, rising labor prices also transformed the Sunshine State's labor market, allowing farmworkers, especially bean pickers, to hold out or move on to higher wages. As a result, growers complained of shortages and sought greater control over migrant workers. The previous year, R. Y. Creech and other Belle Glade area bean growers, several of whom farmed over four thousand acres each, passed a resolution to close all "jook joints," enforce vagrancy laws, and establish wage ceilings. By July 1942, L. L. Chandler, chairman of the USDA board and the agricultural division of the National Defense Council for Dade County, urged Senator Claude Pepper and other Florida congressmen to relieve the "farm labor situation" by supporting the importation of Bahamian workers.

In February 1943, Chandler informed a Senate agricultural subcommittee that "workers are money mad" and that after picking hampers of beans they refused to "give them up until the employer promise[d] to pay them half the selling price of beans in that area." In April 1943, labor tensions mounted in South Florida when bean pickers again refused to accept growers' wages, holding out for a higher price. As chairman of the Labor Division of the Belle Glade Defense Council, R. Y. Creech complained to Senator Pepper that "fifty thousand bushels of beans are being left in the fields today" because the laborers refused to work. Such an "unprecedented" strike incited Creech to warn the WMC that it could "expect the killings to start soon."[30]

Given the variables of race and language that divided migrant workers overall, it is impossible to generalize about the cultural and historical forces that informed migrant families' strategies for survival at the end of the Great Depression. Interracial labor organizations such as the Southern Tenant Farmers Union and the United Cannery, Agricultural, Packing, and Allied

Workers of America (UCAPAWA-CIO) mobilized farmworkers and small farmers to some extent in the rural South and Southwest during the 1930s. In South Texas during the 1930s, Mexican workers continued to feel most comfortable working for economic security through local, working-class, mutualist institutions. Generally, though, successful labor organizing in the Cotton Belt remained elusive for small farmers and rural workers. Certainly, organizers and workers had a lot to contend with in the region. All workers struggled against employers' ability to maintain a labor surplus. Throughout much of the rural South, racialized class boundaries between white tenants and nonwhite wage laborers continued to divide rural southerners who organized under the CIO and the Southern Tenant Farmers Union (STFU).[31]

The overwhelming lack of organized labor activity in the rural South and Southwest during the late 1930s suggests that small farmers and rural workers sought economic security through means other than a national or interracial organized labor movement. In this context of limited organizational ability during the Great Depression and the war, family mobility constituted an important strategy in the struggle for economic security and even social freedom. Migrant families thus acted in their own economic interests by making annual journeys to jobs outside of the state. Whereas their flight from the South's rural industries lacked the overt militancy of an organized strike, the action of moving on nevertheless displayed how migrant workers used their mobility to challenge growers' wage policies. As defense contractors sought workers throughout the nation in 1941 and 1942, great numbers of workers in low-wage rural industries throughout the South contested their employers' economic and social control by migrating to high-wage defense contract jobs.

Work or Fight and the Limits of White Control

Throughout 1942 and 1943, rural employers throughout the Cotton Belt sought a variety of legal and extralegal means to prevent workers from leaving rural areas to seek higher war wages elsewhere. Under the decentralized administration of the WMC, local planters and lumbermen did have some ability to implement labor policies that protected their interests. Since the growth of a large-scale timber industry during the Gilded Age, both groups had united in their support of low taxes, cheap labor, and minimum federal intervention. At the state and national level, these white men's traditional interests were represented in the halls of Congress through powerful trade associations such as the Farm Bureau, the National Cotton Council, the

American Sugar Cane League, and the Southern Pine Association. Yet as employers in these low-wage industries discovered, legal constraints could not suppress workers' quest for defense wages.[32]

Under wartime mobilization efforts, employers opposed centralized federal manpower controls, wage regulation, and the military drafting of rural workers. By 1942, conservative industrialists in the rural South began using their influence on county extension boards and war boards to grant draft deferments to farmworkers, control wages, and allocate rubber and gas rations for farmworkers. Just as they had during the First World War, rural capitalists in the region used decentralized selective service and manpower programs to their own advantage during World War II. As Manuel Gonzales, a San Antonio civil rights attorney, discovered at the beginning of the 1942 cotton harvest, South Texas selective service boards threatened to draft all Mexican workers who did not work for a dollar per day.[33]

By the fall of 1942 the passage of the Tydings Amendment provided the legal basis for such control by giving county selective service boards the power to defer or draft farmworkers.[34] Throughout the war, rural industrialists in the South often served on these boards and therefore had some measure of power in determining the fate of southern rural labor. In the Mississippi Delta, the experiences of blues artist B. B. King illustrate how the Tydings Amendment worked at the local level. According to King, when he was drafted into military training at Camp Shelby near Hattiesburg and then at Fort Benning, Georgia, his Sunflower County boss arranged a deferment to work on the "farm," because King was a good tractor driver who also picked up to five hundred pounds of cotton per day. As King recounted in 1967, "If you left [the county], you had to go back into the army."[35]

In more extreme cases, debt peonage served rural employers as a means of maintaining surplus and cheap labor. Throughout the war, progressive reformers, civil rights and labor activists, and the African American press monitored regional peonage cases to expose the system, which they argued was an embarrassment to the South and the nation.[36] Some of the most notorious cases occurred in 1942 and 1943 in the Clewiston (Everglades) and Del Rey (Palm Beach) areas of Florida, a state with a long history of brutal peonage, where bean and sugarcane growers held hundreds of African American youths from Tennessee and Alabama. One teen from Jackson, Tennessee, fled to Miami, where he informed authorities that recruiters lured the youths with promises of fifty cents per hour chopping sugarcane. However, once the group, which numbered close to five hundred persons, arrived, individuals were not permitted to leave for up to eighteen months and received only thirty to forty cents per day. Another group from Georgia who worked at the massive Buster and Dewitt Bean Farm in Del Rey managed to escape by train only to be arrested by the sheriff at Smyrna Beach.[37]

As employers perceived themselves losing control over black workers, the WMC and the FSA served as obvious targets of southern planters and states' rights politicians agitated over the labor issue. Whereas the FSA recruited southwestern farmworkers for western states, in the Southeast, federal agencies recruited farmworkers for Florida's harvest. Although the FSA kept southern workers within the region, states adjacent to Florida were reluctant to lend their farm labor for the winter harvest.[38]

In 1942, South Carolina governor R. M. Jeffries responded forcefully to federal recruitment officials and ordered the arrest of all labor agents, including federal employees in violation of the state's emigrant agent law.[39] In an incident that caused heated controversy among the region's farming interests and federal manpower officials, a South Carolina sheriff arrested Glenn Huff, an agent with the Fellesmere Sugar Production Association, for trying to persuade farmworkers near Spartanburg to go to Florida. Jeffries used the occasion of Huff's arrest to charge federal manpower officials with "surreptitiously conspir[ing]" to violate the law.[40] Amidst the 1942 harvest and a regional labor market in flux due to high war wages, southern states such as South Carolina, Florida, Georgia, Mississippi, and Texas announced that state emigrant agent laws against outside recruiters would be strictly enforced. Most of the southern states had passed variations of the emigrant agent law earlier in the twentieth century that required out-of-state labor recruiters to apply with the state for a license and fee as a means of discouraging and regulating the recruitment of workers.[41]

During the 1942 harvest and 1943 plantings, southern states issued work-or-fight proclamations that reflected employers' and state politicians' unease with the mobility of southern farmworkers and servants toward war industries. In October 1942, New Orleans ordered the police to arrest any vagrants to provide labor for the sugarcane harvest in South Louisiana.[42] In March 1943, Texas congressman Rogers Kelly of the Lower Rio Grande Valley drafted a new law aimed specifically at emigrant agents from Michigan. That same month, Alexandria, Louisiana's mayor issued a work-or-fight proclamation for black women, while in June, Macon, Georgia, issued a jail-or-work proclamation to help that city's alleged domestic servant shortage. As during World War I, these laws, aimed at black women, were intended to insure a surplus of domestic labor for white women.[43]

In preparation for the coming harvest of 1943, the wave of mandates con-

Chapter Three

tinued. In the fall, Georgia's governor Ellis Arnall issued a work-or-fight order to all local sheriffs and the selective service, while Alabama's governor Chauncy Sparks issued an order for the Jefferson County sheriff department to round up idle African Americans in Birmingham. The enforcement of such orders incited protests from black leaders in both New Orleans and Mobile. In New Orleans, NAACP chairman Daniel Byrd complained to the Justice Department regarding the actions of police in that city, while J. L. LeFlore, chairman of the Mobile NAACP, wrote to NAACP secretary Walter White in New York objecting to the indiscriminate arrest of black citizens. As LeFlore argued, the work-or-fight drive was "believed to be an effort to drive many Negro women back to domestic service and force men into accepting jobs which may be offered at sub-standard wages."[44]

Throughout the winter and spring of 1943, the federal presence in rural areas continued to cause tension among conservative growers.[45] As a result, conservative farm interests in Washington began dismantling the FSA's control of farm placement and rehabilitation through the passage of Public Law 45 and the creation of the Emergency Farm Labor Program. Under this program, the newly created War Food Administration replaced the FSA as the federal agency in charge of farm placement duties. Also under Public Law 45, the Pace Amendment (sponsored by Congressman Stephen Pace of Georgia) stipulated specifically that no government funds could be used to transport farmworkers out of an area without clearance from the county agent.[46] While Pace justified the amendment on the grounds of farm labor needs, as a congressional representative of southern interests he also undoubtedly grasped the social and economic effects of placing worker mobility in the hands of local elites.

As Congress prepared to address the mobility issue that winter, Texas farm manpower official W. B. McFarland warned the regional FSA against continued recruitment of farm laborers from East Texas to areas farther west such as the Texas Panhandle, New Mexico, and the Pacific Northwest. "For the past two years," McFarland declared, "Washington and other states had the idea that Texas has an unlimited labor supply, especially agriculture." Despite receiving assurances from the Farm Security Administration that essential workers in Texas would not be transferred to other areas, McFarland feared that the FSA's continued presence would only intensify friction between Texas farm interests and federal farm agencies.[47]

Indeed, in its last month of activity, the FSA's continued recruitment of Texas labor for the West antagonized at least one county war board in East Texas. In April 1943, C. E. Belk, Texas WMC director in Austin, warned regional WMC officials in Dallas about unauthorized FSA recruiting in Wood County, near Tyler. According to Belk, the Wood County USDA board protested FSA newspaper advertisements for "a good many under-employed farmers who can better themselves and serve the war effort more efficiently" on farms in West Texas, Oregon, and Washington. In the federal homestead program, the FSA sent farmers and their families by train from East Texas and Oklahoma to either work or homestead in the western states. Because the FSA recruitment targeted "under-employed farmers" exclusively, H. W. Dowell, a planter in Golden, Texas, complained to the Wood County War Board that the FSA allegedly took a "farm family" from him. While the WMC classified the family as "part-time" and therefore not beholden to their employer, USDA board officials took offense because such seasonal workers and their families provided the majority of low-wage harvest labor throughout the Cotton Belt.[48]

Farming and lumber interests in Louisiana and Mississippi also objected to the federal export of rural workers. During the winter of 1943 agricultural agents from Bossier and Caddo Parishes, in Louisiana's Red River Valley, warned that continued FSA recruitment to Washington State "would be met with vigorous opposition by farmers."[49] In the Mississippi Delta, a large lumber operator blamed the Yazoo City USES for its "haphazard manner of soliciting labor." Although the USES denied authorizing a labor contractor for nearby Grenada Air Base to recruit workers, an exodus occurred based on rumors of construction wages alone. The next day, L. A. Perry Jr., of nearby Georgia Hardwood Company in Winona, claimed that "all of the men at the mill intend walking off of the job Monday morning . . . to come to Grenada seeking employment on the construction of the Army cantonment." Perry, eager to maintain control, suggested to the Grenada USES office that by implementing a "labor draft" or "freezing the workers," the WMC could "assist him with this problem."[50]

The Lower Rio Grande Valley also experienced intense labor conflicts over federally approved worker recruitment during the spring of 1943. According to the Texas WMC, a hops rancher near Yakima, Washington, contracted with Cabelo Asebedo, a South Texas labor contractor, to recruit former farm laborers in Hidalgo County. Valley growers and packers, through the Water Conservation Association (WCA), reacted immediately when Asebedo recruited in Elsa, Texas, in a "hot spot" area farmed by Vahlsing Gardens, reportedly one of the largest shippers of fruits and vegetables in the world, and Engleman Gardens, one of the largest shippers in the valley. Allegedly, the hops rancher, Lloyd Hughes, wired seventeen hundred dollars to cover transportation, and in response the Hidalgo County ration board re-fused to clear funds for gas and tires. As the Washington State WMC approved the recruitment, the incident led to intense reaction from A. L. Cramer, manager of Engleman Gardens and secretary of the WCA, who authored a res-olution to declare the Lower Rio Grande Valley as an agricultural critical labor area. According to Cramer, "the situation [was] sitting on a powder keg ready for an explosion if gasoline [was] granted to any workers leaving the Valley."[51]

WMC operations in Texas under C. E. Belk and James Bond generally sought to protect the valley's agricultural labor resources. At the same time, however, the Texas WMC did not nominally support South Texas growers' efforts to flood the local labor market with surplus labor. During the spring of 1943, the Water Conservation Association requested the WMC to freeze forty thousand workers for fruit and vegetable production, claiming that a short-age existed from workers migrating to Beaumont and California as well as the northern beet fields. The WMC argued that ample labor existed in the valley to handle the harvest of mixed vegetables and citrus. In fact, by May, federal observers found that the approximately one thousand Mexicans immigrating daily into the valley were causing a "serious depression" of agricultural wages.[52]

Throughout the remainder of the war, Texas produce and cotton growers flooded the labor market with Mexican immigrants, many of whom com-muted daily. As the Texas Extension Service made no effort to determine labor resources or future needs during the summer of 1943, the War Food Administration (WFA) monitored farm labor migration throughout Texas in 1943 and 1944.[53] When the Immigration Service's deportation programs drew the ire of South Texas bosses in the summer of 1944, the former cur-tailed its activities to maintain the surplus growers desired. As the McAllen WFA farm labor camp manager reported, "The Immigration Service [was] being just as lenient as possible in this section," and this policy, combined with local and interstate labor, was "supplying sufficient labor for this sec-tion."[54]

In August 1943, annual cotton harvest migrant trails resumed out of the Lower Rio Grande Valley as they had in previous years. That month, WMC officials observed that from eighteen to twenty thousand workers migrated out of the valley to pick cotton in the Coastal Bend of Texas and farther north. In 1944 the same annual migration stream also occurred as in years past.[55] Seasonal migrant streams also continued their coursing up the East Coast when the WMC and WFA imported 45,000 foreign workers, mostly from the

Bahamas, Jamaica, and Haiti. Thus, the enforcement of Public Law 45 did not eliminate the American migrant worker. In Texas, as on the Atlantic Coast, migrant farmworkers moved about on their own, although they frequently encountered gas and tire shortages. Because many farm operators refused to use federal contract labor, the seasonal migrant trails remained a necessity for the U.S. rural economy during wartime.[56]

After 1943, the WMC never fully relinquished full control of rural labor in the Cotton Belt. Through the expansion of the federal Labor Importation Program under the War Food Administration in the spring of 1943, the two agencies authorized the use of prisoner and foreign labor for growers provided that a "shortage" of domestic labor existed in the local labor market.[57] Throughout the South, the WMC actively assisted cotton, sugarcane, rice, and vegetable growers by supplying both prisoners and foreign labor.[58] To further aid rural employers during the fall of 1943, the Labor Importation Program expanded under the WMC and WFA to include other rural, low-wage industries, such as lumber, grain milling, paper production, and food processing, after these employers complained of labor shortages.[59] In the Southwest, the use of Mexican immigrant workers under contract with the U.S. government became known as the *bracero* program. While the program was originally designed to placate growers in California, growers as far east as Mississippi used *braceros* during the war along with POWs to harvest cotton. In Texas, where rural employers remained especially antagonistic toward federal labor regulation, growers largely avoided the *bracero* program and instead hired undocumented Mexican migrant workers.[60]

Gradually, in 1942, lumber operators in the South joined the state's cotton farmers in protesting the pirating of workers. Like the cotton industry, the southern lumber industry lost mostly low-wage, unskilled, nonwhite workers to national defense industries.[61] While employers hoped to prevent worker turnover, they nevertheless remained cool toward any federal manpower controls. Hence, in the fall of 1942, mill owners reacted with ambivalence to the WMC's "labor freeze," which required lumber workers to obtain authorization from their local USES office in order to leave their job. By implementing the labor freeze in twelve western states, including Texas, WMC officials in Washington hoped to reduce the turnover of lumber workers and thereby stabilize lumber production.[62] In doing so, the WMC freeze order theoretically assisted lumber operators in maintaining control over their unskilled workforce. Yet unlike the Emergency Farm Labor Program, the lumber freeze gave the local USES office and not the county extension agent authority for worker clearance. This USES control was a double-edged sword, since the WMC and

USES generally prioritized the manpower needs of western defense industries over those of southern lumber.

Throughout 1942 and 1943, local, state, and federal governments passed laws restricting the ability of workers in essential industries to leave their jobs. By the spring of 1943, a worsening manpower crisis prompted President Roosevelt and the WMC to extend the western lumber freeze policy to all workers in essential industries throughout the United States. Roosevelt's "Hold the Line" Order, as it became known, required that any person working in an essential war industry, including farming, lumber, and mining, was required to have authorized clearance, through a Statement of Availability, from his or her local USES office. Employers hiring new workers were therefore required to hire only workers who could provide a Statement of Availability. Because all WMC programs were strictly voluntary and without legal merit, however, workers could legally move from job to job, while employers could hire them without fear of penalty.

The Underground Railroad: Worker Mobility and Civil Rights

Despite draft deferments, Roosevelt's "Hold the Line" Order, and legal mechanisms such as the Statement of Availability, rural employers in low-wage states simply could not prevent workers from migrating. From 1942 to 1945, the WMC, along with corporate defense industries and labor unions, subsidized rural workers' transportation to out-of-state work sites. Mexican and African American workers who faced increasing attempts to keep them on the farms and in the mills still managed to get around local control by leaving undercover and without transportation or funds. Continuously during the remainder of the war, labor piracy occurred throughout the Cotton Belt, as railroads, shipyards, and lumber companies sought common labor without following proper procedures established by the WMC.

Because the system provided economic mobility for frozen black workers especially, contemporaries referred to the national recruiting network as the "underground railroad." In May 1944, for example, the *Atlanta Daily World* reported on a particular network that allowed workers "to slip away from county agents charged with enforcing the labor hoarding law." The article assured readers that "the 'railroad' [was] not operated in violation of any law, but through a loophole" and therefore was perfectly legal. Further urging readers to participate, the article even provided contact information for interested persons.[63]

Campbell Soups of New Jersey provided one of the most notable networks on the underground railroad, paying for transportation of farmworkers from Florida, Arkansas, and Tennessee. Beginning in June 1942, the WMC assisted recruiting efforts for Campbell Soups in New Jersey by arranging a contract with Otis Nation, an organizer for the UCAPAWA-CIO union in Florida. Once rural labor freezes went into effect in 1943, however, the program raised the ire of central Florida growers. After some 438 unemployed black workers were shipped out of Florida, the Orange County sheriff arrested Nation on charges of being an emigrant agent without a license. In response, the *Birmingham World* charged Florida growers with maintaining a "slavocracy" by "restricting labor's flow . . . in order to maintain a consistent labor supply to keep wages down and to protect a long-time underpaid labor force." In New Jersey, Campbell's plant manager, James A. Heap Jr., decried the "tremendous resistance against the repeated migration of Negroes to South New Jersey" while "there [was] still unemployment in the South." Despite the protest, in October, an Orange County jury took only seven minutes to declare Nation guilty of the charges, whereby the judge fined the defendant fifteen hundred dollars and sentenced him to a year in the county jail.[64]

The Otis Nation case symbolized the reaction against both CIO activity in rural Florida and any organized attempts to free workers from southern farm jobs. While Campbell Soups lost its labor contract in Florida, beginning in the summer of 1943, the STFU negotiated with the AFL Meat and Cannery Workers Union and Campbell Soups along with Seabrook Farms in New Jersey to import unemployed tenants and sharecroppers from the South. In effect, STFU founder H. L. Mitchell offered a placement service for tenants, sharecroppers, and migrant workers to northern industries. Unlike UCAPAWA's attempts in Florida, the STFU continued the network through the remainder of the war.[65]

Beginning in June 1943, local and state WMC officials in Tennessee were cognizant of the STFU's activities, because H. L. Mitchell notified the Memphis USES office of plans to recruit workers through advertisements in the *Commercial Appeal.* Such an organized recruitment of Delta farmworkers certainly had broad implications for the southern tenancy system and worker dependency. Whereas Mitchell envisioned a system in which union hiring halls around the country hired frozen farmworkers for the "best paying jobs," planters feared that such a plan would not only deplete local labor surpluses but also break down the existing racial, political, and economic order. Under the rationale that farmworkers were essential workers, county agents and rural USES offices in Arkansas denied STFU workers clearance, while the Memphis area WMC declined to assist the STFU in recruiting and placement for the New Jersey industries.[66]

Even with (or perhaps because of) these barriers placed in the Delta, from 1943 to 1944 the STFU system recruited over a thousand farmworkers for New Jersey's food industries. Perhaps due to the decentralized nature of WMC operations, however, it was not until March 1945 that Leo Werts, assistant executive director of the WMC Field Service in Washington, D.C., discovered the unauthorized network. After reading an article in the *Philadelphia Record* that referred to the recruiting system as the "Underground Railroad of 1945," Werts felt obliged to inform the WMC regional director in Philadelphia that he could not "officially approve" of the arrangement. Werts decided not to impose WMC control, despite being in a position to enforce official WMC policy to the benefit of Delta planters. As Werts informed Clinton Golden, WMC vice chair, "as long as Region III [was] willing to overlook any violations of our regulations, I think we should just let the matter stand as it is." Thus, as local and state WMC offices in the South restricted frozen farmworkers' mobility, national and northern WMC officials chose to ignore the freeze to the benefit of New Jersey's industries and STFU members.[67]

During the war, southern African Americans increasingly viewed mobility as a civil rights issue. Because of the connections between slavery, peonage, and wartime labor freezes as a means of controlling labor, workers' freedom of movement took on more meaning during the war. Inevitably, the WMC found itself caught in the middle of a civil rights struggle over the recruiting of southern African Americans for northern industries. In one case, during March 1945, a Delta planter demanded the return of Peter Coates Jr., employed at the International Harvester Plant in Indianapolis. Coates claimed he had worked for a net income of $4.75 per week under lease at his former employer's farm in Mississippi. When his lease expired in 1944, he moved to Yazoo City with his wife and son. Then, early in 1945, the USES recruited him for "temporary" employment at the war plant in Indianapolis. Six weeks later, the USES informed him that "a demand had come from Yazoo City" that he be "sent back home for farm labor."

In Indianapolis, NAACP chapter president Lowell Trice defended Coates. Echoing the sentiments of national civil rights activists, Trice blasted the WMC policy as a "back to the farm movement" in which "southern states may keep Negro farm workers in a state of peonage." By "placing the uneducated and poorly informed Negro farm worker virtually in the hands of the county agent," Trice argued that the WMC policy only reinforced southern peonage. By June, the WMC had consented to Trice's right-to-work arguments and allowed Coates to remain in Indianapolis.[68]

In the Chicago area in 1945, the mobility rights issue also centered on the

WMC's temporary clearance of southern farmworkers to northern industries. In the suburb of Joliet, the Army Air Force 803 Depot offered to employ four black farmworkers in order to save the men from a "return to sharecropper status." According to reports, one worker, Edward Lee Sanders of Indianola, Mississippi, was to be extradited from the Elwood Ordnance Plant, where he made ninety-six cents per hour. The other three men, from nearby Isola, Mississippi, were making close to $1.06 per hour at the Joliet war plants. In Chicago, the issue brought together a network of civil rights activists. Denouncing the WMC policy were local CIO representatives, Baptist and Methodist church pastors, the local NAACP chapter, and FEPC field investigator Virgil Williams. The Chicago NAACP, leading the defense, protested the economic injustice of "returning the workers back to their former $1 a day jobs in Mississippi cotton fields," especially "in the face of [Illinois's] industrial manpower shortage."[69]

Given the controls that southern workers encountered with federal recruitment networks, it is not surprising that many workers avoided formal recruiting networks altogether. For African American and Latino workers especially, informal recruitment outside of the local USES networks provided the least visible means of fleeing rural areas where local law enforcement remained vigilant. In this wartime conflict over worker mobility, the employers' and federal administrators' beliefs are quite evident through the existing correspondence and complaints. Because of the lack of available or existing correspondence among the workers and their families, however, one has greater difficulty understanding the significance of wartime mobility to the workers themselves. Hence, one must view workers' actions and their decisions in order to understand how they and their families responded to both local authority and distant economic opportunities. Through a variety of means, including illicit migration, work slowdowns, and absenteeism, rural workers overcame the barriers to economic and social mobility placed before them.

In the Lower Rio Grande Valley, even as rural employers sought vigorous enforcement and county control, valley workers continued avoiding local attempts to inhibit out-migration. Throughout the war, Great Lakes sugar beet growers utilized correspondence as a means of illicit recruitment and hired pirate trucks to haul workers north in the spring.[70] South Texas workers were not limited to the sugar beet industry in their illicit network for northern jobs. Mexican American workers throughout the region found ample employment in the farm fields of the Pacific Northwest and midwestern industries. In one notable case in 1944, the Texas WMC requested the return of twelve Mexican American workers from Laredo who were recruited without authorization by

Inland Steel of Chicago. The company and its representative, Serefino Alexander in Chicago, had contracted with a local Mexican recruiter by correspondence who then assisted the workers in leaving without clearance from the Laredo USES.[71] Throughout the remainder of the war, Inland Steel continued to recruit more workers from Laredo, thus prompting complaints of labor piracy from both the Laredo Army Airfield and the Texas Mining and Smelting Company. Similar job networks also existed for the Saginaw Malleable Iron Company in Michigan for over two hundred workers in San Angelo, Texas, in 1944.[72]

Beginning in 1942, western railroads initiated the first large-scale recruiting efforts in the Cotton Belt. Southern Pacific Railroad, under the approval of the WMC, emerged as perhaps the most effective recruiter of track labor, much to the chagrin of rural employers throughout the region. In Texas during the war, manpower officials complained to national manpower officials about Southern Pacific's unauthorized advertisement for common labor in Brownsville and the Lower Rio Grande Valley newspapers. In the border region especially, industrial farm operators often resented any federal attempts to recruit local Mexican workers and possibly drive up wages. Yet as employer complaints reveal, Mexicans in the Lone Star State eagerly left farmwork for western railroad work. This flight of workers from Texas occurred in addition to recruitment within Mexico of over eighty thousand Mexican nationals for western railroad work. While railroads were not the only western industry to recruit Mexicans in Texas for war work, the industry nonetheless served as the primary recruiter for thousands of unskilled Latino workers throughout the Southwest.[73]

In addition to South Texas, Southern Pacific recruited heavily throughout much of the Southeast. Because African Americans in the South were often excluded from local war industries, the western railroad recruitment campaign offered a chance for young men to travel and make higher wages. Carey McWilliams, who served as chief of immigration and housing for California during the war, investigated Southern Pacific's recruitment campaign in 1942. McWilliams calculated that African Americans from southern states made up 98 percent of the railroad company's recruits for track labor. He also discovered that most of these workers were illiterate and unskilled and lacked any railroad experience.[74]

While contemporaries were concerned with the general welfare of the migrants as they became stranded or arrived in crowded conditions, black workers' actions suggest that they used the Southern Pacific and other recruitment networks as a means of achieving economic and geographic mobility. Carey

McWilliams reported that approximately 50 percent of the workers actually worked for Southern Pacific once they were recruited, while 15 percent deserted en route, and 20 percent quit after a short time on the job. Even with such unfavorable conditions and high turnover rates, however, only a small minority of workers requested to be shipped back home. Moreover, the workers' willingness to sign up for low-wage railroad work without any real assurances from Southern Pacific regarding the actual nature of steady employment, accommodations, and working conditions attests to the workers' desperation to leave their environment.[75]

Undoubtedly, many such workers were seasonal or unemployed farmworkers from the declining Cotton Belt. Subsequent manpower reports indicated that a large portion of black migrants in Los Angeles originated from the Shreveport, Louisiana, area. As Rev. C. Lopez McAllister reported at the National Baptist Convention in Shreveport in February 1943, "for several months" there had been an "exodus" of "thousands of racial farmers" in Texas and Louisiana who had "gone to California to cultivate the fields and plantations which were formerly utilized by the Japanese." According to the reverend, California growers sent "special trains" to "carry these new home seekers to the West Coast."[76]

In Los Angeles, manpower officials discovered informal job networks among black migrants moving west. In July 1943, for example, agents observed what appeared to be a "mass movement from some areas of the deep south where Negroes have been held under the heels of the white population for many years." Observing that half of these men brought their families, the WMC in California noted that word of western wages and improved social conditions had "traveled back to them by word of mouth from workers who had come to this area previously."[77] As one manpower report on African Americans in Los Angeles indicated, many of those workers rejected by the USES in the South "decided to come on out to the west coast anyway, assuming they might be hired at the gate."[78]

Families' willingness to move to overcrowded war centers revealed just how much southerners, especially African Americans, wanted to leave behind the stifling economic conditions of the rural South. While the promise of a better life may have been deceptive, southern workers believed that the low wages, a declining farming system, and the Jim Crow system in the rural South offered little hope for a better life. By having to leave undercover, however, working families' actions took on extra significance in a region where the power of rural elites often rested on the social and economic control of nonwhite workers.

Chapter Three

As federal interregional recruitment and labor piracy grew in sophistication in 1942 and 1943, the Cotton Belt served as a primary source of manpower for western and northern industries. In an attempt to meet the West Coast's industrial manpower shortage in 1943, the USES and corporate labor contractors sent recruiting teams throughout Texas and adjacent states to help fill western manpower quotas assigned by the WMC in Washington, D.C. Beginning in the summer of 1943, western industries with top military priorities such as Kaiser Industries, Boeing, and Du Pont drew a combined average quota of ten thousand workers per month from Texas, Louisiana, and New Mexico. During this period, the top-secret Manhattan Project sites of the Hanford Engineer Works at Pasco, Washington, and the Clinton Engineer Works outside of Knoxville, Tennessee, emerged as top priorities for WMC recruiters. Under such intensive and federally sanctioned recruiting efforts, rural employers in the Lumber and Cotton Belt faced even greater competition for local labor while their employees found unprecedented opportunity for economic advancement.[79]

Lumber operators especially accused the WMC and local USES offices of pirating their labor. For instance, in early 1943, the Bass-Jones Lumber Company and the Tilford-Hunt Lumber Company protested that the manager of the Nacogdoches USES office continued to issue certificates "entirely without the knowledge or consent of the employer." According to S. R. Stevens, regional lumber advisor of the War Production Board in Houston, the above cases were not isolated instances.[80] In another case in 1944, the Chicago Mill and Lumber Company complained that WMC recruitment advertisements in local papers had caused the loss of some 1,370 workers out of a total of 3,400 from the company's mills in Helena, Arkansas, Greenville, Mississippi, and Tallulah and Waterproof, Louisiana.[81] Such protests illustrated how WMC clearance for lumber workers antagonized employers and, in some cases, offered economic advancement and subsidized mobility for common laborers.

The recruitment of surplus common labor in the South for the Manhattan Project brought the WMC and defense contractors into some of the greatest wartime conflicts with southern planters over control of rural labor. Ironically, in the earliest stages of Clinton recruitment, Region VII officials used the program as a justification for preventing the export of the region's unskilled labor to the industrial Midwest. In both May and June 1943, Region VII placement director W. B. Klugh denied industries in Cleveland and Muskegon, Michigan, an opportunity to "hire colored help from the hinterland," as one industry requested, because of "highly important" army projects.[82] At the same time, however, rural employers and some USES offices actively protected their labor from Hanford and Clinton recruiters. In September 1943, for example, the Shreveport, Louisiana, USES office denied African Americans in the local lumber industry clearance to work at Hanford Engineer Works on the grounds that they were essential workers.[83] In Alabama, Sumpter County planters complained to the Mobile area WMC office that Du Pont recruited two or three laborers from the town of Livingston. In principle, such large landholders in the South understood the consequences of spreading defense job rumors at harvesttime.

In the Mississippi Delta, protection of farm labor from the Manhattan Project was in large part a cooperative effort between planters, local USES offices, and local law enforcement officials. In June, the first month of interregional recruitment, WMC offices received a barrage of complaints from planters regarding labor piracy. In the Yazoo City area, USES officials protested that Stone and Webster, the contracting firm, was corresponding with local black leaders to recruit labor. Likewise, planters in the Greenville area complained about Clinton contractors recruiting farmworkers with the assistance of the USES. According to the Greenville USES manager Orville Horne, a Mr. Niles from Stone and Webster had gone to the "Negro quarters" of the town, where he informed residents of jobs available at Clinton and the attractive wages they could make. Once Greenville USES officials got wind of the activity, they found Mr. Niles at the bus station, where he had bought ten tickets to Knoxville and had twenty-one laborers signed up for Clinton without clearance from the Greenville USES. Mr. Niles admitted that he did not expect the workers to return to Mississippi. The Bolivar County sheriff then arrested him for illicit labor recruitment.[84]

The showdown at Greenville uncovered the conflicting interests of Manhattan Project officials and southern planters. As a formal gesture, the main contractors of the Clinton project, Stone and Webster and J. A. Jones, signed pledges to adhere to proper recruitment and therefore insure proper clearance of essential workers.[85] During the fall of 1943, however, J. A. Jones arrived at Clinton with truckloads of black workers from Louisiana, Mississippi, and Alabama without proper clearance. When pressed on the matter, J. A. Jones's Clinton project manager, W. D. Twing, complained of the difficulty in recruiting for such an important project in rural Mississippi. According to Twing, all Jones's recruiters reported that in many SES offices, refusal of certification was often based on "indefinite and spasmodic and irregular" farm and sawmill work and not on the basis of "present employment or unemployment." Because of "the political pressure and the complaints regarding the yard boys and the like," Twing lamented the "antipathy on the part of many USES local managers to send labor from their locality."[86]

Despite the WMC's efforts to stabilize labor markets in 1943 and 1944, rural employers and manpower administrators began to observe that low-wage workers in the South left their employers without clearance from local USES offices.[87] Employers such as H. N. Grogan, a lumber operator in the East Texas town of Magnolia, reported in August 1944 that even if a worker was denied local clearance, "we have never been able to retain any man who has made an application for release." For that reason, the employer declared, "we don't ever expect to protest another man."[88] Echoing such sentiments, Texas manpower director C. E. Belk believed early in 1944 that clearance proved to be the weakest link in the WMC chain of labor market control.[89]

Workers who received clearance at times did not let a lack of transportation funds, gas, or tire rations prevent them from leaving. In December 1943, the Dallas USES office reported that "four colored laborers" arrived from Henderson, Texas, where the local USES office had cleared them to work for Du Pont as common labor at the Hanford Engineer Works. As was common, the Henderson USES office informed the workers that if they found a way to Dallas, the company would "pay their expenses while in Dallas." The workers hitchhiked to the city with no food and money, and the Dallas USES, working with Du Pont, advanced sustenance costs for such recruits at shipping points.[90]

Often, out-of-town corporations wired money or train tickets to potential rural workers without the knowledge of the employer or the USES office. As James Bond observed, West Coast employers were furnishing transportation to applicants in Texas and Louisiana "who were not referred to the employers by the WMC." Bond speculated that applicants referred and hired by the WMC were then "wiring to their relatives and acquaintances, advising them of the jobs that are open and request[ing] that they come to the west coast." Under such a system, if the worker back home accepted the job, his friend in the West advised the employer, who then made "arrangements for wiring transportation."[91] For African American and Latino workers especially, this more informal recruitment outside of the local USES networks provided the least visible means of fleeing rural areas where local law enforcement prohibited the departure of workers.

In the cotton and lumber regions, where control of African American labor often symbolized traditional white economic and social hegemony, unauthorized flight often challenged employers' racial sensibilities. In April 1943, the Southern Pine Lumber Company in Diboll, Texas, requested assistance from the Beaumont WMC office to retrieve two "colored" employees, Anderson "Sport" Brown and Jim Wilson, who had left for employment with the Meadow Valley Lumber Company in northern California. In May 1945, Southern Pine pleaded with the WMC to take action against the McNary Lumber Company of McNary, Arizona, which had been "sending railroad tickets" to its employees. According to Southern Pine offices, Roosevelt Jenkins, Dave Spurlock, Will Brooks, A. U. Stubblefield, and Pearl Jenkins had "already received their tickets" and had "left for Arizona," while five more workers—C. T. and E. B. Phipps, E. V. Cade, Ira Hill, and Emmitt Taylor— were "now waiting for railroad tickets."[92]

The unauthorized exodus of workers to the naval ordnance works in Camden, Arkansas, proved to be especially offensive to employers in northern Louisiana, who demanded the return of numerous lumber and farmworkers. In November 1944, for instance, the Silas Mason Company, a lumber concern near Shreveport, provided a list of some twenty-six laborers who had left illicitly to work at the ordnance works with the hope that the WMC would track them down and send them back.[93] The following month, G. S. Smith, a farmer near Robeline, Louisiana, expressed considerable annoyance over the flight of a black sharecropper and his family to the Camden works. As Smith told the local USES office, "Even if he doesn't farm at my place like he promised to do, he should be compelled to farm for someone in this critical stage on the farms."[94]

Despite rural employers' accusations of labor piracy and unauthorized rural flight, the federal wage ceilings of fifty cents per hour for southern lumber workers contributed greatly to the westward movement. Because rural workers in the South and Southwest earned the lowest wages in the nation, they served as prime targets for defense industry recruiters. Even as farm wages rose substantially during the war, federal wage ceilings and low wages generally placed southern industries at a disadvantage and helped ease the greater transition to mechanized labor. After the agricultural Wage Stabilization Act passed in 1942, Texas and Florida were the only two southern states where wage boards had established ceilings for farm labor. When Lower Mississippi Valley cotton wages rose to three dollars per hundred pounds in 1944, planters implemented a wage ceiling of two dollars per hundred pounds for the remainder of the war.[95] In 1943, only out of desperation for labor did southern lumber operators agree to the federal wage ceilings of fifty cents per hour for lumber workers. In this context, southern lumber wages averaging forty-three to fifty cents per hour could not compete with western lumber wages, which paid on average one dollar per hour for common labor.[96]

Not surprisingly, nine of twelve African American workers from Mississippi and Louisiana working on the Manhattan Project at Clinton, Tennessee, cited higher wages as the main reason for moving. James Anderson from Philadelphia, Mississippi, admitted that by earning only twenty to twenty-five dollars per week at the lumber yard he "was not making enough to support [his] family." According to Willie Lee Washington, since his job in Lake, Mississippi, was "not regular," he "could not make enough money." Even workers content within their jobs succumbed to the temptation of higher wages. For example, Ellis Holmes of Bogalusa, Louisiana, claimed that while "I liked my job and the company treated me fair," a recruiter still lured him to Tennessee with the promise of a six- to seven-cent-per-hour wage increase over his current job. For workers who planned to leave rural industries, government contract wages and subsidized transportation provided extra incentive to go with recruiters. James Williams, who had intended eventually to quit work at a warehouse in Carthage, Mississippi, and go to New Orleans, signed with J. A. Jones because "my brother was coming to Tennessee" and recruiter Herman Johnson bragged of wages at fifty-seven and a half cents per hour.[97]

Federal control of labor resources during the war directly affected the bargaining power of both management and labor in the rural South. As the WMC Labor Importation Program helped keep wages low for employers, the availability of higher-paying common labor jobs through the USES provided workers with a degree of economic leverage. Moreover, even though lumber and farmworkers generally lacked representation through rural labor organizations, individual bargaining power manifested itself through migration or work slowdowns when such workers remained in common labor jobs during the war. Like growers elsewhere in the South and Southwest, one East Texas lumber operator complained in 1944 that "workers are quite certain that they will not be discharged, because of lack of men to replace them." As a result, "many men, especially the colored workers," have become "indifferent to efficiency." For workers who were unable to leave their rural area, such passive resistance served as an important means of protest.[98]

Workers and employers both discovered during the war that mobilization permanently transformed the cotton and lumber regions by accelerating the influence of outside social, political, and economic forces. As federal wage standards from the 1930s and early 1940s integrated an isolated and low-wage southern labor market into the national labor market, federal manpower policies hastened this transformation in ways that may have been decisive.[99]

The War Manpower Commission's recruiting networks opened numerous rural southern labor markets to defense industries throughout urban America. With the Cotton Belt's peculiar racial labor traditions, deriving from both Latin American and Deep South agricultural folkways, rural employers resisted radical changes in the social order and labor relations. In the changing world of agriculture during the 1940s, national manpower policies demonstrated to rural industrialists in the South that local labor laws could not halt migration or rising wages. For African American and Latino families living in the Cotton Belt from 1943 to 1945, federal recruitment and labor piracy opened new paths to social freedom and at least a modicum of economic democracy.

4. The Segregation Frontier

African American Migrant War Workers
in the Pacific West, 1941–1945

"When they offered me that job to go to Pearl Harbor, that changed my life forever," declared Arthur Chapman, an African American migrant who worked in the United States Navy Yard in Hawaii. Chapman recalled how when he arrived in Pearl Harbor from New Orleans in the fall of 1941, the limits of opportunity were boundless. That summer, Roosevelt had issued Executive Order 8802 establishing fair employment standards and racial quotas for defense contracts. Yet in New Orleans, federal officials refused to give Chapman any skilled position on any local navy jobs, and the local navy recruitment official threw away Chapman's application on the spot to make the point. Not to be deterred by southern racial conservatism, the young carpenter sought a well-paying position at the navy yards at Pearl Harbor, far from the Crescent City. Once he arrived at the navy placement office in Pearl Harbor, Chapman requested and received a position as the "layout man," a position of authority in the carpenter shop at the yards. The placement official also gave Chapman the status of "safety man" and "supervisor," thus providing the twenty-three year old even greater oversight regarding construction safety and regulation.

As Arthur Chapman made clear, in Pearl Harbor "they hired a man if he was qualified for the job."[1] These occupational openings illustrated most vividly to Chapman how race relations were "superb" in Hawaii compared to those in New Orleans. As part of the Pacific West, Hawaii also reflected how defense industrial manpower needs and a greater racial liberalism fostered a refreshing change and, in many ways, a realization of democracy for African American migrants.

The experiences of southern migrants in the American West, especially California, during the Second World War offer a valuable insight into the specific ways that economic opportunity and racial liberalism combined to provide definite economic and social mobility for black southerners. A number of recent scholars have examined the experiences of southern migrants and especially African Americans in the Pacific West during the war, asking sophisticated questions regarding the war's economic and demographic impact on the East San Francisco Bay Area. Marilynn Johnson and Gretchen Lemke-Santangelo have both tapped into the rich histories of African American and southern defense migrants in Oakland and Richmond. Johnson describes how federal housing policies and fundamental racial conservatism limited opportunities of black migrants from the South. Lemke-Santangelo focuses on institution building among black migrant women and how their determination, hard work, and active roles in community institutions created a better life than they had in the South.[2]

Together, these scholars' focus on both the limits and the expansion of opportunities for black migrants in the West defines a distinct regional race relations dynamic, one that historian Quintard Taylor calls the "central paradigm of African Americans" in the West.[3] With these historical observations in mind, this chapter examines war workers' actions and their recollections to determine how the American West, and especially the urban centers of Los Angeles and the San Francisco Bay Area, provided black migrants new opportunities even as their daily lives were defined by racial conservatism. The experiences of southern migrant defense workers in the West provides a complex view of race relations in the region. Certainly, the Pacific West, like much of the United States, contained white conservatives who at times reacted negatively to the arrival and settlement of black migrants. Even so, wartime defense needs provided a unique opportunity for aggressive southern black migrants to challenge successfully the segregated hiring policies of western industries.

The American West and Southern Migration

As many black and white southerners embraced migration as a key strategy for gaining economic mobility, these migrants made their presence felt in many crowded urban defense centers across the United States. And as housing shortages and racial tension escalated in 1943, some boomtown communities were quick to point out southerners as the sources of such problems. In Detroit, especially during the racial conflicts that occurred in the summer of 1943, contemporaries often blamed the violence on the dramatically increased presence of black and white southerners.[4] Walter White, NAACP secretary, emphasized at the time how many newcomers to midwestern industrial centers such as Detroit, Akron, Cleveland, and Toledo were recruited for war work from Mississippi, Arkansas, and Louisiana by the War Manpower Commission. Southerners had been coming to Detroit since before 1940, yet the manpower shortage that developed in some midwestern cities by early 1942 induced the WMC to increase dramatically its recruitment of southern African Americans for industries after that date. Hence, the vast majority of the fifty thousand black migrants had arrived in Detroit during the fifteen months prior to the June 1943 riot. Detroit's increased dependency on African Americans for defense industry work led to dramatic adjustments for white workers, some of whom resented this transformation in the role of the black worker.[5]

Whereas the southern presence in Detroit is now well documented, the experiences of southern defense migrants in the West have only recently come to light.[6] Indeed, because the Pacific West experienced the greatest population growth of any region in the United States during the war, it is only natural that southerners were one of the largest groups to seek new opportunities out west. Many western states' populations swelled dramatically during the 1940s, and California in particular expanded its populace by an unprecedented 50 percent. During this period, some 621,000 whites from southwestern states and some 125,000 black southerners moved to the Pacific West.[7] From 1943 to 1945, the WMC and western defense corporations targeted southern workers for western jobs. At the same time, southern communities' conservative employment policies and low wages continued to drive out both black and white southerners who sought greater social and economic mobility than the South offered.

Hence, recruiters for western defense industries found their most willing workers in cities like New Orleans, where opportunities for advancement were limited for African Americans and wages were comparatively low for all workers. As the WMC's recruitment program matured in 1943, Clarence Johnson, the Minority Division representative of the WMC on the West Coast, realized the West Coast's important role as a region that offered trained black workers employment opportunities in defense industries. During March

1943, Johnson contacted Robert Weaver to actively recruit trained black workers who were excluded from southern industries.[8] Following that date, southern manpower administrators observed how interregional recruitment for West Coast navy yards, and especially Mare Island, California, led workers employed in the Gulf Coast shipyards to relinquish their jobs for those in California.[9]

From 1942 to 1945, recruitment channels drained unskilled workers throughout the Great Plains, the Southwest, and the Southeast, where wages were lowest and opportunities for advancement fewest. For example, white oil workers at a large Philips Petroleum Refinery in Borger, Texas, eagerly left for higher wages at the Mohawk Refinery in Bakersfield. In another case, Felix Pacheco left his meatpacking job at the Cudahy plant in Denver to work for the Oscar Krenz Copper and Brass Works of San Francisco after the latter sent him a bus ticket.[10] Throughout the war, packinghouse workers from the Great Plains and Southwest formed migrant networks within the Los Angeles shipyards.[11]

In the southern lumber industry, where black workers earned some of the lowest wages in the nation, workers were lured from their jobs by western wages despite rules against quitting essential industries without a Statement of Availability. The experiences of African American lumber workers in Arkansas illustrate the tremendous pull that western defense wages had in the South. For example, Willie Davis more than doubled his pay of forty cents per hour at a lumber mill job when he hired on at ninety cents per hour at the Basic Magnesium Plant in Las Vegas, Nevada. According to his employer, a "colored stooge" in Las Vegas facilitated many other workers at the mill to move to Nevada. Two other black lumber workers in Arkansas struck gold in western defense industries. Andrew Wright moved from his job as a car loader at forty-two cents per hour in the South to a shipyard job in Oakland starting at eighty-seven cents per hour. Henry Jenkins, who was a "dogger" at a mill for forty-seven cents per hour in Arkansas, moved to Portland after his brother sent him the train fare of thirty-five dollars. Working at a Douglas aircraft plant there, Jenkins's wages rose to $1.38 per hour.[12]

For many southern migrants, the West and especially California offered a place of hope and renewal, as it had for American families for a hundred years.[13] In the volatile and transformed environment of the wartime workplace, African Americans from the South used strategies to take advantage of western racial progressivism in race relations and a social and political environment where liberalism that blossomed during the 1930s continued to thrive during the war. Indeed, during World War II, African American migrants from the South eagerly sought the Pacific West not only for its economic opportunity but its reputation for social liberalism.

To be sure, race relations in the West manifested many of the same racial ideologies that shaped race relations in the South. Historically, white westerners after the gold rush of the 1850s made attempts to shape the region as a bastion of whiteness, despite economic forces that dictated the opposite. Both Oregon and California attempted to prohibit the settlement of black migrants in the mid–nineteenth century. Western nativism also inspired the passage of several laws in California during the late nineteenth and early twentieth centuries aimed at discouraging immigration and settlement of Chinese and Japanese workers. By the 1920s, federal immigration acts further attempted to prevent future immigration of nonwhites. And during the 1930s, Los Angeles police deported Mexican migrants whom white Americans considered a threat to job opportunities during the depression.[14] Because the West Coast labor market during the Second World War was far from flooded, however, economic competition never served as the motive to keep black and Hispanic migrants from coming west. Even so, white westerners remained ambivalent about the demographic changes that mobilization brought, and they generally hoped to make the settlement of southern migrants temporary.[15]

During the 1920s and 1930s, southerners moved west in greater numbers than ever with the spread of cotton culture into Arizona and southern California. Often, black and white southerners found themselves working side by side in the fields. In the new environment, some whites felt reluctant to concede their racial entitlement, while others began to relinquish their southern ways under the cause of organized labor.[16] With the war, a new wave of southern migrants flooded into California to work in the state's defense industries. The WMC hoped to use these southern migrants specifically to alleviate the regional labor shortage. Hence, throughout the war, the WMC maintained USES recruiting stations at all border checks at the Arizona border crossings, where southern migrants entered the state. Not surprisingly, workers from the Southwest comprised the largest group of regional migrants in southern California defense industries. At the California Shipbuilding (Cal Ship) yards in Los Angeles, for instance, migrants from Texas, Louisiana, Arkansas, and Oklahoma accounted for almost 15 percent of the workforce, more than any other region outside of California. During the war years, the waterfront towns of San Pedro and Wilmington became, in effect, southern migrant communities.[17]

As black migrants began arriving at western defense centers in substantial numbers during war, they often encountered efforts among local whites to prevent their continued in-migration or their permanent settlement. In the Pacific Northwest, for example, white officials hoped to use discriminatory hiring practices to circumscribe opportunities for rural African American and Mexican migrant workers. In July 1944, Texas manpower officials reported that because Oregon lumber camps and mills had no segregated housing, the employers were not accepting African Americans, while Latin American workers were being recruited in small numbers in only one operation.[18]

Discriminatory housing policies existed commonly throughout the large defense centers of the West. After 1942, black workers and their families found themselves in crowded and segregated housing facilities in all of the large defense projects where black workers were recruited by the federal government and where many others came by word of mouth. For example, in 1942, the WMC recruited workers for the Basic Magnesium Corporation in Las Vegas, and black workers there found themselves limited solely to temporary barracks housing. In Fontana, California, where over two hundred black migrants were recruited to work construction and operations at the new Henry J. Kaiser steel plant, black workers found themselves with ten dormitories for forty men and no possibility to rent due to race covenants. These dorms for single men made it impossible for black families to come to Fontana.[19]

The experiences of black southern migrants in the Seattle-Tacoma metro area also typify much of western cities' response to their rapid and sudden population growth. In defense centers such as Tacoma with little or no prewar black population, the sudden presence of recruited black workers exacerbated social tensions. As attorneys representing the nearby small town of Ruston, Washington, complained to the WMC, southern black "customs and manners" proved to be "more than a very tolerant community [could] accept without protest." Ruston resented the influx of black workers and hoped to preserve its prewar social makeup by housing the Tacoma smelter workers in temporary barracks built especially for them. Despite proclaiming that Ruston was not Detroit in terms of racial tension, the town's attorney felt that "the makings of an explosion" were present and that the migrant workers wished to return to the South. Perhaps the cold reception that such communities gave the migrants insured that permanent settlers were not welcome.[20]

For the workers themselves, the process of making a new life in a different land offered both hope and uncertainty. The experiences of southern migrants in Seattle offer a view into the expectations and confusion that accompanied a new life in the West.[21] In September and October 1943, the Seattle area took on a huge influx of persons from rural Louisiana who were recruited to work either in aircraft or the navy shipyards. Both the Committee of War

Services and the Council of Social Agencies became alarmed at the possibility that some workers, some as young as sixteen years of age, from the National Youth Administration (NYA) defense training program were stranded in Seattle without proper housing or welfare.

Migrant workers who expected immediate improvement in their lives were initially disappointed. The Welfare Agency noted how with the closing of the NYA in July "Seattle had reached its saturation point in terms of housing for Negro people." The migrants "arrived without the remotest conception of how to adjust to an urban industrial community," and, worst of all, many of them "seem to have been grossly misled as to what expectations in the way of opportunities—social, economic and otherwise—and the consequent disillusionment made it all the harder for them to make a satisfactory adjustment here." Some of the female migrants verbalized their "reactions to their release from 'Jim Crow' restraints," experiencing first a "feeling of freedom and exhilaration, followed by doubt and anxiety as to what might be expected of them in this new place of apparently unlimited freedom." The migrants then felt "disillusionment and acute anxiety" as they became aware of "the more subtle discrimination and hostility" they faced. Apparently, some of the youths told welfare officials that they felt "safer" in the South, where they knew what was expected of them.[22]

Housing Black Migrants in the West

Carey McWilliams, who studied western race relations carefully during the war, found that urban centers in the West varied generally in terms of housing and race policies. In particular, Portland maintained a rather conservative reputation in regard to its willingness to absorb black migrants, while other cities, such as Los Angeles and Seattle, came across as more liberal in their housing policies. As McWilliams argued in 1945, Washington State had at least a weak civil rights act and had never had a miscegenation statute. In contrast, Portland was "a much more conservative community than Seattle," thus reflecting the "southern exposure" of Oregon, which had no civil rights law and maintained a statute against intermarriage. With a black population of 1,900 in 1940, Portland exemplified the western cities that had only a small prewar black community connected to the railroad industry. With the rapid and dramatic increase in the black population during the war to almost 22,000, the Portland Realty Board tried to maintain prewar residential boundaries by forbidding any realtors to sell or rent property to black families outside of restricted areas.[23]

In Los Angeles, despite its large prewar population of approximately 64,000, the wartime housing issue led to very tense racial relations.[24] The massive waves of black migrants that Carey McWilliams described in 1942 found themselves shut out of new housing and limited to areas that were black or Japanese in 1941. As a quick and temporary solution, the government used abandoned houses in "Little Tokyo" to accommodate the black migrants from the American South as the Japanese families were relocated to internment camps inland. In the process, the area became known as "Bronzeville" and was described by one migrant as having a "ghetto" reputation at the time.[25]

Reports in Los Angeles described the severe overcrowding that forced African American families to double and triple up with other families.[26] During the summer of 1943, another large wave of black migrants from the South arrived at a rate of between 3,500 and 5,000 per month, with some estimates of about 125 per day. Manpower officials pointed to a recruitment campaign by the Southern Pacific Railroad throughout the Deep South in the spring, and the migrants that arrived had "90 cents to 95 cents an hour ideas." Reports also noted the large number of unskilled workers, classified as 4-F due to their illiteracy. Yet recruiting by West Coast firms had also lured a large number of semiskilled and skilled black migrants. Some of these workers claimed to have left Detroit as a result of the race riot and tension in that city, believing that they would be safe in Los Angeles. Of course, with the "zoot suit riots" that summer, black migrants realized that racial tension existed wherever their presence was felt and resented by whites.[27]

This massive wave of in-migrants during the summer of 1943 created a desperate housing situation. In Los Angeles, the overcrowding prompted the *California Eagle,* the city's black newspaper, to describe the housing situation as pure "misery" for "war workers and their families who had been recruited" to southern California. As in Seattle, Los Angeles officials noted how in-migrants had doubled up with the "native Negroes," yet the housing situation reached the saturation point as thousands more migrants poured in. Since June the in-migration had doubled, and local leaders were indeed desperate for a solution to the overcrowding. Furthermore, officials noted how the same trend appeared to be occurring in San Diego and San Francisco.[28] By 1945, officials estimated that some 23,000 black families had migrated into Los Angeles since April 1940 and that 13,700 of these families needed housing. During that year, continued white resistance to black expansion prompted black activists to form the Home Owners Protective Association to fight restrictive covenants.[29]

In Los Angeles, black migrants naturally sought access to residential areas excluded to them. With this process of expansion, the city experienced tremendous tension, as white neighborhoods in South Central Los Angeles reacted by enforcing racial covenants and at times resorting to violence and intimidation. In October and November 1943, the all-white South Los Angeles Home Owners Association, which covered real estate from between 89th to 104th Streets and Avalon to Clovis, attempted to stop a new Federal Housing Administration (FHA) housing project with 465 units. Hacienda Village, as it was known, was an integrated development, where, according to the *California Eagle*, black, Mexican, and white residents lived peacefully together. During the fall, various interracial organizations, including local labor groups, black churches, Jewish religious leaders, and the NAACP Youth Council, protested the action of the homeowners and demanded that FHA projects have no race restrictions for residents. During the war, California liberals and black activists made integrated public housing and expanded private housing their two top goals.[30]

Politically, the recruitment of southern workers also concerned western Republicans, given the former's inclination to vote the Democratic ticket. Republicans' worry became most evident with the fall election of 1944. As Marilynn Johnson details in *The Second Gold Rush,* this political controversy shaped wartime and postwar politics in the San Francisco Bay Area as Democrat politicians gained voters. In Portland, conservatives were no less concerned. C. C. Crow, editor of a regional lumber industry journal, expressed tremendous indignation toward southern migrants after President Roosevelt's 1944 election victory. Arguing that the federal recruitment campaign was designed to disperse Democrats throughout the nation, Crow blasted the "boot-licking, fixed-fee-plus-cost contractors" who recruited the southern Negroes, "hill-billies, Oakies, and other riff-raff" to Oregon. Whereas Portland was "once famed for the fact that it had no slums, scarcely any negroes, a minimum of crime and an unusually high average of citizenry," now "to the casual observer," Crow lamented, Portland "looks like an angel food cake swarming with black ants."[31]

In many cases, western defense centers such as Portland, Oakland, and Los Angeles were reluctant to expand housing for black southern migrants for fear that the workers would stay permanently.[32] As with the lumber camps, western towns and cities used housing shortages during the war as a means of discouraging black migration and settlement. In 1944, for instance, the Kaiser Corporation restricted recruitment of African Americans in Texas based on alleged housing shortages in Richmond and Fontana, California. Such exclusion did not occur without protest, however. In Los Angeles, the NAACP and local activist Rev. Clayton Russell battled a plan by Deputy Mayor Orville Caldwell to stop all black in-migration into the city.[33]

Given these overall limitations, migrants' relentless pursuit of higher wages and improved social conditions reveals the tremendous desire within southern families to improve their lives by migrating. As workers with restricted capital discovered the means of overcoming their economic limitations, their willingness to move to overcrowded war centers suggests just how much African Americans and Latinos sought to leave the stifling conditions of the South. While the promise of a better life may have been an illusion in the West, a declining farming system and Jim Crow laws failed to offer much hope for those seeking a better life for themselves and their children. In the West, and especially in urban California, black migrants from the South created and extended community institutions in their new home. In Los Angeles, black churches played an important role in motivating migrant workers to protest existing discrimination in western industries. As in the South, more militant churches began to take a more demanding posture on the jobs issue specifically.[34]

The lack of adequate housing seems to have deterred few southern migrants heading west during the war. While white separatism manifested itself in restrictive housing covenants and segregation on the shop floor in the West, compared to the South, a more liberal environment existed where black workers got into high-paying skilled positions. The story of southern families' migration to the Pacific Coast during the war has only recently been recognized for its relevance to larger questions of the struggle for equality, democracy, and civil rights in the United States. As recent historians focus on the war as a period of advancement for labor and civil rights advocates, the process of improving economic and social mobility in the West represents an important gain for black southerners during the war. The fact remains that nonwhite workers from the South did find new and greater employment opportunities in numerous western defense industries. The economic gains made in western defense industries certainly raise important questions about the successes and limits of civil rights improvements for black migrants during the war.[35] In the Pacific West, liberal employment practices held tremendous social and economic implications for African Americans and Latinos seeking citizenship and equality during the war.

Chapter Four

Black Migrants and the Jobs Movement in the West

Robert Weaver, noted African American economist and former WMC administrator, argued in 1946 that the occupational and industrial diversification that occurred during the war represented "a departure from older practices" not seen for seventy-five years.[36] Emphasizing this dramatic and symbolic change reinforces many home front historians' contention that the war did in fact bring about positive change in the area of employment discrimination. During the 1930s and 1940s, job inequality emerged as one of the most pressing issues for African Americans. The breaking of traditional job barriers by black workers took on a special significance in labor markets throughout the nation. The change had tremendous symbolic importance to both white workers, some of whom resisted the change, and black workers, who sought economic mobility.[37]

The workplace served as a key site for the struggle over equality. In comparing the various industrial regions, including the South, the Northeast, the industrial Midwest, and the Far West, evidence suggests that workplace activism and the conflict over job equality varied regionally. During the peak labor shortage period, the Fair Employment Practices Committee (FEPC) tracked some ninety-two race-related work strikes throughout the United States.[38] The FEPC was not able to discern the cause of all of these strikes. Yet officials determined that at least twenty involved white workers protesting the training and upgrading of African Americans as well as integrated dressing facilities. Another twenty-one strikes involved African Americans protesting management's failure to upgrade poor work conditions, racialized wage differentials, and segregated facilities.[39] In this struggle for labor and civil rights during the war, black workers sought economic equality and citizenship through organized labor networks and federal wartime labor arbitration. As had been the case during World War I, the National War Labor Board provided some bargaining power to organized labor, as unions enjoyed unprecedented and unsurpassed membership.

In many respects, the civil rights movement during the Second World War is defined by the struggle for equality in the workplace. On the job, black workers often sought equality of opportunity as their right. With the heightened concern with democracy at home, black workers used a variety of strategies to protest discrimination. FEPC statistics indicate that the preponderance of African American workplace activism, in the form of race strikes, occurred in Ohio, Michigan, and Pennsylvania. Such heightened activism may be attributed to the greater overall grassroots support of organized labor and the exceptional organization of Left-led unions in the North. For federal manpower administrators in the WMC during this period, the decentralized structure of the agency also allowed regional offices some latitude in defending or opposing civil rights strikes during the war. More often than not, the more liberal WMC administrators resided in the North. Robert Goodwin, during his tenure as WMC Region V director from 1942 to 1944, was praised by liberals and integrationists for openly advocating the utilization of nonwhite labor and enforcing antidiscriminatory policies.[40] Indeed, Region V, which comprised Ohio, Michigan, and Kentucky, was the site for thirty-one of the ninety-two race strikes during this period.[41] Robert Weaver, as former director of the Negro Manpower Division under the WMC, also noted that the greatest cooperation at the regional level occurred in Region V, Region II (New York), and Region VI (Illinois, Wisconsin, and, to a lesser degree, Indiana).[42]

In stark contrast to the midwestern strikes, the FEPC documented only one strike in the American West during this period. At the Basic Magnesium plant in Las Vegas, Nevada, in October 1943, black workers walked out to protest segregated facilities. Can one assume that the low level of workplace conflict over racial issues in the West reflects a more progressive attitude in the region? Were white southern migrants in the West less likely to protest over black upgrading than those southerners in the South, the border states, and the industrial Midwest? Most fundamentally, how much did the racial progressivism in the Pacific West provide African Americans from the American South economic and social mobility?

The labor market on the West Coast, like the region's race relations, varied largely in terms of tolerating or enforcing the strict economic and social segregation found on the shop floors of the American South. Within the complex ethnic makeup of California's workforce, Chinese, Japanese, Mexican, Filipino, and black workers competed for common labor positions in farming and domestic labor. Outside of the more leftist CIO unions, most AFL unions and employers enforced segregated worker classification based on white entitlement to higher pay and advancement.

The labor market in southern California prior to the war was generally segregated along lines of race and ethnicity. In oral history accounts, several southern migrants and native black Angelenos found that prior to 1942 jobs outside of manual labor and domestic work were largely off-limits to them.[43] In the cotton compress industry of the San Joaquin Valley specifically, southern attitudes shaped employment policies to maintain southern racial customs. George Lee, an organizer for the International Longshoremen's and Warehousemen's Union (ILWU) of the CIO, recalled how "organizing cotton compress workers in the Valley was a little like it must have been in Mississippi." Cotton was a southern industry. Hence, in California, Lee observed that "the supervisors and foremen were mainly from the South, the whole company leadership was southern." Furthermore, Lee found that "many of the workers had worked in the compresses back in Texas, Oklahoma and Arkansas. When they followed the industry out here in the 1920s and 1930s, they brought that whole southern thing with them."[44]

The experiences of Elijah Fifer, a Texas migrant who came to Bakersfield, illustrate the economic changes that the West Coast ILWU provided southern migrants. As Fifer remembered, cotton compresses in Texas paid thirty-five cents an hour while the San Joaquin Compress in Bakersfield paid forty-five cents. Even with the increased wage, the actions of one white foreman named "Tex" motivated the workers to strike for better conditions. "Tex" was "one rough bugger," Fifer recalled. "I'm glad he come here because he was so nasty, he made us organize faster." In 1937 "it was really on account of Tex that we walked out. We wasn't asking nothing and he was just making it so hard on us."[45]

African American and Mexican migrants in the cotton compresses in Fresno and Bakersfield united under the CIO. In 1938, compress workers were assisted by Hursel Alexander, a black organizer from Los Angeles under the United Cannery, Agricultural, Packing, and Allied Workers of America (UCAPAWA) Local 272. Later in 1938 and 1939, the CIO compress organization would form the basis of the ILWU's valley jurisdiction. Ollie Lewis, an ILWU member in the valley during the 1930s, claimed that most of the workers were "really green," but they "tried to learn all they could." "We voted in the union, struck for three days, and won a contract with better wages, overtime, holiday pay, seniority and a grievance system. After that we began to get very particular about hours." As Lewis declared, the workers simply wanted a "fair day's work, that's all."

Black and Mexican workers' grassroots victories with leftist CIO unions in a conservative southern industry illustrated the key role that western labor shortages had in unions gaining concessions. Elijah Fifer remembered that "so many people were afraid that when we walked out [the company] could have fired us all." At that time, however, only a few compresses existed in the state, and "help wasn't plentiful like it was in the South with people who understood the compress." "We got them in the middle of the season and there wasn't anything they could do," Fifer boasted. "Head sewers, lever pullers, cotton tiers, they was hard to get. We knew that. We knew that all the skilled people had jobs. We did our homework, we didn't go into it just blind."[46]

While the cotton industry drew many southern migrants to California in the 1930s, with war mobilization many more southern workers came west specifically to work in the shipyards for the duration of the conflict. As top military priorities, the Kaiser Corporation and navy shipyards and repair facilities in California, Washington, and Hawaii drew the majority of southern migrants. As in the South, however, African American migrants found that opportunities in the western shipyards did not always lead to the promises of advancement for which they hoped. Federal navy yards in Pearl Harbor, Bremerton, Washington, and Mare Island and Hunter's Point, California, provided opportunities for advancement to thousands of southerners. To the dismay of many black migrants, however, privately operated shipyards on the Pacific Coast were largely dominated by the AFL International Brotherhood of Boilermakers (IBB) and, hence, refused to classify black workers in skilled capacities.

This general exclusion policy came to light most dramatically in 1942 when IBB Local 72 in Portland, representing some 45,000 workers, refused to clear some thirty trained black workers for any work above the status of laborer. In the spring, Thomas Ray, the secretary-treasurer of Local 72, agreed to clear only "local Negroes" and refused to grant the privilege to "migrant Negroes." Tensions mounted when a group of 106 trained black welders from New York arrived and were directed to the Laborers and Hod Carriers Union Local 296, regardless of their skills and classifications. Many new arrivals declared in protest that they were only going to refuse such work. As the migrants expressed disgruntlement, conservative whites expressed alarm at the in-migration of black shipyard workers and tried to incite feelings against their presence in the local newspapers. As a town dominated by a powerful conservative shipbuilding union, Portland offered skilled black migrants little opportunity for advancement.[47]

In the majority of shipyard cities on the West Coast, the AFL posed serious barriers to black advancement in the shipbuilding industry. Like the Gulf Coast, the IBB on the Pacific Coast dominated shipyard organizing. Contractors such as Henry Kaiser signed with the AFL in 1941 because the AFL had an unofficial privileged status with such large defense contractors. Hence, the IBB held contracts with Western Pipe and Steel and Henry Kaiser's Cal Ship in Los Angeles, Marinship in Sausalito, the huge Kaiser and Todd shipyards in Oakland and Richmond, and the three large Kaiser yards in Portland and Vancouver, Washington.[48]

The CIO's Industrial Union of Marine and Shipbuilding Workers of America (IUMSWA) also maintained a presence on the West Coast but never really challenged the AFL's organizing dominance during the war. In South Los Angeles, Local 9 out of San Pedro organized workers at the large Bethlehem and Todd shipyards. At twenty thousand members, Local 9 was the largest CIO union in southern California.[49] During the war, it remained the largest IUMSWA local on the West Coast and therefore stood as a symbol of the CIO's potential political power. However, throughout the war, Local 9 was racked by factionalism between leftists, who demanded local union autonomy, and those IUMSWA leaders who allied with the more moderate East Coast leadership. As a CIO union with a sizable leftist membership and a progressive stance on equal employment, Local 9 offered great potential for organizing black workers in the West Coast shipbuilding industry. Harry Bridges, the most vocal proponent of equal membership for black workers in the West Coast CIO, encouraged IUMSWA leaders to take advantage of black and white workers' contempt toward the IBB in the California shipyards.[50] For the most part, however, race and the presence of southern migrants remained a nonissue for CIO shipyard organizers as political factionalism emerged as the most pressing barrier to successful organizing.

For black workers on the coast, the IBB's segregated setup proved to be the most glaring violation of their equal rights on the shop floor. In the western defense centers, the Boilermakers followed its nationally segregated setup by organizing IBB auxiliaries for black workers in Local 26 in Oakland, Local 32 in Portland, Local 92 in Los Angeles, and Local 41 in Sausalito.[51] From 1943 to 1946, African American workers supported a major lawsuit, *James v. Marinship*, against the IBB to protest the discriminatory setup. The desegregation fight mobilized liberals up and down the coast and emerged as part of the broader jobs movement that blossomed in southern California. In this conflict over job equality, feelings existed among some African Americans that southern white migrants were the root of the conservative resistance. In October 1943, for instance, the *California Eagle* feared that white in-migrants from the South had developed a "Klan network" in the shipyards to "set off a holocaust" and thereby thwart the labor movement.[52]

In the West Coast jobs movement during the war, the Negro Victory Committee (NVC) in Los Angeles emerged as the most militant and most organized black civil rights group. Formed in 1942 by Rev. Clayton Russell, pastor of the People's Independent Church in Los Angeles, the NVC hoped to combat the exclusion of African Americans from all defense jobs throughout southern California. Russell had taken over the church in 1935, and he made social outreach in South Central Los Angeles one of the strengths of the church. He also embraced a more progressive and militant agenda of social work and civil rights than most of his contemporaries in the churches of California. Hence, in his political stance, Russell stood apart from more conservative black churches in the city, and he represented the emergence of a new breed of church leader who hoped to use the church aggressively to mobilize African Americans for equal rights and economic opportunity.[53]

Like other progressive black church leaders throughout the nation during the war, Russell sought alliances with organized labor, especially the CIO, to battle the exclusion of nonwhites from defense jobs. The jobs movement in Los Angeles blossomed during July 1942, when Russell mobilized the black community around the Los Angeles USES's statement that black women had no interest in defense jobs. On July 6 Russell held a mass rally with the local NAACP and the Los Angeles CIO to protest employment discrimination. As Russell recalled, "We just challenged them. We said it doesn't make any difference what church you belong to or what faith or religion or no church. If you need a job or hear of a job, meet us here. If you have a problem, regardless of what it is, any kind of discrimination, come to my office."[54]

In a dramatic and unprecedented show of political force, on July 12, 1942, Russell mobilized hundreds of black women to stage a direct action protest at the Los Angeles USES office. Women flooded the employment office and occupied all of the stations in line, while officials of the NVC negotiated the inclusion of black workers in the defense effort. The NVC's bold strategy in July forced USES officials to concede on the jobs issue, and the NVC ultimately claimed a moral and political victory. In the wake of the protest, the War Manpower Commission in Washington established a Temporary Committee on Fair Employment to work in California on the jobs equality issue and appointed Clarence Johnson to head the West Coast Minority Division of the WMC.[55] Because California and the Pacific West were so vital to national defense, and because the NVC strategy could potentially embarrass Roosevelt and the Allied cause, the NVC direct action strategy succeeded.

Following the Negro Victory Committee's campaign at the USES office, jobs movement leaders in California tackled the segregation and exclusion of black workers in the West Coast shipbuilding industry. In February 1943, the NVC sent a telegram to FEPC regional director W. K. Hopkins protesting the "Jim Crowing of Negro Workers into auxiliary unions" by the IBB at Western Pipe and Steel in San Pedro and Cal Ship and Consolidated in Wilmington. As the committee declared, "Negroes [were] being forced into Jim Crow Unions and [were] being denied full insurance rights, employment opportunities especially in Western Pipe and Steel, seniority protection and equal participation in labor guarantees and privileges." The committee urged immediate action.[56]

As the NVC began to address the job discrimination issue in 1943, militant black shipyard workers formed the Shipyard Workers Committee, a group dedicated to battling the segregating of black workers into the IBB auxiliary unions. Shipyard worker and Los Angeles native Walter Williams helped initiate the antidiscrimination movement among the black employees, who viewed equality of opportunity as a civil rights issue. In 1943, Williams became chairman of the Shipyard Workers Committee and thereby represented black workers who demanded equality and who also sought alliances with the NVC in the West Coast jobs movement. At the same time, the revitalized FEPC established an office in Los Angeles to gather and file specific complaints against the Boilermakers and the three big shipbuilding companies.[57]

In its battle against Jim Crow in the shipyards, the Shipyard Workers Committee chose to challenge the IBB with a lawsuit and not with any direct action forms of protest. By doing so, black labor leaders, which comprised a mix of California natives and southern migrants, illustrated their ability to use diverse strategies in their fight for economic and social equality. During the winter and spring of 1943, the Los Angeles Urban League in alliance with the NVC also protested the discrimination at Cal Ship and began building a case against the union. During March, the Negro Victory Committee issued its mandate to W. K. Hopkins. At the same time, Clarence Johnson, the minority field representative of the WMC, began building a case against companies in the San Francisco Bay Area after Rev. Columbus Johnson of Richmond sent him a letter documenting the exclusion of black workers. That spring, the California CIO council also joined the movement when it criticized the apathy of the California WMC on the jobs issue. As Marvyn Rathborne, secretary-treasurer of the state CIO, charged, the WMC had "done nothing effective to stop the spread of discrimination or to correct specific cases" brought to its attention by the newly formed Bay Area WMC Advisory Committee against Discrimination. Together with the Bay Area Council against Discrimination (BACAD), these interracial groups tackled the issue of discrimination in California's defense industries and made equal rights in the workplace a major goal.[58]

The NVC eventually won the suit in 1946. While the jobs movement addressed the concerns of black workers specifically, the legal battle required an interracial effort with support from the CIO and white liberals. Ben Margolis, a leftist lawyer from California, represented Joseph James on behalf of the black workers in *James v. Marinship* and also served as the main counsel for the Los Angeles CIO from 1943 to 1948.[59] During the war, white liberals like Margolis, along with more leftist members of the CIO in California, certainly were important in forming an interracial movement among workers. The effort to desegregate defense industries on the West Coast remained a complex mixture of black workers demanding equality of opportunity and white and Jewish liberals supporting equality in principle. What is less well known, however, is how many shipyard workers overall supported the suit.

In his novel *If He Hollers Let Him Go*, author Chester Himes used the racial tension of the Los Angeles shipyards during the war to address the variety of strategies that black workers faced in their efforts to cope with discrimination in defense industries. As five men on one segregated crew debate how to overcome the injustices of the workplace, they propose a variety of solutions. As Himes wrote, Red said "they all ought to quit." Smitty was "for talking to Mac," the supervisor. Pigmeat thought the crew "ought to mess up the work so it'd have to be done over," and Conway thought "they ought to form a committee to go see some of the big shots in the front office." Lastly, George promoted the idea of organizing "all the colored workers." In the end, however, the workers only vented their frustration and declined to act on their resentment against their lack of power. Himes's fictional account reflects a reality that existed for many black workers in the West as they struggled with the dilemma of keeping their high-paying jobs or fighting against inequality. In Himes's shipyard, the black workers acknowledged the ideal of political strength through an interracial movement among leftist whites and blacks within the union but remained largely separatist in their actions. While they often expressed resentment against the white-dominated union, they nevertheless remained on their jobs for the money.[60]

The shipbuilding industry was the largest employer of black migrants in the West during the war, despite the economic segregation and lack of advancement opportunities available in the shipyards. Indeed, at the war's peak production, close to thirty thousand black men and women found employment in privately operated western yards.[61] While no real figures exist for the navy yards in the Pacific region, WMC records indicate that some of the yards, such as Mare Island and Hunter's Point in the San Francisco Bay Area and those in the Puget Sound area, recruited from two hundred to a thousand workers per month from the South and the Great Plains, the two regions with the greatest surplus of workers.[62] Certainly, discrimination existed at these yards, as FEPC complaint cases suggest. Yet in comparison to the South, many greater opportunities for advancement existed in federal navy yards out west.

As New Orleans migrant Arthur Chapman attested, the Pearl Harbor navy yard employed black workers based on their qualifications. This policy represented a distinct and welcome change for black southern migrants like Chapman.[63]

The California CIO: The Promise of Western Liberalism

Clearly, the majority of black workers chose to stay in the western shipyards even with IBB representation. In doing so, their actions reflected their priority of accepting with clenched teeth high wages over any principles of social equality. Their employment should not be interpreted as an indifference to segregation, however. In many cases, black workers stayed in the shipyards only as long as they felt necessary. As they did so, they kept their eyes and ears open to other opportunities. In California, CIO unions, such as the ILWU, which was committed to building an interracial labor movement, often attracted migrants who refused to settle for the discriminatory working conditions and lack of upward mobility in the shipyards.

Bill Williams, a black worker who migrated from Texarkana, Texas, to Oakland in 1942, received paid training from his employer, Moore's Shipyard, and began work as an electrician's helper; he then joined the International Brotherhood of Electrical Workers (IBEW) of the AFL. The conservative union gave Williams and other black workers permits but not full membership in the union. Hence, as Williams recalled, "they took my money and gave me the right to work. They didn't invite [me] to any meetings and I didn't want to go to any meetings." Despite this discrimination, Williams found that wages, compared to those in Texas, were superior. In the South, he made $1.50 a day as a hotel maintenance worker, while at Moore's he started at 90 cents an hour. Eventually, he convinced his wife to come out, and she got also got hired at Moore's.

Williams found that less overt racism existed on the integrated shop floor at Moore's, where he worked with white, black, and Chinese workers in his gang and where "the emphasis was so heavily on winning the war that the biases were not nearly as sharply felt as it might have been in the Depression times."[64] While he acknowledged the existence of discrimination at Moore's, Williams nevertheless believed that "things were so much better there than where I had come from that I saw, I think, and appreciated the improvements to such a great extent. And then having a regular check."[65]

Eventually, Bill Williams left Moore's to find permanent work on the Oakland waterfront, where he joined the ILWU Local 10. Williams's actions illustrate how migrant workers who were concerned with maintaining a permanent job into the postwar years consciously sought jobs outside the shipyards, where advancement and security were possible and one was paid according to one's qualifications. One worker who left Cal Ship after six weeks complained that he had been working "beneath his skill" as a carpenter at $1.20 an hour, thus "constituting a great hardship for himself and his family." He quit his job at the shipyard to take one at a company in San Pedro, where he received $1.34 an hour as a foreman carpenter. The change provided a welcome advancement in comparison to the race relations and segregated shop floor at Cal Ship that limited his abilities. Specifically, he claimed that he had been required to "do all the dirty work of a carpenter helper" while still being paid regular journeyman wages. At the same time, "white men working close complain all the time about how I make as much as they do." The worker quit because he felt he was entitled to switch jobs after enduring such injustices. Another worker at Cal Ship told the USES that "all I want . . . is to get out of the shipyards," because despite four years of carpentry apprenticeship, the company refused to hire him in a skilled carpentry position. According to the worker, the company instead gave journeyman carpenter wages to whites regardless of their experience.[66]

For some black shipyard workers who were determined to find permanent employment in the West, longshore work offered a sensible avenue for work opportunities. In the move from the shipyards into work on the waterfront, Gulf Coast family networks and familiarity with the industry certainly facilitated the transition. Willie McGee, who migrated from New Orleans to Los Angles in 1941 to work in the shipyards, used his knowledge of longshore work from his years in New Orleans to gain a permanent job and eventual membership in ILWU Local 26 in San Pedro. After working for a Los Angeles shipyard as a rivet heater, McGee picked up part-time work on the docks. From his part-time job, McGee jumped at the chance to join Local 26 after a year. As he recalled, "I had the opportunity to [join] and I had sense enough to know that organized labor was the worker's friend."[67]

Elbert Kelly, who migrated from Texarkana to Los Angeles in 1937, started out in domestic work when he arrived in California. After bouncing from job to job, a friend of his took him down to the waterfront and the ILWU dispatch hall in San Pedro, where he was hired on the spot. According to Kelly, the ILWU gave him a longshore carpentry job, despite the fact that he had no carpentry experience. As Kelly recalled, "I took the job and I went out to work on this carpenter job and it was so easy until I fell in love with it." He made $1.50 an hour and $15 a day, unprecedented wages for the young man.

Chapter Four

While the pay was excellent compared to domestic work, Kelly also appreciated the liberal race relations in California. He left Texas because he "didn't like discrimination." "I was headed for trouble if I stayed down there," he admitted. In California, Kelly made friends with a white Texan on the docks, and to him this enduring friendship symbolized the important social differences between the two states.[68]

Bill Williams, who worked at Moore's Shipyard in Oakland, also joined the ILWU Local 10 on the Oakland waterfront for the purpose of securing permanent employment. Because the contracts at Moore's were "getting slimmer and slimmer," Williams kept his ears open for other jobs. In February 1944, he heard a man at a barbershop talk about longshore work and went down to the ILWU Local 10 hall, where he was hired. When he began work at Pier 23 in Oakland, Williams noticed that there were many black longshoremen, certainly more than in San Francisco. Once on the job, he "ran across fellows from the Gulf Coast who had had experience, and they taught me lots about the work."[69] For these migrants attracted by the western labor shortage, Williams claims that ILWU Local 10 in Oakland was "a utopia." "Even the level of struggle we faced in Local 10," he declared, "was something so high above what most of us had experienced in Arkansas, Texas, and other places in the South that we were willing to get involved and take our chances at the results." According to Williams, "We're talking about a union that gave you a chance to be somebody, to hold your head high."[70]

Bill Williams believes that race relations in the ILWU Local 10 were generally quite decent during the war and without any hostility. On the one hand, some white workers were indifferent to the existence of black workers. Yet other white Communists and liberals "showed a concern about your welfare" by asking about housing and transportation.[71] Black migrants from the Gulf Coast played a prominent role in the struggle for black warehousemen to keep their memberships in 1946 when conservative white ILWU leaders hoped to evict black workers who joined during the war. Williams recalled that in 1946 "there was antagonism between some whites and blacks then, because the new black leaders articulated our vision and our hopes very well." In particular, "Albert James from the Gulf and Johnny Walker from New Orleans were the most vocal." These men brought their "labor background here from their history" with the International Longshoremen's Association (ILA) in the Gulf. "They transferred their skills to the union combats here." According to Williams, Albert James was "so fluent he could take an idea and make it visible," while Johnny Walker "was very courageous." Likewise, Bill Chester "was very methodical" as well. It was from these more militant southern migrants that Williams learned the ropes of shrewd political maneuvering in the ILWU.[72]

For black workers who sought some permanency in the West, the ILWU offered an opportunity to stay in California with some economic security. The ILWU had maintained a reputation for fairness and the promotion of racial equality since 1935. In 1933, Harry Bridges, the leftist leader of the union, demanded that the San Francisco Local 13 of the ILA include black workers as members in the name of worker unity. Bridges eventually left the ILA over the race issue and helped found the ILWU under the CIO. His dedication to racial inclusion reflected the tremendous symbolic changes occurring in race and labor relations during the 1930s, as interracial unity became a key strategy for organizing workers in mass production industries. African Americans in the South were undoubtedly well aware of the union's reputation for fairness through the black media and the ILWU's own organizing efforts along the Gulf Coast after 1937.[73]

The CIO's rise in the U.S. labor movement after 1935 signaled an important shift in American race relations. In many ways, the racial progressivism of the ILWU in San Francisco symbolized most vividly the movement toward interracialism in organized labor within the United States. In the West, leftist leaders and militant rank and file in the CIO promoted racial inclusion in key wartime industries where black workers found jobs. By 1938, the ILWU controlled the docks and warehouses on the Los Angeles harbor and in the San Francisco Bay Area, while after 1941 the United Auto Workers (UAW) organized several large aircraft plants in Los Angeles.[74]

Following the 1934 waterfront strike in the San Francisco Bay Area, the ILWU began its "great march inland" to organize warehouses, packing sheds, and other goods-handling services in the Los Angeles harbor area.[75] ILWU Local 26 in San Pedro was chartered in October 1936. In May 1937, the ILWU made a push to organize the smaller warehouses of Los Angeles, signing up over thirteen hundred new members. During that year, Local 38-134 of the Old Pacific District of the ILA-AFL became the new ILWU-CIO Local 26. By September, the ILWU had organized most of Los Angeles's drug industry warehouses. The AFL Teamsters countered the ILWU gains in warehouses and mills with membership raids, physical intimidation, and Red-baiting, while some employers fired any workers suspected of joining the ILWU.

Between 1937 and 1940, the ILWU managed to hold on to most drug warehouses and mills and eventually moved into organizing hundreds of scrap workers, who were mostly black, Mexican, and Jewish and therefore traditionally excluded from the Teamsters. By organizing these workers, the ILWU illustrated its policy of racial inclusion in the multiethnic Los Angeles area. In 1943, the acceptance of over a thousand black migrants into San Pedro's Local 26 altered dramatically the ethnic composition of the union. Although membership continued to be predominantly white, ILWU organizers in Los Angeles made a concerted effort during the war to continue organizing warehouses and plants with black workers while battling discrimination. In 1943, for instance, ILWU Local 26 won an election for 190 black women at the Aero Reclamation Company plant in downtown Los Angeles. Discovering that local food merchants in that area refused to serve the workers because of their race, the ILWU organizers negotiated with city officials and the merchants to desegregate their establishments in the cause of "equality of treatment."[76]

The United Auto Workers emerged as another important CIO union in southern California when it began organizing southern California's burgeoning aircraft industry in 1940. By 1941, the union's organization of North American Aviation (NAA) in Inglewood became one of the most controversial organizing movements of the defense buildup period when over five thousand workers in UAW Local 683 walked out in an unauthorized strike. After refusing to return to work, President Roosevelt called out the National Guard to reopen the plant for defense purposes. In general, the strike created criticism in the press and among more conservative CIO leaders. Eventually, the workers returned to work after the UAW gained substantial wage increases for them.[77] Although the leftist UAW Local 683 leadership at NAA had considerable influence, racial inclusion never became an issue, because the conservative hiring policies of the aviation industries prior to 1943 largely enforced segregation and exclusion of nonwhite workers.

After 1935, Harry Bridges and the ILWU in California emerged as the power base of the entire western CIO. The ILWU's racial inclusion policy was important in setting a tone of tolerance and inclusion throughout the West. Yet nonwhites represented such a small percentage of workers in many mass industries such as aircraft, shipbuilding, and all industries in the Pacific Northwest that racial conflict rarely became an issue until the mass migration of black workers after 1942. In the industries in which nonwhites were present in large numbers prior to the war, particularly cannery, agriculture, cotton compress, and some warehouses, the CIO did offer black and Hispanic workers a chance to be a part of the organized labor movement.

The ILWU also organized women in small manufacturing plants and the warehouse service industries in California. Although males comprised the majority of union members in the ILWU, women played an important role in the union. Along the West Coast, ILWU Local 6 in Oakland emerged as the most important local for black female migrants. In a recent ILWU oral history project, many women from the South and Southwest affirmed the improvements that the ILWU made in their lives. For example, Lillian Price migrated from Oklahoma to Oakland in 1944 when she was twenty-one years old. In just twenty days she found work through ILWU Local 6. She eventually got hired at the Colgate Ajax plant in Berkeley, where she was "the first black woman that ever done cans" on its line. "Local 6 made it possible for blacks to get where we got," Price declared. "If it hadn't been to the union, we wouldn't have made it. I've been a union member since I've been in California, and I'll still fight for unions."[78]

Another migrant, Virginia Wysinger, who came to northern California from New Orleans in 1930, worked as a domestic until 1942, when she heard about the union and got hired at Colgate as well. Wysinger stated proudly, "I was the first black woman to work in the wash powder department." Like many other southern migrants, she was glad to get the work. "In the beginning there was a difference between men's and women's work and wages. Then I didn't have any feelings about this, I was so glad to get the work. It was better than doin' housework."

Fanny Walker was also one of the first black women to work at Colgate in Berkeley. Growing up in a sharecropping family in Louisiana, her first job was washing dishes for two "old maids" at twenty-five cents a week. Subsequently, she worked as a domestic through her twenties and thirties, earning on average $1.50 a week. In 1940, Walker came to California, and in 1942, she hired on at Colgate. As one of the first black woman at the plant, she encountered a little resistance to her presence from the white women. She recounted that on lunch break some of the white women would take her lunch off the table and put it on the floor. In response, Walker would put it back on the table. She then told the women, "Now, the first one put my lunch on the floor, I'm gonna fight," and they "let me alone." The next day, one "girl" brought Walker a sweater, and they became "friends from then on." She stayed twenty-eight years at Colgate and credited the ILWU with helping improve race relations among the workers. In retrospect she found that "the treatment of black people by the whites changed a lot," and "it changed a lot on account of the union."[79]

The Los Angeles Aircraft Industry: The Test of Western Liberalism

The ILWU in Oakland certainly provided black migrants with security and even dignity. Yet among the large war industries, the aircraft industry was perhaps the most flexible in utilizing African American labor and especially women workers during the war. When aircraft mass production first began in 1942, Lockheed-Vega in Los Angeles and Bell in Buffalo, New York, initiated the first successful integration efforts in the country. Soon thereafter, other plants, such as North American Aviation (NAA) in Kansas City, Glenn L. Martin in Baltimore and Omaha, Curtis-Wright in St. Louis, Grumman in New York, and others on the West Coast integrated black workers in a variety of skills. Boeing in Seattle, however, remained the most resistant. Under a contract with the Machinists (IAM-AFL), Boeing remained notorious for excluding black workers from skilled positions.[80]

Aircraft plants in the American South, from where many of California's wartime workers migrated, lagged behind the rest of the nation in employing black workers in part because the plants were some of the last to be built. The NAA plant in Dallas, the first in the South, was completed in 1941, and management continued to delay integration well into 1943. Among other southern aircraft plants, the Bechtel-McCone-Parsons aircraft modification plant in Birmingham, the Bell bomber plant in Atlanta, and Convair in New Orleans did not begin production until 1943. On the other hand, Fort Worth's Convair plant went on-line in 1942. Some of these plants offered semiskilled and skilled employment to African Americans. Yet the overall percentage of black workers to benefit from these jobs was minuscule compared to the large majority, who found themselves excluded or unable to advance.

In contrast to the South, the West Coast generally offered a flexible and liberal environment for challenging traditional employment policies in the aircraft industry. The case of Herbert Ward, who moved from Houston to Los Angeles, offers an example of this overall ability for both companies and unions to accept black workers with equal status as white workers. At the same time, Ward's experiences also exemplify the ways in which southern migrants brought their own tradition of labor organizing to the West Coast: "My people were longshoremen," and "I came up union all the way." In Texas, Ward's grandfather was in the Knights of Labor, and, hence, Ward was "born into the movement." While in Texas during the 1930s, he felt the call to move out west. As he put it, "things being as restrictive as they were . . . in Houston, . . . I took it on myself with two other fellows to catch a freight train and leave with the whole interest of furthering my education . . . to follow pursuits of art and history" that he could not get in Texas.

In Los Angeles during the early part of the war, Ward continued to find a lack of economic opportunity despite the wartime boom. He eventually signed on with the Los Angeles Urban League training program at Lockheed-

Vega in Burbank. In 1942, Lockheed integrated, and Ward was hired for a menial position as a sandblast operator. Once Ward came on the job, he heard racial slurs in the restrooms, made deliberately "to scare you if possible, or to embarrass you to such an extent that you wouldn't want to stay." Ward remembered encounters and fights during this initial period. In the beginning, "it was there." Yet as time went on, "people came to understand that these feelings couldn't be openly expressed." Eventually, the IAM–AFL recognized that the union "would be defeating [its] purpose" unless it "really worked . . . and accepted everyone" and unless it "brought the blacks and minorities in."

Herbert Ward, like many southern migrants, was well aware of the more liberal racial environment in Los Angeles, and he actively pushed for his rights. As he recalled, "The IAM put black acceptance on the back burner." In particular, "these people who'd come from the South . . . made it pretty difficult for blacks coming in." At the same time, "blacks recognized that they weren't gonna be accepted on the same basis of whites." In March 1942 at Lockheed, a white progressive named Clarence Gibson got Ward into the IAM. Although the union "didn't come seeking us with open arms," he and other black workers "got in and tried to fight the restrictive clause against blacks." The existing rule stipulated that blacks were to be totally excluded from the IAM. As Ward remembered, "It was hard for me to accept it. I felt that here we were engaged in a war for democracy, and it was certainly far less than that in the labor movement."

In 1943, Ward and other black workers decided to work for change within the IAM by forming the Yea Vote Committee "to protect myself and others." The black workers drew from inspirational community leaders in the fight for social equality. As they declared in the *California Eagle,* "We want only one union shop that will justly and adequately represent all workers as full participating members." While the committee's goals may have seemed radical to the IAM initially, its strategy was somewhat conservative in that it chose to work "on the inside" of the system and to avoid a legal suit while encouraging union activism among black workers.[81]

Eventually, the IAM invited all black workers into District Lodge 727. This admission represented a major victory in the desegregation movement of Los Angeles defense industries. Over time, Ward became a respected leader in the white majority union. During his several decades at Lockheed he was elected frequently to office and eventually became the first black special representative on the International Staff of the IAM in the West. At the same time, his workplace activism was transferred to the community at large. Ward eventually became a leading member of the NAACP in Los Angeles and participated in many campaigns for social justice over the years.[82]

The story of desegregation in the Los Angeles aircraft industry during the war is important because it illustrates how the industry in the West offered thousands of southern migrants, especially black women, new economic opportunities and advancements that were largely unavailable in the South. Hence, the stories of black migrant women in the southern California aviation industry reveal how the decision to migrate west proved very worthwhile for numerous women. For example, Katie Mae Miles moved from Houston to Los Angeles in 1942. She was raised in rural Louisiana and Texas and had moved to Houston in 1931. Between 1931 and 1942 Miles moved to Kansas City and Chicago to find work, but the jobs she found never appealed to her enough to stay permanently. At the beginning of the war, she decided to head west for new work opportunities. Once in Los Angeles, Miles found work in the garment industry, where she made fifty dollars per week and she had the opportunity to join the International Fur and Garment Workers Union. In the union, she worked on an integrated shop floor with African American, Italian, Jewish, and Hispanic women, a new experience for her. On a whim in 1943, she went to the Los Angeles USES office, which placed her at Lockheed, where she made ninety-five cents to a dollar an hour for bucking and riveting. On the shop floor she remembered working with both white and black women from the South, but for the most part, the shop floor remained segregated. Because her husband worked at a Los Angeles shipyard, they qualified for public housing, which she discovered was segregated. She lived in the housing project until 1956.[83]

Another migrant, Videll Drake, moved from Dallas to Los Angeles in 1941. In Dallas, she had made $7.75 a week as a maid and waitress at the Hockaday School. She moved to California "to get a better job." Once in Los Angeles, she, like other southern migrants, started out in domestic work. By 1943, she was determined to get a good-paying war job. She went to NAA in Los Angeles and was hired almost immediately as a riveter starting at sixty cents an hour. When she got the phone call asking her to begin work, she was relieved that she did not have to work at the shipyards. In comparison to her previous job, the pay and hours were exceptional in the aircraft industry. Once at NAA, however, Drake observed that the work crews were generally segregated and that there were no black crew leaders. In her words, NAA "didn't let them work together; the coloreds mostly worked together. There always been a kind of discrimination in that plant." Despite the existence of segregation at the plant, Drake valued the economic stability the job offered. Most importantly, in 1945, after the war was over, NAA invited her to become a permanent postwar worker. Hence, the migration and the wartime opportunities gave Drake an unprecedented degree of economic security and mobility that she believed did not exist in the South.[84]

Fanny Christina Hill's experiences illustrate another example of how migration to Los Angeles and employment in the aviation industry during the war offered important economic opportunities to southern black women. Hill moved from Tyler, Texas, to Los Angeles in 1942. She got a job at NAA only a few days after her arrival. At the beginning of her employment, she received job training for sixty cents an hour, a wage that Hill considered "good money" at the time. While the training was generally integrated in regard to both gender and ethnicity, Hill discovered that at the plant the departments were generally segregated. According to Hill, all the black women were sent to Department 17, which involved nothing but "shooting and bucking rivets." In contrast, "I noticed that some of the white girls did not go to that department. They went to better departments where the work was not as strenuous or whatever." Furthermore, Hill averred that "some departments they didn't even allow a black person to walk through there let alone work in there."[85]

Even with the general segregation and discrimination on the shop floor, Hill discovered that she could gain some occupational mobility by requesting to be transferred from any job she did not like. During the war years, Hill moved from assembly work at a bench to rivet work and then to working in the glass department, which she found to be the most comfortable for her. While Hill refrained from being active in the UAW at North American, she nevertheless praised the union for getting results in correcting a complaint. In her words, "You had someone to back you up if you had a grievance." "You should be able to talk back to your boss, tell him the things that he's doing that's not right," Hill declared.[86]

Mostly, Fanny Christina Hill found that the war industry opportunities in California offered her a far better life than the one she left in Tyler, Texas, a town she called "a very prejudiced place." In her and her sister's opinions, "Hitler was the one who got us out of the white folks' kitchens." Through her job at NAA, Hill was able to buy a house in South Central Los Angeles for four thousand dollars in an integrated neighborhood where residents peacefully coexisted. While she never thought the job would last past the war effort, North American kept her on as a permanent employee after the war. Hill continued to save money and have economic security well into the postwar years. By 1951, her husband left Texas to join her in Los Angeles, where he also got a job at NAA and was able to gain some economic security and mobility.[87]

Josephine Houston's experiences provide another vivid example of how black women migrants from the South found a new and better life in California during the war. Houston was raised in Broussard, Louisiana, and migrated to Los Angeles in 1935, well before the wartime migration. Once in Los Angeles, she discovered that race relations were very different from back in the South. Houston found work at North American Aviation during the war. Yet in contrast to other black migrants such as Fanny Christina Hill, Houston recalled that NAA was generally very integrated on the shop floor. "They had all nationalities," she claimed, like a "United Nations." Moreover, Houston believed the UAW integration policy kept shop floor relations generally peaceful. Houston recalled that on a couple of occasions the UAW gave white migrants from the South who refused to work with black women the ultimatum of working in an integrated setup or quitting. She also discovered that her new neighborhood and the schools her children attended were also ethnically mixed. Houston found that in her experiences, California liberalism provided a welcome change from the suffocating segregation of southwest Louisiana.[88]

Another black migrant who identified herself only as "J.K." also found the racial climate of Los Angeles very different from her native home of Little Rock, Arkansas. Yet she also discovered that Jim Crow could and did exist in parts of California. In 1942, when she was in her early twenties, J.K. had an opportunity to receive state-funded aircraft industrial training in Sacramento. In Los Angeles, she had never encountered Jim Crow, but when she was enjoying leisure time in downtown Sacramento, she was refused admission to a theater based on Jim Crow policy. As she recalled, "I had learned the difference between the South and the West, and naturally assumed that there weren't supposed to be prejudices out here." Nevertheless, J.K. questioned the existence of such racial policy, especially in the state capital.

After completing her training, J.K. returned to Los Angeles, where she was hired as the only black woman in a small machine shop operating a drill press for $125 a month. At the shop, she befriended the white male workers, who treated her well. However, after accepting an innocent ride home from one of the workers, J.K. came to work the next day and was terminated without a valid reason. She knew that her firing stemmed from the interracial socializing. Her experience at the machine shop illustrated that even in the West, conservative racial mores circumscribed the economic opportunities that existed for black migrants.

Following her time at the machine shop, J.K. found employment at North

American. In the aircraft industry, she found that while the shop floor was integrated, subtle racism existed in the promotions and job classifications of white women over more experienced black women. Like many migrants, during the war J.K. sought a permanent job for the postwar years. Hence, when NAA fired her for fighting on the job, she used the opportunity to search for long-term employment. In 1943, she began employment as a civil servant for Los Angeles County and in 1946 began a career at the county sheriff's office that she would have the rest of her working life.[89]

The Segregation Frontier

The men and women interviewed for the Rosie the Riveter and the ILWU oral history projects are important because their life histories illustrate the complexities of southern migrants' experiences during World War II. On the one hand, these black workers generally found permanent and relatively secure jobs that they held into the postwar years. This economic mobility thus illustrates how black southern migrants during the war did find new opportunities for economic stability and even advancement through migration to the West. Nevertheless, their experiences should not necessarily reflect on all black migrants to the West. The workers in aircraft and longshore work were a small handful of the tens of thousands of migrants who went west and failed to secure well-paying and permanent jobs into the postwar years. Unfortunately, the workers who failed to secure long-term jobs have not been interviewed, and their story has not been told. One can surmise that their experiences would certainly illustrate a greater complexity of migrant experience overall. If Chester Himes's wartime novel of shipyard work is any indication, many black workers suffered undue discrimination but remained reluctant to endanger their jobs by protesting or were apathetic toward the prospect of racial progress.

Clearly, though, the existing testimonies of migrant war workers suggest that black southerners in the West found both open and more subtle forms of discrimination and racism. Some workers, such as many of the women in aircraft, felt some resentment at the greater opportunities for advancement given white women and men. These migrants dealt with this discrimination in a variety of ways. Some workers chose to switch jobs until they found employment in industries that allowed for greater advancement and the ability to use the skills they had. Other workers who had migrated continued to work at their jobs and enjoy the economic security that their jobs and their unions provided them.

Some of the more militant migrants who left the South to escape the social and economic limitations of Jim Crow chose to fight discrimination and inequality in California. In the general effort to desegregate California war industries and fight for equality on the shop floor, these migrants used a variety of strategies that suited their circumstances and goals. Herbert Ward, the migrant from Houston who began work at Lockheed-Vega during the war, decided to fight for black equality within the IAM. By placing pressure on the union to desegregate from within, black activists in the IAM chose a strategy that avoided the cost and publicity of a legal suit. In the end, they did succeed in their goals when the IAM allowed black workers to be full members of the AFL union.

Many black workers who joined the ILWU during the war were denied permanent membership after the war. In ILWU Local 26 in San Pedro, white conservatives in the union under L. B. Thomas sought to make the union "lily white." Black workers responded by filing a suit against the union for permanent membership. They believed they were denied membership based on their race, and they felt that the ILWU as a liberal institution should honor their wartime contribution. Their story is part of the postwar struggle to maintain the gains made during World War II in the West. Eventually, they did succeed and gained full permanent membership. By hiring Ben Margolis as their legal counsel, their struggle emerged as an outgrowth of the wartime desegregation movement and therefore represented an important bridge to the modern civil rights movement.

In focusing on the experiences of southern migrants in the West, there is no attempt to imply that migration to the North offered less opportunity for many southerners. As recent labor historians have illustrated with their oral histories of workers in Packinghouse Workers Organizing Committee (PWOC-CIO) in the Midwest and the UAW-CIO in Detroit, many southern migrants in northern industrial centers found the same security and opportunities for advancement as their colleagues in the West.[90] Yet because the West as a region attracted the most migrants during the war, it played an exceptionally important role in the strategies of upwardly mobile African Americans from the South. One might view the region as a "race relations frontier," in that the lack of Jim Crow laws made race relations fluid and undefined. In addition, the large presence of newcomers from throughout the Midwest and Northeast also inhibited the existence of southern racial mores that reinforced social castes and a racial hierarchy.[91]

Certainly, racial liberalism in the West played a very important role in establishing an environment that allowed protest against discrimination and also fostered a broad coalition of black, Jewish, and white liberals who actively fought discrimination during the war. In northern California, the Bay Area Council against Discrimination was perhaps the most prominent and active of all interracial civil rights groups. In the Los Angeles area, over sixty civic groups, labor unions, and ethnic institutions mobilized to support the FEPC from 1944 to its demise in 1946.[92] Hence, in the struggle against employment discrimination in California, especially, interracialism flourished much more so than in the South. This open interracial movement illustrates most dramatically the differences between the South and the West in terms of race relations and the ability for civil rights groups to operate during the war without fear of violence and backlash.

Even with a more open and liberal environment, which fostered greater openness for liberal activity, black workers nevertheless sought to work for change within institutions such as the Negro Victory Committee, which fought for equality in Los Angeles war industries, and the Yea Vote Committee, which fought for black admission and equality in the IAM at Lockheed–Vega in Los Angeles. The NAACP emerged as an important institution in the fight for employment equality in both San Francisco and Los Angeles. And while local Urban Leagues were technically interracial organizations, their agendas in western cities such as Los Angeles, Seattle, and Portland reflected the needs of black workers specifically. It was in these urban defense centers that the greatest numbers of workers challenged segregation and discrimination in local industries. San Francisco, Oakland, and Los Angeles emerged as the centers of black presence on the West Coast. In doing so, they continued to draw black migrants from the South well into the postwar years.

Memphis, Tennessee, June 1938. Daily lineup of African American workers outside the Tennessee State Employment Service office. In the years before World War II, the abundance of underemployed workers kept wages low. Photo by Dorthea Lange. (Reproduced from the collections of the Library of Congress)

Homestead, Florida, February 1939. Migrant vegetable pickers waiting after work to be paid. Although many occupations were segregated by race in the South, migrant workers knew no such boundaries in the fields. Photo by Marion Post Wolcott. (Library of Congress)

Starke, Florida, December 1940. Carpenters and construction workers waiting outside the Florida State Employment Service Office trying to get jobs at Camp Blanding. This scene was typical of many construction boomtowns at the beginning of the war when sometimes more than twenty thousand workers arrived at once looking for work. Photo by Marion Post Wolcott. (Library of Congress)

Beaumont, Texas, May 1943. Workers leaving the Pennsylvania shipyards at a shift change. Skilled workers migrated from all over the United States to earn the high wages paid by shipbuilding firms in the South. Photo by John Vachon. (Library of Congress)

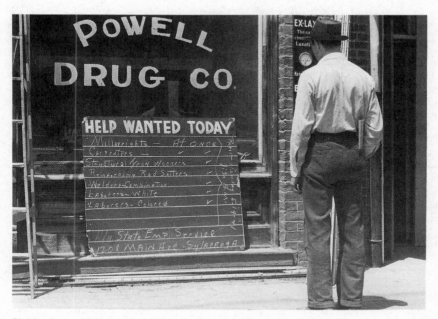

Childersburg, Alabama, May 1941. On Main Street. Alabama State Employment Service advertising construction jobs at the Du Pont ordnance plant. Note that jobs are classified by race and that workers are needed in all categories. Photo by Jack Delano. (Library of Congress)

Millington, Tennessee, December 1940. Unpicked cotton in front of a billboard offering to cash the checks of workers at a nearby ordnance plant. Many workers, especially women, who in previous years would be picking cotton, worked at the ordnance plant. Photo by John Vachon. (Library of Congress)

Childersburg, Alabama, May 1942. Trailer camp for migrant construction workers' families employed at the Du Pont ordnance plant. Rent was three dollars a month. Photo by John Collier. (Library of Congress)

Columbus, Georgia, near Fort Benning, December 1942. Tents, trailers, and shacks in a camp for migrant construction workers' families. Note the contrast of the home-made trailers in this scene with the modern and streamlined trailers used by the families at Childersburg. Photo by Marion Post Wolcott. (Library of Congress)

Arlington, Virginia, April
1942. Farm Security Administration trailer camp project
for African Americans. With
war mobilization, the Farm
Security Administration expanded its housing programs
for migrant farmworkers to
encompass workers em-
ployed in defense industries.
Photo by Marjorie Collins.
(Library of Congress)

Beaumont, Texas, May 1943. Welders at the Pennsylvania shipyards. With very few exceptions, in the shipyards of the South white workers considered welding a white trade and a racial privilege. Photo by John Vachon. (Library of Congress)

Beaumont, Texas, May 1943. A segregated work gang at the Pennsylvania shipyards. On the shop floor, African Americans worked in segregated gangs doing most of the required manual labor. Photo by John Vachon. (Library of Congress)

Negro Defense Training Center, Southern University, Louisiana, 1941. In the fall of 1941, the U.S. defense program began sponsoring Negro defense training centers in the southern states. This center at Southern University was one of the region's first. (National Archive Photo—OWI Negro Division)

Nashville, Tennessee, August 1942. Two women riveting parts at the Convair plant. As shortages of white male workers occurred during 1942, aircraft plants began to hire white females. This transition offered new employment opportunities to women and allowed employers to exclude African Americans from the bulk of aircraft jobs in the South. Photo by Jack Delano. (Library of Congress)

Robert Weaver, Minority Group Services, War Manpower Commission. (National Archive Photo—OWI Negro Division)

Lawrence Oxley and Ben Wilson, Minority Group Services, War Manpower Commission. (National Archive Photo—OWI Negro Division)

Lester Granger, executive director, National Urban League. (National Archive Photo—OWI Negro Division)

5. "We're Not Here to Start a Social Revolution"

Southern Black Workers Define Equality, 1943–1945

In March 1945, Jackson Valtair, a consultant for the Fair Employment Practices Committee (FEPC) in Dallas, held a meeting with the Colored Aircraft Workers Union and white managers at the Convair aircraft plant in Fort Worth. Valtair called the two groups together to discuss a new segregated training program for black workers at the plant. Since the early years of the war, African Americans in Fort Worth had been calling for a training program, and now that Convair agreed to the program, Valtair emphatically assured the management, "We're not here to start a social revolution." Rather, Valtair emphasized that the FEPC's agenda of integrating black workers into skilled jobs "was based upon a simple economic theory—not a radical theory, but a theory that in a war of survival no nation however big or powerful can afford to waste its manpower."[1]

Jackson Valtair's comments underscore the dynamics of labor and race relations in southern defense plants during the last years of the Second World War. African American workers and labor leaders continuously emphasized the conservative nature of their goals by condoning social segregation in the workplace and asking only that qualified workers be hired for skilled positions. At the same time, African Americans mobilized to unprecedented levels of civic and labor organization in their struggle for defense jobs and upgrading. Throughout many southern cities after 1943, the jobs movement and a revitalized FEPC induced new-found alliances among a host of black labor, civic, and church institutions. In Fort Worth, for example, the newly formed Glover Colored Aircraft Workers Union allied with the Colored Women's Club, Packinghouse Workers Union, Brotherhood of Sleeping Car Porters and the Ladies Auxiliary, Railway Shop Workers, Dining Car Employees, beauticians, and the Mount Zion Baptist Church to protest the lack of job opportunities for African Americans in the city.[2] Although black workers in Fort Worth and other southern cities often failed to gain racial equality in the workplace during the war, the bonds formed between black labor unions, civil rights groups, and church leaders established an important organizational link to the modern civil rights movement of the 1950s and 1960s.

During World War II, the majority of southern workers stayed in the region despite the pull of higher wages elsewhere. All workers who remained in the South faced working conditions that were in many ways unique to the region, including a lower wage scale and a more rigidly segregated labor market. Within this conservative labor market, white workers certainly benefited from the racial hierarchy that guaranteed them higher pay and upward mobility. And they defended this privilege through unified action and, at times, violence.[3] The barriers to equal opportunity and advancement did not always prevent African American workers and labor leaders from organizing and protesting discrimination in work-related matters. Indeed, these grievances invigorated a movement to demand equal rights in the workplace. This chapter, then, explores African American efforts during the last three years of the war to define equality and challenge discrimination on the shop floor.

The second half of the war, from 1943 to 1945, was a time of unparalleled labor organizing throughout the United States. After 1942, American workers gained political and economic leverage as a national labor shortage emerged. In the American South, this phenomenon enabled labor unions to continue organizing industries such as textiles, oil, steel, shipyards, automobiles, and aircraft while also organizing previously unorganized industries throughout the region, such as warehouses and wood-based industries. Hence, the war years brought the greatest era of labor organizing and workplace activism in the history of the nation and the American South. As a result of the labor shortage, workers throughout the United States felt emboldened in their ability to protest workplace grievances.

In this overall context, African American war workers in the South became more vocal about racial inequality in the workplace, while black labor leaders became more sophisticated in their use of political networks. During this three-year period, both workers and labor leaders used the political lever-age from the labor shortage to demand concessions in the workplace. Among national institutions, jobs movement leaders in the National Urban League, the NAACP, and labor unions often defined a variety of goals for black work-ers. Since the 1930s, black intellectuals and leftists had been active in chal-lenging barriers to job inequality and pushing for the desegregation of in-dustries as a means of achieving both social and economic equality for African Americans. On the shop floor, many black workers themselves articulated more conservative goals, such as equal pay, wage increases, basic representa-tion, seniority, and job security.

Many skilled black workers sought only the opportunity to practice their industrial craft in a segregated context. As Thomas Mitchell, representing black workers excluded from skilled positions at the Todd-Johnson Dry Docks in New Orleans, declared to the FEPC, "We feel as taxpayers, Ameri-can citizens and qualified workers, we are entitled to employment in our craft where ever work is available, regardless of our racial identity."[4] Black workers' conservative goals and priorities illustrate the changing nature of race and labor relations in the American South during the war. As the war allowed greater economic mobility and emboldened workers to fight for rights in the workplace, black workers usually avoided challenging social segregation out-right. Most black workers prioritized economic security in defense indus-tries, and they worked for these goals through segregated black institutions. Hence, institutions born out of social and economic segregation led a move-ment for greater economic opportunity in a region where black economic mobility had profound political repercussions. As black workers looked to or-ganized labor and especially the CIO for assistance in the fight for citizenship and equality, there emerged within the southern jobs crusade a strong voter registration movement that would carry on into the postwar years.[5]

The Southern Jobs Movement Revitalized, 1943–1945

After 1942, the jobs movement made gradual strides as African American la-bor and civic leaders negotiated carefully for the inclusion of black workers in war industries. Nationally, the greatest gains occurred in northern indus-trial centers, and the process often occurred discreetly. In December 1943, for example, National Urban League executive director Lester Granger, a veteran of the movement, openly addressed the proven techniques of inte-gration in both Chicago and Kansas City. Granger described a process that involved "skillful negotiation with employers and labor leaders, continuing education among both groups," and "community education among the Negro workers themselves." In Kansas City, a locally organized committee interviewed city officials, plant heads, employment service representatives, and federal officials in Washington. After a two-year period, the Kansas City Urban League's campaign of "education and insistent persuasion" brought results in integrating the city's industries. Under a slightly different strategy, Chicago's Urban League worked on a plant-by-plant basis, achieving integration at two hundred plants that had previously employed African Americans only in an unskilled capacity or not at all.[6]

These strategies and methods applied by the Urban Leagues in Kansas City and Chicago established a model for the same eventual process in southern wartime cities, such as New Orleans, Atlanta, and Dallas. Since 1941, the region's new shipbuilding and aircraft industries had emerged as the most sought after jobs for workers who desired good pay and a high-profile defense job. Hence, these two industries became the primary focus of black civic and jobs movement leaders throughout the region. While shipbuilding remained resistant to black demands for jobs and upgrading opportunities, jobs movement leaders found the aircraft industry more compliant to their agenda. By focusing on the aircraft industry, African American leaders in Dallas, Fort Worth, New Orleans, Birmingham, and Atlanta challenged the general exclusion of African Americans from the defense boom. Importantly, aircraft plants in several of these cities bowed under pressure from local activists and other liberal forces to implement a greater plan for the inclusion of black workers. This achievement reveals the ways in which black labor leaders used the labor shortage and enhanced political networks to achieve an important gain in the wartime movement for economic and civic equality.

Indeed, some of New Orleans's most well organized activism during the war occurred in the fight for the integration of the city's Convair aircraft plant. In 1943 and 1944, the New Orleans Urban League (NOUL) under new executive secretary Grady Farley worked closely with the FEPC in Dallas and field examiner Virgil Williams to enforce equal hiring practices at the new Convair plant. In December 1943, Farley served as a liaison at a conference to discuss integration at the plant. The meeting was attended by government and industry officials, including W. H. O'Kelly, the War Manpower Commission (WMC) area director; Everett Clerc, chief of industrial relations for Convair in New Orleans; and Virgil Williams, who represented the FEPC. In addition, the NOUL sponsored a Work Opportunity Committee for the meeting that included local African American activists such as Dr. George Snowden, AFL organizer and economic professor from Dillard University; Rev.

L. L. Haynes, a local activist who had recently transferred from Fort Worth; Ernest Delpit, local AFL carpenter boss; and Dr. F. M. Hammond, professor of philosophy at Xavier University.

For the regional jobs movement, the presence of these leaders from Fort Worth, Dallas, and New Orleans at the Convair conference symbolized the maturation of African American political networks in the Southwest. Even beyond the symbolism, these leaders' convergence in New Orleans produced definite results. While Everett Clerc initially hesitated to make any commitment to use trained black workers, Virgil Williams's and Reverend Haynes's agitation for a specific training and employment timetable forced Clerc's hand. By the end of the rather tense meeting, Clerc conceded to Work Opportunity Committee and FEPC demands for training and upgrading.[7] The success of the NOUL in the Convair case illustrated the potential for Lester Granger's "skillful negotiation" in southern cities.

Several factors helped the NOUL's successful campaign to desegregate the Convair aircraft plant. First, from 1943 to 1945, the decline of a surplus of white male labor ultimately induced greater utilization of African Americans and women in the city's industrial workforce. Additionally, the presence and determination of Virgil Williams from the FEPC gave the NOUL's mission a certain legitimacy and political weight. During the summer of 1943, efforts to upgrade and increase the numbers of African American workers in southern defense industries received a tremendous boost with the rebirth of the Fair Employment Practices Committee under Executive Order 9346. The order reconstituted the FEPC as an independent agency from beneath the shadow of the WMC and created twelve regional offices that were to implement operating agreements with all twelve WMC regional offices. Out of the new southern offices in Dallas and Atlanta, FEPC field staff continued and expanded field-work begun in 1942 prior to the Birmingham and El Paso hearings.

From August 1943 to the months after V-J Day, newly established FEPC Regions IV, VII, and X, with headquarters in Washington, D.C., Atlanta, and Dallas, respectively, provided a state infrastructure that bolstered southern civil rights networks in the struggle for economic advancement.[8] Under the FEPC's expanded program, the new southern regional offices established and strengthened political networks between leading black civic groups and liberal organized labor leaders in the region. With the unprecedented expansion of FEPC field staff and bureaucracy, newly appointed field investigators were recruited from among regional and national integration leaders. At the FEPC regional office in Dallas, for instance, Virgil Williams, former executive director of the Dallas Negro Chamber of Commerce (DNCC), accepted a position as field examiner for Region X. Similarly, in Atlanta, John Hope Jr., a regional civil rights activist, became field examiner for Region VII.[9]

By combining the pressure of local activists with intimate negotiations from the Urban League, Virgil Williams's strategy provided results in New Orleans. Gradually, Convair trained and integrated black workers at its plant. By March 1944, Convair's manager reported to Williams his satisfaction with skilled black workers. And throughout the remainder of the war, the company continued to cooperate in upgrading and utilizing African Americans. From 1944 to 1945, the NOUL served as placement service to Convair for New Orleans's black workers, including some eleven hundred women. In 1944 alone, the proportion of African Americans at the plant jumped from 2 to 18 percent, and job titles increased by 27 percent. Although entry wages were only fifty to sixty cents per hour, the opening of semiskilled and skilled positions represented a gain for black New Orleanians virtually shut out of most skilled trades in defense industries.[10]

Overall, the Convair arrangement in New Orleans reflected the potential for cooperation among African American civic organizations, the War Manpower Commission, and the FEPC on the jobs issue. Throughout the war, jobs movement leaders in the South remained cautiously optimistic toward the federal government's and especially the WMC's ability to implement a federal mandate for industrial integration during the war emergency.[11] With the expansion of the FEPC in 1943, WMC commissioner Paul McNutt made a symbolic effort to address African Americans' concerns, announcing that under the WMC and the FEPC operating agreement, Robert Weaver would serve as director of the WMC's newly established Minority Group Services (MGS). Under Weaver, Cy Record from the FEPC became the southeastern (Region VII) representative of the WMC-MGS in Atlanta. Because the MGS position existed only in the capacity of consultation under the Bureau of Placement, Weaver often felt frustrated over his lack of power within the WMC. Protesting his administrative impotence, Weaver resigned from the directorship within five months of his appointment. Mary McLeod Bethune then declined the position, citing the lack of a detailed agenda. For most of 1944, the WMC-MGS remained in limbo, reflecting conservative WMC officials' indifference toward the division's fate.[12]

Although generally ineffective in opening job opportunities for African Americans, the southern WMC was particularly helpful in Atlanta at the Bell bomber plant, where the Atlanta Urban League (AUL) had sought the upgrading of skilled workers unsuccessfully until 1944. Throughout 1943 and 1944, the AUL worked with the WMC-MGS to recruit local black workers for

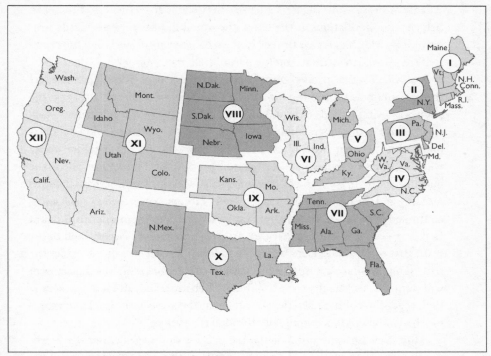

FEPC Regions of the United States, 1943–1944

the plant while helping to place graduates of the Booker T. Washington Aircraft School at Bell and other aircraft companies throughout the nation.[13] Beginning in December 1943, A. Bruce Hunt, director of FEPC Region VII, initiated conferences between Frank Constangy, WMC Region VII attorney, and Margaret Fisher, the newly appointed WMC liaison officer, to work out an operating agreement between the two agencies. In 1944 and 1945, the Atlanta WMC regional personnel actually cooperated with the FEPC in placing African Americans at the local USES office and the Bell bomber and Firestone plants. Relations between the two federal agencies were not always smooth, however.[14]

In February 1944, the first real test of cooperation between the FEPC and WMC in Atlanta occurred when the former attempted to set up a conference with the Bell bomber plant personnel director and a War Department representative. In a rather curt response to the proposal, Bell refused to admit the FEPC examiner into the plant, while the War Department personnel refused to participate in the conference. Nevertheless, over the following months the

Atlanta WMC's involvement as a liaison between management and the FEPC helped smooth relations as the latter attempted to initiate the upgrade program.[15] By May, an excited Bruce Hunt gave Fisher and Constangy full credit for "the change in attitude" on the part of Bell management.[16]

Remarkably, this gradual transformation at Bell occurred despite the fact that Atlanta never faced the threat of a serious labor shortage. By 1945, the plant was using skilled African Americans under white and sometimes black supervision in the subassembly, metal-cleaning, and metal-polishing departments. During that time, black and white workers worked together under white supervision in feeding the hydraulic press, in heat treatment, and in the machine shop. African American workers also served as productive helpers in molding and the foundry/drop hammer operations. Nevertheless, grievances continued from black workers over the lack of advancement opportunities at Bell. For example, in 1945, African American employees complained to the WMC that some supervisors were able to limit upward mobility by claiming that "if one wants to get upgrading, then all of the workers in the department will want it." And, as the WMC's William Shell observed, all black workers at Bell, regardless of their skill level, entered at the same entry level and therefore had to be upgraded gradually through the system.[17]

After New Orleans and Atlanta, the process of desegregating the North Texas aircraft industry represented another important campaign in the southern jobs movement. Under the strong and active leadership of A. Maceo Smith, Virgil Williams, and Maynard Jackson Sr., the DNCC emerged as a powerful but discreet force in the local jobs movement. As the *Dallas Express* declared in January 1944, "Although under the blankets," Smith and the DNCC "have done more to integrate their group into government jobs and other work than Negroes in other cities of this area."[18] In 1942, Virgil Williams, then executive secretary of the DNCC, continued to pressure Dallas officials, the NYA, the WMC, and the Texas Department of Education for proper defense job training. Following three years of the DNCC's pressure and negotiation, the United States Office of Education and the Dallas School Board announced in August 1942 that Dallas's black community would receive training for aircraft manufacturing. After final negotiations in November 1942, the war training plant opened in March 1943, symbolizing a great concession won by the DNCC.[19]

In cities like Dallas, the shortage of white male workers girded local officials to resolve local manpower problems by using local women and African Americans, by reducing turnover rates, and by improving housing. In Dallas, North American Aviation (NAA) adjusted to labor shortages by recruiting and training local white women in large numbers. Aircraft managers preferred such employment practices, because this policy helped resolve local labor shortages without compromising white entitlement to the better defense jobs. At the same time, utilizing a greater number of white women allowed managers to keep wages relatively low. Thus, at North American in 1943, as at Bell in Atlanta, Bechtel-McCone-Parsons in Birmingham, and Convair in Nashville, a tremendous increase occurred in the employment of white women aircraft workers.[20]

Following a June 1943 conference with the Dallas area WMC director, Orville Erringer, DNCC officials, and NAA personnel management, the company initiated greater Negro employment and training opportunities by offering paid training at first in Grand Prairie, the suburb where the plant was located, and eventually in downtown Dallas. By July, the *Dallas Express* reported NAA personnel director Nate Molinarro's praise for African American workers at the plant. By August, NAA and Dallas USES officials claimed that 50 percent of the graduates from the local Negro war training center had been placed at NAA. By January 1944, after continued pressure from the DNCC, the NAA began to hire black women, marking another gain for Dallas's African American community and a concession on the part of Dallas's business community. At the same time, the NAA displayed a serious commitment to hiring black workers in Dallas by placing a company representative in the African American section of the Dallas USES, a practice quite uncommon throughout the South and Southwest.[21]

The rebirth of the FEPC and the placement of the Region X FEPC office in Dallas certainly contributed to the change in hiring policy at North American. After August 1943, when the regional offices were established, the new Dallas FEPC office initiated a steady flow of complaints regarding discrimination at NAA and other local establishments by seeking out grievances from workers at the plant. In 1944, NAA repeatedly complied with FEPC orders and therefore imbued a sense of racial cooperation in the Dallas labor market. Yet NAA's management style also belied a much more conservative reaction among some of the plant's rank and file. Throughout 1943 and 1944, tension existed between some white workers and newly hired black workers. While no outbreaks of violence occurred at the plant, NAA officials used this tension as an excuse to slow the upgrading of black workers.[22]

Overall, the transformation of hiring policies in the southern aircraft industry illustrates several interesting facets of the wartime jobs movement. First, leaders targeted the high-profile and more glamorous industries in an effort to challenge exclusion of black workers in the defense boom. While

African American leaders may have had good intentions, their efforts ultimately led to limited gains, considering the small number of black workers who actually found employment in the industry. One certainly cannot fault the jobs movement leaders for their inability to get a greater percentage of jobs to black workers, considering the generally conservative nature of the southern labor market at the time.

Another important reality of the transformation was the way in which jobs movement leaders compromised on the issue of segregation. Their initial resistance to segregation illustrates the liberal ideology of such leaders and their ultimate goal of dismantling segregation in all its manifestations. In this sense, they foreshadowed the main goal of the modern civil rights movement ten years later. Yet by accommodating on the issue of segregation, these same leaders also embraced a more practical approach to the movement, one that prioritized the economic gains of jobs over the social gains of desegregation.

In the southern aircraft industry, the issue of segregation also posed a dilemma for the United Auto Workers (UAW-CIO). Theoretically, the UAW, as a CIO union, embraced a doctrine of racial equality. Even Robert Weaver argued in 1946 that UAW locals were always "open to Negroes who were accepted as first-class members, and even in some of the southern plants, participated fully and often actively in the affairs of the union."[23] Among locals throughout the United States, UAW Local 600 in Detroit gained notoriety for allying with the Detroit NAACP and placing civil rights at the top of its agenda during the war.[24] In contrast to the predominantly African American Local 600, southern UAW locals in Dallas, Atlanta, and Memphis maintained white majorities, and their agendas did not reflect concerns specific to their black members. Importantly, these locals advocated for basic labor issues, including national wage equality and the enforcement of seniority clauses. However, these southern locals also sanctioned racial segregation and social inequality.[25]

In Atlanta during the summer of 1945, Local 19 at the Bell bomber plant struck for back pay and won, providing workers who had been employed since September 6, 1944, a 10–17 percent wage increase.[26] Local 19 also negotiated with Bell management to permit unskilled African American workers with seniority to receive training at the Booker T. Washington Aircraft School and a chance to be upgraded.[27] However, Local 19's Jim Crow meeting arrangements raised concerns from the national UAW and its African American members. According to some black members, prior to the summer of 1945, union meetings at the Marietta plant had never been segregated. Yet in July 1945, the *Atlanta Daily World* protested that Local 19 officials en forced a Jim Crow seating arrangement during a meeting at the CIO head-quarters on Ivy Street. According to the paper, "because of the large number of Negroes present (over 100), the white workers in private meeting through their officials had the Negroes move to the back of the room." "Each time a black union member sat down," the paper reported, "nearby white workers would get up and move away." While the room was full of "tenseness" and "bulging with attendance," no violence occurred. The following week, the national UAW-CIO demanded a report from the regional CIO head on the incident. And as a show of solidarity at the national level for civil rights within the UAW, George Crockett, the FEPC lawyer hired by the UAW to head its own Fair Employment Division, also criticized Local 19's Jim Crow practice.[28]

In Dallas also, UAW Local 645 officials sanctioned social inequality. In November 1943, the Dallas FEPC investigated a complaint that Local 645 failed to maintain grievance procedures for the nineteen hundred African American members at North American. According to FEPC regional director Carlos Castaneda, because of this discriminatory policy, the black members had "lost confidence in presenting their complaints to the union officials."[29] When FEPC officials met with Local 645 leaders to discuss a resolution to the grievance matter, Mr. Simms, a member of the UAW board, told the federal officials that "here in Texas there shall be no social equality," and, furthermore, "no one is going to tell us that we will have to accept our Negroes as equals." At the close of the conference, Mr. Letner, a regional representative of the CIO, declared that "it was a feeling that the Negro employees at North American were being stirred up by outside agencies" and that if such activities continued "there might be a race riot."[30]

The conservatism of the UAW in the South and Southwest reflected the general conservative leanings of CIO leadership throughout the region. As the CIO made tremendous strides in organizing southern industries during the war, divisions became more and more pronounced between progressive and conservative factions. Generally, more Left-led unions, such as the National Maritime Union (NMU), the International Longshore and Warehousemen's Union (ILWU), United Cannery, Agricultural, Packing, and Allied Workers of America (UCAPAWA), and United Packinghouse Workers (UPWA), found themselves being undermined by more powerful conservative leaders who sought to Red-bait the former out of existence.[31] In 1944, for example, ILWU organizer Howard Goddard found that Bill Taylor, director of the Oil Workers International Union (OWIU) Organizers Committee, and Tim Flynn, CIO regional director for the Southwest, had implemented an anti-ILWU campaign in North Texas. In general, the OWIU remained the most powerful of

CIO unions and also the most conservative in the region. The OWIU leaders' conservatism, like that of the Dallas area's UAW, reflected the overall antileftist sentiment among CIO leaders throughout the state and a general desire to keep Harry Bridges out of the Southwest. In Louisiana, Goddard discovered that the same anti-ILWU and anti-Left dynamics existed under Fred Pieper, the CIO director for New Orleans. According to Goddard, Pieper had directed all his subordinates in the New Orleans CIO to thwart any ILWU organizing efforts as well as the ILWU's participation in the 1944 voter registration drive.[32]

The UAW's racial conservatism in the North Texas aircraft industry differed only slightly from the region's AFL aircraft workers union, the International Association of Machinists (IAM), which held a contract at the Convair aircraft plant in Fort Worth. By June 1944, African Americans represented only 827 of 20,000 workers at the plant. Of these 827 persons, 130 were allegedly semiskilled and skilled. Generally, under the IAM and a separate "colored employees' local," African Americans at Convair in Fort Worth faced difficulty achieving upward mobility. In a telling incident, Don Ellinger, FEPC Region X director, reported that R. C. Carroll, president of the colored local, was terminated after requesting to work in the maintenance department. On investigation, Ellinger observed that the company management maintained a "concerted anti-Negro policy" expressed by such claims that "all [R. C. Carroll and] these niggers want is a chance to work with white people." Similarly, J. D. Smith, business manager for the IAM, commented to Ellinger that "Carroll got out of line by requesting a job in which he would have to work with white people."[33]

Throughout 1943 and 1944, Convair in Fort Worth consistently denied training and upgrading to skilled black workers. As NAA in Dallas integrated with some resistance from UAW officials, African American and white labor activists in the Fort Worth area continued to maintain pressure without success up to March 1945. As a result of Convair management's conservatism and the FEPC's inability to enforce upgrading, Virgil Williams noted that black leaders in Fort Worth "had lost confidence" in the agency. Additionally, a loss of confidence in the union grievance system existed among black union members, because formal complaints had only brought on "needless reprisals from the employer." After three years of continuous out-migration among skilled black workers in Fort Worth, Convair management grudgingly upgraded African Americans into skilled positions from March to August 1945. The belated victory remained bittersweet for the FEPC, however. Don Ellinger referred to Convair's compliance and the closing of the case as a mere "shadow of satisfactory adjustment," as the new operation was segregated, and many upgraded workers were eventually returned to their original positions.[34]

The Limits of Industrial Integration in the South, 1943–1945

The FEPC's and the black workers' decision to accept the segregated setup at Convair represented a compromise won, much like at the Alabama Dry Dock in Mobile two years earlier.[35] Clarence Mitchell, the FEPC's associate director of field operations, in discussing the matter with Will Maslow, the FEPC's director of field operations, acknowledged that he was "not impressed" with the segregated arrangement, but because Don Ellinger felt that it would "represent progress," the case should proceed to close. One month later, in March 1945, Mitchell again contacted Maslow, stating that he had "given considerable thought" to "the weighty problem of segregation," which lay "heavily on the shoulders" of the southern FEPC officials. In opting to accept the company's plans at both the Bell bomber and Convair plants in Fort Worth, Mitchell admitted, "We, of course, are not telling the companies that we approve these programs of segregation. We are merely insisting that they comply with the order."[36]

Clarence Mitchell's and Don Ellinger's acceptance of Convair's segregated plan reflected their willingness to negotiate a compromise with management in order to achieve a semblance of victory rather than see three years' effort wasted. Failing to legally challenge southern state segregation laws, Ellinger realistically felt that black workers sought economic upward mobility more than workplace integration. Hence, the Convair and Bell cases characterize the racial accommodation within southern aircraft jobs movement in 1945.

Likewise, in the southern shipbuilding industry, the Delta Shipyards represented a compromise for jobs integrationists. In January 1945, African American welders at the Delta Shipyards were finally upgraded after four years of pressure from the New Orleans Urban League and the FEPC. While the hiring policy represented a victory of sorts, Don Ellinger observed in February 1945 that Boilermakers referred black workers to welding jobs but not other skilled crafts. Realizing that such practices were discriminatory, Ellinger advised the FEPC's Clarence Mitchell not to push for full compliance because "more harm will come from insistence on details which have been ignored for three years."[37]

To many black aircraft and shipyard workers in the South, these occupations paid some of the highest wages in the region. As the Urban League reported in November 1944, black workers at the Bell bomber plant in Atlanta, regardless of their position level and skill, made better money than even the highest-paying jobs for educated African Americans in Atlanta. In the Gate City, black teachers in the public school system made on average $90 a month and never over $120 per month. Graduates of the Atlanta University School of Social Work employed at the Department of Public Assistance started at around $100 per month and seldom exceeded $120 per month. Yet the overall numbers of black workers employed in the aircraft plants in Dallas, Fort Worth, and Atlanta in July 1944 amounted to roughly 4,500 workers out of a total of 79,000 workers.[38] Such small numbers represent a fraction of southern black workers in those cities. Within this group, the number of skilled workers was even smaller.

Hence, for the lucky ones who were hired, employment opportunities at aircraft plants represented a relatively high living standard within the region. Citing the experiences of a woman graduate of Atlanta University earning eleven dollars a week and fifty dollars a month on a "white collar job," the Urban League described how the woman "cried" when offered a position as a maid at Bell, because she feared losing "her white collar status." Finally accepting the menial position at Bell, the woman began earning $150 per month, three times the level of her previous job. As the League argued, "with her more adequate income" she had "begun to live the full life."[39]

Black aircraft workers' actions in the South during this period often reflect their tenuous position as minorities within a predominantly white industry. In such industries, black workers undoubtedly felt less inclined to endanger their long-term security by challenging segregation. In other industries, such as labor, transportation, and waterfront warehouse work, black workers had greater job security and were more inclined to organize. In these occupations, black workers' jobs were not in danger during the last years of the war, and their heightened concern with labor and equal rights led to an intensive period when black unions mobilized black workers for labor rights and even voter registration.

The southern shipbuilding industry, like aircraft, was one of the higher-paying and attractive jobs in the region. Like the aircraft industry, it was one in which white workers held a majority of the jobs. Generally, shipyard managers and union officials put up a steadfast resistance to black upgrading and wage equality. Hence, the industry enforced wage and classification policies that supported white privilege and divided workers as much as possible by race. Within this context of job segregation, African American civic, church,

Chapter Five

and labor organizations actively mobilized against these injustices in the name of equal rights and economic opportunity for black people. In city after city, however, these groups faced continuous efforts by white civic, industrial, and labor leaders to circumscribe their efforts for equal opportunity.

In Tampa, Florida, for example, the NAACP, the Tampa Urban League, and black industrial unions worked with the FEPC to close complaint cases against the Boilermakers in the Tampa shipyards. As with most coastal cities in the South, the USES and the AFL in Tampa recruited white workers from outside the area while refusing to hire qualified black workers within the area for the skilled jobs. As Tampa suffered from a housing shortage, liberal activists attempted to use the issue as a means of getting black workers upgraded at the yards. In January 1945, Ed Ray, Tampa Urban League (TUL) president and liberal editor of the *Tampa Times*, criticized the Boilermakers and the Tampa Housing Authority for causing racial tension in the community. The previous month, the Tampa Housing Authority had announced plans to move skilled white shipyard migrants into the Lake Avenue Housing Project, built originally for African Americans. Comparing the conflict to that of Detroit in 1943, TUL executive secretary Sidney Miles feared that the "situation would erupt as soon as the whites begin to move into the housing project" and would result in another "Sojourner-Truth situation."[40]

In Jacksonville, by April 1945, skilled African Americans abandoned their pursuits to upgrade at the St. Johns River shipyard and moved on to J. A. Jones in Brunswick, Alabama Dry Dock, and the Charleston Navy Yards. In January and February 1944, skilled African Americans at St. Johns River attempted to organize an auxiliary of the IBB local. Yet by May, management had returned the black workers to the labor department, thus halting any organizing efforts among them. While company officials reasoned that the "Negroes failed to cooperate," John Hope Jr. of the FEPC believed that, more likely, IBB representatives would make no commitment as to whether qualified black workers would be allowed to work above the helper's grade.[41]

Despite these barriers to upgrading, the jobs movement in Tampa and Jacksonville had strengthened ties between the FEPC and Urban League affiliates as well as local March on Washington movement and NAACP chapters. In Tampa specifically, John Hope Jr. worked with M. Gregory, president of both the local March on Washington chapter and the Pullman Porter's Local of Tampa, and Earl James, president of the local Laborer's Union AFL at the Tampa shipyard.[42] Although Hope failed to initiate an FEPC hearing before the war's end, the issue clearly galvanized African American organized labor and civil rights leaders.

In Savannah, black shipyard workers found support from L. E. Carter, chairman of the Savannah NAACP Committee on Labor and Industry, and William "Bill" Smith, a white liberal organizer for the Industrial Union of Marine and Shipbuilding Workers of America (IUMSWA). In 1942, Carter and Smith appealed to the FEPC and Paul McNutt to integrate skilled black workers into Southeastern Shipbuilding's six-thousand-person labor force. In Savannah and nearby Brunswick, however, the AFL maintained power at local shipyards despite pressure from the FEPC and an organizing campaign by IUMSWA in 1942 and 1943. The AFL accomplished this task by various nefarious means. As Bill Smith complained to the FEPC about IUMSWA organizing attempts at Southeastern in November 1942, "any negroe belonging to a CIO union had his card pulled out of the time rack and the only excuse that is given is that his services are either no longer needed or that they are unsatisfactory."[43]

After failing to organize Savannah's black shipyard workers, Bill Smith was ready to "pull out" in the spring of 1943 when he discovered that African American workers in Brunswick had "come to life." According to Smith, a "Negro committee" working at the J. A. Jones shipyard appealed to the CIO "to come in." As the committee informed Smith, the IBB was about to sign a "back-door contract" with J. A. Jones, and the black workers "wanted no part of it." Under J. A. Jones's setup, the entire third shift was African American, and all forty-six workers wanted to sign up with IUMSWA. Organizing attempts in Georgia and Florida resulted in severe violence and reprisals, however. During the winter and spring of 1943, Bill Smith reported that on numerous occasions, the police were "in league with certain reactionary forces, shipyard operators, AFL, and company unions to terrorize and beat every person who might speak for the CIO."[44]

Smith labeled Jacksonville and Savannah as cities where Democratic machines enforced the AFL organizing racket in defense industries through "terrorism." For African American IUMSWA organizer Elijah Jackson, terror occurred when he was almost lynched for organizing workers at the MacAvoy shipyards in Savannah.[45] Surviving the incident, Jackson eventually moved on to organize African American workers at Local 18 in Mobile until he was removed by white organizers for aggressively pressing for civil rights.[46]

Ultimately, the FEPC and the WMC-MGS failed to pressure several large shipyards that refused to pay, classify, or use skilled African Americans. These yards included Tampa Shipbuilding, the St. Johns River shipyard in Jacksonville, the MacAvoy and Southeastern shipyards in Savannah, and Mingledorf in Brunswick, Georgia.[47] In the Southeast, only five large yards—Alabama Dry Dock in Mobile, Delta in New Orleans, J. A. Jones in Brunswick, and the navy yards in Charleston and Norfolk—pursued the hiring of skilled black workers in a segregated setup. Within the private shipyards of Norfolk and Newport News, Virginia, African Americans worked as riveters, a skilled position commonly held by black shipyard workers since the turn of the century. However, black workers were still excluded from the more modern trades in the yards, such as those for electricians, machinists, and welders.[48]

Black Shipyard Workers Define Equality in the South

While African American shipyard workers found limited opportunities in the modern trades, their employment in the yards as laborers and teamsters in segregated work crews gave them a sense of racial and occupational identity. During the last three years of the war, the national labor shortage gave black workers in these segregated occupations some sense of job security. Hence, they felt emboldened to protest a variety of issues, ranging from inadequate protection against violent whites to low wages and general inequality in the yards.

In New Orleans, black workers mobilized a number of times to defend themselves from violent white workers. For example, in August 1943 at the Delta Shipyards, around three hundred concerned black laborers gathered at the plant manager's office to protest a white foreman's threat to kill black workers because one worker allegedly winked at a white woman in the yard. While demanding greater protection, the black workers were quick to blame the attitudes of the white rural migrants from outlying towns. Eventually, investigators determined that white workers had resented the promotion of Aaron Reed, the worker who was threatened, to leader of a black crew. In the yards where segregation defined job classification, conservative white workers viewed any black man in a position of authority as a threat to white privilege.[49]

In another incident in February 1944, white guards at the Delta Shipyards assaulted George Cooper, a black truck driver and World War I veteran, for allegedly trying to run over a white woman in the yard. In response to the white violence, a majority of black workers mobilized a walkout, shutting down the yard until management guaranteed their safety. The Teamsters AFL Local 270 representative backed the strikers and eventually gained Delta management's assurance that the abuse of black workers would stop.[50] Thus, black workers sought protection from violent whites and at times mobilized in large numbers simply to insure their own safety. Such goals were certainly not radical, but they did reflect the priorities of the workers.

African Americans in New Orleans also went beyond the issue of protection to protest unequal conditions that stemmed from segregation and discriminatory policies. In 1944, for example, black employees at Higgins Industries challenged the lack of democracy and equality in company food-service policies. In March a number of black workers protested management policy that required all workers to pay three dollars per week for meals at the plant while prohibiting African Americans from having salads and desserts on Mondays, Wednesdays, and Fridays. When the company threatened to fire any workers who signed a petition in protest, one worker informed local CIO organizer and voting rights activist Ernest Wright that he "was fed up with trying to stay 'in his place.'"[51]

Throughout the war, black workers at Higgins Industries consistently complained of the inequality of working conditions. While some workers, like Ernest Davis, simply left for California shipyards, other frustrated workers who stayed sought grievance through the New Orleans Urban League, the FEPC, or organized labor.[52] In one case in November 1944, a white foreman beat a black union steward for the Hod Carriers Union Local 689 for being "an agitator" and for "stirring up dissent among the men." In turn, the steward, Harry Stewart, sought grievance through Local 689 and the Region X FEPC. In such cases, white conservatives viewed African American attempts to defend themselves or organize for protection as a threat and a form of agitation. In this racially conservative environment, Stewart's actions were in many ways radical to white workers who expected subservience. Hence, when black shipyard workers such as Stewart refused to accept abuse on the job, their efforts to seek support through black institutions and the federal government signified a greater militancy among some black workers.[53]

Perhaps the greatest example of black worker protest in New Orleans occurred at the Delta Shipyards at the end of the war. Beginning in November 1944, from seven hundred to a thousand black truck drivers in Teamsters Local 270 struck for higher wages. As the strike progressed through December, white officials were amazed to find that Local 270 members in other transportation companies throughout the city maintained a solid effort to bargain for higher wages and justified their actions as "a definite Negro problem." Ironically, as the Teamsters sought economic concessions through organized labor activism, the racial fallout over their actions postponed the upgrading of African American welders at Delta. In January and February 1945, plant management conceded to the demands of the strikers and then upgraded the black welders quietly. The Local 270 victory illustrates that within segregated unions, black workers organized successfully for economic motives.

While the welding upgrade remained a symbolic achievement for equality of opportunity, the actions of black teamsters suggest that basic economic issues such as livable wages remained a top priority for many black workers.[54]

At the Todd-Johnson Dry Docks in New Orleans, African American workers responded in numerous ways to the lack of opportunities for economic advancement. Under Todd-Johnson management and the weak IUMSWA Local 29, African Americans performed semiskilled and skilled jobs but were classified nonetheless as laborers. By May 1945, WMC reports indicated a large degree of African American absenteeism and turnover at Todd-Johnson due to disillusionment over the pay policy. As one African American union steward informed Don Ellinger of the FEPC, newly hired "colored employees" wanted to "get out of the company if there [was] no chance of advancement." Hence, most black workers used their ability to job shop as a means of protesting their predicament at Todd-Johnson.[55]

Over a three-year period from May 1943 to March 1945, the number of African American workers at the plant had fallen from 1,201 out of 2,400 (50 percent) to only 386 out of 4,331 (9 percent).[56] At the same time, the WMC recruited white workers from the Piedmont towns in South Carolina, Georgia, and Alabama and other small towns in Texas, Mississippi, and Florida.[57] Over time, black concerns grew less relevant to the agenda of Local 29. Even as white liberal IUMSWA organizers hoped to emphasize the principles of interracial tolerance as part of CIO policy to white rank and file, Local 29's leaders ultimately chose to forgo this education policy for fear of alienating white members and losing the local.[58]

In Local 29, Arthur Colar and Henry Bowser emerged as the most militant African Americans in the struggle for upgrading in 1945. IUMSWA organizer Buster Crist was particularly concerned with Colar and Bowser, whom he viewed as "agitators" at the segregated union meetings. Early that year, Colar and Bowser appealed to both the national IUMSWA office and the FEPC in New Orleans to rectify the upgrading problem at Todd-Johnson. Yet national and local IUMSWA leaders felt reluctant to enforce racial equality at the local level, again for fear of estranging white members. Regionally, white organizers in IUMSWA also remained suspicious of black organizers Elijah Jackson in Mobile and Russell Watson in Norfolk for fomenting black nationalism among workers at the expense of interracialism. The continuous support of white privilege and wage inequality by Local 29 leadership at Todd-Johnson ultimately prompted Arthur Colar's and Henry Bowser's resignation and their switch to organizing for the Boilermakers Local 37-A auxiliary.[59]

The CIO and Black Nationalism

The southern CIO leadership essentially remained uncomfortable with what it viewed as a black nationalist movement emerging in some industrial unions in which large numbers of African Americans held membership during the war. Much of the white leadership's concerns centered on the growing power of black organizers during this period. As the CIO and the AFL reached out to black workers during the war, the white organizing leadership expanded the use of black organizers in transportation, laboring, shipbuilding, laundry, tobacco, railroad, longshore, and warehouse work. In many cases, the appointed black organizers tied the issue of labor organizing and workers' rights into larger concerns within the black community, such as equal rights and voting rights.[60]

The history of ILWU Local 207 in New Orleans during this period illustrates well how the issues of equal rights and democracy emerged prominently in the overall drive to organize black workers in the segregated South. In 1937 and 1938, the ILWU had expanded from its power base on the West Coast into the coastal cities of the Gulf and South Atlantic Coasts along with inland cities such as Memphis and Dallas. In the process, organizers suffered serious setbacks and violence from local law enforcement and AFL thugs bent on preventing the CIO from gaining any foothold in warehouses in the South. Eventually, New Orleans emerged as the most promising center of organization during the early 1940s under an ambitious organizer, Willie Dorsey.[61] Following the violence of the 1938 drive, the ILWU avoided challenging the supremacy of ILA Local 1419, the largest black union in the South, and focused on the smaller unorganized warehouses up and down the Mississippi River. Hence, in 1940, Dorsey began organizing warehouses and by 1941 became known as "the father of the New Orleans CIO movement."[62]

In 1943 and 1944, a jurisdictional battle over the control of Local 207 reflected African American concerns over democratic freedoms within the labor movement. Trouble began in 1943, when Harry Bridges became suspicious of Willie Dorsey's tendency to promote an agenda that Bridges and other white leaders construed as black nationalism within the ILWU, Amalgamated Clothing Workers, and Transport Workers locals of New Orleans.[63] To further complicate matters, during the summer of 1943 ILWU leadership charged Dorsey with embezzling union funds for personal use, just as the West Coast leadership discovered that Dorsey had allied with Father Jerome Drolet, a local Catholic priest and labor activist, in an effort to Red-bait any leftist CIO members in the area. After the ILWU leadership indicted Dorsey on the embezzlement charge, Harry Bridges arranged to have Howard Goddard, a white ILWU organizing veteran, to come into New Orleans and take charge of the local.

Dorsey characterized the Goddard takeover as a direct threat by ILWU West Coast leaders to the autonomy of Local 207. Believing that black unions such as Local 207 were important self-governing institutions in the eyes of black workers, Dorsey portrayed his own resistance to Goddard as a noble effort to maintain democratic control of the union. For one mass meeting at Second Baptist Church, Dorsey made up flyers depicting Goddard leading black workers by chains, as if they were enslaved. In a letter published in the *Louisiana Weekly,* Dorsey also cast "fuehrer" Harry Bridges as a dictator who enslaved Local 207's members. While Dorsey received support from the local black press and, apparently, ILWU members, the local NAACP and some black ILWU leaders who supported an interracial labor movement continued to distrust Dorsey as a labor demagogue. Specifically, the local NAACP chapter refused to support Dorsey on the ILWU jurisdictional conflict, while local black organizer William Spooner and shop steward Willie Chatman both remained critical of Dorsey's leadership and organizing style, which they viewed as disruptive to the overall goals of the CIO.[64]

Following Goddard's takeover of Local 207, in August 1943 Dorsey abandoned his position with the ILWU and took up as an organizer in New Orleans under the United Retail, Wholesale, and Department Store Employees of America (URWDSEA), a much more conservative CIO union led nationally by Sam Wolchok in Chicago. Dorsey's move was, in fact, orchestrated by Father Jerome Drolet as an attempt to avoid ties with the ILWU and to challenge the Left-led union's hold in the city. In the process of establishing a URWDSEA Local 389, Dorsey tried to raid ILWU Local 207 for members, yet he failed to succeed in these endeavors. These maneuvers, naturally, caused much concern among ILWU leaders out west who hoped to make New Orleans a stronghold of ILWU power in the South.[65]

Dorsey's jump to URWDSEA underscored the conservatism within the New Orleans CIO leadership. How much the rank and file supported his switch is not entirely clear. Some discrepancies exist as to how many workers in the warehouses organized by Dorsey transferred their membership to URWDSEA after 1943. Hence, questions arise over whether black workers supported Dorsey and also over their possible disillusionment with the ILWU. Certainly, black workers were aware of the violence that had befallen ILWU members in the 1938 organizing drive. Many rank and file may have viewed the chance to remain with Dorsey under a new union as an opportunity to avoid any repeat of the 1938 violence. In another light, these workers may have indeed viewed the Goddard takeover as a threat to the autonomy and integrity of a union that many workers viewed as their own and that represented their specific needs as black workers.

In this era of disfranchisement, black workers certainly viewed the industrial union movement as a means of realizing democracy at home. Indeed, during this period, a revolt occurred among black AFL members in the Louisiana State Federation of Labor over the issue of union democracy. In effect, black AFL delegates criticized Harvey Netter, black president of ILA Local 1419, and his colleague, "Preacher Jones," for voting against the election of an African American representative on the state federation's executive board. The black delegates protested that under the present setup with an all-white board, minorities paid dues but had no representation. Unhappy delegates then signed a petition that declared that "taxation without representation on the Executive Board has prevailed for the last 32 years in the Louisiana State Federation of Labor as far as Negroes are concerned." Hoping finally to gain representation with the election of a black vice-president to the board, the delegates viewed the issue as one fundamental to their democratic rights.[66]

CIO-PAC and the Voting Rights Movement

The issue of organized labor and democracy became even more relevant to black workers when both the CIO and the AFL began concerted efforts to mobilize union members for voter registration in 1943 and 1944. Throughout the war, black unions in railroads, laundry, and transportation grew in numerical and potential political strength in New Orleans.[67] As black union membership expanded, the momentum for organizing black workers into black voters also increased. In 1943, the CIO began to organize a voter registration movement in the South to assure labor support for the Democratic Party in the upcoming 1944 national election. This campaign, known as the CIO Political Action Committee (CIO-PAC), gained tremendous support among black labor unions with the increased emphasis on democracy because of the war.[68]

After 1942, black industrial unions became one of the greatest driving forces behind the voter registration movement in the city as the People's Defense League (PDL) united militant church leaders with labor leaders in the local black industrial unions. During this period, the PDL emerged as a potent force in making voting rights a priority for African Americans in New Orleans as it brought together A. L. Davis of the Interdenominational Ministers Alliance; Moses Turner of the Brotherhood of Railway Carmen of America AFL Local 200; William Spooner of the ILWU Local 207; and Ernest Wright of the Amalgamated Clothing Workers Association CIO Local 389. This merging of progressive church and labor leaders symbolized the growing sophistication of black institutional networks in urban areas of the South and the heightened concern of African Americans over issues of democracy in the workplace and community.[69]

The labor movement in New Orleans clearly emerged as a movement for democracy and voting rights in 1943 and 1944. In many respects, this democratic development among black industrial unions constitutes the war's greatest legacy for fomenting a modern civil rights movement and the increased demand for voting rights. Fortuitously, this indigenous civil and voting rights movement coincided with the CIO's and AFL's efforts to mobilize voters through the newly created PACs. For the black community of New Orleans, the CIO-PAC movement signaled a potential sea change in the political alignment of the city. As CIO-PAC leaders began to mobilize union members for the 1944 vote, the disenfranchisement of New Orleans's black voters emerged as a political liability to their movement.

In 1943 and 1944, CIO leaders in the New Orleans area began to talk with the local Democratic machine, known as the Old Regulars, about the possibility of registering CIO union members in large numbers.[70] For local and state Democratic party bosses, the potential for increased voter support through the registration of black voters created quite a predicament. The Old Regulars controlled the registrar of voters, and without their approval, there would be no mass registration. When ILWU organizers pressed New Orleans CIO director Fred Pieper on the registration of black voters, Pieper informed them that the United Labor Council, an alliance of AFL and CIO leaders in New Orleans, was working closely with the Old Regulars to sanction the voter registration of organized labor rank and file in the city. On the black vote issue specifically, Pieper declined to take a position, because in his view such a stance would alienate the AFL as well as the Old Regulars.[71]

In the end, the CIO in New Orleans was unable to foster a deal that would allow a mass registration of black CIO members for the 1944 election. Yet the CIO-PAC movement and its coinciding with the PDL's own efforts to promote voter registration unleashed momentum that would not be stopped in the postwar period. As the war incited a greater concern with democracy and civil rights at home, progressive black and church leaders in New Orleans used the opportunity to issue a call for equal rights and the ballot in Louisiana. Hence, while the wartime voter registration campaign encountered resistance, the movement laid the foundation for a voters' rights movement in Louisiana and other southern states that would continue well beyond the war.[72]

After 1942, grassroots African Americans in organized labor, the church, and civil rights organizations sought to use the national labor shortage to gain economic concessions during the war. By focusing on the vital role that black workers played in war production in the South, workplace activists stressed economic mobility and downplayed social advancement. In the struggle for equality, many African American civil rights advocates were willing to forgo literal integration in the workplace and accept segregated arrangements in order to gain some economic mobility through upgrading. Likewise, liberal jobs movement leaders often claimed victory when they pressured defense industries to hire African Americans in unskilled positions for which management had previously hired only white workers.

In 1946, Robert Weaver argued that African American workers in the Second World War embraced organized labor as a means of garnering some economic justice.[73] Although their participation in majority white unions in the South did not always achieve the progress they sought through the system, southern African American workers in the 1940s, more so than during the First World War, sought organized labor and arbitration channels to gain wage increases, upgrading, seniority rights, and even a sense of participatory democracy. Working-class African Americans in the South sought economic concessions through segregated AFL and CIO unions such as the Pullman Car Porters, Teamsters, Longshoremen's, and Laborers locals. By allying with civil rights organizations, such as local Urban League affiliates and NAACP chapters, black workers' new alliances reflected the growth of key networks to maintain a united front for economic equality. This wartime unity among church, organized labor, and formal civil rights groups ultimately displayed how the war galvanized a variety of black community institutions to gain inclusion in the war effort and hence a newfound citizenship.

In assessing the legacy of the jobs and labor movements in the South during World War II, the brief wartime gains made by black workers and industrial integration advocates signified that, unlike during the previous war, African Americans had become more forceful in their demands for equality. Whether, as Robert Weaver claimed, the war brought about a "social revolution" is debatable.[74] In any case, African American industrial integrationists used the war as an opportunity to demand that white southerners and white Americans face the issue of racial inequality in the workplace and within society at large. By actively demanding industrial integration within the segregated South especially and then compromising enough to gain some economic concessions, African Americans illustrated that sophisticated strategies and well-organized campaigns under the proper circumstances could provide economic and social advancement. Because African Americans understood well the important role that manpower played in their wartime successes, industrial integrationists waited with bated breath after August 1945 to see if violence on a level with the Red Summer of 1919 would occur in the aftermath of economic gains made during World War II.

6. "The South Needs the Negro"

Demobilization and Economic Equality
in the South, 1945–1948

In December 1945, an African American woman from Lake Charles, Louisiana, wrote to Sam Jones, the former governor of her state. She was responding to an article Jones had written for the *Saturday Evening Post* in which he advocated raising the standard of living for African Americans in the South as a means of preventing a mass exodus out of the region. The woman, who declined to identify herself, informed Jones that "what the Negro wants is economic opportunity, not social equality." She then relayed how she lay awake many nights trying to decide where to live, "the West with its overcrowded conditions, its opportunities for cultural advancement or the South with its wide open spaces, its embarrassments and insecurity, and its denying of minor opportunities because of racial differences." Signing the letter "a loyal southern Negro," she proclaimed that "the South needs the Negro and the Negro needs the advantages you suggested the South should offer."[1]

After V-J Day, African Americans in the South faced an uncertain future. In many respects, the decision to stay or migrate, to remain loyal or disloyal, as the case may be, depended largely on the South's strategy, or lack thereof, for dealing with segregation and job opportunities in the postwar era. During the war, southern out-migration had forced racial equality to the forefront of a national discourse on race and democracy. As sociologist

Gunnar Myrdal reminded Americans in 1943, with war mobilization "the Negro problem" had "become national in scope after having been mainly a southern problem."[2] Certainly, the wartime racial conflicts in Detroit, Harlem, and to a lesser extent Los Angeles illuminated this fact all too well. Migration would be sure to continue into the postwar era as demobilization of southern industries and agricultural mechanization eliminated the livelihood of many black southerners. Hence, southern racial policies and especially decisions affecting employment would change the entire fabric of race relations in the United States.

At the end of the war, southern liberals and conservatives both agreed that the South needed to provide black southerners with greater educational and economic opportunities. Many African American leaders in the South supported a federal full employment program and continued southern industrialization in order to raise the standard of living for all southern workers and thereby promote racial harmony. At the same time, southern employers, who continued to resist the decline of cheap surplus labor, urged the use of African American labor in southern industries as a means of forestalling outmigration. Ironically, many of these white conservatives who hoped to increase economic opportunity for southern African Americans also sought to draw new industries by exploiting the region's low-wage black labor force. Thus, in the postwar South, most African Americans struggling for economic equality often found themselves with few alternatives but to migrate out of the region in search of greater economic opportunity or accommodate the return of the segregated labor market and their role as unskilled workers within it.[3]

Demobilization: The "Test for Democracy"

In January 1945, as the end of the war approached, Paul McNutt, chairman of the War Manpower Commission, prophesized that demobilization would be a "test for democracy."[4] Indeed, the utilization of African Americans in U.S. industries in the postwar era continued to serve, as it had during the war, as an issue symbolizing economic and racial equality. With the profound changes occurring in southern agriculture from mechanization and New Deal farm programs, postwar employment opportunities for African Americans represented a serious southern and national dilemma. Even before the war, the question of how to provide economic security for this largely unskilled and undereducated group had emerged as a pressing issue. In the years before Pearl Harbor, the federal government through the Farm Security Administration (FSA) had advocated small farm ownership as a possible solution to the problem. Some southern boosters had advocated new industries to employ displaced farmworkers, yet the process of displacement occurred at a faster rate than southern industries offered employment.

As liberals and conservatives both saw industrial employment as a possible panacea for the region's ills, the process of reconversion in 1945 did not bring the economic opportunities envisioned by liberal state planners or African American leaders. Almost immediately, the return of a labor surplus ensuing from military industry cutbacks generally erased the employment gains African Americans had made in the manufacturing sector during the war.

Fair Employment Practices Committee (FEPC) administrators at the national and southern levels recognized the negative effects that reconversion had on employment opportunities for African Americans and the FEPC's efforts to integrate southern industries. As FEPC official Clarence Mitchell noted in February 1945, impending layoffs in the shipbuilding industry were becoming more serious and would "vitally affect" the FEPC's operations. Mitchell hoped to resolve current complaints against a number of yards, including the St. Johns River Shipbuilding Company in Jacksonville, the Southeastern Shipbuilding Company in Savannah, the Todd-Houston Company in Houston, and the Alabama Dry Dock Company in Mobile. More importantly, however, Mitchell expressed concern that the FEPC also faced "a larger problem of what to do with the workers who will be displaced."[5]

Southern FEPC officials made concerted efforts to close active case files, as layoffs and industrial displacement emerged as two of the key issues facing the agency in early 1945. The Todd shipyard in Houston served as an example of how cutbacks affected the FEPC's agenda. In January, on the heels of the FEPC's victory at the Delta Shipyards in New Orleans, the FEPC hoped that Todd-Houston's pending layoffs of twelve thousand workers would not interfere with the agency's efforts to gain compliance on upgrading.[6] By May, however, Don Ellinger admitted that cutbacks had "lessened the possibility of solving discriminatory hiring practices." Citing Todd-Houston specifically, Ellinger predicted that the company "will probably be completely shut down before any effective action could be taken."[7]

African American economic insecurity became apparent when workers' complaints of discriminatory practices filed through the FEPC began to decline in number throughout 1945. In May, Don Ellinger remained optimistic about the consistency of workers' complaints, noting that cutbacks in the southern shipbuilding industry had not produced any unusual number of complaints based on discriminatory hiring practices. By October 1945, FEPC

Region X director Carlos Castaneda offered a differing view of worker complaints. Since June 1945, he had observed that complaints had fallen off in Region X. According to Castaneda, minority groups were "willing to put up with such discrimination" rather than "lose their jobs at a time [of] periodic layoffs and systematic reductions." In effect, the return of the surplus labor market had removed the leverage that minority workers had used during the war.[8]

Reconversion gradually negated African American wartime employment advances, as cutbacks in permanent defense industry plants served as a convenient tool for laying off black workers promoted during the war labor shortage. In Fort Worth, for example, Convair terminated its five-month-old black training program under the aegis of production cutbacks as management trimmed employment from a wartime peak of roughly 23,000 in May 1945 to approximately 7,500 by December 1945.[9] Because the upgrading of black workers had occurred so late in the war, their lack of seniority provided no leverage in guaranteeing postwar employment security. As one FEPC report indicated, "Since all departments are being reduced, the company does not feel that it would be justified in terminating qualified, experienced, white employees in order to make jobs for Negroes." These veteran white workers, the company argued, "should rightfully be placed before other workers who are new to the work."[10]

Black workers' wartime experience and seniority did not guarantee them skilled occupations when the southern labor market returned to prewar surplus levels. At Alabama Dry Dock in Mobile, one of the only permanent shipyards that had upgraded African Americans during the war, black workers were downgraded to unskilled positions as the workforce declined from thirty thousand to three thousand in the postwar period. As historian Bruce Nelson argues, despite ten years of contention and vacillation on civil rights issues, after the war the Industrial Union of Marine and Shipbuilding Workers of America (IUMSWA-CIO) Local 18 "became an instrument to guarantee the privileges of white workers."[11]

The Lone Star ordnance plant near Texarkana, Texas, provides yet another example of how cutbacks in permanent defense industries affected African American workers. In the summer of 1945, the plant was scheduled for a series of production cutbacks, and the hand grenade department, the only department to employ skilled African American women, was eliminated entirely. The plant had nominally offered to transfer workers with seniority to other departments; however, the lack of skilled positions for black women in any other department meant, in effect, that the only postwar employment opportunities for such women were as maids. In July, FEPC regional director Don Ellinger sought to open a case file at the plant based on the above argument. In alerting War Manpower Commission (WMC) Region X director James Bond to the issue, Ellinger requested help from the WMC to prevent discriminatory layoffs. Nevertheless, Ellinger's efforts were futile. Even for the few weeks that the WMC remained in existence, Bond claimed that the WMC "had no control over the cutback determinations and policies in any war industry." Thus, like other permanent war plants, Lone Star used cutbacks and a return of the surplus labor market to eliminate departments in which skilled black workers had found employment.[12]

As management and organized labor in permanent plants successfully eliminated black economic gains brought about from wartime manpower shortages and FEPC pressure, the complete closing of defense plants after the war further hindered postwar employment opportunities for black workers. In February 1945, this industrial displacement was addressed by both William Bell, director of the Urban League's Southern Division in Atlanta, and WMC Minority Group Services director Benjamin Wilson during his publicized visit to that city. Wilson warned that while wartime gains were encouraging, the postwar period provided "the greatest test of Negro job security."

According to Wilson's statistics, between April 1940 and April 1944, employment of black men had increased from 2.9 to 3.2 million, while employment of black women rose from 1.5 to 2.1 million, for a total employment gain of some 900,000 jobs. Despite such employment advances, William Bell pointed out that postwar employment prospects for African Americans did not look promising, because they had made the greatest gains in war industries, such as shipbuilding, aircraft, and ordnance, which faced the greatest postwar declines. "In those industries in which the Negro has made his greatest employment advances," Bell argued, "he was generally among the last to be hired." Therefore, "under seniority rules, he is more likely to be laid off than the average [white] worker in these occupations." Such foreboding was certainly warranted, as the Convair case in Fort Worth illustrated three months later.[13]

In southern FEPC Regions VII, X, and XIII, the vulnerability of black workers was obvious in such temporary "war baby" plants as the Delta Shipyards and Convair in New Orleans, North American Aviation near Dallas, and the Bell bomber plant outside of Atlanta. In New Orleans, the upgrading and integration of black workers at both the Delta Shipyards and the Convair aircraft plant in 1944 and 1945 represented both regional and national victories for African American industrial integrationists. Although New Orleans economic boosters and civic leaders wanted permanent plants, their postwar closings effectively took away employment opportunities for over two thousand African Americans at Delta and approximately seven hundred African Americans at Convair on the lakefront.[14]

At the Bell bomber plant in Marietta, Georgia, following V-J Day, the plant's closing laid off some fifteen hundred black workers and thereby negated the Atlanta Urban League's hard-fought wartime employment gains. From 1946 to 1951, the federal government used the plant as a warehouse for surplus equipment. Not until 1951 did the United States Air Force lease the plant to Lockheed. From 1951 to the 1960s, Lockheed management and the International Association of Machinists (IAM-AFL) enforced a rigid occupational segregation arrangement at the plant.[15] The North American Aviation (NAA) plant in Grand Prairie, Texas, closed operations soon after V-J Day, eliminating 1,182 African Americans (down from peak employment of 2,274 in July 1944) and 5,368 women along with 13,000 white males. After NAA deactivated the plant in August 1945, the Texas Engineering and Manufacturing Company (Temco), a locally established aviation firm, leased a part of the plant from the Reconstruction Finance Corporation and retained twelve hundred "expert maintenance men" from the previous NAA employees for postwar employment.[16]

Ironically, in March 1945, Don Ellinger cited the United Auto Workers (UAW-CIO) Local 645 contract at NAA in Dallas to illustrate how organized labor offered African American workers the best chance for keeping their jobs in the postwar era. As Ellinger informed the *Pittsburgh Courier,* when NAA in Dallas had a recent ten-thousand-worker cutback, the UAW's enforcement of its seniority clause prevented the dismissal of some two thousand white workers and many black workers. As Ellinger concluded, "We have made progress, but if there are not enough jobs in the postwar period, there will be plenty of trouble. If we can have ten years of full employment our race problems will be solved."[17]

The Promise of Full Employment

In the weeks following V-J Day, the job layoff issue emerged as one of the top political and economic issues in the national press. By August 1945, some 9 million of a total of 52 million American workers were employed in defense industries. As layoff fears mounted, economists and supporters of full employment predicted that as many as eight million idle workers would be searching for work by the spring of 1946, creating a situation ripe for racial tension. In the eyes of New Deal liberals, full employment in the postwar era represented the surest way to maintain and foster racial peace in the United States.[18] Until a Full Employment Bill could be submitted to Congress, however, Americans watched uneasily as the nation demobilized millions of workers.

By the middle of August, alarming reports indicated that aircraft plants in New Jersey, Ohio, Illinois, and Connecticut had already laid off some 106,000 workers. In Akron, Ohio, Goodyear had let go 15,000 persons, while U.S. Steel in Pittsburgh had recently let go some 45,000 workers. Detroit as the center of northern defense industries counted between 250,000 to 300,000 jobless persons. As the site of a major wartime race riot and a major center for defense industry layoffs, Detroit served as a national bellwether for how demobilization would affect race relations. By September, however, reports indicated that black workers in Detroit numbering from 100,000 to 350,000 remained calm in the face of bleak employment prospects.[19]

Despite the general calm that prevailed in defense centers, national jobs movement leaders were concerned that black migrants outside of the South remained most vulnerable to unemployment. In the Pacific West, manpower officials observed that USES offices up and down the coast relegated black migrants largely to the hull crafts of the shipyards, and 80 to 90 percent of black workers worked in less than 10 percent of the coastal industries. As West Coast manpower administrators discovered, the USES did not want to "antagonize employers and unions in general and specifically those employers and unions that will remain in existence after the war." For this reason, the FEPC predicted that African Americans and other minorities would be affected by cutbacks "more severely than any other group."[20]

Indeed, these predictions had been realized by the fall of 1946. After V-J Day, WMC officials in California observed that African Americans, 90 percent of whom worked in war industries such as aircraft and shipbuilding, experienced the dramatic effects of postwar layoffs. In shipbuilding around the San Francisco Bay Area, for example, the industry employed 20,587 nonwhite workers in July 1945. Yet by September 1946, that number had fallen to 1,963. During this period, the percentage of African American employment overall fell from 13.1 to 6 percent of the Bay Area work force, while over 90 percent of USES placements for black workers were in unskilled jobs. In fact, by September 1946, food packaging, iron and steel, shipbuilding, transportation, and dock work comprised the only jobs in which African Americans worked in considerable numbers in the California job market.[21]

Even in warehouse and longshore work, where African American migrants found some of the greatest opportunities for long-term employment on the West Coast during the war, black members of the ILWU faced an uncertain future. In a case that created tremendous bitterness among black war workers, L. B. Thomas of ILWU Local 26 in San Pedro led a movement to exclude black members from keeping their permanent membership after the war. In April 1946, Local 26 deregistered the majority of black ILWU members who had become members during the war. Rather than stand idly by, the group of African Americans known as the "Unemployed 500" fought for their permanent membership in the California courts. By 1949, they had eventually won back their membership and in the process continued the wartime battle for equal rights in the workplace.[22] Indeed, in Los Angeles after the war, Rev. Clayton Russell, the Los Angeles Urban League, the local NAACP, and other committed job activists continued to make job opportunities and industrial integration a key issue in the battle against discrimination overall.[23]

Despite postwar layoffs and white efforts to continue enforcing discriminatory housing covenants, many African American migrants to the Pacific Coast resolved to remain in the West.[24] While many white migrants from Texas, Oklahoma, and other Plains states returned home after August 1945, many black migrants from these states as well as most other southern states hoped to stay.[25] In the Pacific Northwest, for example, one federal housing official noted that black migrants were determined not to go "back South."[26] In California, FEPC regional director Harry Kingman believed that "only a small portion of southern born defense workers" would return to the South.[27] In Los Angeles, where over 100,000 southern African Americans had moved during the war, WMC officials Charles Bratt and Lt. Lawrence Oxley warned of a race relations and job crisis. "Job security is the fertile soil in which racial tensions mature," Oxley argued.[28] To meet the needs of black migrants in California, he supported effective job controls and "prompt action by federal, state and local agencies."[29]

Lawrence Oxley's advocacy of greater government action on the West Coast and throughout the nation in 1945 highlighted the emerging national political and ideological debate over the role of the state in minimizing tensions from wartime cutbacks.[30] Looking back at the experiences of the "Red Summer" after World War I, when African Americans were subject to a rash of white violence, liberal state planners and African American leaders like Oxley embraced several strategies to prevent a recurrence of such violence in 1945 and 1946. Many liberals argued specifically for federal control of the la-

bor market through continued federalization of the USES and the establishment of a permanent FEPC. In addition, liberals and state planners supported
the idea of full employment, which for African Americans implied economic
security through industrial employment. From 1944 through 1946, these
three Democratic planks represented the heart of the liberal reconversion
agenda.

In large part, the postwar liberal agenda, as expressed by President Roosevelt in his last term and supported by state planners, organized labor, and
most African Americans, sought to reduce class and racial tensions by creating an economy that theoretically produced enough jobs to employ everyone.
In his 1944 State of the Union address, Roosevelt called for an "economic bill
of rights" to provide Americans with "economic security and happiness." In
the increasingly conservative climate of wartime and the beginnings of the
cold war, the overall liberal agenda of full employment became embodied in
the Serviceman's Readjustment Act of 1944 (more commonly known as the
GI Bill) and the Employment Act of 1946. Despite liberals' hopes, however,
both bills compromised their agenda.

The GI Bill passed through Congress with relative ease. In the House, the
bill caused some controversy when Mississippi congressman John Rankin insisted on amendments that minimized educational and unemployment benefits. Rankin, in essence, feared that the bill's current wording would encourage African Americans in Mississippi to remain unemployed at least a
year after the war.[31] Rankin, in fact, had little to fear. After the war, state and
local government administration of the GI Bill allowed southern elites to regulate unemployment compensation and veterans' benefits for African Americans. In general, the decentralized administration of the GI Bill was undoubtedly a strong selling point of the bill to conservatives throughout the
nation.

In contrast to the GI Bill, the original Full Employment Bill underwent a
more profound transformation that reflected the conservative political climate of 1945 and 1946. In 1944, liberals introduced the bill as "a firm assurance that unemployment never again will be permitted to become a national
problem." Ultimately, the bill ended up as the Employment Act of 1946 and
failed to provide the social insurance, federal public works programs, and
government spending that liberals hoped would insure economic growth.[32]
In the intervening year, southern conservatives had especially come to view
the Full Employment Bill as what the *Manufacturers' Record* called the "modern carpetbaggers' bill." More reactionary southerners' views on the bill
maintained, as the *Knoxville Journal* argued, that full employment was "the

good old communistic line patented in Moscow, being copied in London, and now being slipped over on the people of the United States."[33]

African Americans considered the bill a means of eliminating job competition and racial strife. Walter White of the NAACP saw a "full job bill" as staving off economic depression and "the sinister forces of hate."[34] When the final bill passed in January 1946, however, conservatives and states' rights advocates won a key victory as Kentucky senator Alben W. Barkley inserted a clause returning the USES to state control.[35] African American civil rights organizations and liberal state planners viewed this defederalization of the USES as a return to the prewar status quo and therefore a key setback for the liberal agenda.

Since 1944, state planners and liberal African Americans had supported the continued federal control of state employment services along with full employment as a central ingredient to postwar economic security. Paul McNutt toured the United States promoting this agenda among WMC regional, state, and local administrators.[36] The NAACP urged President Truman to veto the return of the USES to state control. In its view, federal management of the USES eradicated "many injustices" and implemented "equitable referrals to jobs."[37] With the prospect of the USES under state control, liberal African Americans viewed the move as "a menace to the Negro worker" and a restoration of "the old feudal system." One Associated Negro Press (ANP) article charged, "The general idea is to deny [Negroes] unemployment benefits and make them accept any job assigned to them." Furthermore, the southern conservative movement to eliminate "federal interference" placed southern Negroes in a position in which they would "have to take it or else starve."[38]

Leading southern civil rights activists remained critical of both the War Manpower Commission and the USES's wartime record, despite the nominal praise from the NAACP. In the Southwest, the regional FEPC office, the New Orleans Urban League, the Dallas Negro Chamber of Commerce, and the Fort Worth Negro Welfare Council worked with WMC Region X to appoint WMC Negro Advisory Councils (NACs) in large cities in an effort to improve relations between the WMC and black communities. These organizations, as part of a larger effort to improve civil service opportunities for African Americans, also urged the WMC to hire black personnel in their regional office and local USES Negro divisions. However, by the end of the war, no NACs had been established, and the above organizations remained contemptuous of the WMC's lack of concern for African Americans' economic affairs. The New Orleans Urban League, in particular, continued to criticize the WMC for the failed NAC and African American staff issues. In its annual report for 1945, the NOUL accused the WMC of failing to live up to its promises.[39]

The National Urban League's southern division director, William Bell, also remained highly critical of the WMC at the end of the war for failing to effectively insure full utilization of Negro workers. The commission, he insisted, was "apathetic, negligent, and fail[ed] to take reasonable advantage of the opportunity to meet most Manpower's needs by promoting more extensive use of Negro workers." Bell did not see the WMC as hostile to black workers, but he declared, "If a word 'apitheti-Negro' could be substituted for 'anti-Negro' the sense would be crystallized."[40]

The WMC failed to leave a progressive legacy for many African American leaders in the South. In late 1945, the WMC officially dismantled, and Paul McNutt became high commissioner to the Philippines.[41] Four years of southern USES administrators' complicity in preserving the segregated labor market undoubtedly took its toll on the patience of progressive black leaders such as William Bell. Throughout 1944 and 1945, Bell corresponded futilely with WMC officials to insure that African American employment issues remained a priority in the WMC operations. Gradually, the Full Employment Bill replaced the wartime manpower issue as a focus for postwar jobs movement leaders. In this transition, progressive black leaders, such as *Louisiana Weekly* editor C. C. Dejoie, urged all African Americans to press for full employment and industrial integration before "the war's momentum will fade."[42]

Full Employment and Democracy in the South

The struggle for economic security galvanized African American civil rights organizations, educators, local churches, organized labor, and veterans at the regional and local levels in their efforts to maintain their wartime economic gains. Veterans and war workers in many ways provided the black community with a hope for respect and citizenship in the United States. In response, the National Urban League and the NAACP made veterans' employment and voting rights key issues in 1944 and 1945, as local black veterans groups in the South began to emerge simultaneously. Among the leading efforts in this period was the strong civil rights coalition that had emerged in Atlanta during the war. By the summer of 1945, WMC Minority Group Services administrator W. H. Shell, the local NAACP chapter, and the Atlanta Urban League had joined with local church leaders, including Martin Luther King Sr., to sponsor four mass meetings that addressed the benefits and services for veterans and the "GI Bill of Rights."[43]

For African Americans in the postwar years, the GI Bill's provisions replaced many federal programs such as the Works Progress Administration (WPA), the National Youth Administration (NYA), and the Farm Security Administration (FSA). Hence, black jobs movement veterans and activists emphasized the importance of these federal veterans' benefits in maintaining economic security for black families after the war. In the South, however, white conservatives who administered the programs generally thwarted the GI Bill's potential of generating black economic mobility and independence.

Realizing this problem, the Urban League focused on ensuring the fair administration of veterans' training and benefits at the local level. In December 1944, William Bell and Julius Thomas, the NUL industrial relations director in New York and a Mississippi native, pointed out that African American veterans from the First World War had been largely uninformed about their veterans' rights and benefits. According to Bell, most southern states had no American Legion posts for African Americans in 1918. And as he understood a military official's recollection, "17,000 Negro Veterans in Georgia didn't secure their bonuses following the last War largely because they were unable to learn about their rights through the Legion's Educational Program." As Bell argued, the program might have reached black veterans "if there had been more Negro posts or if Negro posts were integrated."[44]

Because southern black and Latino veterans were largely excluded from the more formal white veterans associations, they formed their own institutions to serve the veterans' needs. In Texas, the formation of the GI Forum among returning Latino veterans in the town of Three Rivers illustrated the growing political mobilization of minority veterans. In Atlanta, a group of black veterans in Georgia formed the Georgia Veterans League, an organization allied with the AUL in its effort to serve the welfare and needs of "service folk." According to historian Karen Ferguson, "black veterans in Atlanta became a militant and autonomous force in the African American community from which there emerged a leadership group somewhat separate from the black reform elite."[45] In New Orleans, black veterans organized the Citizens Committee on Services to Veterans under a similar agenda to that of their colleagues in Georgia.[46]

Reflecting this concerted effort to mobilize for postwar jobs, the New Orleans Urban League (NOUL) organized a Community Conference on Job Opportunities for Negroes. Reflecting the growth of southern civil rights networks during the war, the NOUL conference put forth an important regional focus on economic opportunities for both rural and urban African Americans across the South. At the spring gathering, the list of attendees and speakers at the conference read like a who's who of progressive southern black leaders from the local New Orleans networks, the National Urban League, the Southern Negro Youth Congress, the Southern Regional Council, historically black colleges and universities, organized labor, the black churches, and business elites from New Orleans and Memphis.[47]

In a united show of support, the panel presenters all openly supported the full employment program and a permanent FEPC. William Bell, in speaking on "Full Employment—For Negroes Too?" declared that as America had produced the "manpower, machines and money" for the war, the nation could now use these resources to "produce the highest standard of living the world has ever known." Following Bell, Willard Townsend, the United Transport Service Employees (UTSE-CIO) president and National Urban League board member, called for an expanded welfare safety net and federally sponsored "permanent prosperity." "It is only by achieving this program," Townsend argued, "that we can hope to establish a climate that will enable us to continue to improve the economic, social and political status of the Negro."[48] Townsend's belief in federal economic spending to induce racial progress led Carter Wesley, the Houston media mogul, to praise Townsend and the New Orleans Urban League as "the type of Negro leadership which represents our greatest hope."[49]

As part of the postwar full employment agenda, all speakers held consensus on the importance of industrial employment for southern African Americans in the postwar era. As William Bell had acknowledged, the defense jobs opened up by the war clearly provided southern African Americans with unprecedented economic advancement. With the ongoing process of farm mechanization, the conference's Committee on Agricultural Employment Opportunities for Negroes in Louisiana stressed the importance of providing industrial jobs for rural African Americans experiencing the dramatic transformation occurring in southern agriculture. Echoing the concerns of prewar state planners over the issue of massive rural out-migration, the committee argued that "if farm life may be made to 'hold' the youth, the urban unemployment problem may be lessened a great deal." While urging greater farm ownership and a federal farm program that would make the farming market more equitable, the committee also stressed the need to provide industrial enterprises such as sawmills, commercial canning and dehydration plants, and textile industries.[50]

That spring, the United States Department of Agriculture (USDA) also addressed the profound repercussions stemming from the mechanization of the Cotton Belt. Faced with the introduction of the mechanical cotton picker in

1943, USDA planners under Chairman Claude Wickard strove to meet the human fallout from this change. In April 1945, the USDA's liberal planning agency, the Bureau of Agricultural Economics (BAE), issued a report entitled "A Conversion Program for the Cotton South." In it the bureau outlined future problems facing southern agriculture and its rural workforce. As the report urged, "industrial expansion in the South is essential to providing job opportunities for underemployed and displaced agricultural workers." Providing statistics that correlated the per capita income in the South with the level of industrialization, the BAE illustrated that rural southern states with the highest percentage of workers engaged in farming also had the lowest incomes. To combat this problem, the bureau urged a "conversion program" whereby the "the shift of workers from agriculture to industry" would "increase the average income per worker in the South by about half above the 1940 level." Advocating the great need for "off-farm jobs," the report further claimed that "if such a gain were coupled with full employment of the 2,000,000 who were jobless in 1940," then "total regional income could be expected to rise by about 90 percent." Clearly, the report advocated southern industrialization as a key to regional economic uplift.[51]

From 1944 to 1946, African Americans openly endorsed southern industrialization as a solution to ending economic inequality in the South and the racial tensions in the North and West stemming from migration of rural southerners. In October 1945, Carter Wesley cited the USDA Cotton Conversion Program's statistics correlating industry and per capita income in the South as a mandate not only for subsidizing farm wages but also for greater southern industrialization and new job opportunities for rural African Americans in the Cotton Belt. As Wesley urged, "A deliberate and stubborn effort must be made to move these people from their farms to the cities and industries."[52]

In the context of the full employment movement, African American elites and labor leaders viewed industrialization as a positive force in the struggle for economic and political equality. In the winter of 1945, the southern African American press applauded the endorsement by the Southern Governors Conference of southern industrialization as a key item in the postwar agenda. Commenting on the conference, the *Dallas Express* argued that "whatever will help the South and make more jobs in the South is bound to help the Negro."[53] The *Birmingham World* also argued that the proposed industrialization of the South was sure to be a "boon to Negroes" because the spread of unionism would increase economic and political power.[54]

In the summer of 1945, African American columnists in the national black press also addressed what they saw as a new day for black southerners with the dismantling of the regional freight rate system and the introduction of more industries. In August, the Interstate Commerce Commission (ICC) ruled to eliminate discriminatory freight rates for the South and the West. George McCray, in his syndicated column, "On the Labor Front," argued that the ICC decision would "probably cause far-reaching changes in southern race relations as well as in southern industry," because the South would no longer use race to divide southern workers as a means of insuring a docile labor force that could compete with northern industries. Along with many southern black editors, McCray agreed that industrialization would spread the liberal trade union movement, increase the standard of living, and topple the forces of discrimination.[55] Likewise, Dean Gordon Hancock, in his weekly syndicated column, "Between the Lines," argued that the ICC ruling raised questions regarding the "place the Negro will occupy in the New South that parity rates will help to make." Claiming that "the Negro will benefit from the uplifting of the South," Hancock asserted that "as the South becomes industrialized it will become more cosmopolitan and more liberal and tolerant."[56]

The Problem of Postwar Industrialization in the South

In 1945, the Southern Governors Conference, liberal state planners, and conservative and liberal African Americans all agreed on the need for southern industrialization. The consensus nonetheless belied some fundamental differences in the motives of liberals and conservatives in supporting economic development. African Americans often emphasized the liberal effects organized labor and an industrial society brought to the South. More conservative businessmen, such as members of the Southern States Industrial Conference, remained steadfastly opposed to organized labor and federal labor regulation, such as the FEPC and the Fair Labor Standards Act (FLSA). Increasingly, though, southern conservatives realized that the South needed to provide economic opportunity for the region's African Americans to maintain some regional social and economic stability. As the BAE's Cotton Conversion Program argued, while many southern men and women had left the region during the war, "If the South can provide [southerners] good jobs after the war, most of them will come back afterwards."[57]

Among moderate and conservative white southerners who favored industrialization, former Louisiana governor Sam Jones remained one of the most outspoken. In his *Saturday Evening Post* article entitled "The Southern Negro Packs His Bags," Jones argued that "the hope of the South, the hope of the nation, and incidentally the hope of the Negro race is rapid industrialization of the South." He then related the story of a Mississippi Delta general store owner whose diminishing stock of cheap cardboard suitcases indicated "a social shuffle of immense proportions now under way in the South." In Jones's view, economics caused this exodus, for "happy Negroes are Negroes with good jobs, good homes, ample food and a chance for fulfillment within their own social patterns," and "they also know that intelligent southern leaders are willing to go to bat for them to get these things."[58]

While Sam Jones purposely avoided taking a stand on either "keeping" or "getting rid of the Negro," his advocacy of economic equality served mainly to preserve the southern white economic status quo. According to Jones, "migration of the Negro to the industrial centers of the Northeast and West Coast will bring him into direct economic competition with northern laboring men." In contrast, the South has "set aside, so to speak, certain types of labor as belonging to the negro into which fields few white men go." The rural exodus and its effect on the southern economy, not economic equality, held Jones's interest. "Agricultural mechanization," he insisted, merely displaced "'poor whites' and negroes," driving them north and to the Pacific Coast. Most importantly, Jones worried that "the South will become big mechanized farmers with a considerably reduced population" and with "a general slackening of business due to the loss of population as in the mid-West when the same process took place."[59]

Jones's views reflected the attitudes of a growing number of southern conservatives and liberals who tied the future of southern economic development to the future of African American economic opportunity in the region. As he argued, by providing jobs in southern industry for displaced rural southerners of both races, industry would raise incomes and living standards for all southerners.

In many respects, African American out-migration was a central concern to white planters in the southern Cotton Belt who sought to mechanize their operations yet who resisted the social changes inherent in the demise of sharecropping. Recognizing that the share system provided a means of racial, political, and economic control, southern planters feared the implications of a rural African American exodus for their regional hegemony. Thus, they sought to mechanize in order to compete on the global market while discouraging any African American efforts to move away. The Delta Council, an organization made up of leading white bankers, businessmen, planters, and political and civic leaders, sought to induce black workers to stay in the Delta by improving educational facilities and living conditions and by discouraging migration through the press and the urgings of black leaders. And, like Sam Jones, Washington County industrial engineer John W. Lynch argued that the Delta must initiate plans for the kinds of industry that planters wanted in order to keep the region's labor force intact.[60]

Indeed, Delta planters' plans to maintain their local power were in large part consistent with the Southern Governors Conference's agenda for a post-war South that stressed the importance of educational equality and industrialization for black and white southerners.[61] At their meeting in January 1945, as the invention of the mechanical cotton picker made national headlines, Mississippi governor Thomas Bailey addressed the issue of five million rural migrants in the regional economy. Like many of his peers, the governor advocated the need for industry as a solution to this "problem."[62] Later that year at a meeting of the southern governors in New Orleans, a report sponsored by the Committee on Regional Education, consisting of Mississippi's Thomas Bailey, Alabama's Chauncy Sparks, and Virginia's C. W. Daren, advocated improved segregated educational facilities for African Americans in the South. As Sparks declared, "It will be necessary to establish professional colleges and vocational schools for Negroes within their borders."[63]

The emphasis on industrial development and educational equality represented a shift in southern conservative political thought that stressed a more literal interpretation of the separate but equal doctrine. By improving African Americans' standard of living while maintaining social segregation, southern white conservatives and moderates hoped to discourage black migration. In 1944, the *Dallas Morning News* ran a ten-part series by columnist Barry Bishop entitled "Negro Problems Confronting the Nation." Citing the racial problems in northern and western cities, Bishop promoted the ideas of *Richmond Times-Dispatch* editor Virginius Dabney as the model of modern southern thought that embraced both segregation and equality. Claiming that "conservative Negroes of the South . . . are not asking for an over-night revolution in race relations, or anything remotely approaching it," Bishop argued that instead "they wish to obtain for Southern Negroes a better share in the good things in life—better education, better health, better welfare, better jobs, better opportunities." Ultimately, Bishop observed, "they are not seeking social equality but equality before the law."[64]

Advocating a role for African Americans in southern industry, Bishop further urged that "the Negro must try by good work to fit so well into industry that management will see no economic advantage and perhaps even disadvantage in laying him off."[65] An extension of southern racial paternalism, his advice acknowledged a future for African Americans in southern industry, albeit on conservative white terms. It also indicated how southern states' rights advocates sought to isolate race relations as a strictly southern issue. As one editorial from the *High Point (North Carolina) Enterprise* argued, "We are whole heartedly in favor of improving the economic status of the American negro." Looking forward to a time "when capital—far-sighted white capital as well as negro capital—erects plants for colored workers and pays them equal wages for equal work," the paper also anticipated a time when "the improved earning power of negroes results in a great increase in negro capital." However, "we will never see such a day," the paper warned, "as long as the approach to it is attempted by any such law as the Fair Employment Practices Act."[66]

"What Will Be Done with Negro Workers?"

Southern conservatives ultimately hoped to avoid any outside interference in segregation matters. By advocating segregation and equality, white southerners, fearing that the changes brought about by the war would ultimately lead to greater black demands for social equality, hoped to at least buy some time on the segregation issue. Naturally, such white conservatives promoted southern African American support of their agenda. The *Dallas Morning News* in 1944 publicized Carter Wesley's praise for the Bishop series and also pointed to Dr. D. V. Jemison, president of the National Baptist Convention, who argued that "the white and Negro people of the South should be left alone to solve their own problems."[67]

White leaders, however, failed to really spell out specifically the role of black workers in emerging southern industries. In addressing the status of African Americans after the war, Thurman Sensing, of the ultraconservative Southern States Industrial Council, openly opposed the FEPC while he advocated greater economic opportunities for African Americans in the South under segregation. From "all indications [Negroes] are going to remain largely in the South," and "it is therefore to the self-interest of the South that the Negroes improve their financial status to as large an extent as possible." By failing to outline any specific plan for the future role of black workers, however, the council's inaction revealed the uncertain state of black employment in the South after the war.[68] Not surprisingly, the black press recognized the council's lack of commitment and vision. As the *Dallas Express* observed, "The South's bid for industrial power must recognize the Negro as an integral part of the plans." Yet the *Express* concluded that "while all this planning is going ahead, no one has mentioned what will be done with Negro workers."[69]

Even as Mississippi Delta elites advocated greater economic opportunities for African Americans through industrial expansion, sugarcane planters in South Louisiana remained antagonistic to industry and industrial training. In the summer of 1944, an event in New Iberia illustrated planters' contempt for industrial training. New Iberia, located in the heart of sugarcane country, made national news when law enforcement officials ran several black civic leaders out of town. The war had brought a new sense of urgency to local African Americans, who, in 1943 and 1944, formed a credit union and a local NAACP chapter and also helped to establish a welding school for African Americans two weeks before the leaders' ejection. While the violence in New Iberia was in part a response to increased black activism, the existence of the modern industrial training school in the predominantly agricultural area concerned planters, who hoped to maintain a large uneducated labor force and thus keep wages and production costs low.[70]

Even in Sam Jones's back yard, the uneasy relations between sugarcane growers and Baton Rouge petrochemical industries over the control of seasonal black workers underscored the inherent labor conflict. In January 1945, one year before Jones's "The Negro Packs His Bags" article ran, cane planters in West Baton Rouge Parish, working through their Farm Bureau, issued a strong protest to War Manpower officials and Senators Allen Ellender and John Overton regarding the alleged labor hoarding and pirating of sugarcane labor by North Baton Rouge industries. At a meeting of planters at the parish courthouse, Farm Bureau president B. C. Devall complained that several planters had lost workers through migration to local industry, despite planters' efforts to retain workers.[71]

As it had throughout the war, the controversy boiled down to white control over the black migrant workforce. In this context, black harvest workers continued to exercise their ability to move about and job shop seasonally and often discreetly. As the WMC discovered, sugarcane workers in the off season issued false claims about their employment status with the planters in order to gain employment at the North Baton Rouge petrochemical industries. The permanent industries, to the planters' chagrin, gladly overlooked any false claims to gain adequate unskilled labor. In doing so, they illustrated the inherent conflict between southern industries intent on keeping wages low through surplus labor markets.[72]

Despite the uneasy relations between planters and industrialists over labor competition during the war, both groups hoped to keep black workers in the South. Some companies went so far as to take out advertisements that openly discouraged workers from moving out of the region. For example, Shreveport's largest wartime defense industry, the J. B. Beird ordnance plant, urged potential workers not to "be misled by stories of high paying jobs at West Coast manufacturing centers." Realizing that high western wages had caused an exodus of workers from the area, J. B. Beird reminded potential migrants that "although hourly rates of pay may be higher, these cities are crowded, living conditions are poor, living costs are high and the job is for the duration only."[73]

Southern capitalists' fear of a continued mass out-migration became readily apparent in April 1945, when Eleanor Roosevelt discussed a plan to "deliver the Negro from bondage" by establishing a federally funded program that would relocate black southerners outside the South. According to the *Atlanta Daily World*, "southern manufacturers and plantation owners" opposed the plan, which would "deprive them of an estimated five million cheap laborers."[74] While the First Lady's plans may not have been politically viable, black leaders gauging white reactions undoubtedly grasped how even the threat of out-migration gave black southerners some leverage in gaining economic concessions at the end of the war.

As white southern conservatives and moderates began openly advocating economic and educational equality for all southerners, including African Americans, they did so with the understanding that segregation would remain in order to preserve social inequality. Many southern African Americans' general acceptance of economic equality within the larger segregated society represented a continuous thread of thought from Booker T. Washington's Atlanta Compromise to the cold war South. For other southern African Americans, the war had inspired a new sense of urgency to either migrate out of the region or stay and fight segregation.[75]

Race and Worker Mobility in the Postwar South

Since Emancipation, black southerners had used their freedom of mobility to exploit the economic opportunities available to them. Many southern sharecroppers moved annually, looking for a better contract, while seasonal farmworkers often migrated temporarily to southern cities and rural industries in the off-season to supplement their incomes. During World War II, the unprecedented out-migration of black southerners symbolized the economic limitations for regional black workers in the South's segregated and low-wage labor market. Given the large-scale and profound impact of black migration on American race relations during the war, the continued migration of black southerners after the war raised questions among all Americans regarding the long-term impact of this trend.

The issue of migration came to the forefront of debate in the black press in 1946, when Adam Clayton Powell, in his new book *Marching Blacks*, advocated that southern African Americans migrate north as a means of achieving racial progress. Powell's argument represented one thread in a larger discussion on differing African American strategies for gaining equality and a better life. In response to the issues Powell raised, a lively debate ensued over the merits of migration or remaining in the South. A rather heated debate emerged in New Orleans between *Louisiana Weekly* editor C. C. "Connie" Dejoie and Alonzo Willis, owner and editor of the *Negro South*, a nationally syndicated but locally edited magazine. Dejoie openly supported planned migration as a means of realizing justice for southern African Americans, while Willis advocated the Washingtonian "cast-down-your-buckets" argument.[76]

Not surprisingly, Alonzo Willis's plea garnered the support of some fifty southern daily papers as well as a host of southern businessmen who hoped to preach his advice to their own workers. Willis was especially proud of the support he had garnered from Andrew Jackson Higgins, a man he considered to represent the future of industrial race relations in the South. As the New Orleans editor printed in the *Negro South*, Higgins praised "[the Negroes'] aspiration for economic equality" and the fact that Willis had "contributed a great deal to amicable relations" while striving to "obtain economic and industrial equality."[77]

Higgins's endorsement of these terms under a segregated labor market reflected the new southern boosters' mantra of economic equality for African Americans as a means of enticing them to stay in the South. Despite such rhetoric, however, surplus labor markets and local economic conditions in the South largely determined employment opportunities (or lack thereof) for black southerners. As veterans returned home to rural areas especially, they found farmers concerned with rising farmworker wages and, hence, a movement toward cheaper production costs by mechanizing and moving into livestock management. In Caddo Parish, Louisiana, for instance, R. T. Douglas informed *Progressive Farmer* readers, "Instead of $2 per day labor, I am going to use a $40 cow that gets up in the morning to the pasture on her own power and comes back heavier in the evening—with no labor costs to me."[78]

In the Arkansas Delta town of Brinkley, USES manager Dorothy Dalton revealed how rural black workers in the postwar South sought economic security in the postwar economy. As Dalton reported, a number of women filing for unemployment compensation would "not accept work at a lower wage than they have been receiving during the last four years." Moreover, as the office reported, many "colored women" were "interested only in industrial employment" even when there were "no openings whatsoever of that type for colored women." Of the black men returning to the Brinkley area, the USES noted that most were "willing to take jobs here at a lower wage scale than they were receiving in war work." At the same time, the USES observed that of returning black veterans, most were interested in work in the North because of the higher wages and better working conditions. Nevertheless, the USES continued to report that very little out-migration was occurring.[79]

Likewise, in Helena, Arkansas, the local USES noted in October 1945 that migration into the area had shown a gradual increase and that out-migration of workers had actually slowed. According to W. J. Monday, the Helena USES manager, the majority of workers migrating into Helena were black men and women who "left this area to accept war work." Of this group, "a considerable number of those migrating are returning to their farms or other farms in which they were employed prior to their leaving this area." As before the war, black men found some seasonal employment opportunities in the lumber industry, the cotton oil mills, and the vegetable canneries.[80]

In 1945, the Texas USES also noted that 86 percent of all veterans reporting to local USES offices desired work within their own communities, and 75 percent of veterans returned to their former jobs or to some related occupation. Only 10 percent of the veterans left local communities to accept employment elsewhere. Of this group, the majority went to the West Coast, and "of these the larger percentage are Negroes who either worked there prior to their military service or have heard through friends of the higher wages being paid in that area." The USES further observed that workers seeking new jobs were largely unskilled and semiskilled workers and that their decision was largely based on the salary scale regardless of the location. "Having heard of fabulous wages paid, they feel that they should get their share while they can."[81]

The postwar labor market illustrated that war workers and returning veterans sought a mixture of economic mobility and stability. The trend toward stability was evident in Louisiana and Texas during the autumn of 1944, when the WMC noted that workers were "better contented and less interested in higher paying jobs away from home." One man interviewed by the WMC claimed that he had quit a shipbuilding job at $1.10 per hour to go "back home" to drive a logging truck at 50 cents per hour. According to the WMC, the worker declared that he was tired of being away from home and wanted "to be sure of a permanent postwar job" and that "many other workers are doing the same thing."[82] The return of black workers to farm jobs at the end of the war reflected the general pattern of seasonal employment established before the war. As the Alabama WMC noted, migration to and from rural areas often coincided with the farm season and especially cotton planting and harvest.[83]

As black veterans returned to the South, they, along with the Southern Regional Council (SRC), made efforts to have vocational training available under the GI Bill. The SRC established a Division of Veterans Services, headed by George Mitchell, to publicize the bill's benefits and to monitor its application to black veterans. Under the SRC program, eight to ten black veterans traveled throughout the rural and small-town South, contacting official veteran service agencies.[84] At the same time, black civic leaders, such as R. R. Grovey of Houston's Third Ward Civic Club, and black veterans, such as those in the United Negro Veterans in Atlanta, made vocational training a top priority in the struggle for economic security.[85]

While the GI Bill theoretically offered returning black veterans a means of economic mobility by providing training and education opportunities, white southerners' local control of federal veterans' programs insured that such programs did not challenge the status quo. In some southern cities, vocational training was available for black veterans. For instance, in February 1946, seven hundred veterans in Houston received technical training at the Houston Negro College and Dart Vocational School, the site of the former war training school downtown.[86] Likewise, in Atlanta and New Orleans, black veterans received some vocational training at both cities' Booker T. Washington High Schools. However, in Atlanta, social workers discovered that trained veterans still had trouble selling their skills to southern industries. In New Orleans, local activists complained that the training facilities provided were often limited or inadequate for veterans' needs.[87]

Training opportunities for black veterans in the rural South were often limited or nonexistent. In July 1945, the SRC's Committee on Services to Veterans convened to hear reports from SRC representatives who were investigating the administration of the GI Bill in rural Louisiana. According to one SRC agent, Wesley Brazier, colored veterans in the parishes he covered were often not informed of their rights. Although Brazier organized citizens committees, he reported that his efforts received little cooperation from locals, a sign he interpreted as "a lack of interest" in such organizations among rural African Americans. Furthermore, Brazier observed that outside of "farming training" in St. Tammany and Washington Parishes, "on-the-job training was unheard of." In southern Louisiana, some rural African Americans did seek to take advantage of the GI Bill. For instance, Brazier reported that one high school principal in Iberville Parish urged black veterans to return to school and local black businessmen to accept veterans for training. In Lafourche Parish, Brazier reported that officials did an especially good job of informing vets of their rights. However, no job training was available because sugarcane was "the only crop raised." In St. Landry Parish, Brazier observed that white farmers did not cooperate in hiring black veterans.[88]

Throughout 1945, African Americans found that the postwar USES and Veterans Administration offices throughout the United States and especially in the South practiced discrimination. In a report on difficulties that minority veterans experienced under the GI Bill, the American Council on Race Relations (ACRR) criticized the poor services that nonwhite veterans received. The biggest problems centered on prevailing local discrimination patterns, unequal facilities, and local USES and Veterans Affairs offices discriminating in job referrals and job placement, as well as these offices encouraging minority vets to draw unemployment benefits and not work. At the same time, surveys and investigations by organizations such as the NAACP, ACRR, NUL, and SRC proved charges of discrimination, segregation, and indifferent USES officials to the job problems of many black veterans. The ACRR found specifically that minority veterans were "met with cold politeness, ridicule, and open hostility in USES offices in San Francisco, Los Angeles, Nashville, Houston and Atlanta." Without the protection of the FEPC and a labor shortage, there was "a general 'drying up' of job opportunities for returning minority veterans."[89]

"Like a Tidal Wave": The Death of a Permanent FEPC

In 1945 and 1946, as African American veterans and war workers struggled for jobs, the fight to keep the FEPC as a permanent federal agency galvanized African American communities in the South and Southwest. This campaign grew directly out of the wartime jobs movement, and in doing so it represented an important extension of the African American drive for economic equality and democracy in the workplace as the war ended. At the same time, the movement's ultimate failure in the summer of 1946 reflected the overall lack of political leverage that black workers in the South had during the immediate postwar years.

Throughout the region in 1945, black activists in all large cities formed

Committees for a Permanent FEPC to raise money for their lobbying efforts. Beginning in October 1945, *Birmingham World* editor E. O. Jackson chaired the local committee to form a permanent FEPC in that city.[90] In Atlanta, the permanent FEPC movement began in September just before the local headquarters for Region VII closed in November.[91] Local activists in Dallas and Houston formed local committees, and by October 1945, local committees had formed in Fort Worth, San Antonio, and Shreveport.[92] The local FEPC movement in Houston received not only support from black leaders but also financial contributions from the Fifth Ward Civic Club, the Boilermakers AFL auxiliary, and the Southern Pacific Railroad workers. The FEPC's hearings involving the Texas and New Orleans Railroad in 1945 also served as a motivating force for local fair employment activists.[93]

In New Orleans, a local committee organized to maintain the FEPC in December 1944, well before activists in other cities organized. Throughout the winter and spring of 1945, churches, fraternal organizations, and businesses along with black unions, such as carpenters, painters, textile workers, bricklayers, seamen, postal workers, and teamsters, all united to raise money for a permanent FEPC. Within this movement, the Transport Workers CIO along with the Interdenominational Ministers Alliance (IMA) and the AFL carpenters and laborers union representatives contributed over five thousand dollars to the permanent FEPC movement, while the AFL Pullman's local sponsored a dance to raise money for the cause. In August 1945, the local NAACP chapter supported the permanent FEPC movement in cooperation with both the local AFL and CIO. Referring to this positive support as "a sign of the times" in March 1945, E. J. Wright praised the fact that the permanent FEPC movement in the Crescent City had garnered the cooperation of labor, civic, church, business, and educational organizations under a common cause.[94]

Because New Orleans served as the regional FEPC headquarters for Region XIII in 1945, the permanent FEPC movement maintained considerable momentum there. In March, the local NAACP and the local FEPC office under Don Ellinger mobilized workers with a kick-off rally to support the FEPC. That same month, FEPC chairman Malcolm Ross came to New Orleans on a southern public relations tour to meet with representatives from major employers and civic leaders as well as with about fifty local black leaders to discuss the future of the FEPC. During Ross's visit, the New Orleans Council on Race Relations (NOCRR), in cooperation with Don Ellinger, established an advisory committee to aid in establishing a fair employment agency in the city. Local NAACP chapter leaders L. L. Haynes and Daniel Byrd, along with J. Harvey Netter, president of the International Longshoremen's Association

(ILA) Local 1419, and Arthur Chapital, activist leader of the local National Association of Postal Employees (NAPE) interracial union, led the committee. The *New Orleans Item* even endorsed the establishment of a fair employment code for the city based on the principles of equal pay for equal work and equal opportunity to work.[95]

In Texas, the permanent FEPC campaign faced more open resistance to the federal agencies' postwar existence. To be sure, in San Antonio, the new headquarters for the FEPC in the Southwest, regional director Carlos Castaneda attempted to mobilize support for the FEPC among local conservatives and liberals with mixed results. Encouragingly, John C. Granberry, the publisher of the *San Antonio Emancipator*, the local League of United Latin American Citizens (LULAC) chapter, and the Mexican Chamber of Commerce offered their assistance in the campaign. In contrast, Castaneda failed to garner support from Frank Huntress, the owner and publisher of the local *Express* and *Evening News*. Castaneda later described Huntress as a southerner "of the old school" who "really loved a good Negro who knew how to keep his place."[96]

That spring of 1945, FEPC director Malcolm Ross made an unpublicized tour of the Southwest to shore up support for a permanent FEPC. In San Antonio, he met with local industrialists and Governor Coke Stevenson's Good Neighbor Commission. Among liberal groups Ross convened with the San Antonio Negro Chamber of Commerce, the San Antonio NAACP, and the Ministers Alliance as well as with the local LULAC chapter and the Mexican Chamber of Commerce.[97] Moving on to Dallas, the FEPC director then visited with the business elite in the city's Chamber of Commerce, North American Aviation management, and the local media to discuss the future of federal fair employment. Despite such public relations efforts, however, the *Dallas Morning News* continued to oppose the permanent FEPC movement under the banner of states' rights.[98] Amidst the conservative political environment facing FEPC proponents, Castaneda informed the FEPC in Washington that "liberal groups in our area" had become "as rare as hen's teeth."[99]

In the postwar period, liberal activism subsided throughout the South and Southwest as reactionaries used anti-Communism measures to assault fair employment. In March 1946, Carlos Castaneda complained to FEPC officials in Washington of Senator W. Lee "Pappy" O'Daniel's successful attempt to kill the FEPC with Red-baiting propaganda. As a reactionary, O'Daniel charged that the "communist inspired" FEPC only caused "strife and bloodshed in the South." In Castaneda's view, Texas needed a permanent FEPC more than ever because "industrialists and unions alike" had "reverted back to the good old days of the pre-war era and combined to put the Negro and the Mexican back in his place as common laborer, fit only for servile manual labor, dirty undesirable jobs and the lowest paying work." Expressing dejection, Castaneda concluded to the FEPC's Clarence Mitchell that "the antebellum status quo has been restored generally" while "reaction" had "set in like a tidal wave."[100]

The wartime momentum of the fair employment movement led by the FEPC and NUL subsided dramatically with the FEPC's gradual dismantling in 1945 and 1946. The CIO and AFL national offices nominally supported a permanent FEPC, yet ultimately they declined to provide political support for fear of alienating conservatives within the labor movement. Reflecting black labor leaders' dismay toward labor's apathy on the race issue, syndicated labor columnist George McCray decried in February 1946 that "America does not have a democratic form of government" because the AFL was "hypocritical" in its support of the FEPC and the CIO failed to "marshal its usual forces." That same week, columnist B. Robinson declared "the FEPC died because the virtues of this democracy were raped by the rakes of discrimination."[101]

In February and March, A. Philip Randolph threatened to stage a march on Washington to protest the death of the FEPC. Ultimately, however, the return of the surplus labor market in 1946 reduced any real political leverage that Randolph had possessed on the eve of war in 1941.[102] In stark contrast to the tight labor market and the Roosevelt administration's need for black support before Pearl Harbor, Randolph in 1946 had little leverage from which to work, other than the unlikely threat of withholding black support of the Democratic Party. The return of the surplus labor market effectively negated the momentum of activism that Randolph and other jobs movement veterans hoped to carry into the postwar years.

With the political landscape shifting farther to the right, black civil rights and labor activists focused more on voter registration and less on jobs. In the postwar years, the issue of job equality faced a number of barriers in the South, including the surplus labor market, the continuation of Jim Crow on the shop floor, the return of State Employment Service offices to state control, and a wave of conservatism against federal fair employment laws. And, as with the American labor movement overall, the jobs movement in the South succumbed to the rash of antilabor legislation that emerged in the late 1940s. Given the growing power of conservatives and the seemingly apathetic state of liberals and jobs movement activists, black labor leaders in the South used the wartime networks of churches, civic institutions, and unions to mobilize African Americans for the vote across the urban South.[103]

Epilogue

"A Virtual Revolution in Negro Leadership"

In 1946, the CIO initiated Operation Dixie, a campaign to "organize the unorganized" throughout the American South. As Operation Dixie commenced in the spring, many African Americans questioned the CIO's rhetorical support of nondiscrimination and economic equality. George McCray, in his weekly column, "On the Labor Front," observed, "The effort to organize white and Negro workers in southern industry will provide an acid test of the CIO's ability to stick to its policy of equal treatment for Negroes and all other workers." McCray then questioned the "moral strength" of the CIO in the South. Accusing Van Bittner of scaring off the liberal groups whose support the CIO needed to win the South, McCray predicted that "the CIO will be too afraid of the charge of communism to make a bold and convincing attack on discrimination against Negroes in employment." McCray then argued, "Many Negro leaders report that frequently, Negroes in the AFL in the South get a much better 'break' than those in the CIO."[1]

Operation Dixie illustrated to progressives how the CIO had largely forsaken the cause of racial equality after the war yet still offered African Americans access to economic security. George McCray, in observing Operation Dixie in June 1946, understood how a call for "social equality" among black workers appeared radical and therefore politically dangerous in the conservative climate of the postwar South. Realizing that such demands could jeopardize overall gains for organized labor, he underscored how CIO union organizers claimed that "their drives did not seek social equality—only economic equality." In this emphasis on the economic benefits of labor representation, McCray stressed that "as union members, Negroes do get equal pay for equal work."[2]

This acceptance of economic equality at the expense of social equality among black workers was evident in Dallas in March 1945. At the Butane Equipment Company, black members of the local Boilermakers AFL auxiliary lobbied for equal representation under the white local's contract. To the dismay of liberal FEPC officials, the black boilermakers willingly accepted the segregated arrangement, because under a new contract, the company would be required to meet the colored workers' terms of agreement.[3] Indeed, throughout the war, black workers failed to prioritize integration on the shop floor while seeking economic mobility. At Butane Equipment and other plants, African American workers would largely settle for economic equality under a segregated labor market.

Operation Registration: The Voting Rights Movement Matures

By 1946, the failure of the permanent FEPC movement, the national CIO's retreat from racial equality, and the return of a surplus labor market illustrated to both black workers and labor leaders the tentative nature of wartime liberal advancement. In the context of postwar conservatism, black labor leaders nonetheless hoped to use the momentum of wartime economic gains and the labor movement to invigorate a voter registration movement.

In New Orleans especially, CIO organizer Ernest J. Wright argued in his *Louisiana Weekly* column, "I Daresay," that CIO-PAC networks at the parish, ward, and precinct levels in Louisiana offered an unprecedented opportunity for local African Americans to become more politicized. As Wright declared in April 1946, "Nothing like this has happened in my lifetime and in the lifetime of others of us. It is up to us to join progressive and liberal minded white people and help bring about a new day in Louisiana."[4]

The CIO-PAC's "operation registration" offered black and white liberals in the South a chance to come together on the voter issue while politicizing southern workers. Yet the 1946 voter registration movement would generally avoid open interracialism. In the conservative racial climate of 1946, black leaders within the churches and black industrial unions focused on using these segregated black institutions to mobilize the black working class for the vote. In doing so, southern African Americans found that these community institutions often provided the greatest means of achieving economic and even social progress.[5]

Throughout the South in the months after V-J Day, labor-church coalitions mobilizing voters received considerable publicity in the regional black media. In Memphis in September 1945, local CIO representative Henry B. White allied with the Centenary Church to implement a Forum Hour meeting every Tuesday for black Memphians. In Savannah in October, the local NAACP president, together with the pastor of First Baptist Church and the International Longshoreman's Association (ILA-AFL) local, urged African Americans to register for the vote. In Atlanta in September, the Hotel and Restaurant Employees Union Local 629 invited persons to a meeting at the Wheat Street Baptist Church to hear Rev. William Holmes Borders espouse his "fearless defense of organized labor" along with Solon C. Bell, international representative from Chicago.[6] In New Orleans, the People's Defense League (PDL) symbolized the strong church-labor coalition that had emerged from the war. By 1944, the militant actions of Rev. A. L. Davis, pastor of Mount Zion Baptist, and Ernest J. Wright along with other black labor leaders in New Orleans garnered front-page news in the *Atlanta Daily World*.[7]

The voter registration movement in Birmingham also received regional attention in June and July 1944 when local CIO, AFL, and United Mine Workers (UMW) leaders competed with the NAACP to register Negro voters during the Alabama state registration period.[8] The Jefferson County, Alabama, CIO-PAC, which formed in 1944, sought to register black voters by capitalizing on Governor Chauncy Sparks's efforts to get the "soldier vote." As one labor leader declared, the movement's aim was "liberation of the ballot." The NAACP, in contrast to the CIO, was largely dominated by Birmingham's business elites, such as executive board member A. G. Gaston, owner of a local burial insurance agency and hotel, and other local businessmen. Nevertheless, the overall vote effort in Birmingham largely crossed class lines.[9] In 1945, the NAACP's and the CIO's voter registration efforts were further bolstered by support from the Registration League of the South Elyton Civic League with the cooperation of the black Baptist church and the local Elks.[10]

Commenting on this trend in January 1946, Maida S. Springer, former educational director of the International Ladies Garment Workers Union (ILGWU), declared that "a virtual revolution in Negro leadership" had occurred over the past ten years. "Practically every big town branch of the NAACP and the NUL today gives increasing attention to workers' problems," Springer argued, "while Negro ministers—long regarded as the bulwark of conservative leadership—no longer hesitate to address union meetings."[11]

Indeed, the southern voter registration movement, like the permanent FEPC movement, grew largely out of cooperation among church, labor, and civil rights leaders.

In the postwar South, interracialism remained a vision within organized labor under the CIO and within organizations such as the National Urban League, the Southern Regional Council, and the Southern Conference for Human Welfare. Interracialism in these institutions helped bring together black and white liberal intellectuals and labor leaders throughout the South. For working-class southerners, the CIO, through the Highlander School, made tremendous efforts to educate workers about the economic benefits of interracial cooperation and unity in the labor movement. At the local level, however, biracial unity within the CIO's industrial unions often became an accommodation between racialized factions.

Southern CIO unions representing workers in steel, oil, aircraft, autos, and shipbuilding, where white majorities ruled, generally made white workers' concerns a priority. Yet where the CIO and the AFL represented workers in maritime shipping, railroads, laundry, trucking, and laboring, where black majority unions predominated, such institutions provided an environment conducive to serving black economic and political aspirations. In the postwar urban South, African Americans continued, as they had throughout the war and before, to fight for political and economic equality largely within the black church and black-led unions such as laborers, Pullman porters, laundry, railroad and dock workers, teamsters, warehouse, and transport workers.[12] Out of this institutional and occupational segregation, majority black AFL and CIO unions emerged at the center of voter registration and labor-organizing drives in 1946.

During the war the organizing of southern laundry workers, the majority of whom were female, illustrated the growing presence of organized labor in both low-wage industries and black urban communities. In Memphis in 1943 and 1944, local Urban League executive secretary Ben Bell Jr., a former organizer for AFL tobacco workers, attempted to organize laundry workers in that city. His aggressive tactics offended Memphis's city leaders and the Edward Crump political machine, however, and eventually led to Bell's resignation from the Memphis Urban League.[13]

In contrast to the Memphis experience, in 1943 the Atlanta Urban League (AUL), with the support of the AFL Laundry Workers International, successfully coordinated a laundry strike that gave some three thousand workers wage raises up to fifty cents per hour, paid vacations, and a fifty-hour work week. Earlier that year, the AUL made concerted efforts to fuse ties with organized labor and black churches. After an AUL-sponsored discussion on organized labor revealed a "lack of education and coordinated leadership among Negro workers," the AUL stepped up its commitment to organizing Atlanta's black industrial workers. Although the AUL's industrial relations secretary, Amos Ryce, lamented the "apathy of workers" and the "aloofness of church leaders," the AUL did organize laundry workers while also appealing to the AFL and CIO to hire black organizers.[14]

In New Orleans during Operation Dixie, Ernest Wright, as an organizer for the Amalgamated Clothing Workers of America (ACWA-CIO) Local 389, made a concerted but unsuccessful attempt to unseat the black-led AFL laundry workers union. The fact that Wright, a major leader in voter registration, threatened to organize the city's black laundry workers under the CIO must have unnerved the city's AFL and political establishment.[15] William Spooner, an organizer for ILWU Local 207 in New Orleans, likewise became active in mobilizing African Americans in New Orleans for voter registration under the CIO-PAC campaign of 1944. Together, Wright and Spooner were committed leaders of the PDL's voter registration movement in the New Orleans area. Despite New Orleans CIO director Fred Pieper's refusal to sanction any registration of some fifteen thousand black union members in 1944, Wright and Raymond Tillman of Transport Workers Union CIO Local 206 continued efforts to register voters throughout 1945 and 1946 through the CIO-PAC.[16]

Segregated AFL union leaders also participated actively in the New Orleans voter registration movement. Moses Turner, head of the segregated Brotherhood of Railway and Carmen AFL Local 200, emerged as an influential organizer within the PDL. A respected regional labor leader, Turner encouraged voter registration in the black community while networking among AFL black labor networks throughout the South. Preceding the 1946 midterm election, International Longshoremen's Association (ILA) Local 1419, one of the largest black locals in the nation with some 3,500 members, also organized its members for registration through the PAC system.[17]

Despite their institutional differences, after 1943 the more progressive leaders of black AFL and CIO unions allied within the PDL to make it one of the most organized and visible church-labor coalitions in the southern voter registration movement. This cooperation across institutional lines illustrates that black labor leaders at the local level were able to use the labor movement as a vehicle for politicizing the black working class. Thus, while such local organizers lacked a voice in national CIO and AFL affairs on racial equality, they nevertheless exploited their labor institutions to mobilize black workers in search of economic equality and voting rights.[18]

As the voter registration movement spread across the South during the summer of 1946, black registered voters totaled over 23,000 in Alabama and over 35,000 in Florida, including over 12,000 new voters in Jacksonville. Atlanta led the urban South in black voters by registering nearly 24,000 new voters under a well-coordinated effort among the NAACP, the Urban League, churches, and the CIO-PAC. Over 10,000 black voters registered in Macon, while over 5,000 registered in Savannah. One report even indicated that over 100,000 African Americans had voted in Georgia's July primary.[19]

In comparison to Atlanta, New Orleans lagged in voter registration numbers in 1946. Despite the efforts of the PDL, the CIO- and AFL-PACs, and the local NAACP to mobilize black voters, only 4,822 out of a general population of 200,000 African Americans had successfully registered for the November 1946 election.[20] New Orleans's meager 5,000 registrants for the 1946 election paled in comparison to Atlanta's 24,000. Yet, two years later, in 1948, NUL southern field office investigator William Valentine reported 12,000 and perhaps even 20,000 registered African Americans in New Orleans. Valentine claimed that the exact number was not divulged because "it is not considered desirable that the Negroes know their voting strength."[21] Of the voters in New Orleans who did register in 1946, the largest concentration came from the outer black wards with a mix of middle and working classes. The seventh ward, the center of the Creole middle class and elite, led with 644 voters, while the three uptown wards (eleventh, twelfth, and thirteenth) combined for a total of over 1,500. The ninth ward, a largely working-class neighborhood on the industrial canal, registered 324 voters.[22]

The voting of African Americans in southern primaries largely occurred without violence. As Carter Wesley observed after the Texas primary in August 1946, "The Negroes' right to vote in the primary is now generally accepted" and, therefore, "the Texas vote had come of age."[23] Registered African Americans generally voted without interference at the polls. However, conservative white registrars continued to make registration difficult in large cities such as New Orleans, Birmingham, and Atlanta. The *Louisiana Weekly* complained in 1946 that four veterans were denied the vote after the registrar allegedly asked them arbitrary questions on the exam. In Birmingham, veterans denied the vote marched through the streets of the city protesting the denial of democracy at home. In Atlanta in July 1945, the registrars barred several black elites, including Ira De A. Reid and other Atlanta University faculty members.[24]

The Postwar Jobs Movement Struggles

The immediacy of the voter registration issue for urban southern African Americans in 1945 and 1946 prompted the southern Urban League affiliates' participation in the movement. This policy shift reflected the growing importance the voting rights movement assumed as the jobs movement took a back seat. Historically, the Urban League avoided overt political activism and focused largely on social welfare and industrial relations through World War II. The southern regional office sought to influence the white community to accept the objectives of the NUL, namely, improving health, education, and employment opportunities for southern African Americans.[25] This somewhat apolitical strategy existed at the local level until 1945 because most Urban League affiliates received funding from their local Community Chest, which was often dominated by conservative white elites who avoided funding any organization with obvious political activities as a matter of policy. Nevertheless, in 1945 southern Urban League affiliates in New Orleans and Atlanta began campaigns to actively register African American voters.

Lester Granger questioned in 1946 the political role of the NUL at the local level. In April, Grady Farley, the industrial secretary for the New Orleans Urban League (NOUL), responded to Granger's inquiry about local southern affiliates' plans to register voters. According to Farley, in the summer of 1945 the NOUL wanted to open a registration school, like the NAACP. However, the local Community Chest director did not favor the NOUL conducting such an institution because he "feared that such a procedure would affect some of the large white donors making their chest contributions." At the same time, the NOUL board of directors and Mrs. Joseph Friend, president of the board and a local white liberal, became furious at the Community Chest's stance on the issue. The NOUL executive committee decided that the constitution of the Community Chest prohibited any interference with the policies or programs of any of its agencies. Together, the board "favored registration and voter education," and Farley stood "ready to launch a project for the distribution of registration and voting educational material, and to encourage voting in every way."[26]

In Atlanta, the NUL southern regional director, Nelson Jackson, also responded to Lester Granger's questions regarding the role of the NUL in voter registration. As Jackson informed Granger, the AUL was "working very close with this problem" and had "set up plans for getting every Negro registered in the city." Most encouraging to Jackson was the existence of a "super organization" composed of Democrats, Republicans, the NAACP, and others organizing the city into wards, precincts, census tracts, and blocks. As Jackson admitted coyly to Granger, "Of course the crackers are frantically discussing methods of saving the white primary." Because Atlanta's most powerful white leaders supported the AUL's voter agenda, the Atlanta Community Chest, despite these white fears, did not object to the registration program.[27]

The Tampa Urban League (TUL) affiliate also participated in the voter education and registration movement. The TUL was in large part influenced by its president, Edgar Ray, the white liberal editor of the *Tampa Daily Times* and a protégé of Louisville journalist Mark Ethridge. Under Ray's leadership after the war, the TUL secured a Negro USES office, and African Americans were hired on the Tampa police force. Under his influence, the Don Thompson Vocational High School continued operating after the war. Ray also lobbied the local Community Chest to appoint its first black member. However, in the process he discovered that the conservative Community Chest maintained what he called a "passive resistance" toward the growth of the TUL. In Ray's opinion, there was "too much vested interests and old-line Southern thinking on the Chest Board." Moreover, both the trustees and the executive had been fearful of "giving the Urban League a primary place of importance in the community."[28] As the TUL discovered, local conservative control of Community Chest budget allocation in the postwar period often presented the greatest barrier to advancement for southern Urban League agendas and activities.

In other southern cities, the Urban League faced considerable obstacles in establishing local affiliates, largely because local white elites resisted the creation of liberal African American organizations. Beginning in 1943, the NUL made a concerted effort to expand into the Southwest, specifically into Houston, Dallas, and Fort Worth as well as southern cities such as Birmingham, Jacksonville, and Charleston. William Bell enthused that Houston, "while it is a southern city, . . . lacks some of the provincial features characteristic of some of the cities in the Deep South." Citing the origins of the white primary fight with *Smith v. Allwright* within the state, Bell further contended that "Texas still operates under the spirit of the frontier and has the courage to take great strides forward." Therefore, the state and its larger cities held some potential for Urban League progress.[29]

White conservatives in Texas, however, largely objected to the establishment of local NUL affiliates. By 1946, Fort Worth had received an Urban League charter, while the effort in Houston failed. In Dallas, A. Maceo Smith, the progressive leader of the Dallas Negro Chamber of Commerce, served as local coordinator between the NUL and the Dallas Community

Chest, which remained wary of the liberal role and influence that an Urban League affiliate would bring to Dallas. During the final negotiations in July 1946, Smith assured conservative whites on the Community Chest that the Urban League's activities would not include "a possibility of political intrigue." Smith also informed Nelson Jackson that some white conservatives on the Chest were "of the opinion that the urban league was dominated by northern influences and would be a haven for the distribution of CIO and communist propaganda." In another meeting with Smith, white businessmen on the Chest's executive committee also feared that a Dallas Urban League would "cause a considerable amount of trouble and at the same time would cause Negroes to demand certain rights which they hitherto had not enjoyed."[30]

After receiving a report from Smith that compared various Urban League affiliates' roles, accomplishments, and constitutions throughout the United States, the Dallas Community Chest vetoed the establishment of the Dallas Urban League in December 1946.[31] Jackson blamed the failure in part on Smith's strategies, informing Lester Granger that he had "asked Maceo time and time again" to work very closely with "the powers that be" in the southern field office to insure the establishment of a Dallas Urban League. Smith, however, sought to keep the field office at arm's length, fearing that Jackson's presence would offend local conservatives. In Jackson's opinion, Smith's strategy had backfired.[32]

Nelson Jackson nevertheless understood the effects of reactionary politics in the cold war South. In a letter to Cenoria Johnson, executive secretary of the new Fort Worth Urban League, Jackson observed that "the whole field of race relations [was] going through a 'tightening up' period." Agreeing with Jackson, Johnson responded by claiming that "seemingly, there is a wave of resistance in many areas." Not only did Johnson feel obstruction "in the matter of race relations," but she also observed "a tenacious effort on the part of community leaders to hold everything in its place." Johnson further noticed that conservative whites were "strongly resisting the union movement in Fort Worth and their ultimate desire is to maintain 'status quo.'" Nevertheless, Johnson persisted and ultimately viewed such trends as a challenge to overcome.[33]

Throughout the entire South, regional and local NUL administrators struggled with the conservative political and racial climate in their efforts to maintain and expand wartime economic and social gains. During the spring of 1945, William Bell, in his last month as southern regional director for the NUL, expressed some pessimism about the future of Urban League growth in the South. As he wrote to Ruby Yearwood at New York headquarters, the NUL's recent failure to establish community relations projects in Houston, Oklahoma City, Charleston, Jacksonville, and Birmingham did not bode well for the postwar NUL agenda.[34] Indeed, by 1948, many southern affiliates had weakened considerably since the active days of the wartime fair employment and industrial integration movements. In the two years since V-J Day, limited budgets under conservative Community Chests had handicapped southern Urban League activities dramatically. Of the seven affiliates in the South in 1948, only Atlanta and Richmond maintained industrial secretaries.[35]

The sudden weakening of the New Orleans Urban League from 1946 to 1948 represented the most dramatic turnaround in the southern jobs movement. At the beginning of the war the New Orleans Urban League under Clarence Laws and the Atlanta Urban League under William Bell emerged as the two strongest and most active regional industrial relations forces. In early 1943, when Clarence Laws served in the armed forces, his able successor, Grady Farley, had coordinated and overseen the integration of the Convair and Delta Shipyards. Laws again assumed his role as New Orleans Urban League executive secretary when he returned in 1946. As a veteran, Laws received the Bronze Star from the army and a formal congratulations from "Chep" Morrison, the newly elected reformist mayor and a war veteran himself.[36] Yet by November 1946, coinciding with the veto of the Dallas Urban League and Republican electoral victories, Laws resigned as industrial secretary, saying he was "'fed up' trying to do an impossible job with little or no outside assistance." Nelson Jackson and Ed Ray, president of the Tampa Urban League, sought in vain to remove New Orleans Community Chest restrictions on fund raising for the NOUL in order to raise money for an additional staff person.[37] Yet with Laws's successor, Alvin Jones, the NOUL struggled to maintain basic services throughout 1947 and 1948.

The decline of the NOUL did not go unnoticed among national black activists. The *Pittsburgh Courier* in July 1948 addressed what it identified as "some insidious problem within the ranks of the New Orleans Urban League." According to the paper, Alvin Jones, who was appointed executive secretary in 1946, felt "that his views in favor of equal rights for Negroes [were] not held in esteem by key board members."[38] As Ernest Wright asked at the time, "What is wrong with the New Orleans Urban League?" Arguing that "certainly, there is a need for an Urban League in New Orleans," Wright suggested that NOUL board members who did not approve of Alvin Jones and the Urban League's objectives should resign and "permit another who is in sympathy with the objectives to serve."[39] The NUL southern field office conducted an investigation that revealed Alvin Jones was the source of the controversy, in spite of accusations against the board.

Southern NUL field investigator William Valentine visited New Orleans to examine personally the NOUL's troubles. Citing obvious friction between Jones and the board, Valentine observed that the board's attitude "stemmed from the executive's inactivity, un-cooperativeness, untruthfulness, and beligerant [sic] resistance to board pressures to get something done." Labeling Jones's demeanor as resistant, dilatory, and lethargic while carrying "a constant chip on his shoulder," Valentine further argued that Jones had a "very unfortunate personality" and seemed to make enemies on "every occasion" and "in purely social relationships." In conferring with board members, Valentine agreed with them that Jones should resign "in order to break the long period of silence and inactivity on the local League's part."[40]

In the field of NOUL industrial relations, William Valentine observed that in 1947 and 1948, Alvin Jones had conducted only "a half-dozen placements and random visits to a handful of employers" in New Orleans. Unfortunately for southern urban African Americans seeking industrial opportunity, the NOUL's pitiful industrial relations program reflected the overall state of the National Urban League's industrial relations in the urban South. Jones's inactivity combined with white business elite's apathy toward black gains failed to insure any black employment opportunities in the postwar era.

During his visit, Valentine generally agreed with various New Orleans industrial establishments' criticism of unskilled black industrial workers. "Poor work habits on the part of Negro workers in many places throughout the city," Valentine argued, imposed "a threat [to] the security of jobs." The Lane Cotton Mills had a capacity of 2,400 and was one of the biggest mills in the South. However, management had trouble finding enough workers to operate full shifts. As Valentine characterized the problem, the workers were "predominantly rural people, former farm laborers, who haven't the manual dexterity required for spinning and weaving operations." As a result, their "sloppy work habits" consistently frustrated Lane's management.[41]

William Valentine's condescension toward the rural and seasonal textile workers with poor work habits reflects some of the cultural gulf between Urban League officials and the grassroots workers in these postwar years. This distancing of low-wage workers and the Urban League was only one of many problems besetting the jobs movement, however. The biggest problem was the lack of manufacturing jobs that provided economic mobility. With three hundred African Americans out of a total workforce of sixteen hundred, the Lane Cotton Mills employed in 1948 the largest number of black workers for one operation in New Orleans. According to William Valentine, Lane Mills utilized African Americans in some skilled positions and therefore offered upward mobility to a few persons. However, in shipbuilding, one of New Orleans's principal postwar industries, Todd-Johnson Dry Docks and Avondale Marine Ways did not use skilled black workers, while Higgins Industries, which had reverted to pleasure craft production after the war, employed only a few black carpenters.

In investigating the key role of job placement in New Orleans, Valentine visited the New Orleans LSES office and discovered to his surprise that the current district supervisor, a Mr. Thames, had been a WMC minority division chief during the war and was sympathetic to "the UL philosophy and approach." Thames boasted that the Louisiana SES "handled a load of 15,000 Negroes per month" and that the state agency "placed a number of Negroes in the building trades due to a shortage of skilled mechanics and the waiving of union qualifications." The LSES also claimed that black workers had cornered the supply of carpenters, bricklayers, and plasterers and that the agency placed a large number of truck drivers and helpers and some skilled and unskilled factory help.[42]

In New Orleans, black workers in longshore work and the building trades and teamsters held their ground reasonably well after the war. Labor unions in these occupations continued to politicize their members through the election of representatives who served on local, state, and regional union councils. In the case of the ILA Local 1419, for example, the 3,200-member union played an important role in mobilizing black workers for voter registration into the 1950s.[43] Yet the manufacturing jobs in shipbuilding did not open to black workers until the 1960s. Indeed, the failure of the city to hold on to its wartime industrial gains, such as the Delta Shipyards and the Convair aircraft plant, certainly limited employment prospects for African Americans in the New Orleans area. The city's inability to manage manpower effectively during the war led many branch industries to perceive that New Orleans's labor market was not conducive to large-scale manufacturing. Ironically, Higgins Industries, with one of the city's most progressive management styles, closed in 1959 after suffering from poor administration and financial difficulties after the war.[44] As George Decket of the New Orleans Association of Commerce admitted to William Valentine in 1948, because New Orleans was not "an industrial city," it would "probably always maintain a degree of unemployment."[45]

In contrast to the older coastal ports such as New Orleans, Mobile, and Charleston, newer cities such as Atlanta, Dallas, Fort Worth, and Houston successfully maintained and even expanded wartime manufacturing plants after the war. Much of the postwar industrial expansion occurred in labor markets where a surplus existed and where the city had managed local manpower resources effectively during the war. By the fall of 1945, the *Manufacturers' Record* foresaw postwar growth in textiles, tobacco manufacture, rubber products, iron and steel, paper and allied products, food and kindred products, and apparel manufacturing. As southern cities reconverted their wartime production, this new wave of growth reflected national corporate concerns' hopes of capitalizing on expanded southern consumer markets, a return of the South's surplus labor market, and southern states' political support of antilabor legislation.

Atlanta, a regional financial center, emerged after the war as a manufacturing center for expanding Deep South markets, in part because of the Federal Reserve Bank that had been located in the city during the 1930s. In October 1945, Frank K. Shaw, secretary of the Atlanta Industrial Bureau, reported that seventy industrial firms were poised to expand, spending a total of $71 million in construction, and another 119 firms were "actively considering" the greater Atlanta area as a site for establishing businesses. In 1946, the city witnessed assembly plant expansions at Ford and GM, while several corporations, including Owens-Illinois Glass, E. I. Du Pont, Sherwin-Williams, and Kraft Foods, planned new plants in the area. In Savannah, Union Bag and Paper expanded its facilities, while in Macon, the Southern Newspaper Publishers Association planned an enormous newsprint mill in the area. As the *Manufacturers' Record* predicted, "labor-starved retail and service establishments of textile and lumber" would absorb "displaced war veterans."[46]

In the postwar climate of growth, the Atlanta Urban League continued to pressure industrial plants to integrate black workers in all classifications. Nelson Jackson and AUL industrial secretary Robert Thompson visited the Ford and General Motors assembly plants to negotiate upgrading for black workers. GM, under contract with the UAW, refused to upgrade black workers despite Ford's commitment to hiring skilled black labor. At the old Bell bomber plant, taken over by Lockheed in 1951, the International Association of Machinists (IAM-AFL) also limited any upgrading opportunities for black workers until the early 1960s.[47]

After the death of the FEPC, the Atlanta Urban League continued to manage industrial relations within the Gate City. Nevertheless, the Georgia SES, under state labor commissioner Ben Huiet, provided plenty of challenges for the AUL. Huiet opposed hiring African American employees at the Georgia

SES and writing a nondiscrimination clause in the Georgia SES placement service guidelines. The AUL had negotiated successfully in 1945 for a separate Negro USES office with its own personnel staff and management to better serve veterans and workers. Eugene Talmadge's return as governor, however, threatened this important gain. Ben Huiet's refusal to meet with the AUL on the issue illustrated the Georgia Department of Labor's apathy and even antagonism toward the employment concerns of local black workers.[48]

As they had before the war, in the postwar era State Employment Services and Unemployment Compensation offices used their agencies to deny workers unemployment benefits and thus bolster a surplus labor market to the benefit of employers seeking low-wage labor. For example, Ben Huiet announced in September 1945 that veterans who returned to sharecropping were ineligible for readjustment allowances under the Veterans Administration. That same month in Alabama, the state Department of Industrial Relations disqualified workers for unemployment compensation benefits because the workers refused to take low-paying jobs. In one publicized case, the Unemployment Compensation office disqualified an African American woman who had never worked below fifty cents an hour because she refused to take a job at thirty cents an hour. According to the CIO, which protested the agency's policy, the woman would have made only sixty dollars a month. While the union symbolically supported the woman and other disqualified persons in their cause, the tenor of the Alabama Department of Industrial Relations's policy indicated a return to a prewar labor market.[49]

In response to these unsettling developments, Nelson Jackson urged greater action in industrial relations for the Urban League's southern field office throughout 1947 and 1948. As Jackson observed, "New industries are moving south," and the "efforts to integrate Negroes into southern industries coming south" were dependent on NUL industrial secretaries. Nelson urged an expansion of these positions in Memphis and New Orleans.[50] By September, his unfulfilled plans had prompted him to continue lobbying for greater industrial relations from the Urban League's southern field office. Citing a recent positive meeting with a manufacturer's representative in Atlanta, Jackson continued to express hope that "the League program could be sold to industry." However, even he conceded that "there has been very little done with the Negro labor supply in terms of attempting to utilize the skills to their fullest" in Atlanta's industries.[51]

The postwar years in Dallas and Fort Worth witnessed tremendous growth in the military aerospace, petroleum, and finance industries that fueled the economies and the growth of the white middle class. Black workers, however, did not see a return of the great wartime gains in the aircraft and aerospace industry until the modern civil rights movement. In the postwar southern auto industry, the United Auto Workers (UAW-CIO) in Dallas (as in Memphis and Atlanta) provided black workers with economic security while ignoring the national UAW's nondiscrimination policies. Black and Latino workers found greater employment opportunities in the meatpacking industry rather than the white-dominated auto industry.[52]

Under the Packing House Workers Organizing Committee (PWOC-CIO) in Fort Worth, black and Latino workers, with significant support from PWOC's progressive Chicago office, mobilized successfully after the war to end Jim Crow in area plants operated by Swift and Armour. White workers, who once held a majority, lost out to an emerging bloc of motivated black and Chicano workers. Many of these more aggressive postwar workers were military veterans whose wartime experience had altered their views about the place of black workers in southern society. As war veteran and labor leader Eddie Humphrey recalled, "Being in that type of a war, and what we were fighting for . . . when I came back, I just couldn't see myself being segregated and discriminated against the way we were." Remarkably, under black and Latino leadership, PWOC provided minority workers in the Fort Worth area social equality, economic security, and advancement.[53]

In many of the largest southern manufacturing centers, the lack of an NUL industrial relations program certainly limited the postwar economic advancement of urban African Americans. In older manufacturing centers like Birmingham, the local Community Chest refused to consider the establishment of a Birmingham Urban League (BUL). The city's conservative climate did not deter local liberals. Robert Durr, the editor of the *Birmingham Weekly Review*, led a local effort to establish a BUL. Like Maceo Smith in Dallas, he questioned the success of any social agency in Birmingham that had an "allegiance to any outside group." In December, the agenda continued as Dr. Henry L. Edmonds, director of the Loveman, Joseph and Loeb Department Store, agreed to serve and organize a board. By 1950, however, the majority of members on the Birmingham Community Chest board made it clear that they opposed any organization that was interracial in nature.[54]

As the Urban League's southern director, Nelson Jackson, informed Lester Granger, the failure to establish an affiliate in Birmingham illustrated the weak position that the League held in overcoming conservative opposition to "outsiders" and "communists" in one of the South's most industrialized urban centers. Alabama had voted heavily Dixiecrat in the 1948 election "in an attempt to maintain the status quo." Race relations in Birmingham, according to Jackson, were "traditionally paternalistic" on the part of whites, with "an expected subservience on the part of the Negro." In these postwar years, Birmingham's black citizens watched with alarm the violence and brutality of Bull Connor's police department. When local African Americans complained to the governor, city commissioners, congressmen, and the attorney general, Bull Connor labeled the petition "a move by a communist front organization."[55]

In the face of conservative opposition, Birmingham African Americans persisted in their struggle for civil rights, especially in the steel industry, where black workers continued in the postwar years to struggle for advancement within the United Steel Workers of America (USWA-CIO). During the cold war years, black and white workers united with national union representatives in the battle to bring Birmingham's steel wages and classifications in line with northern steel plants. Like other CIO affiliates in the South, however, the USWA, despite its rhetorical commitment to antidiscrimination, remained reluctant to push for civil rights gains for fear of alienating its white members. As Bruce Nelson has argued, the CIO in these years chose not to allow civil rights concerns to jeopardize the institutional survival of their organization.[56]

The expansion in steel, petrochemical, and refining industries made the Texas and Louisiana Gulf Coast one of the South's largest industrial centers. In Houston, the Urban League's southern field office attempted to establish a community relations project during the war to gain a foothold. Yet the city remained without an Urban League throughout the 1940s and early 1950s. As had African Americans in the Birmingham and Atlanta steel industries, black and Latino workers seeking economic opportunities in the Texas steel and oil industries worked within the established channels of segregated organized labor institutions. At Hughes Tool and Sheffield Steel, two of Houston's largest employers, the Independent Metal Workers (IMW) union and the USWA represented black workers under Jim Crow wage classifications. Black and Latino workers also encountered in the oil and petrochemical industry a segregated labor market that, combined with a conservative leadership in the Oil Worker International Union (OWIU-CIO), limited upward mobility. Consequently, these minority workers in southern coastal cities, including Houston, Galveston, New Orleans, Mobile, and Savannah, continued to find their greatest political labor strength in the railway, longshore, teamsters, and building trades AFL unions in which black concerns found a voice and national representation.[57]

The Failed Promise of Separate and Equal

As rising wages brought the South into the American economic mainstream after the war, black workers found that the maintenance of Jim Crow in the labor movement, in the southern wage structure, and on the shop floor reflected the overall failed promise of economic equality. With this failure, the growing militancy among black veterans and war workers would lead directly to the racial conflicts of the 1950s and 1960s. Working-class whites naturally defended their privileges in the labor marketplace and in society at large during this period. As journalist Agnes Meyer observed in 1944, "much of the white man's cruelty, callousness and injustice toward the Negro are due to the fact that he, himself, does not feel secure in the precarious, competitive world."[58]

As long as white workers felt economically insecure in the South, they generally embraced segregation in the workplace because it provided security. To be certain, the existence of white workers in black majority CIO unions during these years represented a major advance for interracial unionism in the South. And in the postwar years, interracialism would exist within organized labor, local Urban Leagues, and liberal organizations such as the Southern Conference for Human Welfare and the Southern Regional Council. Yet the decline of civil rights as an issue within the CIO and organized labor generally after the war signified to African American workers that the majority of white labor leaders could afford to ignore black demands for equal representation, the elimination of Jim Crow, and wage equality overall.

In the immediate postwar years, the failure of Operation Dixie symbolized this overall conservative swing in labor and race relations. In this move to the right, historians often point to Operation Dixie leader Van Bittner's role in opposing leftist and racially progressive groups such as the Southern Conference and the Highlander School. Under Bittner's leadership, Operation Dixie essentially avoided the issue of racial equality and nondiscrimination and openly Red-baited leftist CIO organizers and sympathizers who were often proponents of racial equality. This general organizing environment signaled to African Americans that no real differences existed between the AFL segregationist policies and those of the postwar CIO. While Bittner and national CIO organizing director Alan Haywood undoubtedly sought to appeal to conservative whites in the South, the Red-baiting strategy also reflected the decline of the Left within the CIO during these early cold war years.[59]

The passage of the Taft–Hartley Act and the sanctioning of the anti-Communism pledge in unions after 1946 drove out many leftist organizers who prioritized racial equality in the labor movement. At the same time, numerous western and southern states banned the closed shop, while arbitration court costs over contract negotiations drained the weak budgets of many unions.[60] In the South and Southwest, the effects of antilabor legislation were apparent in the eventual complete disappearance or decline of liberal CIO unions, including the ILWU and UCAPAWA. In 1946, for example, the ILWU eventually withdrew altogether from its tentative gains in Texas, Louisiana, Mississippi, Tennessee, and Virginia as it retrenched in its main base of political power on the Pacific Coast. UCAPAWA (renamed the Food, Tobacco, Agricultural and Allied Workers) also suffered setbacks in the postwar South. In one of the union's biggest blows, Local 22 in Winston-Salem, North Carolina, where the union had made its greatest gains in the South among some eight thousand black tobacco workers, was essentially neutralized when companies automated stemming operations and laid off close to seven hundred workers.[61]

In these years the southern labor movement lost most of the liberal gains made during the war, while the racial caste system remained intact on the shop floor and in wage divisions. Overall, this preservation of a segregated labor market in the South kept wages low in the competitive global labor market and thereby helped to lure new branch industries to the region with the promise of low production costs.[62] Under the South's racialized occupational structure, unions focused on securing wage concessions that would move the southern labor market into the American economic mainstream. Despite the overall maintenance of a segregated labor market, southern industrial workers experienced important economic gains as wage differentials based on region and race gradually became less common after the war.[63]

Even so, as southern workers organized, employers consistently sought cheaper means of production by gradually closing southern urban plants and moving operations off-shore or into rural areas in industries such as sugar refining, textiles, meatpacking, tobacco processing, and garment manufacturing.[64] Other industries that remained unionized such as longshore and woodwork also succumbed to mechanization. All along the Atlantic, Gulf, and Pacific Coasts, shipping lines and dock boards switched to containers and thereby eliminated thousands of jobs for African Americans in the port cities of the South, East, and West.

For rural southern families, opportunities for economic advancement remained limited in the postwar years. In some rural areas, the cold war led to a prolonged life for some federal military bases and defense-related industries such as munitions plants and ordnance depots. In these small towns and rural communities, southerners held jobs in the federal public sector and hence gained some economic security. Even for white women and African Americans, the expanded wartime presence of federal military facilities such as munitions depots and airbases provided important new economic opportunities into the postwar years. Yet well-paying rural jobs were hard to come by as industries and especially agriculture became more mechanized and farmworkers failed to gain the same bargaining rights as workers in urban manufacturing industries.[65]

Rural workers and their families therefore remained on the lowest rungs of the American occupational ladder. With agricultural commercialization and the accompanying large-scale mechanization and displacement of farmworkers, state and small-town economic boosters throughout the Cotton Belt actively sought industrial manufacturing to offset the rapid decline of farm employment. Yet the arrival of low-wage rural industries such as garments and textiles, food processing, and raw material refining offered only limited economic advancement for rural southerners. Because of the overall lack of industrial manufacturing opportunities for rural black and Latino farmworkers, the 1940s and 1950s witnessed the peak of out-migration to the urban centers of the South, the West, and the North as workers continued to seek economic advancement through geographic mobility.

Throughout the early cold war years, black workers certainly entered southern industries and organized labor, even as upward mobility under the segregated labor market proved difficult for most. As Bruce Schulman argues, African Americans remained largely in the shadow of the Sunbelt.[66] While many black southerners generally had difficulty achieving occupational mobility, black industrial workers continued to use labor institutions to gain economic equality as they had done during the war. As middle-class black leaders focused on the dismantling of social segregation in the 1950s, the black workers who chose to remain in the South increasingly combined the NAACP's segregation battle with their own quest for economic equality. Southern migrants in the North and West also played a key role in this battle to insure equality and an end to discrimination on the shop floors of industries and within organized labor.[67]

After the immediate postwar years, when conservatives battled the fair employment and organized labor movements with a renewed enthusiasm, African American labor and civil rights activists responded by recommitting themselves to the battle for equality in the workplace and increasingly within society at large. The formation of the National Negro Labor Congress (NNLC) in 1950 signaled a renewed spirit in this national battle for black labor and social equality. Importantly, the NNLC's agenda in the early 1950s fore-shadowed the modern civil rights movement's goal of dismantling social seg-regation, yet it did so in the context of the fight for economic equality and la-bor rights. In this reinvigorated labor and civil rights movement, southern labor activists played key roles. It was no accident that the NNLC's southern delegates' local efforts to mobilize for labor and social progress drew largely from the institutional alliances that had emerged so prominently during the war. For example, delegate Asbury Howard, regional director of the Mine, Mill, and Smelter Workers for Alabama and Mississippi and a native of Bessemer, Alabama, was a clerk of the Starlight Baptist Church, a member of the Masons, and vice-president of the Bessemer NAACP. Likewise, Estelle Holloway, who represented tobacco workers from North Carolina, was an ac-tive member of the St. James Baptist Church and her local NAACP as well as a charter member of the Tri-State Negro Labor Council.[68]

As the National Negro Labor Congress's founding reflected a renewed commitment to labor and civil rights among African American labor activists, the Supreme Court's rulings on racial equality in the workplace during the early 1950s reflected a liberal shift in legal opinion that would later emerge prominently in *Brown v. Board of Education*.[69] And, with the eventual estab-lishment of President John Kennedy's Equal Employment Opportunity Commission in 1961, the federal government emerged once again to actively enforce industrial integration, just as the FEPC had done during World War II.[70] Thus, as segregation fell in public accommodations, black workers in the South (and throughout the nation) benefited from the desegregation of the industrial labor market and the decline of Jim Crow on the shop floor.

Most historians agree that the modern civil rights movement of the late 1950s and early 1960s emerged largely as a church- and student-based effort to fight social inequality by challenging Jim Crow. Yet the roles and ideologies of working-class African Americans in the black church after the war reveal a continuous campaign for economic equality that bridged the wartime and modern civil rights eras. Recently, Judith Stein has argued that African American workers after the war protested job barriers to obtain more income, but not because they wanted to work with white men. Specifically, she writes that "postwar movements fighting discrimination and seeking economic equality and justice have attempted to improve black lives, not to make ex-plicit statements on racial associations."[71] For black workers emerging from the jobs movement of World War II, the conservative political and racial cli-mate of the postwar South did not permit an open assault on social segrega-tion. Nevertheless, the legacy of the civil rights gains as well as the unprecedented economic advancement achieved during the war certainly helped to raise expectations among many southern African Americans for a better life. For this reason, black southerners after the war continued to seek economic opportunity and, to some degree, social equality by migrating outside of the South and by supporting the NAACP, the church, and organized labor within the South.

Notes

Introduction

1. Meyer, *Journey through Chaos*, 373–74.
2. Lange and Taylor, *An American Exodus;* Agee and Evans, *Let Us Now Praise Famous Men;* Shindo, *Dust Bowl Migrants.*

The geographic terms *South* and *Southwest* are used throughout this book. However, there is no precise designation of where one region begins and the other ends. Certainly, one may be inclined to differentiate the regions based on environmental or demographic characteristics. In this respect, then, the drier climate, open spaces, and large Hispanic population of Central Texas and all points west to southern California would distinguish the Southwest as a region from the area that stretches from East Texas to Virginia, which is more humid and heavily timbered and has a large African American population. Yet, as this work makes clear, despite the environmental and demographic differences between the South and the Southwest, both regions also shared much in common. The rural areas in both regions were largely dependent on a cotton economy during the 1940s, hence, the term *Cotton Belt.* Rural employers in both regions (the Cotton Belt) enjoyed a surplus labor market that kept wages low and organized labor activity to a minimum. Employers in both regions also maintained a rather strict racial caste system that distinguished whites from Mexicans and African Americans through occupational classification and wage structure.

3. Tindall, *The Emergence of the New South.* Tindall was perhaps the first U.S. historian to examine comprehensively the war's impact on the South. Historians have generally agreed with Tindall's overall emphasis on the war's transformative effect on the region. See, for example, Grantham, *The South in Modern America;* Bartley, *The New South;* and McMillen, ed., *Remaking Dixie.*

4. Sosna, "More Important"; Cobb, "World War II and the Mind of the Modern South."

5. Cobb, "Beyond Planters and Industrialists," 45–68; Cobb, *The Selling of the South.*

6. For a characterization of the war as a second New Deal, see Cobb, "World War II and the Mind of the Modern South," 9. For Daniel's characterization of the New Deal in the South, see Daniel, "The New Deal and Southern Agriculture"; Daniel, *Breaking the Land;* Schulman, *From Cotton Belt to Sunbelt.*

7. Works that focus on rural workers include the following: Woodruff, "Pick or Fight"; Woodruff, "Mississippi Delta Planters"; Daniel, "Going among Strangers"; Hahamovitch, *The Fruits of Their Labor.* The following works concentrate on urban workers: Honey, *Southern Labor and Black Civil Rights;* Obadele-Starks, "Black Labor"; Obadele-Starks, *Black Unionism;* Korstad and Lichtenstein, "Opportunities Found and Lost"; Nelson, "Organized Labor"; Zamora, "The Failed Promise"; Halpern and Horowitz, *Meatpackers;* Johnson, *The Second Gold Rush;* Lemke-Santangelo, *Abiding Courage;* Phillips, *Alabama North.*

8. Finkle, "The Conservative Aims"; Takaki, *Double Victory.*

9. Reed, *Seedtime;* Reed, "The FEPC and Federal Agencies"; Reed, "The FEPC, the Black Worker, and the Southern Shipyards"; Zamora, "The Failed Promise"; Obadele-Starks, *Black Unionism,* 112–28; Honey, *Southern Labor and Black Civil Rights.*

10. Kryder, *Divided Arsenal.*

11. Lange and Taylor, *An American Exodus;* Anderson, *Men on the Move;* Volanto, "Burying White Gold"; Whayne, *New Plantation South;* Seavoy, *The American Peasantry;* Weber, *Dark Sweat;* Gregory, *American Exodus;* Kirby, *Rural Worlds Lost;* Grubbs, *Cry from the Cotton.*

12. Sullivan, *Days of Hope.*

13. Carlton and Cochlanis, eds., *Confronting Southern Poverty;* Mertz, *New Deal Policy;* Cobb, *The Selling of the South.*

14. "Farm-Factory South" (editorial), *New Orleans Times-Picayune,* April 4, 1939; "Economy Drive under Fire" (editorial), *Dallas Morning News,* February 7, 1940, sec. 1, 9; "Newsprint Now Being Made in the South," *Manufacturers' Record* (January 1940): 25; Finlay, "The Industrial Utilization," 41–52. Begun in 1939 as one of four regional labs in the nation, the USDA lab promoted chemurgy, the term coined by the burgeoning national farm chemurgic movement for the scientific research of industrial uses for agricultural products.

15. "More Industries Held Needed for Southern States," *New Orleans Times-Picayune,* November 23, 1939, sec. 1, 2; "Temporary Distress" (editorial), *New Orleans Times-Picayune,* December 27, 1940; Victor Schoffelmeyer, "Aggressive Governors Unite to Bring More Industries to Southern States," *Dallas Morning News,* August 26, 1940, sec. 3, ii; Schulman, *From Cotton Belt to Sunbelt,* 89, 101.

16. Daniel, "Going among Strangers," 888–91; Daniel, *Breaking the Land,* 104, 109.

17. Lange and Taylor, *An American Exodus;* Anderson, *Men on the Move.*

18. The Texas State Employment Service cited 600,000 migrants in "Origins and Problems of Texas Migratory Farm Labor," 42, September 1940, Texas State Employment Service, Archives Division, Texas State Library, Austin. The Texas Agricultural Workers Association estimated in 1940 that there were 350,000 migratory

farmworkers in Texas; see *Dallas Morning News,* February 7, 1940, sec. 1, 9. In Florida, some forty to sixty thousand migrants, many of whom were cotton refugees from Georgia and other southeastern states, traveled to the state annually. See Anderson, *Men on the Move,* 209, 215.

19. "Pick Cotton or Do Not Eat (in Alabama)," *Louisiana Weekly,* September 29, 1934, 8; "Economic Discrimination against Negro Reflected in Relief Work Figures," *Louisiana Weekly,* December 1, 1934, 4; "Suspend WPA Jobs for Miss. Negroes" and "Police Force Negroes to Pick Cotton," *Louisiana Weekly,* September 19, 1936, 1; "Cane Cutters vs. WPA" (editorial), *Louisiana Weekly,* November 21, 1936, 10; "Negro vs. White Cane Cutters" (editorial), *Louisiana Weekly,* November 28, 1936, 10; "Florida Negroes Jailed for Refusing Jobs," *Louisiana Weekly,* February 13, 1937, 1; "Armed Georgia Farmers Hold Negro Cotton Pickers on Job at Starvation Wages" and "Peonage in Georgia Laid before U.S.," *Louisiana Weekly,* October 2, 1937, 2; "Close WPA Projects to Send Workers to Cane Field," *Louisiana Weekly,* November 27, 1937, 1, 8; "Explanation of Seasonality Determinations by the Florida Industrial Commission," file 6, box 5, Florida Industrial Commission, series 1477; Weber, *Dark Sweat,* 126–36, 162–79; Foley, *The White Scourge.*

20. Baldwin, *Poverty and Politics.*

21. See W. B. Klugh to Ralph Walton, May 28, 1943, Labor Mobilization and Utilization 10-1—Negro Recruitment file, box 8, and W. B. Klugh to J. K. Johnson, July 7, 1943, Labor Mobilization and Utilization 10-2 file (1 of 2), box 3, series 11, War Manpower Commission, RG 211, National Archives and Records Administration, East Point, Georgia (hereafter cited as NARA EP).

Astonishingly, during the war, some 3.2 million people left rural areas of the South, while over 1.5 million southerners left the region. See Daniel, "Going among Strangers," 886; Cobb, "World War II and the Mind of the Modern South," 11.

Chapter One: Tents, Trailers, and Shack Towns

1. "Army Building," *Life Magazine,* January 20, 1941, 33–36.

2. For statistics on Camp Blanding placement, see the Interstate Conference on Migratory Labor, Atlanta, December 17–18, 1940, Department of Industrial Relations file, box 12257, Frank Dixon Administration Files.

3. According to Southern Tenant Farmers Union (STFU) figures, southern cotton pickers made from 11 to 22 cents per hour, based on $1.50 per hundred pounds. See "Cotton Pickers Ask 30 Cents/Hour Minimum," *New Orleans News Digest,* October 5, 1942, 3. Wages in the southern and southwestern traditional industries in 1941 generally varied from 35 to 50 cents per hour, while new southern defense industries paid at least 75 cents per hour. By 1942, southern shipyard jobs paid as much as $150 per week. See Report on Freeport-Velasco, Texas War Production Area, February 25, 1942, Labor Market Report—Freeport file, 16–17, box 6, series 277, War Manpower Commission, RG 211, National Archives and Records Administration, Fort Worth, Texas (hereafter cited as NARA FW); "Housing for War," *Fortune Magazine* (October 1942): 93–96, 190–98.

4. *Life Magazine,* January 20, 1941, 33–36; "National Defense vs. V.D.," *Life Magazine,* October 13, 1941, 178–81; "Vast Traffic Jam Daily Engulfs Workers outside Baltimore Bomber Plant," *Life Magazine,* December 8, 1941, 51–55; "Housing for War," *Fortune Magazine* (October 1942): 93–96, 190–98.

5. Schmidt, "The Impact of Camp Shelby"; Morgan Jr., "Craig Air Force Base"; Interstate Conference on Migratory Labor, December 17–18, 1940, Department of Industrial Relations file, box 12257, Frank Dixon Administration Files; Lotchin, ed., *The Martial Metropolis;* Strickland, "Remembering Hattiesburg."

6. Report on Texarkana, Texas and Arkansas Defense Area, February 5, 1942, 27, Labor Market Report—Texarkana file, box 6, series 277, War Manpower Commission, RG 211, NARA FW; Childersburg Operations file, box 12262, Frank Dixon Administration Files; McClane, "The Radford Ordnance Works"; "The South's War Effort in Private Industry: Ordnance," *Manufacturers' Record* (January 1942): 20–21.

7. Report on Freeport—Velasco, Texas, 16–17, box 6, series 277, War Manpower Commission, RG 211, NARA FW.

8. Meyer, *Journey through Chaos,* 172, 372–73.

9. For a brief history of the National Resources Planning Board, see Brinkley, *The End of Reform,* 245–61.

10. Draper, "Urban Development"; Labor Market Report—Beaumont-Orange file, June 30, 1942, 23, and Labor Market Report—Texarkana file, 27, 28, boxes 6, 7, series 277, War Manpower Commission, RG 211, NARA FW. For an analysis of planning for mobilization on the West Coast, see Johnson, *The Second Gold Rush,* 101–5; and Abbott, "Planning for the Home Front." See also Alan Brinkley's discussion of the NRPB's plans for the "Seven Little TVAs," or regional planning authorities, during 1938 and 1939 (*The End of Reform,* 256).

11. See letter to the editor regarding Neosha, Missouri, in *Life Magazine,* February 2, 1942, 2–3, for a discussion of boom-and-bust dam-building projects in the 1930s. See also Dunbar and McBride, *Building Hoover Dam.*

12. See Labor Market Reports and National Resource Planning Board Reports, boxes 5 and 6, series 277, War Manpower Commission, RG 211, NARA FW.

13. Report on Killeen Military Area, Labor Market Report 7 Survey Belton, Killeen, Temple file, box 5, series 277, War Manpower Commission, RG 211, NARA FW.

14. Meyer, *Journey through Chaos,* 201–2.

15. For a recent analysis of the expansion of the state in the South during World War II, see Spinney, "Municipal Government."

16. A. Keith to Hon. Sam Hobbs, March 25, 1941, and A. Keith to President F. D. Roosevelt, Sen. W. B. Bankhead, and Sen. Lister Hill, March 26, 1941, Childersburg Operations file, box 12262, Frank Dixon Administration Files.

17. Report on Alexandria-Pineville, 51–52, Labor Market Report—Alexandria file, box 6, series 277, War Manpower Commission, RG 211, NARA FW.

18. Report on Shreveport-Minden, 68–69, Labor Market Report—Shreveport file, box 6, series 277, War Manpower Commission, RG 211, NARA FW.

19. Report on Texarkana, 72.

20. Report on Alexandria-Pineville, 51–52. Dewey Grantham reports that in Alabama, Georgia, and South Carolina, the federal government displaced some 25,000 persons in its acquisition of military facilities during the war (*The South in Modern America*, 172). See also "Trailer City—Home Is Anywhere You Find It," *New Orleans Item*, December 21, 1942, 1.

21. "Complain over Labor," *New Orleans Item*, May 18, 1941, 3; Labor Market Report, Louisiana Department of Labor, September–October 1941, 15, in P. J. Charlet file, folder 13, box 16, Sam Houston Jones Papers; ES 270 Labor Market Report for Alabama, Division of Labor file (2), box 12268, Frank Dixon Administration Files.

22. C. F. Anderson addresses Alabama's Employment Service Program, July 1939; and "What Representative Alabama Employers Think of the ASES," ASES file, box 12236, Frank Dixon Administration Files.

23. GSES Third Annual Report, January 9, 1940, box 1, Department of Labor, RG 16.

24. Breen, *Labor Market Politics*, 157–58; "Origins and Problems of Texas Migratory Farm Labor," and "Supplement to Origins and Problems of Texas Migratory Farm Labor," Texas State Employment Service, Archives Division, Texas State Library, Austin; FSES Farm Placement Manual, file 4, box 3, Florida Industrial Commission, series 1477; Louisiana Division of Employment Security Annual Report, 1940, Tulane University.

25. "20,000 Will Lose Jobs in Plow-Up," *New Orleans Times-Picayune*, March 31, 1940, sec. 1, 1; "Louisiana Farmers Plow Up Cane—On Orders from U.S.," *New Orleans Item*, April 28, 1939, B-1; Volanto, "Burying White Gold."

26. "Farm Tenants Ask U.S. Aid at Conference," *Dallas Morning News*, January 16, 1940, sec. 1, 7.

27. Victor Schoffelmeyer, "Negro and Agriculture," *Dallas Express*, January 18, 1941, 11; "Farm Future Bright despite Bleak Present," *Dallas Morning News*, January 12, 1940, sec. 1, 2; "Plans to Aid Poor Farmer Are Discussed," *Dallas Morning News*, August 27, 1940, sec. 2, 1; Anderson, *Men on the Move*, 199–234. See also Kirby, *Rural Worlds Lost*, 13–22, 238–44; Foley, *The White Scourge*, 118–40.

28. "Farm Labor Problems" (editorial), *New Orleans Item*, April 19, 1941; "Labor Disruptions, Crowded Housing in Defense Boom Cited," *New Orleans Item*, May 18, 1941, Metro, 1.

29. Brinkley, *The End of Reform*, 181–82; Schulman, *From Cotton Belt to Sunbelt*, 94, 100–101; Vander Meulen, "Warplanes, Labor," 39; Combes, "Aircraft Manufacturing"; Tindall, *The Emergence of the New South*, 696.

30. "Origins and Problems of Texas Migratory Farm Labor," 31–32; Tentative Organization Chart of the Bureau of Employment Security, file 8, box 3, Florida Industrial Commission, series 1477; Georgia Department of Labor files, Department of Labor, RG 16; file ASES, box 12236, Frank Dixon Administration Files.

31. Louisiana Division of Employment Security Annual Report, 1940, Tulane University; Georgia Department of Labor 4th Annual Report, box 1, Department of Labor, RG 16; "Reduced Unemployment in Alabama," newspaper clipping, ASES file, box 12242, Frank Dixon Administration Files.

32. Sam Jones to F. E. Hebert, January 2, 1941, F. E. Hebert file, and Sam Jones to Hale Boggs, Hale Boggs file, box 28, Sam Houston Jones Papers; "Our #1 Empty Stocking" (editorial cartoon), *New Orleans Item*, November 17, 1940. During the fall of 1940, a Texas delegation from the House of Representatives complained that the "industrial states" benefited disproportionately from the National Defense Program, while Texas had "greater need and larger unemployment." See "Increased WPA Allotment Asked for Texas Clients," *Dallas Morning News*, July 24, 1940, sec. 1, 2; Labor Market Report—Alexandria file, 54–55; "Defense Has Put Burden on Welfare," *New Orleans Item*, October 16, 1941, 12.

33. "Drop 4,000 from Rolls of WPA," *New Orleans Item*, July 6, 1941, Classified, 4; "Many Quit WPA Rolls Voluntarily," *New Orleans Item*, August 25, 1941, 22; "WPA, NYA Drop Thousands, No Defense Jobs Yet," *Louisiana Weekly*, August 9, 1941, 1; "Defense Situation in Dallas—G. F. Porter, Sec. of the Dallas NAACP—Fights Local NYA Policy of Dropping Negroes from Rolls," *Dallas Express*, March 29, 1941, 1.

34. Resolution from Jackson NAACP to President F. D. Roosevelt et al., April 18, 1942, Committee on Fair Employment Practices (COFEP) cases 1941–42 (A–M) file, box B-11, part 2, National Association for the Advancement of Colored People Collection.

35. Explanation of Seasonality Determinations by the Florida Industrial Commission, file 6, box 5, Florida Industrial Commission, series 1477.

36. "City Feels Unusual Labor Pinch," *New Orleans Item*, August 11, 1941, sec. 1, 1; Louisiana Labor Market Report, September–October 1941, 22, Department of Labor file 5, box 9, Sam Houston Jones Papers; "Labor Disruptions, Crowded Housing in Defense Boom Cited," *New Orleans Item*, May 18, 1941, Metro, 1.

37. "Labor Supply Key Question," *New Orleans Item*, August 9, 1941, 21; "Labor in the South," *Manufacturers' Record* (September 1940): 48–50.

38. "Dallas Gets Naval Air Base; Factory Has Six Units," *Southwest Business* (October 1940): 16–17; "Factory Draws Labor from Wide Area," *Southwest Business* (October 1940): 23; "Employment Policies Outlined," *Southwest Business* (October 1940): 40; *Dallas Morning News*, August 27, 1940, sec. 1, 3; Barksdale, *Genesis of the Aviation Industry*, 9; Combes, "Aircraft Manufacturing."

39. Schulman, *From Cotton Belt to Sunbelt*, 100. For Louisiana Department of Labor concerns over shipbuilding manpower in New Orleans, see Louisiana Department of Labor, Labor Market Reports, December 1941, February 1942, P. J. Charlet file, folder 13, box 16, Sam Houston Jones Papers.

40. Employment—Local Personnel file, box 4, F. Edward Hebert Papers.

41. Department of Industrial Relations Release No. 5-41, March 1, 1941; F. Dixon to M. H. Branyon, June 12, 1941; F. Dixon to T. Ehlers, September 24, 1941; F. Dixon to C. F. Anderson, September 24, 1941; C. F. Anderson to F. Dixon, September 29, 1941; all in ASES file, box 12253, Frank Dixon Administration Files.

42. For the importation of skilled workers from Ohio for Delta Shipbuilding, see LSES meeting transcript, July 31, 1941, 3, and D. F. Johnson to H. R. Bishop, March 19, 1941, in P. J. Charlet file, folder 14, box 16, Sam Houston Jones Papers. For the importation of skilled workers from Southern California into the NAA plant at Grand

Prairie, see "Employment Policies Outlined," *Southwest Business* (October 1940): 40. For Taylor's and Lange's discussion of out-of-state plates, see *An American Exodus,* 118.

43. For placement at Fort Bragg, North Carolina, and Camp Blanding, Florida, see the Interstate Conference on Migratory Labor, Atlanta, December 17–18, 1940, Department of Industrial Relations file, box 12257, Frank Dixon Administration Files.

44. Schmidt, "The Impact of Camp Shelby," 43–44; Report on Texarkana, Texas and Arkansas Defense Area, February 5, 1942, Labor Market Report—Texarkana file, box 6, series 277, War Manpower Commission, RG 211, NARA FW.

45. Report on Brownwood, 15–16, Labor Market Report—Survey Brownwood file, box 5, series 277, War Manpower Commission, RG 211, NARA FW.

46. Breen, *Labor Market Politics.*

47. W. O. Hawke, president of the conference and the most outspoken on the subject, urged state administrators to actively resist federalization, warning, "We might well expect some rather radical departure from the present Federal-State relationship." See W. O. Hawke to P. J. Charlet, October 14, 1941, P. J. Charlet file, folder 13, and *Advisor* (August 1941), P. J. Charlet file, folder 14, box 16, Sam Houston Jones Papers.

48. See miscellaneous correspondence, files 1–4, box 12274, Frank Dixon Administration Files; S. Holland to Florida congressmen, January 24, 1942, FIC file, box 57, series 406, FSA. Governors' willingness (or lack thereof) to cooperate with the federal mobilization efforts had relatively little bearing on the amount of new industries their respective states procured during the war. Even as Frank Dixon remained somewhat antagonistic toward the process of federalization, Alabama's steel industry underwent a dramatic expansion. By 1945, Alabama and Louisiana had both received roughly similar amounts of federal war contracts throughout the war ($2 billion). See "Steel Industry's Capacity over 95,500,000 Tons," *Manufacturers' Record* (May 1945): 40; and "Major War Contracts and Facility Projects Southern States," *Manufacturers' Record* (July 1945): 56. See also P. J. Charlet to Sam Jones, January 5, 1942, P. J. Charlet file, folder 13, box 16, Sam Houston Jones Papers, for Jones's stance on federalization.

49. Flynn, *The Mess in Washington,* 3–23.

50. Special Committee Investigating the Interstate Migration of Destitute Citizens, press release, June 28, 1940, Interstate Migration file, box 12248, Frank Dixon Administration Files. The committee came south in August 1940 to hold its southern hearings in Montgomery, Alabama. The committee held the other regional hearings in New York City, Chicago, Oklahoma City, San Francisco, and Lincoln, Nebraska. In publicizing the tour, the committee contended that migration should be regarded as a national problem, one that "must be solved by action initiated by the Federal government, in collaboration with State and local authorities." For testimonies, see *Interstate Migration Hearings, Part 2;* for the political context of the Tolan Committee, see Sullivan, *Days of Hope,* 103–4.

51. For SGC and Delta Council statements at the Tolan Hearings regarding migrant labor, see *Interstate Migration Hearings, Part 2,* 518, 602–11.

52. W. R. McDonald to E. D. Rovers, August 16, 1940, Interstate Migration file, box 12248, Frank Dixon Administration Files; Hahamovitch, *The Fruits of Their Labor;* Grubbs, "The Story."

53. Interstate Conference on Migratory Labor, Atlanta, December 17–18, 1940, Department of Industrial Relations file, box 12257, Frank Dixon Administration Files.

54. Recommendations of the Interstate Conference on Migratory Labor, Atlanta, December 17–18, 1940, file 6, box 5, Florida Industrial Commission, series 1477.

55. The commission itself included military procurement officials, representatives of the Departments of Labor and Agriculture, and the War Production Board to serve as an advisory board on mobilization policies. See Brinkley, *The End of Reform*, 221; Flynn, *The Mess in Washington*, 17; Lichtenstein, *Labor's War at Home*, 36–43, 89–95.

56. Alabama Department of Industrial Relations press release, April 5, 1941, Department of Industrial Relations file, box 12253; Interstate Conference on Migratory Labor, Atlanta, December 17–18, 1940, 5, Department of Industrial Relations file, box 12257, Frank Dixon Administration Files.

57. "Ship Labor Accord Sought," *New Orleans Item*, May 14, 1941, 1–3; "Ship Firms, Unions in No Strike Pact," *New Orleans Item*, May 18, 1941, sec. 1, 1; "Delta Men Leaving Graft-ridden AFL," *New Orleans News Digest*, August 24, 1942, 1; "Delta Workers Rush to CIO," *New Orleans News Digest*, August 31, 1942, 1; "Delta in the Bag, IUMSWA Goes in for Big Game," *New Orleans News Digest*, October 19, 1942, 1.

58. "Important Labor Conference to Be Held in Atlanta," *Mobile Register*, January 10, 1943, 9–13; "War Labor Confab Slated in Atlanta," *Mobile Register*, January 14, 1943, 1.

59. Milkman, *Gender at Work*, 49–50.

60. Weaver, *Negro Labor*, 21–23; Arthur Krock, "The Baltimore Survey of Manpower Problems," *New York Times*, November 13, 1942, in War Manpower Commission 1942 file, box A665, part 2, National Association for the Advancement of Colored People Collection; "Vast Traffic Jam," *Life Magazine*, December 8, 1941, 51–54; Moore, "No Room"; Flynn, *The Mess in Washington*, 39, 60–61.

61. Flynn, *The Mess in Washington*, 60.

62. "U.S. Planning Board, Fortune Magazine Tell Mobile's Story," *New Orleans News Digest*, October 19, 1942, 4; ES 270 Labor Market Report, April–May 1942, Division of Labor file (2), box 12268, Frank Dixon Administration Files.

63. "1,000s of Wartime Housing Units Completed," *Mobile Register*, December 27, 1942, 1.

64. See the FSA-OWI photograph collection, Library of Congress. For a discussion of FSA photographers in California, see Shindo, *Dust Bowl Migrants;* Gregory, *American Exodus*. For contemptuous views of southern defense community residents, see Meyer, *Journey through Chaos*, 172, 373.

65. "Gulf Shipbuilding—Vital Industry Booms in the South," *Life Magazine*, May 26, 1941, 94–95.

66. Report on Waco, 16, Labor Market Report—Waco file, box 6, series 277, War Manpower Commission, RG 211, NARA FW; and Report on Texarkana, January 10, 1942, 5.

67. "City Commission to Discuss Plan for Trailer Camps," *Mobile Register*, November 12, 1942, 14; "Trailer Parking Violations Probed," *Mobile Register*, December 11, 1942, 5, 13; "1,000s of Wartime Housing Units Completed," *Mobile Register*, December 27, 1942, 1; "Housing for War," *Fortune Magazine* (October 1942): 190.

68. Gregory, *American Exodus;* Johnson, *The Second Gold Rush*, 60–82; Archibald, *Wartime Shipyard*.

69. *New Orleans News Digest* lists NLRB and WLB election results and percentages of elections won and lost by the CIO from 1940 to 1943.

70. "CIO Will Demand Pay Differential Be Eliminated," *Mobile Register*, November 26, 1942, 16; "Manpower Supply Main Issue up at Labor Conference," *Mobile Register*, January 18, 1943, 1; "CIO Will Seek Wage Increases," *Mobile Register*, January 24, 1943, 1; "Closed Shop Ban Opposed by AFL," *Mobile Register*, January 30, 1943, 12; "Universal Price Ceilings Favored by Labor Chiefs," *Mobile Register*, February 4, 1943, 3; "New Worker Order Revokes Labor Contracts," *Mobile Register*, February 11, 1943, 1; "Judge Sets aside Tampa Shipbuilding Co. Closed Shop Rule," *Mobile Register*, February 12, 1943, 9.

71. "Draft Boards Punish Men Who Quit War Jobs," *New Orleans New Digest*, November 2, 1942, 3; "Approach to the Manpower Problem" (editorial), *Mobile Register*, November 21, 1942, 4; "Absent Workers Will Be Drafted," *Mobile Register*, February 16, 1943, 12.

72. ES 270 Labor Market Report for Alabama, April 15–May 15, 1942, 34–35, Division of Labor file (2), box 12268, Frank Dixon Administration Files. See also Nelson, "Organized Labor." For an interpretation of worker mobility nationally, see Meyer, *Journey through Chaos*, 362.

73. "War Workers Are Forced to Yield Their Jobs—Trailerites Form Committee to Fight Move to Stop Parking in Backyards of Private Homes," *New Orleans News Digest*, January 25, 1943, 4; "City Commission to Discuss Trailer Camps," *Mobile Register*, November 12, 1942, 14; "Trailer Parking Violations Probed," *Mobile Register*, December 11, 1942, 5.

74. "Housing for War," *Fortune Magazine* (October 1942): 193.

Chapter Two: "Empty Sermons"

1. "Delta Shipyard Catastrophe" (editorial), *Louisiana Weekly*, October 24, 1942.

2. Paul Dixon to Paul McNutt, November 25, 1942, Minority—Negroes—Discrimination file, box 1, series 278, War Manpower Commission, RG 211, NARA FW.

3. John Beecher to Lawrence Cramer, March 7, 1942, 4, New Orleans file, box 473, John Beecher office files, Division of Field Operations (hereafter cited as DFO), Fair Employment Practices Committee, RG 228, National Archives and Records Administration, College Park, Maryland (hereafter cited as NARA CP).

4. This chapter breaks from previous works on the fair employment struggle in the

South in several important ways. First, whereas Merl Reed's *Seedtime* looks largely at administrative history of the FEPC at the national level, and works such as Zamora's "The Failed Promise" examine local struggles for fair employment, this chapter focuses on the regional movement for fair employment and jobs initiated by Urban Leagues, NAACP chapters, and other black civic institutions across the urban South. In doing so, this study contributes to a growing body of works on the FEPC at the regional level, including Daniel, *Chicano Workers*, and Kersten, *Race, Jobs, and the War*.

Second, with the focus here on a regionwide jobs movement, the black struggle for equality within the South assumes a more organized and militant character at the local level than previous civil rights and labor historians have acknowledged. Adding to the recent findings of Patricia Sullivan in *Days of Hope*, I argue that this southern movement for jobs during the war grew directly out of the militant campaign by black leaders to gain inclusion and racial quotas in federal relief programs during the New Deal.

Lastly, by examining to a greater degree the political negotiations between the WMC and urban black leaders during the war, I hope, as Daniel Kryder has done in *Divided Arsenal*, to expand the historical focus on federal race and labor policy to include not only issues of fair employment but also federal recruitment for war industries. In general, the WMC's role in providing southern African American workers with economic mobility has been woefully underappreciated by historians.

5. "McNutt Addresses Staff of Manpower Service," *Dallas Express*, August 1, 1942, 3; Reed, *Seedtime*, 53; Flynn, *The Mess in Washington*, 149–71; "McNutt Announces Negro Manpower Service Formed," *Louisiana Weekly*, June 27, 1942, 1.

6. In WMC Region X, which covered Texas, Louisiana, and New Mexico, the regional War Manpower (Labor-Management) Committee included representatives from the Texas and Louisiana AFL and CIO as well as a railroad labor representative; Atchison, Topeka and Santa Fe Railroad management; Charles O'Connell, president of Southwestern Life Insurance in Dallas; George Newman, president of Consolidated-Vultee in Fort Worth; George Brown, president of Brown Shipbuilding; and Lester Alexander, president of shipbuilding interests in New Orleans. Throughout the war, with the exception of Convair in Fort Worth from March to August 1945, the above industries failed to utilize African American and Latino workers in any position above common labor. For a list, see John Hilliard to Region X staff, March 27, 1943, Reports file, box 6, series 269, War Manpower Commission, RG 211, NARA FW. In WMC Region VII, which covered the Southeast, the regional WMC board was comprised of Oscar Johnston, president of the Delta, Land and Pine Company; T. M. Forbes, executive vice president of the Georgia Cotton Manufacturers Association; Harrison Jones, president of Coca-Cola; McGregor Smith, president of Florida Light and Power Company; N. H. Lassiter, director of personnel for the Nashville, Chattanooga and St. Louis Railway; as well as regional representatives of the AFL and CIO. For a list, see Committee 3-1942 file, box 1, series 6, War Manpower Commission, RG 211, NARA EP.

7. John Beecher to Lawrence Cramer, March 7, 1942, 1, New Orleans file, box 473, John Beecher office files, DFO, Fair Employment Practices Committee, RG 228, NARA CP.

8. In 1934, for instance, acting NUL executive secretary T. Arnold Hill emphasized how the Atlanta affiliate followed a "reasonable course" that promised "the greatest security of Negro workers." See "NUL SRO Office Is Raided," *Louisiana Weekly*, November 3, 1934, 1.

9. Weiss, *The National Urban League*, 163–64; introduction, Dallas Negro Chamber of Commerce Collection finding aid, Dallas Negro Chamber of Commerce Collection.

10. "Senator Wagner Seeks to Bar RFC Job Jim Crow," *Louisiana Weekly*, June 10, 1933, 1; "Discrimination Barred on All Public Works," *Louisiana Weekly*, October 14, 1933, 2; "Clark Foreman Addresses 2,000 at Meet; 1st Speech since Appointment," *Louisiana Weekly*, October 21, 1933, 2.

11. "Labor Supports Old Age Pension," *Louisiana Weekly*, February 24, 1934, 4; "Labor Hails Resolution on Workers," *Louisiana Weekly*, October 20, 1934, 1; Cohen, *Making a New Deal*, 251–89.

12. "A New Deal for Domestics," *Louisiana Weekly*, August 5, 1933, 8; "What about a Code for Domestics," *Louisiana Weekly*, August 12, 1933, 1, 4; "Local Committee Attempts to Place Negroes in All Recently OK'd Projects" and "Negroes of Dallas Show the Way for Others to Receive CWA Benefits," *Louisiana Weekly*, December 23, 1933, 1; "An Object Lesson" (editorial), *Louisiana Weekly*, December 30, 1933, 8; "The Unemployment Councils" (editorial), *Louisiana Weekly*, June 23, 1934, 8. See Foner, ed., *The Era of Post-War Prosperity*, 537–39 for accounts of laundry workers organizing in Birmingham.

13. "AFL Appoints Southern Man as Organizer," *Louisiana Weekly*, December 2, 1933, 1; "Violation of NRA Code Is Charged," *Louisiana Weekly*, December 22, 1934, 1; "Brotherhood Organizer Here," *Louisiana Weekly*, December 14, 1935, 2; Ferguson, "The Politics of Inclusion," 425–26; Ambrose, "A Revolution of Hope," 135–81.

14. Sullivan, *Days of Hope*, 69–101; Foner, ed., *The Era of Post-War Prosperity*.

15. "Highlights of the 24th Conference of the NAACP," *Louisiana Weekly*, July 15, 1933, 8; "NAACP Urges Action and Cooperation on Industrial Codes," *Louisiana Weekly*, July 29, 1933, 7; "Fight for Jobs under New Deal Marked NAACP 1933 Program," *Louisiana Weekly*, January 20, 1934, 1; *Louisiana Weekly*, June 30, 1934, 1; "NAACP Scores Abandonment of FERA Wage Scale in Southern Pay," *Louisiana Weekly*, December 1, 1934, 1; "Peonage in Georgia Laid before U.S.," *Louisiana Weekly*, October 2, 1937, 2.

16. "New Kind of Radicalism Faced," *Louisiana Weekly*, July 1, 1933, 1.

17. "AUL's Janitor Night Class," *Louisiana Weekly*, February 11, 1933, 6; "NUL SRO Office Is Raided," *Louisiana Weekly*, November 3, 1934, 1.

18. Accomplishments of the NOUL during 1940, Affiliates—New Orleans file, box 111, series 1, part 2, National Urban League Collection; introduction, Dallas Negro Chamber of Commerce Collection finding aid, Dallas Negro Chamber of Commerce Collection; Moore Jr., *A Search for Equality*, 80–85; "NUL Asks Workers to Organize," *Louisiana Weekly*, April 28, 1934, 1; "NUL Appeals to USES for Negro Workers," *Louisiana Weekly*, September 21, 1935, 3.

19. In New Orleans, the Colored Domestic and Allied Service Association and

the Methodist Ministerial Alliance were the most active in uniting labor leaders and local churches to demand fair wages for domestic workers. See "A New Deal for Domestics," *Louisiana Weekly*, August 5, 1933, 8; "What about a Code for Domestics?" *Louisiana Weekly*, August 12, 1933, 1; "Job and Jobless Unite for Quick Action," *Louisiana Weekly*, August 19, 1933, 1; "Minimum Salary $10 Minimum Wage Requested," *Louisiana Weekly*, August 26, 1933, 1; "Code for Domestics Is Considered by NRA," *Louisiana Weekly*, September 16, 1933, 1; "Domestics to Meet Thursday," *Louisiana Weekly*, October 7, 1933, 1. New Orleans's black population in 1940 stood at 494,537 persons.

20. "LW Launches Drive for Welding School," *Louisiana Weekly*, August 9, 1941, 1; "TWU Supports Welding Fight," *Louisiana Weekly*, August 23, 1941, 1; "CIO Head Makes Stand Clear on Welding School," *Louisiana Weekly*, September 27, 1941, 1; "Shakespeare Park the Scene of Protest Mass Meet," *Louisiana Weekly*, October 4, 1941, 1; "Lambast Supt. Bauer at Protest Meet," *Louisiana Weekly*, October 11, 1941, 1; "500 Negroes Swamp Soule Building to Register," *Louisiana Weekly*, November 22, 1941, 1; "PDL Continues Efforts to Register for Democracy and Four Freedoms," *Louisiana Weekly*, December 6, 1941, 1; *Louisiana Weekly*, January 24, 1942, 1; "4th of July Declaration by Negro Youth," *Louisiana Weekly*, July 4, 1942, 2; *Louisiana Weekly*, September, 19, 1942, 1; *Louisiana Weekly*, October 3, 1942, 7; "ILWU Thanksgiving Fest to Give 500 Baskets to the Poor," *Louisiana Weekly*, November 14, 1942, 3.

21. Sullivan, *Days of Hope*, 70–71, 89, 99; Fairclough, *Race and Democracy*, 58–61. For articles on the League for Civil Rights and Justice, see "History of the Federation of Civic Leagues Reveals City's Most Active Group," *Louisiana Weekly*, June 30, 1934, 1; "Group Hopes to Establish Right to Vote," *Louisiana Weekly*, September 1, 1934, 2; "CLCRJ Petitions State Heads," *Louisiana Weekly*, May 4, 1935, 1; "LCRJ Meets at Ladies of Charity Hall," *Louisiana Weekly*, July 13, 1935, 1; "Support the League" (editorial), *Louisiana Weekly*, September 5, 1936, 6; "League for Civil Rights and Justice," *Louisiana Weekly*, April 17, 1937, 1.

22. Obadele-Starks, "Black Labor," 53–65.

23. NAACP National Assistant Secretary to Dr. B. E. Howell, May 3, 1941, Dallas—1943 file, box C 190, National Association for the Advancement of Colored People Collection; see Hill, *Dallas*, 129–61.

24. Foner, ed., *The Black Worker*, 251–60; Kryder, *Divided Arsenal*, 55–66; Pfeffer, *A. Philip Randolph*, 45–88.

25. C. Laws to Eugene Jones, May 29, 1940, Local NULs—N through W, 1940 file, box 9, series 6, part 1, National Urban League Collection.

26. Accomplishments of the NOUL during 1940, Affiliates—New Orleans file, box 111, series 1, part 1, National Urban League Collection; C. Laws to E. Jones, May 29, 1940, Local NULs—N through W, 1940 file, box 9, series 6, part 1, National Urban League Collection; C. Laws to J. Thomas, September 17, 1941, C. Laws file, box A-65, Southern Regional Office, National Urban League Collection; C. Laws to P. J. Charlet, June 19, 1941, P. J. Charlet file, folder 14, box 16, Sam Houston Jones Papers.

27. "Atlanta Urban League Gets Defense Jobs for Negroes at Camp Gordon,"

Oklahoma City Dispatch, March 8, 1941; "Race Workers Hired on Jobs in Arkansas," *Norfolk Journal and Guide*, January 11, 1941, as cited in Kryder, *Divided Arsenal*, 42, 44.

28. *Richmond Urban League Annual Report* 10, no. 1 (January 1943), Richmond 1941–55 file, box 26, series 13, part 1, National Urban League Collection.

29. *Frontier* (April 1943), Little Rock 1940–57 file, box 14, series 13, part 1, National Urban League Collection; Granger, "Techniques in Race Relations," 323–26.

30. Program and Accomplishments of the Dallas NAACP, 1940–41, Dallas—1943 file, box C 190, National Association for the Advancement of Colored People Collection; M. H. Jackson to presidents of colleges, November 1940, M. H. Jackson to A. W. Motley, November 13, 1940, and J. W. Rice to M. H. Jackson, November 28, 1940, file 1940, box 1, Dallas Negro Chamber of Commerce Collection. As of September 15, 1941, Texas NYA maintained Negro training centers in Marshall, Center Point, Itasca, Huntsville, Prairie View, Cuero, and Pittsburg; see *Houston Informer*, September 28, 1940, 2. For advocacy of Negro NYA state representative, see "Texas Needs NYA Negro Project Supervisor" (editorial), *Dallas Express*, January 20, 1940. For advocacy of more than five Negro home and farm supervisors in the state Farm Security Administration, see "Farm Security for Negroes" (editorial), *Dallas Express*, March 9, 1940.

31. Ross, "Mary McLeod Bethune"; Sullivan, *Days of Hope*, 46–50; Kryder, *Divided Arsenal*, 51–52.

32. "L. A. Oxley Appointed as New Commissioner," *Louisiana Weekly*, March 10, 1934, 1; "Lt. Oxley Has Conference Here with Railway and River Men," *Louisiana Weekly*, June 2, 1934, 1; "Straight from the Capital," *Louisiana Weekly*, March 13, 1937, 8; "Oxley Says Church Fails Negro Worker," *Louisiana Weekly*, October 16, 1937, 7; "Oxley Finds Louisiana Labor Question a Problem," *Louisiana Weekly*, February 12, 1938, 1. Also, in 1934, Eugene Kinkle Jones, advisor of Negro Affairs in the Commerce Department, helped secure federal jobs for African Americans in the Civil Works Administration. See "Eugene Kinkle Jones Secures Justice in Commerce PWA Jobs," *Louisiana Weekly*, January 6, 1934, 1.

33. "Intervention of S. W. Green Helps Secure Jobs in California," *Louisiana Weekly*, December 16, 1933, 2; "Skilled Labor to Register at Pythian Temple," *Louisiana Weekly*, December 23, 1933, 2; "Dallas Negroes Show the Way," *Louisiana Weekly*, December 23, 1933, 1.

34. "The FERA in New Orleans" (editorial), *Louisiana Weekly*, June 23, 1934, 8.

35. On the housing front, by 1940, A. Maceo Smith was appointed race relations advisor for the USHA in Region VI. Through this federal position, Smith helped Clarence Laws and the NOUL secure black management of the city's new segregated housing projects in the summer of 1940. In 1939, Smith traveled to Washington to attend a national NYA conference with Mary McLeod Bethune while also garnering support for federal programs in Dallas that would benefit the local black community. In Washington Smith met with United States Post Office officials regarding black civil service opportunities in Dallas and also with the United States Housing Authority (USHA) regarding the establishment of housing projects in both Dallas and

Fort Worth. See "Attends DC Conference," *Dallas Express*, January 14, 1939; "Adviser Here," *Louisiana Weekly*, July 13, 1940, 1; "Magnolia Housing Project to Have Negro Personnel," *Louisiana Weekly*, August 3, 1940, 1; Accomplishments of the NOUL during 1940, Affiliates—New Orleans file, box 111, series 1, part 1, National Urban League Collection.

36. M. H. Jackson to R. Weaver, June 3, 1941, file 1941, box 1, Dallas Negro Chamber of Commerce Collection. For an analysis of Mary McLeod Bethune's power within the NYA, see Ross, "Mary McLeod Bethune," 1–28.

37. "WPB to Probe Shipyard Bias," *Louisiana Weekly*, January 31, 1942, 1; "WPB Aide Pays Visit to City," *Louisiana Weekly*, February 21, 1942, 2; "UL Urges Registration for War Industry Jobs," *Louisiana Weekly*, April 25, 1942, 3; "WPB Commends Local Urban League Sec'y," *Louisiana Weekly*, May 2, 1942, 2; "Housing Project Doesn't Hire Negro Carpenters," *Dallas Express*, October 25, 1941, 1; "Carpenters Protest FEP on Housing Project Discrimination," *Dallas Express*, December 13, 1941, 1; "Fair Employment Investigators in Dallas," *Dallas Express*, February 7, 1942, 1; "Carpenters Await Move by FEPC," *Dallas Express*, February 21, 1942, 1; "Hoping for Defense Jobs—And Training" (editorial), *Dallas Express*, June 13, 1942, 10; transcript of Louisiana USES and NOUL conference, March 26, 1942, Irving Wood file, box 473, John Beecher office files, DFO, Fair Employment Practices Committee, RG 228, NARA CP.

38. J. Beecher to L. Cramer, April 30, 1942, Cramer confidential file, box 470, John Beecher office files, DFO, Fair Employment Practices Committee, RG 228, NARA CP.

39. "Wesley Asked to Head Defense Drive," *Houston Informer*, March 1, 1941, 1; "Texans Rally to Defense Program," *Houston Informer*, March 8, 1941, 1; "Fair Employment Committee Hears Wesley's Report on Kindleberger," *Dallas Express*, August 16, 1941, 1.

40. Reed, *Seedtime*, 175–204. For detailed information on the NCDT, see Ferguson, "The Politics of Inclusion."

41. See numerous letters in COFEP cases 1941–42 (A–M) file, box B-11, and COFEP cases 1941–42 (M–Z) file, box B-12, part 2, National Association for the Advancement of Colored People Collection.

42. Ennis Crawford to NAACP, August 1942; Charlotte NAACP to Walter White, May 19, 1942; W. H. Blackman to F. D. Roosevelt, Congress, Secretary of War, COFEP, and OPM, April 18, 1942, COFEP cases 1941–42 (A–M) file, box B-11, part 2, National Association for the Advancement of Colored People Collection.

43. For Beecher's assessment of New Orleans and Atlanta leadership, see George Streator's comment in transcript of Louisiana USES and NOUL conference, March 26, 1942, Irving Wood file, box 473, and J. Beecher to L. Cramer, March 25, 1942, Bell Aircraft—Atlanta file, box 471, John Beecher office files, DFO, Fair Employment Practices Committee, RG 228, NARA CP. For an example of Ira De A. Reid's early involvement in the fair employment movement, see Ira De A. Reid, "Job Opportunities for Negroes," *Dallas Express*, October 4, 1941, 2.

44. Memphis UL executive secretary B. J. Searcy informed FEPC field examiner

John Beecher that "he would not dare to appear at the Birmingham hearings and describe the Memphis situation, since he most certainly would lose his position and be driven from Memphis as a consequence." See Field Report, John Beecher, Memphis file, box 470, John Beecher office files, DFO, Fair Employment Practices Committee, RG 228, NARA CP. For an analysis of the Crump machine's stance on civil rights, see Honey, *Southern Labor and Black Civil Rights*.

45. C. Laws, "Au Revoir," *Louisiana Weekly*, January 23, 1943, 6.

46. J. Beecher to L. Cramer, April 11, 1942, 3, Training—General file, box 470, John Beecher office files, DFO, Fair Employment Practices Committee, RG 228, NARA CP; "UL Urges Registration for War Industry Jobs," *Louisiana Weekly*, April 25, 1942, 3; "WPB Commends Local Urban League Sec'y," *Louisiana Weekly*, May 2, 1942, 2.

47. W. Moses to NAACP in New York, December 10, 1940, COFEP protests 1942 (M–Z) file, box B-12, part 2, National Association for the Advancement of Colored People Collection. For a later example involving black masons being replaced at Fort McPherson, Georgia, see Atlanta NAACP to NAACP, November 3, 1942, COFEP cases 1941–42 (A–M) file, box B-11, part 2, National Association for the Advancement of Colored People Collection. For the AFL painters at Ingalls shipyard, see C. Record to R. Weaver, April 18, 1942, Pascagoula, Miss., file, box 473, John Beecher office files, DFO, Fair Employment Practices Committee, RG 228, NARA CP.

48. Hill, *Dallas*, 129–61; Ambrose, "A Revolution of Hope," 138–40; Nelson "Class and Race"; Honey, *Southern Labor and Black Civil Rights*, 145–73.

49. Irving Wood to J. Beecher, April 8, 1942, Irving Wood file, box 473, John Beecher office files, DFO, Fair Employment Practices Committee, RG 228, NARA CP; Nelson, "Organized Labor," 965, 970–71; C. Record to R. Weaver, April 18, 1942, May 1942, Pascagoula, Miss., file, box 473, John Beecher office files, DFO, Fair Employment Practices Committee, RG 228, NARA CP.

50. J. Beecher to L. Cramer, March 7, 1942, New Orleans file, box 473, and J. Beecher to L. Cramer, February 13, 1942, Mobile file, box 471, John Beecher office files, DFO, Fair Employment Practices Committee, RG 228, NARA CP; Kryder, *Divided Arsenal*, 8.

51. Northrup, *Organized Labor*, 228–31; *Shipyard Bulletin* 7–9 (1940–42) (a quarterly published by the Newport News Shipbuilding and Dry Dock Company, Newport News, Virginia).

52. Raper and Reid, *Sharecroppers All*, 89–103.

53. Northrup, *Organized Labor*, 210–31. Northrup claimed that in 1918 skilled black shipyard workers comprised approximately 20 percent of shipyard workers nationally, while by 1942 skilled black workers comprised only 3.1 percent (213). See also Weaver, *Negro Labor*, 99–100. Weaver also cites the fact that in 1930 black workers constituted some 8.5 percent of southern shipyard workers, while by 1940 they constituted only 6.5 percent.

54. In Texas, open shop ruled with the exception of IBB locals at Todd-Galveston and eventually Pennsylvania shipyards in Beaumont. In New Orleans, the IBB Local 37 had become the main bargaining agent at Delta and Higgins Industries, while Avondale Marine Ways remained open shop, and Todd-Johnson Dry Dock remained

under contract with IUMSWA-CIO Local 29. Further to the east, the IBB organized the Ingalls shipyards in Pascagoula, the all-white Gulf shipyards in Mobile, and the Tampa Shipbuilding Company, while IUMSWA Local 18 in Mobile represented workers at the ADDSCO plant.

55. Northrup, *Organized Labor,* 210–31; Ambrose, "A Revolution of Hope," 182–98.

56. Ambrose, "A Revolution of Hope," 182–98. See correspondence 1938 and correspondence 1939 files, box 69, series 5, Industrial Union of Marine and Shipbuilding Workers of America Papers; Nelson, "Organized Labor," 988. White majorities existed in the most powerful CIO unions, including the United Auto Workers, Oil Workers International Union, and United Steel Workers of America.

57. Northrup, *Organized Labor,* 213–19.

58. "Negro Ship Workers to Hold Defense Jobs Meeting on Sunday," *Louisiana Weekly,* February 14, 1942, 6; Northrup, *Organized Labor,* 216.

59. J. Beecher to L. Cramer, March 7, 1942, 4, New Orleans file, box 473, John Beecher office files, DFO, Fair Employment Practices Committee, RG 228, NARA CP.

60. Bell Aircraft—Atlanta file, box 471, John Beecher office files, DFO, Fair Employment Practices Committee, RG 228, NARA CP; "To Offer Defense Course," *Dallas Express,* March 22, 1941, 1; "Defense Situation in Dallas," *Dallas Express,* March 29, 1941, 1; "Capacity Crowd Hears DNCC Report on Defense Training Fight," *Dallas Express,* August 1, 1942, 1; "Bottleneck in Defense School Being Removed," *Dallas Express,* January 9, 1943, 1; "Dallas Boasts One of the South's Best War Schools," *Dallas Express,* March 27, 1943, 1; "Welding School Drive Gains Support," *Louisiana Weekly,* August 16, 1941, 1; "Welding School Fight Gets Nation's Attention," *Louisiana Weekly,* August 23, 1941, 1; "NYA Announces Welding Classes to Begin Nov. 1," *Louisiana Weekly,* September 20, 1941, 1; "Shakespeare Park the Scene of Protest Mass Meeting Sunday," *Louisiana Weekly,* October 4, 1941, 1; Mobile, Alabama, file, box 471, John Beecher office files, DFO, Fair Employment Practices Committee, RG 228, NARA CP.

61. Summary of the Hearings of the President's Committee on Fair Employment Practice Held in Birmingham, Alabama, June 20, 1942; Delta 10-BR-128 file, Active Cases, Fair Employment Practices Committee, RG 228, National Archives and Records Administration, Fort Worth, Texas (hereafter cited as NARA FW); Reed, *Seedtime,* 71–72.

62. J. Beecher to W. Alexander, February 27, 1942, National Defense Training file, box 470; L. Cramer to J. Beecher, March 31, 1942, and May 2, 1942, Cramer file, box 472, John Beecher office files, DFO, Fair Employment Practices Committee, RG 228, NARA CP.

63. Associated Industries of Florida to Gov. S. Holland, August 5, 1942, Labor Problems file, series 406, box 66, Spessard Holland Administration Files.

64. See Report on Race Relations in Alabama, August 5, 1942, box 12277, and hundreds of letters of support in file ASES, Department of Industrial Relations, box 12264; Delta Ship-FEPC file and Race Segregation file, box 12277; FEPC file, box 12278, Frank Dixon Administration Files; Reed, *Seedtime,* 73, 90–91.

65. J. Beecher to L. Cramer, and report of interviews, February 15, 1942, Mobile, Alabama, file, box 471, DFO, Fair Employment Practices Committee, RG 228, NARA CP. In the wake of Dixon's Kiwanis speech, influential southern liberal Howard Odum sought some compromise with Dixon on the FEPC issue. Odum had served as an informal consultant to the FEPC when it came South in February. In August, Odum wrote to Dixon seeking a private and unpublicized audience with the Southern Governors Conference, specifically seeking a solution to the issue of segregation in southern defense industries. "What I should like to talk about," Odum informed Dixon, "is how we can be masters of our own situation without letting outside interference goad us into unwise action." See H. Odum to F. Dixon, August 21, 1942, Labor Problems file, box 66, series 406, Spessard Holland Administration Files.

66. F. Dixon to E. Talmadge, September 11, 1942, Alabama Manpower Committee file, box 12277, Frank Dixon Administration Files.

67. "Record Ship Deal Here—Work for 40,000 in New Plant," *New Orleans Item*, March 14, 1942, 1; "Housing to Smash Record—100,000 Population Increase Predicted within Year for City," *New Orleans Item*, March 30, 1942, 1; "My Day" clipping in Southern Conference on Human Welfare file, box 472, John Beecher office files, DFO, Fair Employment Practices Committee, RG 228, NARA CP.

68. A. J. Higgins to E. Trimble, June 16, 1942, loose papers, box 469, Ernest Trimble office files, DFO, Fair Employment Practices Committee, RG 228, NARA CP; "Higgins Tells Plans to Hire Negroes at Conference," *Louisiana Weekly*, May 2, 1942, 8. See also "Higgins Says There Will Be No Discrimination," *Louisiana Weekly*, April 18, 1942, 1; "Urban League Sec. Posits Way to Relieve Local Housing Shortage," *Louisiana Weekly*, April 25, 1942, 3; Northrup, *Organized Labor*, 216. For later comments, see "Headline Highlights: 'Higgins Again,'" *Louisiana Weekly*, October 31, 1942, 6; "Higgins Will Train Workers—Leases School Site in Uptown," *New Orleans Item*, April 27, 1942, 1.

69. "Higgins Says There Will Be No Discrimination," and "Headline Highlights," *Louisiana Weekly*, April 18, 1942, 1, 10.

70. "Labor in the South," *Manufacturers' Record* (September 1940): 49–50; Birmingham Report, 7th Regional Labor Supply Conference file, box 470, John Beecher office files, DFO, Fair Employment Practices Committee, RG 228, NARA CP.

71. Birmingham Report; C. Laws to J. Thomas, October 6, 1941, C. Laws file, box A-65, Southern Regional Office, National Urban League Collection; V. Williams to G. Johnson, December 15, 1942, NAA file, box 802, Closed Cases, Fair Employment Practices Committee, RG 228, NARA FW. For similar attitudes toward social equality in the Mississippi Delta, see Reverend H. H. Humes's views in Woodruff, "Mississippi Delta Planters."

72. Reed, *Seedtime*, 75–76. The FEPC's Ernest Trimble wrote Lawrence Cramer on August 15, "We were all very shocked at the news that we had been transferred lock-stock and barrel to McNutt." Consequently, Trimble admitted, "Our morale has dropped almost to zero for a while." See E. Trimble to L. Cramer, August 15, 1942, loose papers, box 469, Ernest Trimble office files, DFO, Fair Employment Practices Committee, RG 228, NARA CP.

73. For housing issues, see "U.S. Clinches 30,000 New Homes to Be Built Here," *New Orleans Item*, April 1, 1942, 1; "Millions to City for New Homes," *New Orleans Item*, April 10, 1942, 1; "100s Trying to Find Homes Here with Housing Office Swamped," *New Orleans Item*, April 15, 1942, 9; *New Orleans Item*, July 3, 1942, 18. For various reactions to the contract cancellation, see "Probe Shipyard Closing," *New Orleans Item*, July 20, 1942, 1; "Raps Closing of Shipyard—Domengeaux Charges Plot against Higgins," *New Orleans Item*, July 25, 1942, 1.

74. "Extra! Extra! Read All about Higgins Shipbuilding Mystery," *Louisiana Weekly*, August 8, 1942, 3; Northrup, *Organized Labor*, 217.

75. J. Beecher to L. Cramer, April 11, 1942, Training—General (April 13 hearing) file, box 470, John Beecher office files, DFO, Fair Employment Practices Committee, RG 228, NARA CP; E. J. Wright, "Symbol of Rampart," *Louisiana Weekly*, October 17, 1942, 1.

76. Finkle, "The Conservative Aims," 692–713. See also Sitkoff, "African American Militancy."

77. C. Laws, "Headline Highlights," *Louisiana Weekly*, August 29, 1942, 10; "Negroes Still Shut out of War Work Here, Reveals UL Sec'y," *Louisiana Weekly*, October 17, 1942, 1; "Delta Shipyard Catastrophe" (editorial), *Louisiana Weekly*, October 24, 1942, 10.

78. Transcript of NOUL and Louisiana USES conference (March 24, 1942) and J. Beecher to I. Wood, April 23, 1942, Irving Wood file, box 473, John Beecher office files, DFO, Fair Employment Practices Committee, RG 228, NARA CP.

79. "U.S. Irked at South's Attempt to Block Manpower," *Louisiana Weekly*, November 7, 1942, 9; "Slavery 1942" (editorial), *Louisiana Weekly*, November 14, 1942, 9; "For Farm Labor" (editorial), *Dallas Express*, September 19, 1942; "Reveal New Facts on Freezing Colored Labor in Far South," *Dallas Express*, November 14, 1942, 1.

80. Transcript of Louisiana USES and NOUL conference, March 26, 1942.

81. Reed, *Seedtime*, 192–93; "Day Shift of War School under NYA," *Dallas Express*, June 12, 1942, 2; "First Defense Training for Negroes Promises Much Success," *Dallas Express*, November 7, 1942, 1; "Dallas Boasts One of the South's Best War Schools," *Dallas Express*, March 27, 1943, 3. For a list of black training programs in the South during 1943, see Training Negroes file, box 19, series 11, War Manpower Commission, RG 211, NARA EP.

82. "Dallas Boasts One of the Best War Schools," *Dallas Express*, March 27, 1943, 3.

83. Weaver, *Negro Labor*, 26.

84. Statement Regarding War Training, Todd-Houston file, box 808, Closed Cases, Fair Employment Practices Committee, RG 228, NARA FW.

85. "3 NYA Welders Leave for Work in Virginia Shipyard," *Louisiana Weekly*, May 30, 1942, 1; P. Dixon to P. McNutt, November 23, 1942, Minority—Negroes—Discrimination file, box 1, series 278, War Manpower Commission, RG 211, NARA FW.

86. J. H. Bond to A. Fleming, January 16, 1943, Minority—Negroes—Discrimination file, box 1, series 278, War Manpower Commission, RG 211, NARA FW.

87. "Day Shift of War School under NYA," *Dallas Express*, June 12, 1943, 2; Statement Regarding War Training, Todd-Houston file, box 808, Closed Cases, Fair Employment Practices Committee, RG 228, NARA FW.

88. "Training Women as War Workers," *Atlanta Daily World*, March 11, 1943, 3; "Rapid Placements Given Graduates of Florida Normal War Training Courses," *Atlanta Daily World*, May 10, 1943, 10; "Shipyard Workers Are Badly Needed for West Coast," *Atlanta Daily World*, May 23, 1943, 6; "Atlanta Negro NYA Office in State of Apprehension," *Atlanta Daily World*, July 6, 1943, 1; "Aircraft School Graduates Getting Jobs at Bell," *Atlanta Daily World*, October 7, 1943, 1; "Aircraft School Holds First Anniversary," *Atlanta Daily World*, December 4, 1943, 4; Memorandum on Negro Employment at Bell Aircraft Company, 1944 Labor General file, box A-70, Southern Regional Office, National Urban League Collection; Milkman, *Gender at Work*, 65–83; Berger-Gluck, *Rosie the Riveter Revisited*.

89. F. McSherry to J. Bond, November 23, 1942, Minority—Negroes—Discrimination file, series 278, War Manpower Commission, RG 211, NARA FW.

90. "Day Shift of War School under NYA," *Dallas Express*, June 12, 1943, 2; "Negro War Training School Ordered Closed," *Dallas Express*, September 11, 1943, 1.

91. Mertz, *New Deal Policy*. Mertz argues that the New Deal poverty programs had minimal long-term effect in reducing southern poverty. While that may be true, the WMC recruitment policies certainly illustrate how federal war programs offered southerners new avenues toward economic opportunity.

92. During this time, McSherry responded to complaints by Paul Dixon, Thurgood Marshall, and the Galveston NAACP over lack of NYA defense training for black women and another complaint filed by a training graduate of Prairie View A&M alleging discrimination by the Houston USES. McSherry also investigated the Savannah NAACP's on-going complaint over discriminatory employment practices at the Southeastern Shipbuilding Company in that city. See Minority—Negroes—Discrimination file, box 1, series 278, War Manpower Commission, RG 211, NARA FW; Southeastern Shipbuilding Co.—7-BR-58 file, box 1, Closed Cases, War Manpower Commission, RG 211, NARA EP. McSherry responded sympathetically to DNCC executive secretary Virgil Williams's suggestion that the Dallas WMC office include Negroes on the staff. According to Williams, McSherry "pointed to the recognition of the need for additional personnel to work in the field of Negro employment and training." See V. Williams to Paul McNutt, October 5, 1942, 1942 file, box 1, Dallas Negro Chamber of Commerce Collection. In a few cases, Robert Weaver, then chief of the Negro Employment and Training Branch of the WMC, effectively challenged discrimination. For instance, Weaver helped Carpenters AFL Local 2216 in Chattanooga, Tennessee, obtain war construction employment in various projects in Tennessee and Georgia. See press release, May 17, 1942, War Manpower Commission 1942 file, box A665, part 2, National Association for the Advancement of Colored People Collection. For a few other examples, see Kryder, *Divided Arsenal*, 78–85.

Chapter Three: "On the Train and Gone"

1. George Franklin to Leonard Steidel, June 28, 1944, Louisiana Employment Complaints file, box 652, series 270, War Manpower Commission, RG 211, NARA FW.

2. According to Southern Tenant Farmers Union (STFU) figures, southern cotton pickers made between 11 and 22 cents per hour, based on $1.50 per hundred pounds; see "Cotton Pickers Ask 30 Cents/Hour Minimum," *New Orleans News Digest*, October 5, 1942, 3. In fact, some growers in South Texas paid only 60 cents to $1 per hundred pounds. On average, one person could pick one to two hundred pounds per day. In comparison, wages for unskilled workers in defense industries during 1942 varied from 40 to 75 cents per hour.

3. Most recent works addressing the issue of worker mobility in rural areas during the war are either local, state, or subregional studies. As new scholarship, this chapter sets out to examine worker mobility (and immobility) as it affected the entire South and Southwest and also to focus on the ways that rural nonwhite workers used both federal and more informal labor recruitment programs to gain leverage within this regional labor market during the war. See Daniel, "Going among Strangers"; Woodruff, "Pick or Fight"; Woodruff, "Mississippi Delta Planters"; Cobb, *The Most Southern Place;* Hahamovitch, *The Fruits of Their Labor;* Weber, *Dark Sweat;* Gregory, *American Exodus.*

4. "Origins and Problems of Texas Migratory Farm Labor," 31–32; for development of farm placement system in Texas after 1934, see 22, 44, 71, 85. See also "Supplement to Origins and Problems of Texas Migratory Farm Labor," 1–3, 30.

5. Nash, *The American West Transformed,* 44–45; Flynn, *The Mess in Washington,* 68–70. In June 1943, at the outset of the program, the War Manpower Commission determined that the Great Plains and the Ozark regions (WMC Regions VIII and IX) had a surplus labor supply of 210,835 persons, while the South and Southwest from Maryland to New Mexico (WMC Regions IV, VII, and X) had a surplus supply of 178,829 persons. In contrast, WMC Region V (Michigan, Ohio, and Kentucky) had a shortage of 38,525 workers, while WMC Region XII (the Pacific West) had a manpower deficit of 199,685 workers. See Revised Program for Interregional Recruitment, June 1943, Labor Market Reports, 1943 file, box 7, series 156, War Manpower Commission, RG 211, National Archives and Records Administration, College Park, Maryland (hereafter cited as NARA CP).

6. For the meaning of African American mobility in the South, see Cohen, *At Freedom's Edge;* Daniel, *Shadow of Slavery;* Shenk, "Race, Manhood, and Manpower."

7. Anderson, *Men on the Move,* 215, 209.

8. Louisiana Weekly Agricultural Labor Summary, October 10, 1942, Weekly Agricultural Labor Summary Reports file, box 5, series 282, War Manpower Commission, RG 211, NARA FW.

9. TSES cited 600,000 migrants in "Origins and Problems of Texas Migratory Farm Labor," 42. The Texas Agricultural Workers Association estimated in 1940 that there were 350,000 migratory farmworkers in Texas; *Dallas Morning News*, February

7, 1940, sec. 1, 9; Foley, *The White Scourge*, 163–82; *Migratory Labor in American Agriculture*, 3. The report indicates that by 1940 there were an estimated 1 million migrant workers in the United States. Jacqueline Jones estimates that during the 1930s, from 500,000 to 1 million farm families in the South were affected by farm displacement (*The Dispossessed*, 171–72); see also Saville, "Economics."

10. "Origins and Problems of Texas Migratory Farm Labor," 70; Foley, *The White Scourge*, 163–82; Montejano, *Anglos and Mexicans*. For ethnic breakdown, see *The Farm Labor Situation in Texas*, U.S. Department of Agriculture, Bureau of Agricultural Economics 5 (May 1940), Texas State Library, Austin.

11. Lange and Taylor, *An American Exodus*, 51; Weber, *Dark Sweat*, 141; Gregory, *American Exodus*, 3–35, 166–67; Shindo, *Dust Bowl Migrants*.

12. In Texas, the Farm Security Administration built permanent camps in Robstown, Sinton, El Campo, Vernon, La Mesa, and Lubbock; see "Origins and Problems of Texas Migratory Farm Labor," 70. In Florida, the FSA built a permanent camp at Belle Glade. See Hahamovitch, *The Fruits of Their Labor*, 156–72.

13. During the 1938 and 1939 cotton strikes, many African American and Mexican migrants embraced the more active and militant farmworker organizations under the West Coast CIO. Some white migrants also joined the CIO in rural California. Yet largely, southern white migrants viewed migration and wage labor and not organized labor as a means toward economic independence. See Weber, *Dark Sweat*, 137–61; Gregory, *American Exodus*, 154–64; Morgan, *Rising in the West*, 97–112.

14. McWilliams, "Mexicans to Michigan," 5–18; Valdes, *Al Norte*, 80–88.

15. See Bureau of Labor Statistics, Sixteenth Biennial Report, September 1, 1938, to August 31, 1940, 26–33, Texas State Library, Austin. For license fees, see also McWilliams, "Mexicans to Michigan," 8. For the growth of licensing, see Report of the Bureau of Labor Statistics, Fifteenth Biennial Report, 1937–38, 24–25, Texas State Library, Austin.

16. McWilliams found that Frank Cortez, a local entrepreneur, was the "kingpin" of licensed Texas emigrant agents. During the 1941 season, Cortez recruited some 6,000 workers at $1 per head, while S. P. Acosta, another major contractor, recruited close to 2,500 workers for the Mount Pleasant Sugar Company of Michigan. Other local contractors included Simon Vasquez, with the Great Lakes Sugar Company of Ohio, and F. de la Garza, with the Great Northern Sugar Beet Company of Bay City, Michigan. Both of these men contracted for 2,500 workers each (McWilliams, "Mexicans to Michigan," 5–18). For accounts of worker exploitation and recruiting in Dallas churches, see "Supplement to Origins and Problems of Texas Migratory Farm Labor," 7–14, 29.

17. McWilliams, "Mexicans to Michigan," 7–9.

18. "Supplement to Origins and Problems of Texas Migratory Farm Labor," 67.

19. Raper and Reid, *Sharecroppers All*, 45. See also Garcia, *Desert Immigrants*, 62. Garcia argues that as early as 1904, growers in Mississippi and Louisiana began recruiting Mexican migrants for farmwork.

20. J. H. Bond to Arthur Fleming, January 1, 1943, unlabeled file, box 1, series 269, War Manpower Commission, RG 211, NARA FW. Bond cited statistics from 1942

USES records indicating an acceptance of agriculture clearance orders for other states such as Arizona and in the Great Lakes exceeded 50,000, while acceptance of clearance orders in nonagricultural industries exceeded 70,000.

21. Jones, *The Dispossessed*, 172; *Migratory Labor in American Agriculture*, 3; Foley, *The White Scourge*, 205; Allen, *East Texas Lumber Workers*, 54. Allen lists 36,000 lumber workers in Texas during 1940. WMC records indicate that by 1945, there were only 16,000 in the state. See "Manpower Situation in Logging and Lumber Industry, Region X," Special Manpower Problems file, box 7, series 80, War Manpower Commission, RG 211, NARA CP.

22. WMC Regional LMC, December 1943, Committee 3-1942 file, box 1, series 6, War Manpower Commission, RG 211, NARA EP.

23. References to James Bond as director of TSES include "Supplement to Origins and Problems of Texas Migratory Farm Labor," 41; and TSES-1941 file, 4-14/128, Coke Stevenson Governor's Papers.

24. In September 1940, the TSES Farm Placement Service bragged that it had a national reputation as "the leading agency" in attacking both "regular" and "migratory" employment problems of farm labor. TSES officials also claimed that "Farm Placement Procedure had taken its place as an established technique in Employment Service operations" ("Origins and Problems of Texas Migratory Farm Labor," 63–64). See also Breen, *Labor Market Politics*, 157–58.

25. As an extreme example of exploitation, the Bureau of Agricultural Economics documented one case near Amarillo in 1937 where close to three hundred migrant African Americans became stranded on a nine-thousand-acre cotton operation. The workers, who had arrived with the fall cotton harvest, lacked transportation facilities, lived in dugouts, and survived throughout the winter on food from the farm's commissary, to which they became indebted. Only when one worker walked to the county seat to apply for relief did county officials discover that two workers had already died from pneumonia. In response to officials' concerns for the workers, the grower replied that "there was nothing to be alarmed about" and that "as soon as the weather warmed up, the Negroes would fade out." See "Origins and Problems of Texas Migratory Farm Labor," 67–68; *The Farm Labor Situation in Texas*, 12.

26. Astonishingly, during this period the TSES Farm Placement program for cotton growers placed over 400,000 workers in 1938 and over 593,000 workers in 1940 ("Supplement to Origins and Problems of Texas Migratory Farm Labor," 81).

27. For example, when one community in the Brownsville area sent out a call for two thousand pickers, the TSES sent an investigator to the community only to find that names of specific growers were not forthcoming from local officials. After every grower had been contacted and all rumors tracked down, the TSES determined that only eighty-five workers were needed in the community ("Origins and Problems of Texas Migratory Farm Labor," 44–45).

28. "Supplement to Origins and Problems of Texas Migratory Farm Labor," 65–66, 83–86; Lange and Taylor, *An American Exodus*, 28; Weber, *Dark Sweat*, 141–42.

29. "Summary and Analysis of Labor Problems in the Lower Rio Grande Valley,"

2–17, in Farm Labor—W. B. McFarland Reports file, box 1, series 283, War Manpower Commission, RG 211, NARA FW.

30. R. Y. Creech to Claude Pepper, April 23, 1943, Labor Mobilization and Utilization 10-2 file (1 of 2), box 3, series 11, War Manpower Commission, RG 211, NARA EP; Report of the Meeting Held at Camp Osceola, Belle Glade, Florida, May 15, 1942; L. S. Rickard to L. L. Chandler, July 8, 1942; L. L. Chandler to C. Pepper, July 23, 1942; Labor Problems file (1 of 2), box 66, series 406, Florida State Archives, Tallahassee, Spessard Holland Administration Files; "FSA Regional Director E. S. Morgan Responds to L. L. Chandler Accusations of 'Orgies,'" *Mobile Register*, February 23, 1943, 7; Hahamovitch, "Standing Idly By," 15–36.

31. Foley, *The White Scourge*, 183–202; "Farmers Meeting Is Step towards Big Campaign," *Houston Informer*, January 27, 1940, 3; Zamora, *The World of the Mexican Worker*, 204; Mooney, *Farmers and Farm Workers' Movements*, 123–49.

32. For a discussion of similarities between growers and industrialists, see Cobb, "Beyond Planters and Industrialists," 65–66; Schulman, *From Cotton Belt to Sunbelt*, 124–25.

33. M. Gonzales to E. Trimble, August 10, 1942, miscellaneous file, Ernest Trimble office files, DFO, Fair Employment Practices Committee, RG 228, NARA CP. For more on Gonzales, see Daniel, *Chicano Workers*.

34. Flynn, *The Mess in Washington*, 137–45.

35. Dance, "King of the Blues," 18.

36. Daniel, *Shadow of Slavery*, 179–80; Percy, *Lanterns on the Levee*, 281.

37. "Workers Cite Peonage on Florida Cane Farms," *Birmingham World*, October 16, 1942, 1; "Escaped Workers Tell Tale of Horror—\$ Youths Escape from Plantation Semi-Slavery," *Birmingham World*, February 12, 1943, 1; "Workers Fined for Escaping Bean Plantation," *Birmingham World*, March 5, 1943, 1. See also Daniel, *Shadow of Slavery*, 184–85.

38. G. M. Simmons to R. Sullivan, January 5, 1943, Labor Mobilization and Utilization Clearance—1F1 general file, box 2, series 11, War Manpower Commission, RG 211, NARA EP. In January 1943, the FSA sought to transport black farmworkers from Mississippi to Sanford, Florida, north of Orlando, where bean growers signed a labor contract agreement with the FSA. Orlando's USES manager, G. M. Simmons, assured Mississippi WMC state director Raymond Sullivan that there would be "no monkey business" about returning the farmworkers to Mississippi after the harvest. Simmons also assured Sullivan that the Florida growers were "experienced in handling and caring for Negroes" and that "each employer has Negro leaders as foremen." To guarantee the health of the crew, the FSA would furnish subsistence and medical care en route.

39. "Charge Dixie Blocks Manpower Use—Negro Labor in South Frozen," *Birmingham World*, November 3, 1942, 1.

40. Frank Constangy to J. J. Bush, October 21, 1942, and James McGinnis to John Corson, November 12, 1942, 533.2 Special Problems—South Carolina file, box 12, series 2, War Manpower Commission, RG 211, NARA EP.

41. "U.S. Irked at South's Attempt to Block Manpower," *Louisiana Weekly*, November 7, 1942, 9; "Reveal New Facts on Freezing Colored Labor in Far South," *Dallas Express*, November 14, 1942, 1.

42. "Work or Jail Police" (editorial), *Louisiana Weekly*, October 24, 1942, 10. In the Alexandria area, unskilled migrant workers had moved on to construction jobs at Leesville, Louisiana, and Centerville, Mississippi. Under competition from the construction boom, cane harvest wages varied between 17 and 25 cents per hour in 1942. See Louisiana Weekly Agricultural Summary, September 5, 1942, and October 17, 1942, Weekly Agricultural Summary—Louisiana file, box 5, series 282, War Manpower Commission, RG 211, NARA FW.

43. *Dallas Times Herald*, March 19, 1943, Regional, State, and Area Office Press Releases file, box 1, series 279, War Manpower Commission, RG 211, NARA FW; "Alex. Mayor Threatens to Run Negro Women out of Town Who 'Quit' Their Jobs," *Louisiana Weekly*, April 24, 1943, 1; "Macon's Drastic 'Work or Jail' Law Points toward Effort to Straight Jacket Race Labor," *Birmingham World*, June 25, 1943, 4; "Work or Fight Orders Get Teeth," *Birmingham World*, August 20, 1943, 1; "Work or Fight, Governor Orders," *Birmingham World*, September 10, 1943, 3. Shenk provides an excellent overview of "work or fight" legislation in Georgia during World War I ("Race, Manhood, and Manpower," 653–55).

44. T. Clark to D. Byrd, September 10, 1943; Report of Indiscriminate Arrests of Colored Citizens in Mobile's Work-or-Fight Drive, September 26, 1943, and J. L. LeFlore to W. White, October 2, 1943, Work-or-Fight Laws 1943 file, box B221, part 2, National Association for the Advancement of Colored People Collection.

45. In Region X, WMC farm placement director W. B. McFarland, a TSES veteran in South Texas, became the target of verbal attacks from J. E. McDonald, Texas agricultural commissioner, who was an extremely outspoken opponent of federal farm programs and rural labor regulation. At the same time, H. H. Williamson, Texas Extension Service director, laid plans to give county agents sole responsibility of recruiting and placement and thus out of the WMC's and especially the FSA's hands. See W. B. McFarland to E. R. Speer, January 6, 1943, Farm Labor—McFarland Reports file, box 1, series 283; A. D. Stewart to J. H. Bond, January 1943; C. E. Belk to J. H. Bond, February 24, 1943; H. H. Williamson to M. L. Wilson, February 22, 1943; Extension Service—General Correspondence—Texas file, box 10, series 283, War Manpower Commission, RG 211, NARA FW.

46. Woodruff, "Pick or Fight," 79.

47. W. B. McFarland to E. R. Speer, February 3, 1943, FSA Regional Conference, Dallas file, box 1, series 269, War Manpower Commission, RG 211, NARA FW. McFarland informed E. R. Speer, "Our relationship with the FSA and other departments of Agriculture in Region VIII has been harmonious and so far we have been fortunate enough in having the farmer associations and the growers themselves go down the line with us." Nevertheless, McFarland warned: "I am sure you realize what will happen if the FSA starts taking workers from areas in Texas where they can be used."

48. According to the *Wood County Echo*, April 8, 1943, farmers from Oklahoma in the FSA farm labor program received eighty dollars, a cow, a garden plot, and a place

to live from the FSA. C. E. Belk to J. H. Bond, attn. E. R. Speer, April 17, 1943, Regional, State, and Area Office Press Releases file, box 1, series 279, War Manpower Commission, RG 211, NARA FW. Large cotton growers in West Texas also opposed FSA activities in their area, particularly the FSA's plan to convert CCC camps into FSA labor camps. Like their counterparts in California, the growers claimed such camps would "be a hot bed for labor agitators." See W. B. McFarland to E. R. Speer, February 13, 1943, unlabeled file (Texas agricultural placement), box 1, series 271, War Manpower Commission, RG 211, NARA FW.

49. Report on the Recruitment of Dairy Hands for the State of Washington, March 1, 1943, Extension Service—General Correspondence—Texas file, box 10, series 283, War Manpower Commission, RG 211, NARA FW.

50. James Pritchard to Raymond Sullivan, June 19, 1942, and Irene D. Elliot to Raymond Sullivan, June 18, 1942, 533.2 Special Problems—Mississippi file, box 12, series 2, War Manpower Commission, RG 211, NARA EP.

51. C. E. Belk to J. H. Bond, March 27, 1943, Labor—General Correspondence—Louisiana file, box containing 283 and 285, War Manpower Commission, RG 211, NARA FW.

52. Ibid. See also "Rio Grande Valley Farmers Await Word from WMS on Requested Freeze of 40,000 Laborers," *Corpus Christi Caller Times*, March 28, 1943; J. B. Wear to E. R. Speer, March 26, 1943; and Lawrence Appleby (F. W. Hunter) to director, Region X, May 27, 1943, Lower Rio Grande Valley file, box 668, series 270, War Manpower Commission, RG 211, NARA FW. Johnny McCain argues that in July 1943 the WMC and WFA certified a need of 5,000 *braceros* despite Coastal Bend growers' requests for 63,000 ("Texas and the Mexican Labor Question," 51–52). WMC records indicate that H. H. Williamson approved growers' requests for 21,900 workers in Nueces County and 14,395 workers in San Patricio County, making a total of 36,295 workers for the cotton harvest. See Philip Bruton to J. H. Bond, July 1943, Mexicans file, box 1, series 669; and J. B. Wear to E. R. Speer, July 12, 1943, unlabeled file, box 653, series 270, War Manpower Commission, RG 211, NARA FW.

53. Flynn, *The Mess in Washington*, 141–42.

54. McAllen report, July 3, 1944, and October 1944, Narrative Reports—Farm Labor Supply Center-TX 6-12/44 file, box 2, series 6, RG 224, NARA CP.

55. Weekly Agricultural Labor Market Report for Texas, August 13, 1943, and August 27, 1943, Region X—Texas—1943 file, box 13, series 199, War Manpower Commission, RG 211, NARA CP; and monthly narrative reports, C2—R36 TX file, box 2, series 6, RG 224, NARA CP.

56. Hahamovitch, *The Fruits of Their Labor*, 174–78.

57. Ibid., 151–81; McCain, "Texas and the Mexican Labor Question"; Scruggs, "The Bracero Program," 149–68; Gamboa, *Mexican Labor*. See miscellaneous correspondence during the summer of 1943, POW Groups file, box 648, series 270, War Manpower Commission, RG 211, NARA FW. Texas rice farmers gradually began the transfer to imported labor during the summer of 1943. One of the first areas in the Southwest to utilize the program was the Lower Colorado River Valley in Texas. See progress report on agricultural development, May 8, 1943, Progress Reports—Texas

file, box 5, series 271, War Manpower Commission, RG 211, NARA FW. For the first use of *braceros* in Texas, see miscellaneous correspondence, unlabeled file (*bracero* agricultural placement), box 653, series 270; and Mexicans file, box 1, series 269, War Manpower Commission, RG 211, NARA FW.

58. For Texas POWs, see miscellaneous correspondence during the summer of 1943, POW Groups file, box 648, series 270, War Manpower Commission, RG 211, NARA FW. The actual number of POWs varies according to historians. According to Dewey Grantham, the majority of the nation's 250,000 POWs were located in the South (*The South in Modern America*, 178).

59. J. R. Reagor to Orville Carpenter, December 9, 1943, and E. R. Speer to J. H. Bond, November 17, 1944, Placement Program Reports file, box containing series 283 and 285, War Manpower Commission, RG 211, NARA FW; Hahamovitch, *The Fruits of Their Labor*, 176. See also Fickle and Ellis, "POWs in the Piney Woods," 695–724.

60. McCain, "Texas and the Mexican Labor Question," 60–64.

61. WMC records indicate that from 1942 to 1943, Texas lumber operators together employed roughly 43 percent nonwhites; in July 1943, they employed roughly 53 percent nonwhites. Rough averages taken from "Table II: Trend in Employment of Women and Non-White Workers in Selected Industries by Locality and Industry," Texas, Louisiana, and New Mexico file, box 5, series 277, War Manpower Commission, RG 211, NARA FW. Other WMC statistics indicate that in June 1945, African American workers comprised 6,138 out of 14,317 workers in the Texas lumber industry. See "Manpower Situation in Logging and Lumbering, June 1945," Special Manpower Problems file, box 7, series 80, War Manpower Commission, RG 211, NARA CP. Vernon Jensen states that in 1937 the Southern Pine Lumber Company employed a total of 149,000 persons and was the largest employer of black labor outside of agriculture in the region. In 1934, African Americans made up approximately 60 percent of this labor force. According to Jensen, black workers generally comprised around 50 percent of the lumber labor force in the western Gulf states, while in Florida, Georgia, and South Carolina black workers outnumbered white workers (*Lumber and Labor*, 76–77).

62. Allen, *East Texas Lumber Workers*, 83; Jensen, *Lumber and Labor*, 277–78.

63. "New Underground Gets Farm Workers to Jobs," *Atlanta Daily World*, May 24, 1944, 1.

64. "Workers Attempting to Migrate to Camden, New Jersey Jailed in Florida," *Birmingham World*, June 16, 1944, 4; "Accuse Florida of 'Slaveocracy' Labor Practices," *Birmingham World*, August 31, 1943, 1; unidentified article attached to letter from G. Hay to F. Constangy, October 26, 1943, Region VII file, box 2, series 157, War Manpower Commission, RG 211, NARA CP.

65. Hahamovitch, *The Fruits of Their Labor*, 182–99.

66. E. M. Norment to Paul Jessen, June 4, 1943, Labor Mobilization and Utilization 10-2 file (1 of 2), box 3, series 11, War Manpower Commission, RG 211, NARA EP; Woodruff, "Mississippi Delta Planters," 268–75; Hahamovitch, *The Fruits of Their Labor*, 198, 243–44.

67. Leo Werts to C. Golden, March 21, 1945, Farmers, Southern Tenant—1945

file, box 12, series 11, War Manpower Commission, RG 211, NARA CP; Hahamovitch, *The Fruits of Their Labor,* 188–89, 243–44.

68. "Says War Manpower Policy Threat to Negro's Rights," *Birmingham World,* March 20, 1945, 4; press release, March 12, 1945; and pamphlet, *Here's Your Indianapolis NAACP,* Indianapolis, Indiana, 1945–47 file, box C55, part 2, National Association for the Advancement of Colored People Collection.

69. "Demand Workers Return to Farms," *Atlanta Daily World,* March 24, 1945, 1; "Military Groups Offer Jobs to Threatened Mississippi Workers," *Atlanta Daily World,* March 28, 1945, 1.

70. See miscellaneous correspondence in Farm Labor Situation, 4-14/153 file, Coke Stevenson Governor's Papers. See also Orville Carpenter to Robert Goodwin, February 7, 1944; C. E. Belk to John Reagor, February 2, 1944; and Great Lakes Growers Employment Committee to Louis Trejado, Laredo, Texas, January 27, 1944, Labor Agricultural file, box 648, series 270, War Manpower Commission, RG 211, NARA FW. In letters to South Texas workers, the Beet Company informed them: "We will have work for you continuously from the time you arrive here."

71. C. E. Belk to J. R. Reagor, chief of placement, Region X, April 20, 1944; R. L. Coffman to Sam Wynn, January 17, 1945, Unauthorized Recruitment file, box 676, series 270. USES also recruited Latino workers in South Texas for Hanford. One report indicated that in May 1944, the Texas WMC recruited fifteen out of twenty-four Latino interviewees in Brownsville for the Hanford Engineer Works; see C. E. Belk to E. R. Speer, June 15, 1944, Hanford Recruitment file, box 661, series 270, War Manpower Commission, RG 211, NARA FW.

72. C. E. Belk to E. R. Speer, April 2, 1945, Unauthorized Recruitment file, box 676, series 270, War Manpower Commission, RG 211, NARA FW. In March and April 1945, the East Chicago USES requested fifty workers for Inland. See C. E. Belk to E. R. Speer, July 11, 1944, Unauthorized Recruitment file, box 676, series 270, War Manpower Commission, RG 211, NARA FW.

73. C. E. Belk to J. R. Reagor, April 20, 1944, Unauthorized Recruitment file, box 676, series 270, War Manpower Commission, RG 211, NARA FW; Nash, *The American West Transformed,* 54–55. See also Railroad Retirement Board files, series 270; and Unauthorized Recruitment file, box 676, series 270, War Manpower Commission, RG 211, NARA FW. For the canning industry recruitment, see Labor Recruitment— General 1943 file, box 27, series 269, War Manpower Commission, RG 211, National Archives and Records Administration, San Bruno, California (hereafter cited as NARA SB).

74. Report on Importation of Negro Labor to California, August 10, 1942, Labor Employment of Negroes file, 1942, box 291, series 269, War Manpower Commission, RG 211, NARA SB.

75. Ibid.

76. "Negro Farmers Deserting the South, Lopez Says," *Atlanta Daily World,* February 26, 1943, 2.

77. D. Roney to W. K. Hopkins, 4-2 Negro Labor Mobilization and Utilization 1943 file, box 34, series 269, War Manpower Commission, RG 211, NARA SB.

78. C. E. Belk to E. R. Speer, November 11, 1944, Stabilization—Violation—Texas file, box 653, series 270, War Manpower Commission, RG 211, NARA FW. For the Los Angeles report, see D. Roney to W. K. Hopkins, July 20, 1943, 4-2 Negro Labor Mobilization and Utilization 1943 file, box 34, series 269, War Manpower Commission, RG 211, NARA SB.

79. For statistics on interregional recruitment, see correspondence in file pattern correspondence, box 666, series 270, War Manpower Commission, RG 211, NARA FW. Throughout 1943 and into 1944, Kaiser, Boeing, and Du Pont (Hanford) maintained average quotas of two to three thousand workers per month from Region X. See J. H. Bond, October 1943, Searches XII—Oregon and California file, box 663, series 270, War Manpower Commission, RG 211, NARA FW.

80. S. R. Stevens to Harold Holman, March 3, 1943, unlabeled file (lumber stabilization), box 652, series 270, War Manpower Commission, RG 211, NARA FW.

81. J. C. Brill to Leonard Steidel, November 14, 1944, in Chicago Mill and Lumber file, box 1, series 283, War Manpower Commission, RG 211, NARA FW.

82. See W. B. Klugh to Ralph Walton, May 28, 1943, Labor Mobilization and Utilization 10-1—Negro Recruitment file, box 8, and W. B. Klugh to J. K. Johnson, July 7, 1943, Labor Mobilization and Utilization 10-2 file (1 of 2), box 3, series 11, War Manpower Commission, RG 211, NARA EP.

83. J. R. Reagor to J. B. Wear, July 16, 1943, Hanford Recruitment file, box 661, series 270, War Manpower Commission, RG 211, NARA FW.

84. Orville Horne to R. Sullivan, June 26, 1943 and June 28, 1943; R. Sullivan to J. H. White, June 26, 1943, Unauthorized Recruitment 10-3, Tennessee file, box 3, series 11, War Manpower Commission, RG 211, NARA EP. The correspondents cite the name of Congressman James Whittington, which undoubtedly referred to Jaime Whitten.

85. J. H. Bond to B. F. Ashe, July 10, 1943, and Raymond Welch to B. F. Ashe, July 10, 1943, Labor Mobilization and Utilization 10-2 file (1 of 2), box 3, series 11, War Manpower Commission, RG 211, NARA EP.

86. WMC Knoxville to Maj. J. Shackleford, September 21, 1943, and W. D. Twing to Atlanta WMC, September 29, 1943, Unauthorized Recruitment 10-3, Tennessee file, box 3, series 11, War Manpower Commission, RG 211, NARA EP.

87. C. E. Belk to E. R. Speer, November 11, 1944, Stabilization—Violation—Texas file, box 653, series 270, War Manpower Commission, RG 211, NARA FW. For examples of ways in which workers in Buffalo, New York, avoided stabilization regulations, see Meyer, *Journey through Chaos,* 9–10.

88. H. N. Grogan to WMC Houston, August 2, 1944, Stabilization—Violation—Texas file, series 270, War Manpower Commission, RG 211, NARA FW.

89. Belk criticized the system for its "lack of integrity" and the fact that "in the absence of a National labor policy the USES has to set its sails in a sea full of pirates, barnacled old wind-jammers, stumps and ignorance." See C. E. Belk to J. R. Reagor, Acting Chief of Placement, Region X, February 2, 1944, Clearance—Texas file, box 667, series 270, War Manpower Commission, RG 211, NARA FW. For other southern lumbermen's reactions to labor piracy, see Fickle, *The New South,* 306–8.

90. C. E. Belk to W. L. Crawford, December 14, 1943, Hanford Recruitment file, box 661, series 270, War Manpower Commission, RG 211, NARA FW.

91. J. H. Bond to WMC in Washington, August 2, 1944, Louisiana Employment Complaints file, box 652, series 270, War Manpower Commission, RG 211, NARA FW.

92. C. E. Belk to E. R. Speer, May 31, 1945, Unauthorized Recruitment file, box 676, series 270, War Manpower Commission, RG 211, NARA FW. According to the lumber company, these workers fled Angelina County without securing a certificate of separation, and their employer, the Southern Pine Lumber Company, one of the largest in Texas, was convinced that Meadow Valley Company, "or someone connected with them," had sent the two men transportation money.

93. R. D. Reeves to E. R. Speer, November 9, 1944, and November 13, 1944, Unauthorized Recruitment file, box 676, series 270, War Manpower Commission, RG 211, NARA FW.

94. G. S. Smith to John Howard, April 8, 1943, unlabeled file (lumber stabilization), box 652, series 270; W. H. Elliot to manager, USES Leesville, December 30, 1944, Stabilization—General Correspondence file, box 648, series 270, War Manpower Commission, RG 211, NARA FW. The Southern Pine Lumber Company employed on average 725 persons from July 1942 to January 1944, making it perhaps the largest lumber employer in rural Texas; see "Table I: Employment Trend in Selected Establishments by Primary Area and Industry," Texas, Louisiana, and New Mexico file, box 5, series 277, War Manpower Commission, RG 211, NARA FW.

95. Woodruff, "Pick or Fight," 83–84; "Southern Cotton Pickers Back Wage Ceiling—Forced to Vote by Big Planters," *Atlanta Daily World*, September 18, 1945, 1; "Cotton Pickers Lose Fight on Price Ceilings," *Atlanta Daily World*, September 29, 1945, 1.

96. Allen, *East Texas Lumber Workers*, 83.

97. W. B. Robertson to Maj. James Shackelford, September 21, 1943, Unauthorized Recruitment 10-3, Tennessee file, box 3, series 11, War Manpower Commission, RG 211, NARA EP.

98. Factors Affecting Lumber Production, Third Quarter 1944, Logging and Lumbering file, box containing series 283 and 285, War Manpower Commission, RG 211, NARA FW. For attitudes among West Texas growers, see Report for El Paso Agricultural Labor to J. H. Bond, January 19, 1943, El Paso Area file, box 668, series 270, War Manpower Commission, RG 211, NARA FW. Although farmworkers in the rural South and Southwest did organize under both the Southern Tenant Farmers Union (STFU) and the United Cannery, Agricultural, Packing and Allied Workers of America (UCAPAWA-CIO), I have not found evidence of labor organizing in the Texas lumber industry during the war by the International Woodworkers of America (IWA-CIO).

99. Wright, *Old South, New South*, 12, 240–43; Schulman, *From Cotton Belt to Sunbelt*, 65–84. Both authors focus on the effects of the National Industrial Recovery Act, the Fair Labor Standards Act, and minimum wage laws.

Chapter Four: The Segregation Frontier

1. Arthur Chapman interview, October 14, 2000, in possession of author.

2. Lemke-Santangelo, *Abiding Courage;* Johnson, *The Second Gold Rush;* Broussard, *Black San Francisco,* 133–204; Taylor, *The Forging of a Black Community,* 159–84; Sides, "Working Away"; Spickard, "Work and Hope."

Whereas numerous recent works have explored the experiences of black migrants at the local level (in particular, Los Angeles and the East San Francisco Bay Area), this chapter provides more of a regional synthesis of the black migrant worker experience in the Pacific West during the war years. Furthermore, by emphasizing the role of the extreme labor shortage, federal recruitment networks, high wages, occupational mobility, and racial liberalism in the Pacific West, I argue that the region held a particular draw for many African Americans from the South and Southwest. And as black migrants played integral roles in the wartime jobs movement on the Pacific Coast, I argue further that migration to the region represented a key strategy for aggressive southern African Americans who hoped to gain both economic and social mobility through the war.

3. Taylor, *In Search of the Racial Frontier,* 17.

4. Meier and Rudwick, *Black Detroit;* Capeci Jr., *Race Relations;* Clive, *State of War.*

5. White, "What Caused the Detroit Riots?"

6. Johnson, *The Second Gold Rush;* Gregory, *American Exodus;* Lemke-Santangelo, *Abiding Courage;* Sides, "Working Away."

7. Gregory, *American Exodus,* 174.

8. C. Johnson to R. Weaver, March 8, 1943, Labor—Negro—General and Discrimination file, box 27, series 269, War Manpower Commission, RG 211, NARA SB.

9. W. H. O'Kelly to J. H. Bond, March 27, 1943, Reports file, box 6, series 269, War Manpower Commission, RG 211, NARA FW; Louisiana Progress Report, September 1943, Meetings—General file, box 1, series 269, War Manpower Commission, RG 211, NARA FW; L. Levine to J. H. Bond, November 20, 1943, LM and U-15-8 file, box 31, RG 183, National Archives Record Administration at College Park, Maryland (hereafter cited as NARA CP). In 1944, New Orleans's congressman Edward Hebert attacked the War Manpower Commission's West Coast recruitment policy in Congress. Specifically, Hebert took offense to the federal manpower policy whereby "expert" recruiters from the regional office "put on a house to house recruiting campaign in all Negro neighborhoods" for workers for the Hanford Engineer Works in Pasco, Washington, while "New Orleans industrial establishments badly in need of Negro labor" had never benefited from these programs. Speech of Hon. F. Edward Hebert, May 22, 1944, New Orleans Office file, box 640, series 270, War Manpower Commission, RG 211, NARA FW.

10. J. McCusker to W. K. Hopkins, September 22, 1943, and J. H. Bond to W. K. Hopkins, August 14, 1943, Labor Pirating FEP 1943 file, box 32, series 269, War Manpower Commission, RG 211, NARA SB.

11. Walter Pollard Sr. to P. Van Gelder, March 30, 1943, Correspondence, March

1943 file, Local 9, series V, box 29, Industrial Union of Marine and Shipbuilding Workers of America Papers.

12. A. Emmerling to F. Sharp, June 26, 1943, and E. Cook to L. Glazer, April 29, 1943, Labor Pirating FEP 1943 file, box 32, series 269, War Manpower Commission, RG 211, NARA SB.

13. Lemke-Santangelo, *Abiding Courage,* 49–68.

14. Romo, *East Los Angeles,* 154–65.

15. McWilliams, "Critical Summary," 189–94.

16. Kirby, *Rural Worlds Lost;* Harvey Schwartz, ed., "Into the Valley," *Dispatcher* (January 1996): 6. See also Gregory, *American Exodus,* 162–69.

17. Darling, "Controlled Manpower," 48–49, 98–99; Kraus, *In the City,* 24–25.

18. C. E. Belk to E. R. Speer, July 13, 1944, Searches XII—Northwestern Lumber Industry file, box 663, series 270, War Manpower Commission, RG 211, NARA FW.

19. Housing at Fontana, November 15, 1943, Negro Housing 1943 file, box 33, series 264, War Manpower Commission, RG 211, NARA SB. Despite housing shortages and Jim Crow laws, the only suggestions that the WMC offered was for the migrants to be housed in the "Negro sections" of Fontana and other nearby towns.

20. J. H. Binns to P. McNutt, July 8, 1943, Negro Housing 1943 file, box 33, series 264, War Manpower Commission, RG 211, NARA SB.

21. Taylor, "Blacks and Asians," 401–29.

22. O. Whitebrook to C. Taft, September 30, 1943, 6-2 Migration of Workers—Labor Mobilization and Utilization 1943 file, box 37, series 269, War Manpower Commission, RG 211, NARA SB.

23. McWilliams, "Critical Summary," 193; Berry, "Profiles: Portland," 160–61. For an example of San Francisco's conservatism on housing, see Johnson, *The Negro War Worker,* 32–33. For an analysis of Seattle's relative liberalism, see Taylor, *The Forging of a Black Community,* 168–70.

24. See Minority Group Population Distribution, Minorities—F. W. Hunter file, box 2958, series 269, War Manpower Commission, RG 211, NARA SB. In comparison, the black populations of other western cities during 1940 were as follows: the San Francisco Bay Area had a population of 19,759; Portland had a population of approximately 2,000; and Seattle's black population was close to 5,000.

25. Fanny Christina Hill interview by Jan Fischer, June and July 1980, February 1981, transcript 111, Rosie the Riveter Oral History Project; "Little Tokyo No More, Bronzeville Balls!" *California Eagle,* November 4, 1943, 1; Reddick, "The New Race Relations Frontier," 141.

26. Taylor, *In Search of the Racial Frontier,* 267; Josephine Houston interview by Jan Fischer, July 1980, transcript 79, Rosie the Riveter Oral History Project.

27. D. Roney to W. K. Hopkins, July 20, 1943, 4-2 Negro Labor Mobilization and Utilization 1943 file, box 34, series 269, War Manpower Commission, RG 211, NARA SB.

28. Ibid.

29. "Committee Reports: Housing for 11,000 Negro Families Needed," *California Eagle,* July 26, 1945, 20; "Mass Meet on Residential Restrictions Set for Sunday," *California Eagle,* September 13, 1945, 1; Bratt, "Profiles: Los Angeles," 179–86.

30. "Anti-Negro Plot—Try to Stop Housing Project in Watts," *California Eagle*, October 28, 1943, 1; "Protest Watts Homeowners Assoc.," *California Eagle*, November 4, 1943, 1; "Dedication of California Housing Projects," *Opportunity: Journal of Negro Life* 22, no. 4 (fall 1944): 177. This article claimed that three new Los Angeles housing projects dedicated during 1944 (Jordan Downs, Pueblo Del Rio, and Imperial Courts Annexes) were integrated with African American, Mexican, and white families. Jordan Downs's first manager was L. L. Hoffman, formerly manager of "the large Negro Housing Project in New Orleans." See also Kraus, *In the City*, 23–32, for the attitudes of residents toward residential integration in one integrated housing project in San Pedro. Josh Sides addresses the issue of housing during and after the war ("Working Away," 115–29, 187–248).

31. Johnson, *The Second Gold Rush*, 191–92; "Packing the Voters Booth," *Crow's Pacific Coast Lumber Digest*, November 15, 1944, Article file, box 31, Sam Houston Jones Papers.

32. Johnson, *The Second Gold Rush*, 222–33; Lemke-Santangelo, *Abiding Courage*, 69–106.

33. C. E. Belk to E. R. Speer, July 13, 1944, Searches XII—Northwestern Lumber Industry file, box 663, series 270; E. R. Speer to C. E. Brindson, June 1, 1944, Searches XII—Oregon and California file, box 663, series 270, War Manpower Commission, RG 211, NARA FW. In February 1944, C. E. Belk complained to acting regional placement chief J. R. Reagor that Hanford Engineer Works and the Olympic Commissary at Pasco, Washington, and Standard Oil of Alaska placed orders discriminating against Latin Americans. See C. E. Belk to J. R. Reagor, February 2, 1944, Clearance—Texas file, box 667, series 270, War Manpower Commission, RG 211, NARA FW. For Fontana, California, see Negro Housing 1943 file, box 33, series 264, War Manpower Commission, RG 211, NARA SB; "NAACP Fights Plan—Halt Negro Stand Hit by NAACP," *California Eagle*, November 18, 1943, 1. See also Second Baptist Church advertisement to migrant workers from Texas, *California Eagle*, December 9, 1943, 16; "Mass Meet on Residential Restrictions Set for Sunday," *California Eagle*, September 13, 1945, 1.

34. "CIO's Townsend, Gus Hawkins Appear Here," *California Eagle*, October 7, 1943, 1; "Labor Honors Local Pastor," *California Eagle*, October 7, 1943, sec. A, 6; Johnson, *The Negro War Worker*, 86–87.

35. Korstad and Lichtenstein, "Opportunities Found and Lost"; Goldfield, "The Failure of Operation Dixie," 166–89; Draper, "The New Southern Labor History Revisited"; Honey, *Southern Labor and Black Civil Rights;* Zamora, "The Failed Promise," 232–350.

36. Weaver, *Negro Labor*, 78.

37. Reed, *Seedtime*. See also Korstad and Lichtenstein, "Opportunities Found and Lost," 786.

38. Strikes Occurring over Racial Issues during Period July 1943–December 1944, Field Letters #31 file, box 476, DFO, Fair Employment Practices Committee, RG 228, NARA CP. Perhaps because of the South's reluctance and refusal to challenge segregation on the shop floor, industries in southern states (Texas, Louisiana, Mis-

sissippi, Tennessee, Alabama, Georgia, and Virginia) accounted for twenty of the strikes, while thirteen occurred in border states (Missouri, Kentucky, Maryland, and Delaware).

39. Ibid. Of the twenty white strikes, resistance to the upgrading of Negroes accounted for eighteen, while protests over integrated facilities accounted for two. Of the twenty-one African American strikes, seven occurred over the failure to upgrade, and seven were over discriminatory work conditions, while five occurred over wage differences, and two over segregated facilities.

40. "WMC Regional Chief Urges Full Use of Manpower," *Atlanta Daily World*, June 14, 1943, 1; "V-J Day Sees Intensification of Job Discrimination on West Coast," *Atlanta Daily World*, August 22, 1945, 1. Andrew Kersten finds that black gains in Detroit during the war were "among the largest in the Midwest and the nation" (*Race, Jobs and the War*, 110–11).

41. Strikes Occurring over Racial Issues during Period July 1943–December 1944, Field Letters #31 file, box 476, DFO, Fair Employment Practices Committee, RG 228, NARA CP.

42. Weaver, *Negro Labor*, 139–40. As Weaver observed, the WMC secured "consideration for minorities" most often in areas where "minority group employment could be achieved without upsetting other phases of the program and without endangering relations with management groups (as in New England) and where the labor market was tight."

43. Elbert Kelly interview by Lynn Hay and Edna Daley, November 17, 1983, transcript 2, and Walter Williams interview by Tony Salcido, November 10, 1988, transcript 28; International Longshoremen's and Warehousemen's Union Local 13 Oral History Project; Videll Drake interview by Jan Fischer, September and November, 1980, Rosie the Riveter Oral History Project.

44. International Longshoremen's and Warehousemen's Union Local 13 Oral History Project, part 13; "Into the Valley," *Dispatcher*, January 17, 1996, 6; LaSeur, *Not All Okies Are White*.

45. "Into the Valley," *Dispatcher*, January 17, 1996, 6.

46. Ibid.

47. J. Bryant to W. K. Hopkins, November 4, 1942, Minority Group 1942 file, box 2913, series 269, War Manpower Commission, RG 211, NARA SB.

48. Northrup, *Organized Labor*.

49. See official report, October 1942, October 1942 file, box 29, series 5, Industrial Union of Marine and Shipbuilding Workers of America Papers.

50. See miscellaneous correspondence from 1943 to 1945, Local 9 1943–45 files, box 29, series 5, and William Smith correspondence files, box 11, series 2, Industrial Union of Marine and Shipbuilding Workers of America Papers.

51. Taylor, *In Search of the Racial Frontier*, 259.

52. "Klan at Work in Shipyards," *California Eagle*, October 21, 1943, 1; "Danger Signal—KKK Is Busy Here!" *California Eagle*, October 21, 1943, sec. A, 8.

53. Anderson, "The Development of Leadership," 165–78.

54. Ibid., 178–82. Although Russell was born in Los Angeles in 1910, he main-

tained direct ties to the South when he got his doctorate in divinity from Houston-Tillotson College in Texas during 1945 (178–79).

55. Ibid., 184–86.

56. NVC to W. Hopkins, February 22, 1943, Labor Discrimination General 1942 file, box 25, series 264, War Manpower Commission, RG 211, NARA SB.

57. "Shipyard Workers Must File Complaints," *California Eagle,* October 14, 1943, sec. A, 3; "Local FEPC Office," *California Eagle,* October 14, 1943, sec. A, 8; Sides, "Working Away," 157–68.

58. M. Rathbrone to W. Hopkins, March 2, 1943; D. Selvin to W. Hopkins, March 5, 1943; UAW Resolution, January 15, 1943, Labor Discrimination General 1942 file, box 25, series 264; see also files 4–5, Negroes—Employment 1943 file, series 269, box 32, War Manpower Commission, RG 211, NARA SB.

59. Ben Margolis interview by Gregory Perkins, spring 1980, Labor History Collection. See also Taylor, *In Search of the Racial Frontier,* 258–59; Sides, "Working Away," 157–68.

60. Himes, *If He Hollers,* 98.

61. Taylor, *In Search of the Racial Frontier,* 259.

62. See recruitment statistics in Inter-regional Recruitment Patterns file, box 1, series 79, and April 1944 file, box 2, series 193, War Manpower Commission, RG 211, NARA CP. See also Inter-regional Recruitment Patterns 11-12/44 file, box 671, series 270, War Manpower Commission, RG 211, NARA FW.

63. Arthur Chapman interview. FEPC Region XII Closed Case files contain nine complaints for unnamed navy dry docks, fourteen for Mare Island navy yard, and sixteen complaints for Hunter's Point navy dry dock.

64. Cleophus "Bill" Williams interview by Harvey Schwartz, April 8, 1998, tape 1, side 2, transcript 18–19, and tape 2, side 3, transcript 2, Oral History Project for the Coast Labor Relations Committee, International Longshoremen's and Warehousemen's Union Archives.

65. C. Williams interview, tape 2, side 3, transcript 1, International Longshoremen's and Warehousemen's Union Archives.

66. Darling, "Controlled Manpower," 55–56, 65–66.

67. Willie McGee interview by Tony Salcido, February 25, 1991, tape 1, transcript 4–11, International Longshoremen's and Warehousemen's Union Local 13 Oral History Project.

68. Elbert Kelly interview, tape 1, transcript 6–7, International Longshoremen's and Warehousemen's Union Local 13 Oral History Project.

69. C. Williams interview, tape 2, side 3, transcript 4–6, International Longshoremen's and Warehousemen's Union Archives.

70. Harvey Schwartz, ed., "Struggle and Triumph: Pioneer Black Longshore Leader Cleophus Williams," *Dispatcher* (August 1998): 6–7.

71. C. Williams interview, tape 2, side 3, transcript 6, International Longshoremen's and Warehousemen's Union Archives; Schwartz, "Struggle and Triumph," 6–7.

72. Schwartz, "Struggle and Triumph," 6–7.

73. Zieger, *The CIO*, 70–73.

74. Lichtenstein, *Labor's War at Home*, 53–66.

75. Zieger, *The CIO*, 70–73.

76. Harvey Schwartz, ed., "Making It Work in Southern California," *Dispatcher* (November 1996): 6; *Proceedings of the First Annual Conference of the ILWU*, April 4–17, 1938, 126–28; *Proceedings of the Third Annual Conference of the ILWU*, April 1–11, 1940, 114–16; and *Proceedings of the Fifth Annual Conference of the ILWU*, June 4–10, 1943, 179, International Longshoremen's and Warehousemen's Union Archives. During this period, the ILWU in Los Angeles also founded Local 13 in Wilmington and Local 60 in San Pedro for cotton compress workers. Walter Williams estimated that beginning in 1943, from a thousand to fifteen hundred black members joined Local 26 in San Pedro during the war. See W. Williams interview, transcript 63–64, International Longshoremen's and Warehousemen's Union Local 13 Oral History Project.

77. Zieger, *The CIO*, 128–30; Lichtenstein, *Labor's War at Home*, 58–63.

78. Harvey Schwartz, ed., "'We Were There': A Woman's Place Is in the Union—ILWU Warehouse Local 6, 1936–1946," *Dispatcher* (June 1996): 6.

79. Ibid.

80. Northrup, *Organized Labor*, 205–8; "Plane Factory Hires First Colored Help," *Dallas Express*, July 19, 1941, 1; "Negroes Get More Defense Jobs Says Weaver," *Dallas Express*, March 7, 1942, 2; "21,000 Negroes Now Employed in West Coast Aircraft Plants," *Dallas Express*, August 22, 1942, 2; Granger, "Techniques in Race Relations," 323–27.

81. Herbert Ward, interview by Gregory Perkins, spring 1980, Labor History Collection; "Attention Aircraft Workers," *California Eagle*, October 28, 1943, sec. A, 2.

82. Herbert Ward biography, Labor History Collection.

83. Katie Miles, interview by Sherna Berger-Gluck, June and July 1980, Rosie the Riveter Oral History Project.

84. Videll Drake, interview by Jan Fischer, September and November 1980, May 1981, Rosie the Riveter Oral History Project.

85. Fanny Christina Hill, interview by Jan Fischer, June and July 1980, February 1981, transcript 56, 90, 107, Rosie the Riveter Oral History Project.

86. Ibid., transcript 69.

87. Ibid., transcript 88, 101.

88. Josephine Houston, interview by Jan Fischer, July 1980, Rosie the Riveter Oral History Project.

89. J. K., interview by Jan Fischer, March 31, 1980, Rosie the Riveter Oral History Project.

90. Halpern and Horowitz, *Meatpackers*. See also Korstad and Lichtenstein, "Opportunities Found and Lost," 786–811.

91. L. D. Reddick coined the phrase "race relations frontier" in 1945 in his article "The New Race Relations Frontier." Reddick writes: "The West, we know, is the youngest of our sections and as such has escaped most of the historical aspects of the Negro question" (136).

92. See FEPC Committee Conference, October 2, 1945, in FEPC California 1944–

46 file, FEPC box, ILWU History of World War Two, International Longshoremen's and Warehousemen's Union Archives.

Chapter Five: "We're Not Here to Start a Social Revolution"

1. Jackson Valtair, before the membership of the Glover Colored Aircraft Workers Union in Fort Worth, March 25, 1945, Region XIII file, box 403, Carol Coan office files, Division of Review and Analysis (hereafter cited as DRA), Fair Employment Practices Committee, RG 228, NARA CP.

2. See "Please Attend FEPC Meeting," flyer in ILWU Organization—South and Gulf #218 Dallas Warehouse, 1943–48 file, ILWU organizer files, International Longshoremen's and Warehousemen's Union Archives.

3. One of the most drastic instances of white unity occurred on the morning of July 17, 1945, when over three thousand white workers at the Todd-Johnson shipyards in New Orleans walked off their jobs to protest the upgrading of John Gutter, a black welder from Magnolia, Mississippi, who had graduated from the Xavier University welding program. See "The Todd-Johnson Walkout," *Louisiana Weekly*, July 28, 1945, 10; "Boilermaker Reports for Naval Repairs—3500 Quit," *Atlanta Daily World*, July 26, 1945, 1, newspaper clipping, Boilermakers file, New Orleans 1942, box B-5, part 2, National Association for the Advancement of Colored People Collection. For other instances, see Strikes Occurring over Racial Issues during Period July 1943–December 1944, Field Letters #31 file, box 476, DFO, Fair Employment Practices Committee, RG 228, NARA CP.

4. T. Mitchell to M. Ross, September 4, 1945, Todd-Johnson Closed Cases, Fair Employment Practices Committee, RG 228, NARA FW.

5. As does chapter 2, this chapter breaks from previous works on the fair employment struggle by focusing on the intersection of grassroots workers' actions and federal labor and fair employment policies at the local and regional levels within the South. Like Daniel Kryder (*Divided Arsenal*), I emphasize the importance of the tight labor market in providing black leaders and workers with greater political leverage. Yet, whereas Kryder focused on this political negotiation largely at the national level (and especially Washington, D.C.), this chapter again looks at the struggle over jobs and equality across the urban South. With this focus on the FEPC and its alliances with local jobs movement organizations, this work serves as a southern counterpart to Andrew Kersten's *Race, Jobs, and the War*. Like Kersten in the Midwest, I find that the pressure and negotiation strategies practiced by jobs movement leaders in the South did lead to significant (though temporary) gains for black workers in defense industries during the war.

Importantly, too, this chapter adds to growing scholarship on the role of organized labor in the black struggle for equality during the war. See, for example, Korstad and Lichtenstein, "Opportunities Found and Lost"; Honey, *Southern Labor and Black Civil Rights*, 212–13; Zamora, "The Failed Promise"; Nelson, "Organized Labor." Whereas most of these scholars have explored the role of interracialism within the CIO, I argue here that segregated black unions in both the CIO and the AFL served as important community institutions that enabled black workers to articulate specific concerns central to them (as African Americans) and mobilize for political action through voter registration. By shifting the focus from interracial unionism to segregated institutions, I hope to emphasize the importance of local labor, church, and civic organizations in mobilizing southern African Americans for job equality and voting rights during the war.

6. Granger, "Techniques in Race Relations," 323–27.

7. Transcript of Meeting, December 17, 1943, CVAC—New Orleans, Closed Cases, Fair Employment Practices Committee, RG 228, National Archives and Records Administration, East Point, Georgia (hereafter cited as NARA EP).

8. Region IV included Washington, D.C., West Virginia, Maryland, Virginia, and North Carolina. Region VII included South Carolina, Georgia, Florida, Tennessee, Alabama, and Mississippi. Region X included Louisiana, Texas, and New Mexico. In December 1944, FEPC Region X was divided into two regions. East Texas, Louisiana, and southern Mississippi were formed into a new Region XIII with regional headquarters in New Orleans. Region X subsequently covered Central and West Texas and New Mexico, and the headquarters moved from Dallas back to San Antonio.

9. September 25, 1943, Weekly Reports, Texas file, DFO, RG 226, NARA CP; "John Hope II Named to FEPC," *Atlanta Daily World*, December 23, 1943, 1.

10. "Types of Services the UL Performs," *Louisiana Weekly*, January 22, 1944, 10; "A Word about Women in Industry," *Louisiana Weekly*, March 18, 1944, 5; "Women in Skilled War Jobs Prove They're Capable," *Louisiana Weekly*, June 30, 1945, 5; *Challenge* (December 1944), New Orleans 1939–69 file, box 18, series 13, part 2, National Urban League Collection.

11. "McNutt under Fire from Every Side," *Atlanta Daily World*, March 4, 1943, 1; Flynn, *The Mess in Washington*, 149–71.

12. "WMC Reestablishes Race Office," *Louisiana Weekly*, September 25, 1943, 2; "Bob Weaver Leaves WMC January 31—Eyes Successor," *Louisiana Weekly*, January 15, 1944, 3; "Weaver Job Is Turned down by Mrs. Bethune," *Atlanta Daily World*, March 8, 1944, 1; "Say White House Prods McNutt to Name Race WMC Assistant," *Birmingham World*, June 9, 1944, 4; "May Abolish High Job in WMC," *Atlanta Daily World*, August 13, 1944, 1; B. F. Ashe to B. Bell Jr., June 15, 1943, Labor Mobilization and Utilization—Negro—4-2 file, box 13, series 11, NARA EP. For a description of functions for Consultants on Minority Groups and Consultants on Negro Manpower, see Industrial and Agricultural Division—Consultant Services Functional Chart, Placement Bureau file, box 4, series 80, War Manpower Commission, RG 211, NARA CP.

13. "Aircraft School Graduates Getting Jobs at Bell," *Atlanta Daily World*, October 7, 1943, 1; "Forward with the AUL" (editorial), *Atlanta Daily World*, April 13, 1944, 6.

14. A. Bruce Hunt to W. Maslow, December 24, 1943, Weekly Reports— C. Mitchell file, box 459, DFO, Fair Employment Practices Committee, RG 228, NARA CP; D. Lasseter to All State Directors, July 31, 1944, Reports to Regional Director and Miscellaneous Memoranda file, box 1, series 20, War Manpower Commission, RG 211, NARA EP.

15. C. Mitchell to W. Maslow, February 28, 1944, Weekly Reports—C. Mitchell file, box 459, DFO, Fair Employment Practices Committee, RG 228, NARA CP; Amos Ryce to Julius Thomas, May 31, 1944, 1944 Atlanta UL file, box A-69, Southern Regional Office, National Urban League Collection.

16. A. Bruce Hunt to W. Maslow, May 27, 1943, Weekly Reports— C. Mitchell file, box 459, DFO, Fair Employment Practices Committee, RG 228, NARA CP.

17. W. H. Shell to D. Lasseter, June 30, 1945, 7 BC 160 et al.—Bell Aircraft Correspondence file, box 1, series 20, War Manpower Commission, RG 211, NARA EP; Memorandum on Negro Employment at Bell Aircraft Company, November 3, 1944, 1944 Labor General file, box A-70, Southern Regional Office, National Urban League Collection. See also Ferguson, "The Politics of Inclusion," 497–98.

18. "Militant NAACP—Rev. Lucas Tops in Houston for 1943," *Dallas Express*, January 1, 1944, 1.

19. "Capacity Crowd Hears DNCC Report on Defense Training," *Dallas Express*, August 1, 1942, 1; "1st Defense Training School for Negroes Promises Much Success," *Dallas Express*, November 7, 1942, 1; "Dallas Boasts One of the South's Best War Schools," *Dallas Express*, March 27, 1943, 3; NAA, Closed Cases, Fair Employment Practices Committee, RG 228, NARA FW.

20. Recruiting and Advertising Campaigns Conducted in Dallas Labor Market Area, Regional and State Analysis Studies and Surveys file, box 1, series 283, War Manpower Commission, RG 211, NARA FW; Fairbanks, "Dallas in the 1940s," 147; Flynn, *The Mess in Washington*, 39–40, 60; Milkman, *Gender at Work;* Vander Meulen, "Warplanes, Labor," 46. For the utilization of women at Bechtel-McCone-Parsons in Birmingham, see Thomas, "Rosie the Riveter," 196–212.

21. Monthly Field Operating Report for Dallas Area, February 1944, Evaluation of Area Reports file, box 5, series 269, War Manpower Commission, RG 211, NARA FW; "WMC and NAA Officials Meet with Express on Training and Jobs for War Workers," *Dallas Express*, June 19, 1943, 1; "NAA Official Makes Statement on Hiring and Status of Negro Workers," *Dallas Express*, June 26, 1943, 1; "North American Proves It" (editorial), *Dallas Express*, July 17, 1943, 10; "NAA Hires Grads of Negro War Training School," *Dallas Express*, August 21, 1943, 1; "Women Slated for Training and Skilled Jobs at NAA," *Dallas Express*, January 22, 1944, 1.

22. See NAA, boxes 802 and 803, Closed Cases, Fair Employment Practices Committee, RG 228, NARA FW.

23. Weaver, *Negro Labor*, 128–29.

24. Korstad and Lichtenstein, "Opportunities Found and Lost."

25. Honey, *Southern Labor and Black Civil Rights*, 212–13; Zamora, "The Failed Promise." Honey and Zamora both argue that many CIO unions in the South denied social equality to African American and Latino members.

26. "Bell Workers to Get Back-Pay," *Atlanta Daily World*, August 17, 1945, 6.

27. From W. H. Shell to D. Lasseter, February 13, 1945, Reports to Regional Director and Miscellaneous Memoranda file, box 1, series 20, War Manpower Commission, RG 211, NARA EP.

28. "UAW-CIO Workers Jim-Crowed at Meet," *Atlanta Daily World*, July 15,

1945, 1; "UAW Seeks Report on Jim Crow Meet July 14," *Atlanta Daily World,* August 2, 1945, 1; Korstad and Lichtenstein, "Opportunities Found and Lost," 799.

29. C. Castaneda to W. Maslow, November 27, 1943, Texas file, box 482, DFO Weekly Reports, DFO, Fair Employment Practices Committee, RG 228, NARA CP.

30. Texas file, DFO Weekly Reports, DFO, Fair Employment Practices Committee, RG 228, NARA CP.

31. Howard Goddard to J. R. Robertson, May 18, 1944, ILWU and Other Unions—URWDSEA—Dallas file, ILWU History—Jurisdiction, International Longshoremen's and Warehousemen's Union Archives.

32. ILWU and Other Unions—URWDSEA—Dallas file, ILWU History—Jurisdiction, International Longshoremen's and Warehousemen's Union Archives.

33. D. Ellinger to W. Maslow, June 29, 1944, CVAC—Fort Worth file, box 70, Closed Cases, Fair Employment Practices Committee, RG 228, NARA FW.

34. D. Ellinger to C. Mitchell, July 16, 1945, CVAC—Fort Worth file, box 70, Closed Cases, Fair Employment Practices Committee, RG 228, NARA FW.

35. Nelson, "Organized Labor."

36. C. Mitchell to W. Maslow, February 14, 1945, and March 20, 1945, Weekly Reports—C. Mitchell file, DFO, Fair Employment Practices Committee, RG 228, NARA CP.

37. D. Ellinger to C. Mitchell, February 15, 1945, Delta file (2 of 2), Active Cases, Fair Employment Practices Committee, RG 228, NARA FW.

38. Memorandum on Negro Employment at Bell Aircraft Company, November 3, 1944, 1944 Labor General file, box A-70, Southern Regional Office, National Urban League Collection; Employment in Selected Aviation Plants, July 1944, Minority Workers by Industries file, Wilfred Leland office files, DRA, Fair Employment Practices Committee, RG 228, NARA CP. The report indicates that black workers represented 2,274 of 34,621 workers at NAA in Dallas, 730 of 22,524 workers at Convair in Fort Worth, and 1,502 out of 23,637 workers at Bell Bomber in Atlanta.

39. Memorandum on Negro Employment at Bell Aircraft Company, November 3, 1944, 1944 Labor General file, box A-70, Southern Regional Office, National Urban League Collection.

40. L. Brin to W. Dodge, January, 3, 1945, Boilermakers, Iron Shipbuilders and Helpers of America, AFL Tampa—7—UR—3121 file, box 2, Closed Cases, Fair Employment Practices Committee, RG 228, NARA EP.

41. J. Hope Jr. to W. Dodge, April 1, 1945, Boilermakers, Iron Shipbuilders and Helpers of America, AFL Tampa—7—UR—3121 file, box 2, Closed Cases, Fair Employment Practices Committee, RG 228, NARA EP.

42. Ibid.

43. W. Smith to G. Johnson, November 13, 1942, and L. E. Carter to Paul McNutt, November 5, 1942, Southeastern Shipbuilding Correspondence—7-BR-58 file, box 1, Active Cases, Fair Employment Practices Committee, RG 228, NARA EP; L. E. Carter to NAACP headquarters, November 30, 1942, COFEP cases 1941–42 (A–M) file, box B-11, part 2, National Association for the Advancement of Colored People Collection.

44. W. Smith to T. J. Gallagher, April 9, 1943, Organizers Reports—Florida file, March–May 1943, box 18, subseries 4, series 2, Industrial Union of Marine and Shipbuilding Workers of America Papers.

45. W. Smith to T. J. Gallagher, May 10, 1943, Organizers Reports—Florida file, March–May 1943, box 18, subseries 4, series 2, Industrial Union of Marine and Shipbuilding Workers of America Papers.

46. Nelson, "Organized Labor," 985–88.

47. Closed cases, Fair Employment Practices Committee, RG 228, NARA EP. See also Reed, "The FEPC, the Black Worker, and the Southern Shipyards," 446–67.

48. Northrup, *Organized Labor,* 229; *Shipyard Bulletin* 7–9 (1940–42).

49. "Race Trouble Averted at Delta," *Louisiana Weekly,* August 21, 1943, 1.

50. "War Vet Victim of Mob at Delta," *Louisiana Weekly,* February 5, 1944, 1.

51. E. Wright, "I Daresay," *Louisiana Weekly,* March 25, 1944, 3.

52. E. Davis to FEPC, July 25, 1945, Todd-Johnson file (1 of 2), Active Cases, Fair Employment Practices Committee, RG 228, NARA FW.

53. E. Cook statement, November 16, 1944; D. Ellinger to C. Mitchell, Final Deposition Report, Higgins Industries, March 8, 1945, Higgins Industries file, case 10-BR-428, Closed Cases, Fair Employment Practices Committee, RG 228, NARA FW.

54. D. Ellinger to C. Mitchell, January 26, 1945; D. Ellinger to W. Maslow, August 22, 1944, Delta file (2 of 2), Active Cases; and D. Ellinger to G. Singleton, March 15, 1945, IBB Galveston file, Closed Cases, Fair Employment Practices Committee, RG 228, NARA FW; "700 to Walk out at Delta Shipyard—Internal Strife within the Union Is Cause of Action," *Louisiana Weekly,* November 4, 1944, 1; "Workers Stick to Position; Still out at Delta," *Louisiana Weekly,* November 11, 1944, 1; "Delta Puts 100 Negro Welders on at Shipyard," *Louisiana Weekly,* January 27, 1945, 1; "Teamsters Get New Charter in Delta Walkout," *Louisiana Weekly,* February 3, 1945, 3.

55. D. Ellinger to Procurement Officials, May 17, 1945, FEPC Complaint against Todd-Johnson Dry Dock file, series 278, War Manpower Commission, RG 211, NARA FW.

56. Ibid.

57. R. D. Reeves to E. R. Speer, August 13, 1945, Todd-Johnson Dry Dock file; and R. D. Reeves to E. R. Speer, November 14, 1944, Todd-Johnson Search file, box 660, series 270, War Manpower Commission, RG 211, NARA FW.

58. M. Shapiro to T. Gallagher, August 24, 1945, Correspondence, July–August 1945 file, box 70, series 5, Industrial Union of Marine and Shipbuilding Workers of America Papers.

59. W. T. Crist to T. Gallagher, March 21, 1945, and June 18, 1945, Correspondence, July–August 1945 file, box 70, series 5, Industrial Union of Marine and Shipbuilding Workers of America Papers.

60. Korstad and Lichtenstein, "Opportunities Found and Lost."

61. *Proceedings of the First Annual Conference of the ILWU,* April 1938; *Proceedings of the Second Annual Conference of the ILWU,* April 1939; *Proceedings of the Third Annual Conference of the ILWU,* April 1940; *Proceedings of the Fourth Annual Conference of the ILWU,* April 1941; *Proceedings of the Fifth Annual Conference of the ILWU,* April

1943; *Proceedings of the Sixth Annual Conference of the ILWU*, March–April 1945, International Longshoremen's and Warehousemen's Union Archives; Ambrose, "A Revolution of Hope," 215–16, 267–68.

62. *Proceedings of the Third Annual Conference of the ILWU*, April 1940, 140; *Louisiana Weekly*, June 14, 1941, 1.

63. Howard Goddard to J. R. Robertson, January 21, 1943; J. R. Robertson to H. Bridges, February 8, 1943, ILWU History—Jurisdiction files, International Longshoremen's and Warehousemen's Union Archives. Robertson wrote to Bridges: "The weak position of the national administration in regard to the problems of the Negro people and their relationship to the war is primarily responsible for the racism that is rampant in this community and that naturally reflects itself in the Negro membership of all our Unions here."

64. Wells, "The ILWU in New Orleans," 41–48. See also J. R. Robertson to H. Bridges, February 8, 1943, and ILWU and Other Unions—URWDSEA—New Orleans file, ILWU History—Jurisdiction files, International Longshoremen's and Warehousemen's Union Archives; "Dorsey's Request for Support Is Tabled by NAACP," *Louisiana Weekly*, June 19, 1943, 2; "NAACP Explains Action in Not Aiding Dorsey," *Louisiana Weekly*, July 31, 1943, 3; Willie Dorsey, "An Open Letter," *Louisiana Weekly*, September 25, 1943, 10.

65. Wells, "The ILWU in New Orleans," 41–48; "Workers Move to Sever Relations with Local Union," *Louisiana Weekly*, March 4, 1944, 3; "Donaldson Workers Win Out," *Louisiana Weekly*, April 15, 1944, 1; "CIO Union Wins Bargaining Rights," *Louisiana Weekly*, April 22, 1944, 3; "CIO Local Makes Agreement with Letellier-Philips," *Louisiana Weekly*, April 29, 1944, 3.

66. "Charge Netter with Double Cross at AFL Meet—Delegates Say Labor Chief Blocked Negro Vice-President Resolution," *Louisiana Weekly*, April 15, 1944, 1.

67. C. Laws, "Headline Highlights," *Louisiana Weekly*, June 6, 1942, 10; *Louisiana Weekly*, May 1, 1943, 2; "Laundry Workers Seek Pay Increase," *Louisiana Weekly*, May 15, 1943, 6; "Cleaners, Pressers to Hold Organizing Meeting Sunday," *Louisiana Weekly*, June 12, 1943, 2; "Transport Workers Get Pay Raise," *Louisiana Weekly*, December 4, 1943, 3; "Amalgamated Clothing Workers Praise Union for Securing Back Wages," "Labor Unites for Political Action—Ballot Is Sought," *Louisiana Weekly*, September 11, 1943, 1; "Ministers Alliance Supports Political Action Drive for Vote," *Louisiana Weekly*, October 16, 1943, 1; "Ballot Rally Mass Meeting to Be Held in Shakespeare Park," *Louisiana Weekly*, October 23, 1943, 1; "5,000 Hear Leaders in Plea of Right to Vote," *Louisiana Weekly*, November 6, 1943, 1; "Leaders Discuss Right to Vote," *Louisiana Weekly*, December 11, 1943, 2; "Moses Turner Is Making Progress in Labor Circles," "Announce Drive Here to Organize Laundry Workers," *Louisiana Weekly*, March 4, 1944, 3.

68. Sullivan, *Days of Hope*, 172–73.

69. "PDL Holds Rally for City Election," *Louisiana Weekly*, January 24, 1942, 1; "PDL to Hold a Public Meeting Wednesday," *Louisiana Weekly*, September 19, 1942, 1; "NAACP President Believes Move on Foot to Undermine Program of Local Branch," *Louisiana Weekly*, March 20, 1943, 1; "Labor Unites for Political Action—

Ballot Is Sought," *Louisiana Weekly,* September 11, 1943, 1; "Ministers Alliance Supports Political Action Drive for Vote," *Louisiana Weekly,* October 16, 1943, 1; "Ballot Rally Mass Meeting to Be Held in Shakespeare Park," *Louisiana Weekly,* October 23, 1943, 1; "5,000 Hear Leaders in Plea of Right to Vote," *Louisiana Weekly,* November 6, 1943, 1; "Leaders Discuss Right to Vote," *Louisiana Weekly,* December 11, 1943, 2; "CIO Will Try to Get out the Vote in the South—PAC," *Louisiana Weekly,* January 29, 1944, 1; "'We Want the Ballot' Program Arouses Cross Section Support of City," *Louisiana Weekly,* March 18, 1944, 1; "L&N Employees Observe Their 4th Anniversary," *Louisiana Weekly,* April 1, 1944, 6; "Third 'We Want the Ballot' Conference Held," *Louisiana Weekly,* May 6, 1944, 9; "Union to Instruct Its Members How to Register to Vote," *Louisiana Weekly,* July 1, 1944, 1; "Lead Defense League Membership Drive," *Louisiana Weekly,* August 5, 1944, 3; "Many Negroes Vote in Orleans Primary," *Louisiana Weekly,* September 30, 1944, 11; "Negroes Must Contend for Ballot Now," *Louisiana Weekly,* February 17, 1945, 1.

70. Letters from August Harris to J. R. Robertson, September 4, 1944, and September 25, 1944, August Harris, Intl. Re, New Orleans, 1944–45 file; and Wm. Spooner Report on activities, January 14, 1944, ILWU Organization—South and Gulf—Correspondence and Reports—Wm. Spooner—Local 207, 1944 file, in ILWU organizer files, box 14, International Longshoremen's and Warehousemen's Union Archives.

71. Confidential Report on the New Orleans Situation and Pieper's Activities, 1943, ILWU History—Jurisdiction files, International Longshoremen's and Warehousemen's Union Archives.

72. Sullivan, *Days of Hope,* 193–220, 249–75.

73. Weaver, *Negro Labor,* 240.

74. Ibid., 236.

Chapter Six: "The South Needs the Negro"

1. "A Loyal Southern Negro to S. Jones," December 11, 1945, Article file, box 31, Sam Houston Jones Papers. For black skepticism of Jones, see "Sam Jones—American" (editorial), *Louisiana Weekly,* November 30, 1946, 10.

2. "Not the Satevepost Jones," *Louisiana Weekly,* April 24, 1943, 10; "Gov. Jones Makes Another Speech," *Louisiana Weekly,* May 22, 1943, 10; G. Myrdal, "America's Uneasy Conscience," *Louisiana Weekly,* December 25, 1943, 10.

3. Woodruff, "Mississippi Delta Planters," 263–84; Schulman, *From Cotton Belt to Sunbelt,* 112–34.

While many recent works have focused on the war years and their effect on black economic mobility, this chapter traces the process of demobilization as it reflected the loss of wartime industrial employment gains made by African Americans. Some recent econometric literature (see Collins, "Race, Roosevelt and Wartime Production") has addressed the economic mobility and long-term economic gains of African Americans in this period. This chapter focuses more on the community level of demobilization and also how southern white conservatives used antilabor laws and control of federal welfare and employment service agencies to combat the fair employment movement and reduce African American workers' leverage in the southern labor market after the war.

4. "Demobilizing Negro Soldiers to Test Democracy, McNutt Says," *Atlanta Daily World*, January 7, 1945, 1; "Demobilizing Soldiers to Test Democracy—WMC Chief McNutt Says There Must Be Jobs for All in Post-war Period," *Louisiana Weekly*, January 13, 1945, 1.

5. C. Mitchell to W. Maslow, February 20, 1945, Weekly Reports—C. Mitchell file, box 459, DFO, Fair Employment Practices Committee, RG 228, NARA CP.

6. H. Beall to W. D. Ellinger, January 27, 1945, Todd-Houston file, box 808, Closed Cases, Fair Employment Practices Committee, RG 228, NARA FW. For an overview of the Todd Corporation's postwar cutback program, see Mitchell, *Every Kind of Shipwork*. For an overview of the postwar U.S. shipbuilding industry generally, see Mack-Forlist and Newman, *The Conversion of Shipbuilding*.

7. W. D. Ellinger to W. Maslow, May 12, 1945, Biweekly Reports—FEPC file, box 641, series 270, War Manpower Commission, RG 211, NARA FW.

8. W. D. Ellinger to W. Maslow, May 12, 1945, Biweekly Reports—FEPC file, box 641, series 270, War Manpower Commission, RG 211, NARA FW; C. Castaneda to E. Davidson, October 29, 1945, unlabeled file (Weekly Reports 1945), box 456, Will Maslow office files, DFO, Fair Employment Practices Committee, RG 228, NARA CP. For more on Castaneda as FEPC Region X director, see Daniel, *Chicano Workers*, and Obadele-Starks, *Black Unionism*.

9. For May 1945 statistics, see Texas Labor Market, February 1945, ES Texas—Employment file, box 198, RG 183, NARA CP. For employment statistics for CVAC in December 1945, see Walter Humphrey, "Queen of Skies to 'Graveyard,'" unspecified newspaper, December 15, 1945, and "B-36 Production Set Here—5,000 More Workers to Be Employed by Convair," *Fort Worth Star-Telegram*, August 15, 1946, in Convair vertical file, Fort Worth Public Library.

10. Memorandum for Commanding General, Army Service Forces, June 21, 1945, CVAC—Fort Worth file, box 70, Closed Cases, Fair Employment Practices Committee, RG 228, NARA FW.

11. Nelson, "Organized Labor," 988.

12. D. Ellinger to Lone Star Defense Corporation, July 30, 1945; J. H. Bond to D. Ellinger, July 24, 1945; D. Ellinger to J. H. Bond, July 18, 1945, FEPC Region XIII file, box 639, series 270, War Manpower Commission, RG 211, NARA FW.

13. William Y. Bell, "News of Atlanta's Negro Community," *Atlanta Journal*, February 25, 1945, in Reports to Regional Director and Miscellaneous Memoranda file, box 1, series 20, War Manpower Commission, RG 211, NARA EP.

14. George W. Healy Jr., "The Deep South: Delta Shipyard Workers Hope to Keep Jobs," *New York Times*, April 22, 1945, in New Orleans file, box 447, tension files, DRA, Fair Employment Practices Committee, RG 228, NARA CP; D. Ellinger to E. Davidson, July 27, 1945; and D. Ellinger to C. Mitchell, January 19, 1945, Delta Shipbuilding Company file (1 of 2), box 792, Active Cases; Final Disposition Report for CVAC-NO, CVAC—New Orleans file, Closed Cases, Fair Employment Practices Committee, RG 228, NARA FW.

FEPC Region XIII was created in January 1945 when the main office in Washington decided to divide the old Region X in half, making New Orleans the headquarters for Region XIII, covering Louisiana and East Texas, and designating San Antonio as the headquarters for a new FEPC Region X, covering West Texas and New Mexico.

15. Employment in Selected Aviation Plants, July 1944, Minority Workers by Industries file, box 384, Wilfred Leland office files, DRA, Fair Employment Practices Committee, RG 228, NARA CP; Combes, "Aircraft Manufacturing"; Marshall, *The Negro and Organized Labor*, 226–31.

16. For NAA statistics for July 1944, see Employment in Selected Aviation Plants, July 1944, Minority Workers by Industries file, box 384, Wilfred Leland office files, DRA, Fair Employment Practices Committee, RG 228, NARA CP. For NAA employment statistics for 1945, see Texas Labor Market February 1945, ES Texas—Employment file, box 198, RG 183, NARA CP; Barksdale, *Genesis of the Aviation Industry*, 4–7, 13–16; Fairbanks, "Dallas in the 1940s," 141–53.

17. John H. Young III, "Firms Spurn Welders," *Pittsburgh Courier*, March 17, 1945, in Region XIII file, box 403, Carol Coan office files, DRA, Fair Employment Practices Committee, RG 228, NARA CP.

18. Asher Lauren, "Labor and Industry," *Detroit Daily News*, August 12, 1945, 9; "7 Million Unemployed Forecast by End of 1945," *Detroit Daily News*, August 14, 1945, 14; "'Brief' Jobless Period Is Promised by U.S.," *Detroit Daily News*, August 15, 1945, 1; "Ask Full Job Bill to Halt Racial Strife," *Louisiana Weekly*, September 8, 1945, 1.

19. "Job Losses Are Rising by the Thousands," *Detroit Daily News*, August 18, 1945, 2; "Detroit Negroes Calm Despite Layoffs," *California Eagle*, September 6, 1945, 1.

20. E. Rutledge to H. Kingman, April 25, 1945, WMC-FEPC Relations file, box 459, DFO, Fair Employment Practices Committee, RG 228, NARA CP. FEPC Region XII included California, Oregon, and Washington.

21. "Negro Population and Employment in the Bay Area," November 1946, and "Non-White Employment in S.F. Bay Area Statistics," September 1946, in FEPC California 1944–46—miscellaneous material file, FEPC box, ILWU History of World War II, International Longshoremen's and Warehousemen's Union Archives.

22. See International Longshoremen's and Warehousemen's Union Local 13 Oral History Project interviews; Ben Margolis interview, Labor History Collection.

23. "Citizens Mobilize to Fight Bias," *California Eagle*, August 30, 1945, 1; "L.A. NAACP Maps All-out Drive for Jobs—Group Seeks Full Integration of Industries," *California Eagle*, September 13, 1945, 1; "NAACP to Hold Job Clinic," *California Eagle*, October 11, 1945, 4; "NAACP Supports Lockheed Group Bias Campaign," *California Eagle*, October 25, 1945, 1; "Jim Crowism at Navy Dry Docks," *California Eagle*, November 1, 1945, 1; "Rev. Russell Urges Negroes to Join Hands with Labor," *California Eagle*, November 1, 1945, 2.

24. "Marshall Field III Studies Coast Race Relations," *California Eagle*, July 19, 1945, 1; "Mass Meet on Residential Restrictions Set for Sunday," *California Eagle*,

September 13, 1945, 1; "NAACP Head Urges Labor to Support Housing Fight Here," *California Eagle*, September 20, 1945, 3.

25. "California Here We Go! Migrants Are in the Money," *Detroit Daily News*, August 17, 1945, 1.

26. "Negroes Say They Will Not Return South," *Dallas Express*, January 6, 1945, 2.

27. "Problem of Jobs Seen as Number One Problem," *Atlanta Daily World*, November 3, 1944, 1.

28. "Oxley Studies Post-war Job Prospects on Coast," *Dallas Express*, September 16, 1944, 2; "V-J Carries Increase in Job Discrimination," *California Eagle*, August 23, 1945, 1.

29. "V-J Day Sees Intensification of Job Discrimination on West Coast," *Atlanta Daily World*, August 22, 1945, 1; Johnson, *The Second Gold Rush*, 92–96, 210–11.

30. Lawrence Oxley, "Negroes in the Post-war Period," *Manpower Review* (February 1945): 9–10, in WMC Post-war Plans file, box 380, Wilfred Leland office files, DRA, Fair Employment Practices Committee, RG 228, NARA CP. See also "Negro Workers Face Layoffs in Nine Areas," *Atlanta Daily World*, August 26, 1945, 7; "Survey Finds Jobs Spotty—NAACP," *Atlanta Daily World*, August 28, 1945, 1; "Workers Hit with Cutbacks but Opportunities Better—Over 150,000 Temporarily Idle in Five Areas," *Atlanta Daily World*, August 31, 1945, 1; "Cutbacks Trap Workers in Louisiana, Delaware and Oregon," *Birmingham World*, September 11, 1945, 1.

31. Brinkley, *The End of Reform*, 257–62.

32. Ibid., 261–62.

33. "Modern Carpetbaggers Bill," *Manufacturers' Record* (October 1945): 40.

34. "Ask Full Job Bill to Halt Racial Strife—Legislation Would Stave off Economic Depression," *Louisiana Weekly*, September 8, 1945, 1. For a discussion of the National Urban League's support of the liberal agenda, see Moore Jr., *A Search for Equality*, 128–32. As a black worker's caption in an Associated Negro Press cartoon stated regarding Full Employment, "Gosh, that will solve all my problems" (*Louisiana Weekly*, September 22, 1945, 10).

35. "Emergency Job Bill Passed—After Clause Inserted that USES Will Return to State Control," *Dallas Express*, September 29, 1945, 1.

36. "Continued Federal Job Control Urged Here by McNutt," *Houston Post*, May 27, 1945, in unlabeled file (miscellaneous reports), box 456, Will Maslow office files, DFO, Fair Employment Practices Committee, RG 228, NARA CP. See also Flynn, *The Mess in Washington*, 248.

37. "(NAACP) Urges Truman Veto on USES Return to States for Control," *Louisiana Weekly*, December 29, 1945, 11; "NAACP Meets with US DOL at Labor-Management Conference," *Atlanta Daily World*, November 25, 1945, 1.

38. "Shift of Employment Agencies to States Menace to Negro Workers," *Dallas Express*, November 24, 1945, 8; "Negro Workers Are Victimized by White Supremacy Revival," *Louisiana Weekly*, January 5, 1946, 1; "Return of USES to States Presents Greater Problems," *Birmingham World*, August 24, 1945, 4.

39. NOUL Annual Report, 1945, New Orleans 1939–60 file, box 19, series 13, part 2, National Urban League Collection.

40. W. Y. Bell to P. McNutt, March 26, 1945, and P. McNutt to W. Y. Bell, May 19, 1945, War Manpower Commission file, box A-77, Southern Regional Office, National Urban League Collection. McNutt defended the WMC's record, stating that WMC and USES "personnel all along the line, including the work of the (MGS)," had "gone a long way to increase the utilization of Negroes in practically every war industry." While "our work may be short of perfect and far from completed," such shortcomings were "due I think to the fact that none of us is perfect and the problem is one that cannot be solved overnight."

41. Harry McAlpin, "FSA Vacancy," *Birmingham World*, September 11, 1945, 1.

42. War Manpower Commission file, box A-77, Southern Regional Office, National Urban League Collection; "Can't Wait Longer to Solve Problems" (editorial), *Louisiana Weekly*, September 22, 1945, 10.

43. W. H. Shell to Col. J. N. Keelin Jr., June 30, 1945, Bell Aircraft Corporation file, box 1, series 20, War Manpower Commission, RG 211, NARA EP.

44. W. Y. Bell to J. Thomas, December 19, 1944, 1944 Labor Legislation file, box A-70, Southern Regional Office, National Urban League Collection.

45. "Georgia Vets from WWII Organize Georgia League," *Atlanta Daily World*, September 9, 1945, 1; Ferguson, "The Politics of Inclusion," 552–53. See also McMillen, "Fighting for What We Didn't Have."

46. "Atlanta Vets March on City Hall," *Louisiana Weekly*, March 16, 1946, 3; "Two Day Vets' Institute Ends: Form Permanent Committee to Deal with G.I. Problems," *Louisiana Weekly*, March 16, 1946, 3; "Veterans, Where Are You?" (editorial), *Louisiana Weekly*, July 27, 1946, 10.

47. Report of the Community Conference on Employment and Employment Opportunities for Negroes in New Orleans, March 5–7, 1945, Affiliates New Orleans file, box 111, series I-D, part 2, National Urban League Collection.

48. Ibid.

49. "Willard Townsend" (editorial), *Dallas Express*, March 17, 1945, 10. By 1945, Wesley owned the *Houston Informer*, the *Dallas Express* (see *Dallas Express*, April 13, 1940, 1), the *New Orleans Informer-Sentinel* (see *Dallas Express*, July 25, 1942, 1), and the *San Antonio I-Day* (see *Dallas Express*, July 29, 1944, 1).

50. Report of the Community Conference.

51. "A Conversion Program for the Cotton South—by the USDA-BAE," April 1945, miscellaneous file, box 361, John Davis office files, DRA, Fair Employment Practices Committee, RG 228, NARA CP; "USDA Survey Gives Post-war Picture," *Atlanta Daily World*, March 3, 1945, 1.

52. "Interesting Southern Facts" (editorial), *Dallas Express*, October 6, 1945, 1; "Too Much Cotton" (editorial), *Dallas Express*, October 27, 1945, 10.

53. "Industrialized South" (editorial), *Dallas Express*, February 10, 1945, 10.

54. "Proposed Industrialization of the South Termed Boon to Negroes," *Birmingham World*, October 17, 1944, 1; "Plan Postwar Industrialization of the South," *Birmingham World*, January 19, 1945, 1.

55. George McCray, "Southern Industrial Progress and Better Race Relations," *Louisiana Weekly*, June 16, 1945, 10.

56. Dean Gordon Hancock, "The South's Freight Rate Victory and the Negro," *Louisiana Weekly*, August 4, 1945, 10.

57. "A Conversion Program"; Meyer, *Journey through Chaos*, 365–66.

58. Sam Jones, "The Southern Negro Packs His Bags," Article file, box 31, Sam Houston Jones Papers.

59. S. Jones to J. Aswell, April 30, 1945, May 19, 1945, June 9, 1945, Article file, box 31, Sam Houston Jones Papers.

60. Woodruff, "Mississippi Delta Planters," 268, 272, 275–81; "Delta Council Seeks Educational Improvements," *Atlanta Daily World*, August 24, 1945, 1. See also Lemann, *The Promised Land*, 49–52, 70–71.

61. "Two Encouraging Moves," *Louisiana Weekly*, January 13, 1945, 10.

62. "Dixie Governors Plan to Industrialize the South—To Compete with the North and East," *Dallas Express*, January 20, 1945, 9; "Industrialized South," *Dallas Express*, February 10, 1945, 10; "Plan Post-war Industrialization of the South—Governors Plan to Industrialize the South," *Birmingham World*, January 19, 1945, 1.

63. "Governors Hear Need for Schools," *Atlanta Daily World*, December 9, 1945, 1.

64. "Negro Problems Confronting the Nation," *Dallas Morning News*, November 20–29, 1944, FEPC Newspaper Publicity file, box 641, series 270, War Manpower Commission, RG 211, NARA FW.

65. Ibid.

66. "Negro Economic Status," *Manufacturers' Record* (September 1945): 44.

67. "Race Problem," *Dallas Morning News*, December 10, 1944; "Negroes Told to Solve Ills South's Way," *Dallas Morning News*, September 8, 1944, FEPC Newspaper Publicity file, box 641, series 270, War Manpower Commission, RG 211, NARA FW.

68. Thurman Sensing, "The South Has No Race Problem," *Manufacturers' Record* (July 1944): 28, 54–55.

69. "Dixie Governors Plan," 9.

70. Fairclough, *Race and Democracy*, 86–98; "New Iberia NAACP Branch Installed," *Louisiana Weekly*, July 31, 1943, 2; "Wright in New Iberia NAACP Rally Speaker," *Louisiana Weekly*, March 18, 1944, 1; *Louisiana Weekly*, May 27, 1944, 1; "Plantation Philosophy" (editorial), *Birmingham World*, July 25, 1944, 8.

71. J. H. Bond to V. McGee, January 30, 1945; V. McGee to J. H. Bond, January 6, 1945; William Caldwell to R. D. Reeves, January 13, 1945; and Eugene Hill to W. Caldwell, January 13, 1945, Louisiana Employment Complaints file, box 652, series 270, War Manpower Commission, RG 211, NARA FW.

Like cotton, the cane industry in South Louisiana underwent mechanization during the war. Even with the employment of POWs to harvest their crop after 1943, planters continued to complain of labor shortages during harvest. See "Plan for Labor to Harvest Cane Outlined Here," *Baton Rouge Advocate*, September 16, 1943, sec. B, 8, in Clippings and Releases file, box 1, series 279, War Manpower Commission, RG 211, NARA FW.

72. Eugene Hill to W. Caldwell, January 13, 1945, Louisiana Employment Complaints file, box 652, series 270, War Manpower Commission, RG 211, NARA FW.

73. Advertisement from *Shreveport Journal*, October 28, 1944; see E. R. Speer to R. D. Reeves, November 1, 1944, Unauthorized Advertising file, box 676, series 270, War Manpower Commission, RG 211, NARA FW.

74. "Mass Migration Plan Disclosed," *Atlanta Daily World*, April 19, 1945, 1.

75. Roscoe Dunjee and Ira De A. Reid were two leaders who openly opposed segregation during 1945. Their stance became public when John T. Graves, liberal white editor of the *Birmingham Age-Herald*, advised southern African Americans to accept segregation. Both Dunjee and Reid responded in opposition to the advice. See "Accept Segregation, Alabama Liberal Journalist Advises," *Atlanta Daily World*, March 3, 1945, 1.

76. "Negroes Should Leave the South" (editorial), *Louisiana Weekly*, July 14, 1945, 10; "Negroes Should Read but Not Run" (editorial), *Dallas Express*, August 28, 1943, 10. The latter editorial addressed *New Republic* editor Thomas Sancton's article, entitled "Go North, Black Man," from the August 1943 *Readers Digest*. See *Atlanta Daily World*, reprinted editorial from "Why Not Migration?" *Columbia (South Carolina) Lighthouse and Informer*, September 30, 1945; "Migration and the Negro" (editorial), *Louisiana Weekly*, April 13, 1946, 10; *Negro South* (April 1946): 4, 42–48, (July 1946): 18, (January 1947): 18, in Special Collections, Tulane University.

77. *Negro South* (May 1946): 26–27.

78. "How Can Farmers Succeed in the Post-war?" *Progressive Farmer* (December 1944): 54. For other calls for mechanization, see "How Can We Farm More Profitably under Post-war Conditions?" *Progressive Farmer* (July 1944): 42; "Farmers Speak out on Our Post-war Problems," *Progressive Farmer* (October 1944): 12.

79. D. Dalton to D. O. Rushing, October 9, 1945, ES Arkansas Reports 7-1 file, box 183, RG 183, NARA CP.

80. W. J. Monday to D. O. Rushing, October 6, 1945, ES Arkansas Reports 7-1 file, box 183, RG 183, NARA CP.

81. Employment Problems of Veterans, Thomas L. Ward, ES Texas—Employment file, box 198, RG 183, NARA CP.

82. Factors Affecting Lumber Production, Third Quarter 1944, Logging and Lumbering file, box 1, series 285, War Manpower Commission, RG 211, NARA FW.

83. Birmingham WMC Field Operation Report, December 1943, Reports—Alabama—13 file, box 14, series 11, War Manpower Commission, RG 211, NARA EP.

84. George Mitchell, "If Vets Don't Want School, They Can Get Job Training," *Louisiana Weekly*, February 9, 1946, 8; "SRC Pushing 3 Point Program to Aid Vets," *Louisiana Weekly*, September 7, 1946, 7. See also Moore Jr., *A Search for Equality*, 130–31.

85. "Emphasis upon Training" (editorial), *Dallas Express*, December 23, 1944, 10; "Unite with United Negro Veterans," *Atlanta Daily World*, December 16, 1945, 2.

86. "Houston Vets Get Training," *Dallas Express*, February 9, 1946, 10.

87. Ferguson, "The Politics of Inclusion," 539; "Request Vet Trade School for Negroes," *Louisiana Weekly*, February 23, 1946, 1.

88. "Vets Face Appalling Lack of Opportunities," *Louisiana Weekly*, July 27, 1946, 1.

89. William R. Simms, "Minority Veterans and Their Problems," part 1, *Louisiana Weekly*, May 11, 1945, 13; part 2, *Louisiana Weekly*, May 18, 1945, 13.

90. "Jackson Appeals for Funds for Perm FEPC," *Birmingham World*, October 9, 1945, 1.

91. "Perm FEPC Council Sets Confab September 12–13," *Atlanta Daily World*, September 4, 1945, 1; "Atlanta and 6 Other FEPC Offices Close December 15," *Atlanta Daily World*, November 15, 1945, 1.

92. "Plans for FEPC Set-up Made," and "Toward a Permanent FEPC" (editorial), *Dallas Express*, April 14, 1945, 1, 10; "Local Perm FEPC Drive to Begin October 14," *Dallas Express*, October 13, 1945, 1, 10. See also *Houston Informer*, April 28, 1945, Weekly Reports—April–May file, box 403, Carol Coan office files, DRA, Fair Employment Practices Committee, RG 228, NARA CP.

93. "SP Employees Give $400 to Permanent FEPC Fund," *Houston Informer*, May 12, 1945, Field Research—Houston, Texas, Employment file, box 50, series 6, part 2, National Urban League Collection; "Houston Scene of Hearings—FEPC to Hear Cases of 27 RR Switchmen," *Dallas Express*, May 5, 1945, 1.

94. "AFL Leaders See Perm FEPC as Vital Weapon against Racism," and "Orleanians Form Council for a Perm FEPC," *Louisiana Weekly*, December 2, 1944, 1; "Ministers Back N.O. Council for Perm FEPC," *Louisiana Weekly*, December 16, 1944, 1; "N.O. Council for FEPC Gains Momentum," *Louisiana Weekly*, December 23, 1944, 1; "Transport Workers Contribute to Fund for Permanent FEPC," *Louisiana Weekly*, January 27, 1945, 3; "Pullman Porters Sponsor Benefit Dance for FEPC," *Louisiana Weekly*, February 3, 1945, 6; E. J. Wright, "Sign of the Times," and "N.O. Council for Permanent FEPC Active in Fight," *Louisiana Weekly*, March 3, 1945, 3.

95. D. Ellinger to W. Maslow, March 3, 1945, March 10, 1945, Region XIII file (Weekly Reports); D. Ellinger to W. Maslow, April 14, 1945, Weekly Reports April–May 1945 file; and D. Ellinger to W. Maslow, June 23, 1945, unlabeled file (Weekly Reports); box 403, Carol Coan office files, DRA, Fair Employment Practices Committee, RG 228, NARA CP; "N.O. Advisory Committee on FEPC Is Named," *Louisiana Weekly*, August 25, 1945, 1.

96. C. Castaneda to W. Maslow, April 30, 1945, Weekly Reports April–May 1945 file, box 403, Carol Coan office files, DRA, Fair Employment Practices Committee, RG 228, NARA CP. For an examination of the FEPC and its dealings with Chicano workers and civil rights leaders in Texas, see Daniel, *Chicano Workers*, and Zamora, "The Failed Promise."

97. C. Castaneda to W. Maslow, March 3, 1945, Region X Weekly Reports file, box 403, Carol Coan office files, DRA, Fair Employment Practices Committee, RG 228, NARA CP.

98. D. Ellinger to W. Maslow, March 3, 1945, Region XIII Weekly Reports file,

box 403, Carol Coan office files, DRA, Fair Employment Practices Committee, RG 228, NARA CP.

99. C. Castaneda to W. Maslow, April 16, 1945, Weekly Reports April–May 1945 file, box 403, Carol Coan office files, DRA, Fair Employment Practices Committee, RG 228, NARA CP.

100. C. Castaneda to C. Mitchell, March 15, 1945, miscellaneous loose material, box 46, C. Mitchell office files, DFO, Fair Employment Practices Committee, RG 228, NARA CP.

101. "Condemn Deal on FEPC Bill by Senate," *Louisiana Weekly*, February 16, 1946, 1; G. McCray, "Was FEPC 'Death' Due to Poor Strategy?" and B. Robinson, "Notes and Notations," *Louisiana Weekly*, February 23, 1946, 10.

102. Pfeffer, *A. Philip Randolph*, 104–5; "Three Orleanians Attend FEPC Strategy Meet," *Louisiana Weekly*, March 9, 1946, 1.

103. Pfeffer, *A. Philip Randolph*, 118–19.

Epilogue

1. G. McCray, "Does the CIO Have the Moral Strength to Win the South?" *Louisiana Weekly*, May 11, 1946, 10.

2. G. McCray, "Only Economic Equality for Negro Workers in the South," *Louisiana Weekly*, June 1, 1946, 10.

3. D. Ellinger to W. Maslow, March 3, 1945, Region XIII file, box 403, Carol Coan office files, DRA, Fair Employment Practices Committee, RG 228, NARA CP.

4. E. Wright, "I Daresay: 'Action Speaks Louder than Words,'" *Louisiana Weekly*, April 27, 1946, 11.

5. "Operation Registration," and "Registration Is a Must Audience Told," *Louisiana Weekly*, July 13, 1946, 1. Marilynn Johnson describes similar voter mobilization efforts for southern black migrants in Oakland, California, from 1944 to 1946 (*The Second Gold Rush*, 185–208).

6. "Labor Meet at Wheat Street," *Atlanta Daily World*, April 16, 1944, 1; "Labor Speaks at Wheat Street," *Atlanta Daily World*, September 1, 1945, 4; "CIO Will Hold Meet at Centenary Church," *Atlanta Daily World*, September 23, 1945, 1; "Savannah Negroes Show a Renewed Voting Interest," *Atlanta Daily World*, October 10, 1945, 1.

7. "Urges Southern Negroes to Get Ready for Vote—Registration Battle Head Minister Asserts," *Atlanta Daily World*, April 21, 1944, 1; Pfeffer, *A. Philip Randolph*, 172.

8. "Negroes and Labor Join in Alabama Drive for Voters—Political Action Group Stirs All to Get Qualified," *Birmingham World* and *Atlanta Daily World*, July 7, 1944, 1.

9. "Labor Leaders Pledge Aid in Registration Drive," *Birmingham World*, June 20, 1944, 1; "CIO Political Committee Maps Voter Registration," *Birmingham World*, June 27, 1944, 1; "Speakers Urge Group Action in Fight to Become Registered Vot-

ers Here," *Birmingham World*, July 4, 1944, 1; "CIO Pushes Voter Registration," *Birmingham World*, August 15, 1944, 1; "Plans Set to Mobilize Registered Voters," *Birmingham World*, November 24, 1944, 1.

10. "Seek to Register Many for Voting," *Birmingham World*, March 30, 1945, 8; "(J. H. Green, Chair of Birmingham NAACP) Directs Registration," *Birmingham World*, June 5, 1945, 1; "Massing for Big Registration Drive in August," *Birmingham World*, July 17, 1945, 1.

11. "Trend in Negro Leadership" (editorial), *Louisiana Weekly*, January 26, 1946, 10.

12. For interpretation of interracial unionism in the South during the war, see Honey, *Southern Labor and Black Civil Rights*, 216–17; Zieger, *The CIO*, 83–85, 154–61; Ambrose, "A Revolution of Hope," 1–40. For an account of the National Maritime Union (NMU-CIO) in the South, see "Maritime Union Refutes Belief Negro and White Will Not Work Together," *Louisiana Weekly*, September 25, 1943, 1; and for the Rodmen-AFL in New Orleans, see "Workers Resent Unfair Union Practice—Protest FEPC Committee—Seek League's Help," *Louisiana Weekly*, October 23, 1943, 1.

13. F. Nichols to L. Granger, Memphis Report, Memphis UL 1943–48 file, box 106, series 1-5, part 1, National Urban League Collection; Moore Jr., *A Search for Equality*, 152–53; "Organizer for AFL," *Birmingham World*, November 24, 1942, 1; "Job Discrimination Charged against USES," *Atlanta Daily World*, August 22, 1943, 6; "McNutt Promises USES Probe in Memphis," *Atlanta Daily World*, September 27, 1943, 1; "Memphis Laundry Workers on Strike," *Atlanta Daily World*, October 15, 1943, 2.

14. "Forum on Labor to Be Held at Wheat Street," *Atlanta Daily World*, February 28, 1943, 1; "The Church and Labor," *Atlanta Daily World*, September 11, 1943, 2; "1,200 Laundry Workers Strike for Higher Pay," *Atlanta Daily World*, October 8, 1943, 1; "Laundry Union Favors AUL Strike Program—Management Has Not Yet Replied to Proposals," *Atlanta Daily World*, November 5, 1943, 1; Ferguson, "The Politics of Inclusion," 426–27.

15. "CIO Drive in New Orleans," *Louisiana Weekly*, August 10, 1946, 8; "All out Drive to Organize Clothing Workers Started," *Louisiana Weekly*, September 7, 1946, 1; "I Daresay: 'Victory at Rutter-Rex Plant,'" *Louisiana Weekly*, September 14, 1946, 10; "Wright Charges AFL Organizations with Scabbing," *Louisiana Weekly*, October 5, 1946, 1; "AFL Continues Scabbing Says Organizer," *Louisiana Weekly*, October 12, 1946, 2; "Is This the AFL?" (editorial), *Louisiana Weekly*, October 26, 1946, 10.

16. Marshall, *Labor in the South*, 209–10; "PDL to Hold Political Rally Sunday Eve," *Louisiana Weekly*, April 15, 1944, 3; "(CIO) Union to Instruct Its Members How to Register to Vote," *Louisiana Weekly*, July 1, 1944, 1; "Dorsey Points out Benefits of CIO," *Louisiana Weekly*, December 23, 1944, 1. For the Transport Workers' CIO PAC organization in New Orleans, see "Transport Workers Form Committee for Political Action," *Louisiana Weekly*, October 27, 1945, 2; "(Tillman) Speaks on PDL Forum," *Louisiana Weekly*, June 15, 1946, 3; Report on Activities, ILWU Local 207, January 14,

1944, ILWU Organization—South and Gulf—Correspondence and Reports—Wm. Spooner—Local 207, 1944 file, box 14, ILWU organizer files, International Longshoremen's and Warehousemen's Union Archives.

17. "Moses Turner Is Making Progress in Labor Circles," *Louisiana Weekly*, March 4, 1944, 3; "L&N Employees Observe Their 1st Anniversary," *Louisiana Weekly*, April 1, 1944, 6; "Railway Carmen Send Turner to B'ham Meet," *Louisiana Weekly*, May 27, 1944, 1; "Turner Named to AFL Exec. Board," *Louisiana Weekly*, June 10, 1944, 1; "Wright Congratulates Turner on His Election," *Louisiana Weekly*, June 17, 1944, 9; "Labor Leaders Urge Members to Register Now," *Louisiana Weekly*, December 1, 1945, 2; "E. J. Wright Speaks at Shakespeare Park on Registration," and "50,000 Registered Voters for Coming Election Is Goal," *Louisiana Weekly*, June 8, 1946, 1; "ILA Political Committee Gets Its Union Members Registered," *Louisiana Weekly*, July 6, 1946, 2; "Operation Registration," *Louisiana Weekly*, July 13, 1946, 1; "Union Leader Stirs Interest in Registration," *Louisiana Weekly*, July 20, 1946, 8; Maney, "Hale Boggs," 250. For the history of ILA Local 1419, see Ambrose, "A Revolution of Hope," 82–134.

18. "Defense League to Meet Sunday," *Louisiana Weekly*, October 9, 1943, 1; "Ministers Alliance Supports Political Action Drive for Vote," *Louisiana Weekly*, October 16, 1943, 1; "Ballot Rally Mass Meeting to Be Held in Shakespeare Park," *Louisiana Weekly*, October 23, 1943, 1; "10,000 Attend Right to Vote Rally," *Louisiana Weekly*, October 30, 1943, 1; "Leaders Discuss Right to Vote," *Louisiana Weekly*, December 11, 1943, 2; "'We Want Ballot' Program Arouses Cross Section Support of City," *Louisiana Weekly*, March 18, 1944, 3; "Third 'We Want the Ballot' Conference Held," *Louisiana Weekly*, May 6, 1944, 9; "Wright Congratulates Turner on His Election," *Louisiana Weekly*, June 17, 1944, 9; "Lead Defense League Membership Drive," *Louisiana Weekly*, August 5, 1944, 3.

19. "24,000 Registered in Georgia County," *Louisiana Weekly*, May 18, 1946, 1; "Georgia Seeks 100,000 More Voters—Negro Democrats Start Statewide 60 Day Drive," *Louisiana Weekly*, May 25, 1946, 16; "Mississippi Starts Drive to Organize Voters," *Louisiana Weekly*, June 1, 1946, 1; "50,000 Registered Voters," 1; "Political Action" (editorial), *Louisiana Weekly*, June 8, 1946, 10; "Georgia Sets the Pace for Louisiana," *Louisiana Weekly*, July 27, 1946, 1; Bartley, *Keeping the Faith*, 27.

20. "A Voteless People Is a Hopeless People," *Louisiana Weekly*, November 2, 1946, 1.

21. W. Valentine to N. Jackson, May 7, 1948, Affiliates New Orleans file, box 111, series I-D, National Urban League Collection.

22. "A Voteless People," 1.

23. "Texas Vote Comes of Age" (editorial), *Louisiana Weekly*, August 10, 1946, 1.

24. "Four Vets Given 'Run-Around,'" *Louisiana Weekly*, August 10, 1946, 1; "Alabama Denies Voting Rights to Negro Veterans," *Louisiana Weekly*, February 2, 1946, 1; "Atlantans Barred at Democratic Polls," *Birmingham World*, July 11, 1945, 1.

25. National Urban League Southern Regional Office finding aid, 6, National Urban League Collection.

26. G. Farley to L. Granger, April 10, 1946, 1946—NOUL file, box A-81, Southern Regional Office, National Urban League Collection.

27. N. Jackson to L. Granger, March 28, 1946, Southern Office Correspondence, January–July 1946 file, box 73, series I-C, part 1, National Urban League Collection; Ferguson, "The Politics of Inclusion," 556–57.

28. N. Jackson to L. Granger, March 28, 1946, Southern Office Correspondence, January–July 1946 file, box 73, series I-C, part 1, National Urban League Collection; Report on TUL March 22–May 1946, by E. K. Newman, Tampa 1946–48 file, box 131, series 1-5, part 1, National Urban League Collection.

29. W. Y. Bell to W. Banner, April 3, 1945, CRP Houston 1945–47 file, box 25, series 6, part 1, National Urban League Collection.

30. A. M. Smith to N. Jackson, July 15, 1946, and July 31, 1946; N. Jackson to L. Granger, August 5, 1946; Dallas—April 1946 file, box A-78, Southern Regional Office, National Urban League Collection.

31. N. Jackson to A. M. Smith, June 4, 1946, Southern Office Correspondence, January–July 1946 file, box 73, series I-C, part 1, National Urban League Collection.

32. N. Jackson to L. Granger, December 10, 1946, Southern Office Correspondence, January–August 1948 file, box 73, series I-C, part 1, National Urban League Collection.

33. C. Johnson to N. Jackson, December 14, 1946, Fort Worth UL—January–December 1946 file, A-78, Southern Regional Office, National Urban League Collection.

34. W. Y. Bell to R. Yearwood, May 4, 1945, Miami 1947–54 file, box 16, series 13, part 1, National Urban League Collection.

35. N. Jackson to L. Granger, April 9, 1948, Southern Office Memos and Reports—1948 file, box 74, series I-C, part 1, National Urban League Collection. NUL southern affiliates in 1948 included Richmond, Atlanta, Tampa, New Orleans, Memphis, Little Rock, and Fort Worth.

36. See photo of Nelson Jackson and C. Laws, *Louisiana Weekly*, August 31, 1946, 1; "C. A. Laws Receives Bronze Star Award," *Louisiana Weekly*, October 26, 1946, 1.

37. N. Jackson to L. Granger, November 27, 1946, Southern Office Correspondence, August–December 1946 file, box 73, series I-C, part 1, National Urban League Collection. After resigning from the New Orleans Urban League, Clarence Laws never regained momentum in the jobs movement campaign. During 1955, local political boss and prosegregationist Leander Perez and New Orleans congressman Edward Hebert accused Laws of being a Communist because of his membership in and affiliation with the Southern Negro Youth Congress and the Southern Conference on Human Welfare in the 1940s. See Clarence Laws file, box 7, F. Edward Hebert Papers.

38. "Louisiana This Week," *Pittsburgh Courier*, July 10, 1948, New Orleans—1939–60—Special Reports file, box 18, series 13, part 1, National Urban League Collection.

39. E. J. Wright, "'New Orleans Urban League Inactive'—Wright," *Pittsburgh*

Courier, August 21, 1948, New Orleans—1939–60—Special Reports file, box 18, series 13, part 1, National Urban League Collection.

40. W. Valentine to N. Jackson, May 7, 1948, Affiliates New Orleans file, box 111, series I-D, part 1, National Urban League Collection.

41. Ibid.

42. Ibid.; "Blacks in Labor Unions: New Orleans, 1950," in Foner, ed., *The Black Worker,* 529–31.

43. "Blacks in Labor Unions: New Orleans, 1950," in Foner, ed., *The Black Worker,* 530.

44. Strahan, *Andrew Jackson Higgins,* 334–55.

45. W. Valentine to N. Jackson, May 7, 1948, Affiliates New Orleans file, box 111, series I-D, part 1, National Urban League Collection.

46. John Mebane, "Reconversion Progresses in Southeast," *Manufacturers' Record* (October 1945): 44, 70.

47. N. Jackson to L. Granger, April 9, 1948, Southern Office Memos and Reports—1948 file, box 74, series I-C, part 1, National Urban League Collection; Marshall, *The Negro and Organized Labor,* 178–79, 227–29.

48. N. Jackson to L. Granger, December 10, 1946, Southern Office Correspondence, August–December 1946 file, box 73, series I-C, part 1, National Urban League Collection; "Make USES Complaints to Ben Huiet, Commissioner of Georgia DOL," *Atlanta Daily World,* September 21, 1945, 1. For information on the establishment of a separate Negro USES office, see Ferguson, "The Politics of Inclusion," 521–22; and "Timeless: AUL Annual Report 1945," Atlanta 1940–50 and 1960 file, box 4, series 13, part 1, National Urban League Collection.

49. "Sharecroppers Ruled Ineligible for Government Readjustment Allowances—Benefits Denied by V.A.," *Atlanta Daily World,* September 27, 1945, 1; "CIO Protests State Practice in Denying Unemployment Pay—Charges Workers Being Forced to Low Paying Jobs," *CIO News Digest,* September 19, 1945, 1, in Industrial Union of Marine and Shipbuilding Workers of America Papers. See also the account of Estelle Holloway regarding the North Carolina Unemployment Compensation policy on cutting black workers from welfare during 1950, in Foner, ed., *The Black Worker,* 562.

50. N. Jackson to L. Granger, January 14, 1948, Southern Office Correspondence, January–August 1948 file, box 73, series I-C, part 1, National Urban League Collection.

51. N. Jackson to L. Granger, September 13, 1948, Southern Office Correspondence, September–December 1948 file, box 73, series I-C, part 1, National Urban League Collection.

52. Barksdale, *Genesis of the Aviation Industry;* Convair vertical file, Fort Worth Public Library; Marshall, *The Negro and Organized Labor,* 178–83.

53. Horowitz, *"Negro and White, Unite and Fight";* Halpern, "Interracial Unionism," 158–82; Halpern and Horowitz, *Meatpackers* (for Humphrey quote, see 108).

54. N. Jackson to L. Granger, February 28, 1950, Birmingham 1950 file, box 81, series 1-5, part 1, National Urban League Collection.

55. Ibid.; N. Jackson to L. Granger, March 10, 1948, and June 25, 1948, Southern Office Correspondence, January–August 1948 file, box 73, series I-C, part 1, National Urban League Collection.

56. N. Jackson to L. Granger, February 28, 1950, Birmingham 1950 file, box 81, series 1-5, part 1, National Urban League Collection; Stein, "Southern Workers"; Bruce Nelson, "CIO Meant One Thing."

57. Botson, "No Gold Watch"; Zamora, "The Failed Promise"; Green, "Labor in the Western Oil Industry"; Marshall, *Labor in the South*, 230–33; Marshall, *The Negro and Organized Labor*, 149–51 (OWIU), 185–88 (USWA).

58. Meyer, *Journey through Chaos*, 386.

59. Griffith, *The Crisis of American Labor;* Honey, *Southern Labor and Black Civil Rights*, 228–31; Honey, *Black Workers Remember*, 177–236; Goldfield, "The Failure of Operation Dixie."

60. "Closed Shop Already Banned in 11 States," *CIO News Digest*, April 2, 1947, 4; "Bittner Tells Unions to Organize Despite Bills," and Alabama CIO Advertisement, *CIO News Digest*, April 9, 1947, 3, in International Union of Marine and Shipbuilding Workers of America Papers.

61. Schwartz, *The March Inland*, 170–71; Korstad and Lichtenstein, "Opportunities Found and Lost," 786–811.

62. Cobb, *The Selling of the South*, 206–21.

63. "Blacks in Labor Unions: New Orleans, 1950," in Foner, ed., *The Black Worker*, 529–31.

64. See, for example, Korstad and Lichtenstein, "Opportunities Found and Lost," for the tobacco industry's response to UCAPAWA organizing during the war. See also Honey, *Black Workers Remember*, 322–68.

65. Rick Halpern, "The CIO and the Limits of Labor-based Civil Rights Activism."

66. Schulman, *From Cotton Belt to Sunbelt*, 206–21.

67. For an example of NAACP and organized labor coalitions after the war, see Lichtenstein, "Scientific Unionism," 77; Marshall, *The Negro and Organized Labor*, 57–61, 71, 145, 185–87, 197, 228. For examples of southern migrants in the northern and western postwar jobs movement, see Foner, ed., *The Black Worker*, where he cites the examples of Coleman Young and William R. Wood, who were active in the Detroit labor movement. In the San Francisco Bay Area, southern migrants active in the ILWU included Bill Chester, Johnny Walker, and Albert James; see Schwartz, ed., "Struggle and Triumph," 6–7. In the northern meatpacking industry, see Halpern and Horowitz, *Meatpackers*.

68. Foner, ed., *The Black Worker*, 559–60.

69. Ibid., 541–43. See also Pfeffer, *A. Philip Randolph*, 172. Pfeffer found that under A. Philip Randolph's leadership, the Brotherhood of Sleeping Car Porters donated some $4,000 to the NAACP's Legal Defense and Educational Fund during 1953 and 1955.

70. Nelson, "CIO Meant One Thing," 136–37; Honey, *Southern Labor and Black Civil Rights*, 245–77; Marshall, *The Negro and Organized Labor*, 184, 187, 228–39.

71. Stein, "History of an Idea." Stein writes that "postwar movements fighting discrimination and seeking economic equality and justice have attempted to improve black lives, not to make explicit statements on racial associations."

Bibliography

Archival Collections

Bell, Lamar Q. Collection. Georgia Department of Archives and History, Atlanta.

Caldwell, Millard Filmore. Administration Files. Series 576. Florida State Archives, Tallahassee.

Cone, Frederick P. Administration Files. Series 368. Florida State Archives, Tallahassee.

Dallas Negro Chamber of Commerce. Collection. Texas/Dallas Room, Dallas Public Library.

Department of Labor. Record Group 16. Georgia Department of Archives and History, Atlanta.

Dixon, Frank. Administration Files. Alabama Department of Archives and History, Montgomery.

Executive Office Incoming Correspondence. Record Group 1. Georgia Department of Archives and History, Atlanta.

Fair Employment Practices Committee. Record Group 228. National Archives and Records Administration, College Park, Maryland.

Fair Employment Practices Committee. Record Group 228. National Archives and Records Administration, East Point, Georgia.

Fair Employment Practices Committee. Record Group 228. National Archives and Records Administration, Fort Worth, Texas.

Fair Employment Practices Committee. Record Group 228. National Archives and Records Administration, San Bruno, California.

Florida Industrial Commission. Series 1477. Florida State Archives, Tallahassee.

Hebert, F. Edward. Papers. Special Collections, Tulane University.

Holland, Spessard. Administration Files. Series 406. Florida State Archives, Tallahassee.

Industrial Union of Marine and Shipbuilding Workers of America. Papers. Maryland Room, University of Maryland at College Park.

259

International Longshoremen's and Warehousemen's Union. Archives. San Francisco, California.

International Longshoremen's and Warehousemen's Union. Local 13 Oral History Project. Special Collections, California State University, Northridge.

Jones, Sam Houston. Papers. Special Collections, Tulane University.

Labor History Collection. Special Collections, California State University, Long Beach.

National Association for the Advancement of Colored People. Collection. Manuscript Division, Library of Congress.

National Urban League. Collection. Manuscript Division, Library of Congress.

Rosie the Riveter Oral History Project. Special Collections, California State University, Long Beach.

Stevenson, Coke. Governor's Papers. Archives Division, Texas State Library, Austin.

United States Employment Service. Record Group 183. National Archives and Records Administration, College Park, Maryland.

War Food Administration. Record Group 224. National Archives and Records Administration, College Park, Maryland.

War Manpower Commission. Record Group 211. National Archives and Records Administration, College Park, Maryland.

War Manpower Commission. Record Group 211. National Archives and Records Administration, East Point, Georgia.

War Manpower Commission. Record Group 211. National Archives and Records Administration, Fort Worth, Texas.

War Manpower Commission. Record Group 211. National Archives and Records Administration, San Bruno, California.

Selected Works

Abbott, Carl. "Planning for the Home Front in Seattle and Portland, 1940–1945." In *Martial Metropolis: U.S. Cities in War and Peace,* edited by Roger Lotchin. New York: Praeger Publishers, 1984. 163–90.

Agee, James, and Walker Evans. *Let Us Now Praise Famous Men: Three Tenant Families.* New York: Houghton Mifflin, 1960; originally published 1941.

Allen, Ruth. *East Texas Lumber Workers: An Economic and Social Picture.* Austin: University of Texas Press, 1961.

Ambrose, Edith R. "A Revolution of Hope: New Orleans Workers and Their Unions, 1923–1939." Ph.D. diss., Tulane University, 1998.

Anderson, Ernest F. "The Development of Leadership and Organization Building in the Black Community of Los Angeles from 1900 through World War II." Ph.D. diss., University of Southern California, 1976.

Anderson, Nels. *Men on the Move.* Chicago: University of Chicago Press, 1940.

Archibald, Katherine. *Wartime Shipyard: A Study in Social Disunity.* Berkeley: University of California Press, 1947.

Baldwin, Sidney. *Poverty and Politics: The Rise and Fall of the Farm Security Administration.* Chapel Hill: University of North Carolina Press, 1968.

Barksdale, E. C. *Genesis of the Aviation Industry in North Texas.* Austin: University of Texas Press, 1958.

Bartley, Abel. *Keeping the Faith: Race, Politics, and Social Development in Jacksonville, Florida, 1940–1970.* Westport, Conn.: Greenwood Press, 2000.

Bartley, Numan. *The New South, 1945–1980.* Baton Rouge: Louisiana State University Press, 1995.

Berger-Gluck, Sherna. *Rosie the Riveter Revisited: Women, the War, and Social Change.* Boston: Twayne, 1987.

Berry, Edwin C. "Profiles: Portland." *Journal of Educational Sociology* 19, no. 3 (November 1945): 158–65.

Botson, Michael. "No Gold Watch for Jim Crow's Retirement: The Abolition of Segregated Unionism at Houston's Hughes Tool Company." *Southwestern Historical Quarterly* 51 (April 1998): 497–522.

Bratt, Charles. "Profiles: Los Angeles." *Journal of Educational Sociology* 19, no. 3 (November 1945): 179–86.

Breen, William. *Labor Market Politics and the Great War: The Department of Labor, the States, and the First U.S. Employment Service, 1907–1933.* Kent, Ohio: Kent State University Press, 1997.

Brinkley, Alan. *The End of Reform: New Deal Liberalism in Recession and War.* New York: Vintage, 1995.

Broussard, Albert. *Black San Francisco: The Struggle for Racial Equality in the West, 1900–1954.* Lawrence: University of Kansas Press, 1993.

Burran, James. "Urban Racial Violence in the South during World War II: A Comparative Overview." In *From the Old South to the New: Essays on the Transitional South,* edited by W. Fraser and W. Moore Jr. Westport, Conn.: Greenwood Press, 1981. 167–77.

Butler, Joseph T., Jr. "Prisoner of War Labor in the Sugar Cane Fields of Lafourche Parish, Louisiana: 1943–1944." *Louisiana History* 14 (summer 1973): 283–96.

Capeci, Dominic, Jr. *Race Relations in Wartime Detroit: The Sojourner Truth Housing Controversy of 1942.* Philadelphia: Temple University Press, 1984.

Carlton, David, and Peter Cochlanis, eds. *Confronting Southern Poverty in the Great Depression: The Report on the Economic Conditions of the South with Related Documents.* Boston: Bedford Books of St. Martin's Press, 1996.

Clive, Alan. *State of War: Michigan in World War II.* Ann Arbor: University of Michigan Press, 1979.

Cobb, James. "Beyond Planters and Industrialists: A New Perspective on the New South." *Journal of Southern History* 54 (February 1988): 45–68.

———. *The Most Southern Place on Earth: The Mississippi Delta and the Roots of Regional Identity.* New York: Oxford University Press, 1992.

———. *The Selling of the South: The Southern Crusade for Industrial Development, 1936–1990.* Urbana: University of Illinois Press, 1993.

————. "World War II and the Mind of the Modern South." In *Remaking Dixie: The Impact of World War II on the American South,* edited by Neil McMillen. Jackson: University of Mississippi Press, 1997. 3–20.

Cohen, Lizabeth. *Making a New Deal: Industrial Workers in Chicago, 1919–1939.* Cambridge: Cambridge University Press, 1990.

Cohen, William. *At Freedom's Edge: Black Mobility and the White Quest for Racial Control.* Baton Rouge: Louisiana State University Press, 1991.

Collins, William. "Race, Roosevelt and Wartime Production: Fair Employment in World War II Labor Markets." *American Economic Review* 91, no. 1 (March 2001): 272–86.

Combes, Richard. "Aircraft Manufacturing in Georgia: A Case Study of Federal Industrial Investment." Paper presented at the Second Wave: Southern Industrialization, 1940–1970 Conference, Georgia Tech, Atlanta, June 5, 1998. <www.gatech.edu/hts/cssi/2ndwave>.

Cronenberg, Allen. *Forth to the Mighty Conflict: Alabama and World War II.* Tuscaloosa: University of Alabama Press, 1997.

Dance, Stanley. "King of the Blues: B. B. King" (interview). *Jazz* 6, no. 2 (February 1967): 15–21.

Daniel, Clete. *Chicano Workers and the Politics of Fairness: The FEPC in the Southwest, 1941–1945.* Austin: University of Texas Press, 1991.

Daniel, Pete. *Breaking the Land: The Transformation of Cotton, Tobacco, and Rice Cultures since 1880.* Urbana: University of Illinois Press, 1985.

————. "Going among Strangers: Southern Reactions to World War II." *Journal of American History* (December 1990): 888–91.

————. "The New Deal and Southern Agriculture." In *Problems in American Civilization: The New Deal,* edited by David Hamilton. New York: Houghton Mifflin, 1999. 126–44.

————. *Shadow of Slavery: Peonage in the South, 1901–1969.* Oxford: Oxford University Press, 1972.

Darling, Kenneth Tuttle. "Controlled Manpower: A Study of the Activities of the War Manpower Commission in the Los Angeles Harbor Shipbuilding Industry." Master's thesis, University of Redlands, California, 1951.

Draper, Alan. "The New Southern Labor History Revisited: The Success of the Mine, Mill and Smelter Workers Union in Birmingham, 1934–1938." *Journal of Southern History* 62 (February 1996): 87–108.

Draper, E. S. "Urban Development in the Southeast: What of the Future?" *Social Forces* 19 (October 1940): 17–22.

Dunbar, Andrew J., and Dennis McBride. *Building Hoover Dam: An Oral History of the Great Depression.* New York: Twayne, 1993.

Fairbanks, Robert. "Dallas in the 1940s: The Challenges and Opportunities of Defense Mobilization." In *Urban Texas: Politics and Development,* edited by Char Miller and Heywood Sanders. College Station: Texas A&M University Press, 1990. 141–53.

Fairclough, Adam. *Race and Democracy: The Civil Rights Struggle in Louisiana.* Athens: University of Georgia Press, 1995.

Ferguson, Karen J. "The Politics of Inclusion: Black Activism in Atlanta during the Roosevelt Era, 1932–1946." Ph.D. diss., Duke University, 1996.

Fickle, James. *The New South and the "New Competition": Trade Association Development in the Southern Pine Industry.* Urbana: University of Illinois Press, 1980.

Fickle, James, and Donald Ellis. "POWs in the Piney Woods: German Prisoners of War in the Southern Lumber Industry, 1943–1945." *Journal of Southern History* 56 (November 1990): 695–724.

Finkle, Lee. "The Conservative Aims of Black Militant Rhetoric: Black Protest during World War II." *Journal of American History* 60 (December 1973): 692–713.

Finlay, Mark. "The Industrial Utilization of Farm Products and By-Products: The USDA Regional Research Laboratories." *Agricultural History* 64 (spring 1990): 41–52.

Flynn, George. *The Mess in Washington: Manpower Mobilization in World War Two.* Westport, Conn.: Greenwood Press, 1979.

Foley, Neil. *The White Scourge: Mexicans, Blacks, and Poor Whites in Texas Cotton Culture.* Berkeley: University of California Press, 1997.

Foner, Philip, ed. *The Black Worker from the Founding of the CIO to the AFL-CIO Merger, 1936–1955.* Vol. 7 of *The Black Worker: A Documentary History from Colonial Times to the Present.* Philadelphia: Temple University Press, 1983.

———. *The Era of Post-War Prosperity and the Great Depression, 1920–1936.* Vol. 6 of *The Black Worker: A Documentary History from Colonial Times to the Present.* Philadelphia: Temple University Press, 1983.

Gamboa, Erasmo. *Mexican Labor and World War II: Braceros in the Pacific Northwest, 1942–1947.* Austin: University of Texas Press, 1990.

Garcia, Mario T. *Desert Immigrants: The Mexicans of El Paso, 1880–1920.* New Haven, Conn.: Yale University Press, 1981.

Goldfield, David. *Black, White, and Southern: Race Relations and Southern Culture, 1940 to the Present.* Baton Rouge: Louisiana State University Press, 1990.

Goldfield, Michael. "The Failure of Operation Dixie: A Critical Turning Point in American Political Development?" In *Race, Class, and Community in Southern Labor History,* edited by Gary Fink and Merl E. Reed. Tuscaloosa: University of Alabama Press, 1994. 166–89.

Granger, Lester. "Techniques in Race Relations." *Survey MidMonthly* 79 (December 1943): 323–26.

Grantham, Dewey. *The South in Modern America: A Region at Odds.* New York: Harper, 1995.

Green, George. "Labor in the Western Oil Industry." *Journal of the West* (1986): 14–19.

Gregory, James. *American Exodus: The Dust Bowl Migration and Okie Culture in California.* Oxford: Oxford University Press, 1989.

Griffith, Barbara. *The Crisis of American Labor: Operation Dixie and the Defeat of the CIO.* Philadelphia: Temple University Press, 1988.

Grubbs, Donald. *Cry from the Cotton: The Southern Tenant Farmers' Union and the New Deal.* Chapel Hill: University of North Carolina Press, 1971.

———. "The Story of Florida's Migrant Farm Workers." *Florida Historical Quarterly* 40 (October 1961): 103–22.

Hahamovitch, Cindy. *The Fruits of Their Labor: Atlantic Coast Farm Workers and the Making of Migrant Poverty, 1870–1945.* Chapel Hill: University of North Carolina Press, 1997.

———. "Standing Idly By: 'Organized' Farmworkers in South Florida during the Depression and World War II." *Southern Labor in Transition, 1940–1995,* edited by Robert H. Zieger. Knoxville: University of Tennessee Press, 1997. 15–36.

Halpern, Rick. *The CIO and the Limits of Labor-based Civil Rights Activism: The Case of Louisiana's Sugar Workers, 1947–1966.* In *Southern Labor in Transition, 1940–1995,* edited by Robert Zieger. Knoxville: University of Tennessee Press, 1997. 86–112.

———. "Interracial Unionism in the Southwest: Fort Worth's Packinghouse Workers, 1937–1954." In *Organized Labor in the Twentieth-Century South,* edited by Robert H. Zieger. Knoxville: University of Tennessee Press, 1991. 158–82.

Halpern, Rick, and Roger Horowitz. *Meatpackers: An Oral History of Black Packinghouse Workers and Their Struggle for Racial and Economic Equality.* New York: Monthly Review Press, 1999.

Hill, Patricia Evridge. *Dallas: The Making of a Modern City.* Austin: University of Texas Press, 1996.

Himes, Chester. *If He Hollers Let Him Go.* New York: Signet, 1971; originally published 1945.

Honey, Michael. *Black Workers Remember: An Oral History of Segregation, Unionism, and the Freedom Struggle.* Berkeley: University of California Press, 1999.

———. *Southern Labor and Black Civil Rights: Organizing Workers in Memphis.* Urbana: University of Illinois Press, 1993.

Horowitz, Roger. *"Negro and White, Unite and Fight": A Social History of Industrial Unionism in Meatpacking, 1930–1990.* Urbana: University of Illinois Press, 1990.

Interstate Migration Hearings before the Select Committee to Investigate the Interstate Migration of Destitute Citizens, Part 2. Washington, D.C.: U.S. Government Printing Office, 1941.

Jensen, Vernon. *Lumber and Labor.* New York: Farrar and Rinehart, 1945.

Johnson, Charles S. *The Negro War Worker in San Francisco: A Local Self-Survey* (May 1944).

Johnson, Marilynn. *The Second Gold Rush: Oakland and the East Bay in World War II.* Berkeley: University of California Press, 1993.

Jones, Jacqueline. *The Dispossessed: America's Underclasses from the Civil War to the Present.* New York: Basic Books, 1992.

Kersten, Andrew. *Race, Jobs, and the War: The FEPC in the Midwest, 1941–1946.* Urbana: University of Illinois Press, 2000.

Kirby, Jack Temple. *Rural Worlds Lost: The American South, 1920–1960.* Baton Rouge: Louisiana State University Press, 1987.

Korstad, Robert, and Nelson Lichtenstein. "Opportunities Found and Lost: Labor, Radicals, and the Early Civil Rights Movement." *Journal of American History* 75 (December 1988): 786–811.

Kraus, Henry. *In the City Was a Garden: A Housing Project Chronicle.* New York: Renaissance Press, 1951.

Kryder, Daniel. *Divided Arsenal: Race and the American State during World War Two.* Cambridge: University of Cambridge Press, 2000.

Lange, Dorthea, and Paul Schuster Taylor. *An American Exodus: A Record of Human Erosion.* New York: Reynal and Hitchcock, 1939.

LaSeur, Geta. *Not All Okies Are White: The Lives of Black Cotton Pickers in Arizona.* Columbia: University of Missouri Press, 2000.

Lemann, Nicholas. *The Promised Land: The Great Black Migration and How It Changed America.* New York: Vintage Press, 1991.

Lemke-Santangelo, Gretchen. *Abiding Courage: African American Migrant Women in the East Bay Community.* Chapel Hill: University of North Carolina Press, 1996.

Letwin, Daniel. *The Challenge of Interracial Unionism: Alabama Coal Miners, 1878–1921.* Chapel Hill: University of North Carolina Press, 1998.

Lichtenstein, Alex. "'Scientific Unionism' and the 'Negro Question': Communists and the Transport Workers Union in Miami, 1944–1949." In *Southern Labor in Transition, 1940–1995,* edited by Robert Zieger. Knoxville: University of Tennessee Press, 1997. 58–85.

Lichtenstein, Nelson. *Labor's War at Home: The CIO in World War II.* Cambridge: Cambridge University Press, 1982.

Lotchin, Roger, ed. *The Martial Metropolis: U.S. Cities in War and Peace.* New York: Praeger Publishers, 1984.

Mack-Forlist, Daniel, and Arthur Newman. *The Conversion of Shipbuilding from Military to Civilian Markets.* New York: Praeger Publishers, 1970.

Maney, Patrick. "Hale Boggs, Organized Labor, and the Politics of Race in South Louisiana." In *Southern Labor in Transition, 1940–1955,* edited by Robert Zieger. Knoxville: University of Tennessee Press, 1997. 230–50.

Marshall, Ray. *Labor in the South.* Cambridge, Mass.: Harvard University Press, 1967.

———. *The Negro and Organized Labor.* New York: John Wiley and Sons, 1965.

McCain, Johnny. "Texas and the Mexican Labor Question, 1942–1947." *Southwestern Historical Quarterly* 75 (July 1981): 45–64.

McClane, Debra A. "The Radford Ordnance Works: War and Rural Transformation, 1940–1995." Paper presented at the Second Wave: Southern Industrialization, 1940–1970 Conference, Georgia Tech, Atlanta, June 5, 1998. <www.gatech.edu/hts/cssi/2ndwave>.

McMillen, Neil. *Dark Journey: Black Mississippians in the Age of Jim Crow.* Urbana: University of Illinois Press, 1990.

———. "Fighting for What We Didn't Have: How Mississippi's Black Veterans Remember World War II." In *Remaking Dixie: The Impact of World War II on the American South,* edited by Neil McMillen. Jackson: University of Mississippi Press, 1997. 93–110.

———, ed. *Remaking Dixie: The Impact of World War II on the American South.* Jackson: University of Mississippi Press, 1997.

McWilliams, Carey. "Critical Summary." *Journal of Educational Sociology* 19, no. 3 (November 1945): 187–97.

———. "Mexicans to Michigan." *Common Ground* 2 (autumn 1941): 5–18.

Meier, August, and Elliot Rudwick. *Black Detroit and the Rise of the UAW*. New York, 1979.

———. *From Plantation to Ghetto*. New York: Hill and Wang, 1976.

Mertz, Paul. *New Deal Policy and Southern Rural Poverty*. Baton Rouge: Louisiana State University Press, 1978.

Meyer, Agnes. *Journey through Chaos*. New York: Harcourt Brace and Company, 1944.

Migratory Labor in American Agriculture: Report of the President's Commission on Migratory Labor. Washington, D.C., 1951.

Milkman, Ruth. *Gender at Work: The Dynamics of Job Segregation by Sex during World War II*. Urbana: University of Illinois Press, 1987.

Mitchell, C. Bradford. *Every Kind of Shipwork: A History of Todd Shipyards Corporation, 1916–1981*. New York: Todd Shipyards Corporation, 1981.

Montejano, David. *Anglos and Mexicans in the Making of Texas, 1836–1986*. Austin: University of Texas Press, 1987.

Mooney, Patrick. *Farmers and Farm Workers' Movements*. New York: Twayne, 1995.

Moore, Jesse Thomas, Jr. *A Search for Equality: The National Urban League*. University Park: Pennsylvania State University Press, 1981.

Moore, John Hammond. "No Room, No Rice, No Grits: Charleston's 'Time of Trouble.'" *South Atlantic Quarterly* (winter 1986): 23–50.

Morgan, Carl C., Jr. "Craig Air Force Base: Its Effect on Selma, 1940–1977." *Alabama Review* (April 1989): 83–96.

Morgan, James. *Rising in the West: The True Story of an "Okie" Family in Search of the American Dream*. New York: Vintage Books, 1992.

Nash, Gerald. *The American West Transformed: The Impact of the Second World War*. Lincoln: University of Nebraska Press, 1985.

Nelson, Bruce. "'CIO Meant One Thing for the Whites and Another Thing for Us': Steelworkers and Civil Rights, 1936–1974." In *Southern Labor in Transition, 1940–1995*, edited by Robert Zieger. Knoxville: University of Tennessee Press, 1997. 113–45.

———. "Class and Race in the Crescent City: The ILWU, from San Francisco to New Orleans." In *The CIO's Left Led Unions*, edited by Steve Rosswurm. Rutgers: Rutgers University Press, 1992. 19–45.

———. "Organized Labor and the Struggle for Black Equality during World War II." *Journal of American History* (December 1993): 952–88.

Nelson, Lawrence. *King Cotton's Advocate: Oscar G. Johnston and the New Deal*. Knoxville: University of Tennessee Press, 1999.

Northrup, Herbert. *Organized Labor and the Negro*. New York: Harper, 1944.

Obadele-Starks, Ernest. "Black Labor, the Black Middle Class, and Organized Protest along the Upper Texas Gulf Coast, 1883–1945." *Southwestern Historical Quarterly* 103, no. 1 (July 1999): 53–65.

———. *Black Unionism in the Industrial South*. College Station: Texas A&M University Press, 2000.

Percy, William Alexander. *Lanterns on the Levee: Recollections of a Planter's Son*. Baton Rouge: Louisiana State University Press, 1941.

Pfeffer, Paula F. *A. Philip Randolph: Pioneer of the Civil Rights Movement*. Baton Rouge: Louisiana State University Press, 1990.

Phillips, Kimberly L. *Alabama North: African-American Migrants, Community, and Working-Class Activism in Cleveland, 1915–1945*. Urbana: University of Illinois Press, 1999.

Pratt, Joseph A. *The Growth of a Refining Region*. Greenwich, Conn.: JAI Press, 1980.

Raper, Arthur, and Ira De A. Reid. *Sharecroppers All*. Chapel Hill: University of North Carolina Press, 1941.

Reddick, L. D. "The New Race Relations Frontier." *Journal of Educational Sociology* 19, no. 3 (November 1945): 129–45.

Reed, Merl. "Black Workers, Defense Industries, and Federal Agencies in Pennsylvania, 1941–1945." *Labor History* 27 (summer 1986): 356–84.

———. "The FEPC and Federal Agencies in the South." *Journal of Negro History* (winter 1980): 43–56.

———. "The FEPC, the Black Worker, and the Southern Shipyards." *South Atlantic Quarterly* (autumn 1975): 446–67.

———. *Seedtime for the Modern Civil Rights Movement: The President's Committee on Fair Employment Practice, 1941–1946*. Baton Rouge: Louisiana State University Press, 1991.

Romo, Ricardo. *East Los Angeles: History of a Barrio*. Austin: University of Texas Press, 1983.

Ross, B. Joyce. "Mary McLeod Bethune and the National Youth Administration: A Case Study of Power Relationships in the Black Cabinet of Franklin D. Roosevelt." *Journal of Negro History* 60 (January 1975): 1–28.

Saville, R. J. "Economics of Southern Agricultural Labor." *Southwestern Social Science Quarterly* 20 (September 1939): 175–92.

Schmidt, William T. "The Impact of Camp Shelby in World War II on Hattiesburg, Mississippi." *Journal of Mississippi History* (February 1977): 41–51.

Schulman, Bruce. *From Cotton Belt to Sunbelt: Federal Policy, Economic Development, and the Transformation of the South, 1938–1980*. New York: Oxford University Press, 1991.

Schwartz, Harvey. *The March Inland: Origins of the ILWU Warehouse Division*. Los Angeles: University of California, Los Angeles, Institute of Industrial Relations, 1978.

Scruggs, Otey. "The Bracero Program under the Farm Security Administration, 1942–1943." *Labor History* 3 (spring 1962): 149–68.

Seavoy, Ronald. *The American Peasantry: Southern Agricultural Labor and Its Legacy, 1850–1995: A Study in Political Economy*. Westport, Conn.: Greenwood Press, 1998.

Shenk, Gerald. "Race, Manhood, and Manpower: Mobilizing Rural Georgia for World War I." *Georgia Historical Quarterly* 81 (fall 1997): 622–62.

Shindo, Charles. *Dust Bowl Migrants in the American Imagination.* Lawrence: University of Kansas Press, 1997.

Sides, Josh A. "Working Away: African American Migration and Community in Los Angeles from the Great Depression to 1954." Ph.D. diss., University of California, Los Angeles, 1999.

Sitkoff, Harvard. "African American Militancy in the World War II South: Another Perspective." In *Remaking Dixie: The Impact of World War II on the American South,* edited by Neil McMillen. Jackson: University of Mississippi Press, 1997. 70–92.

Smith, Calvin. *War and Wartime Changes: The Transformation of Arkansas.* Fayetteville: University of Arkansas Press, 1986.

Sosna, Morton. "More Important Than the Civil War? The Impact of World War II on the South." In *Perspectives on the American South: An Annual Review of American Society, Politics, and Culture,* edited by James Cobb and Charles Wilson. Vol. 4. New York: Gordon and Breach Science Publishers, 1987. 145–62.

Spickard, Paul R. "Work and Hope: African American Women in Southern California during World War II." *Journal of the West* (July 1993): 70–79.

Spinney, Robert G. "Municipal Government in Nashville, Tennessee, 1938–1951: World War II and the Growth of the Public Sector." *Journal of Southern History* 61 (February 1995): 77–112.

Stein, Judith. "History of an Idea." *Nation,* December 14, 1998, 12–17.

———. "Southern Workers in National Unions: Birmingham Steelworkers, 1936–1951." In *Organized Labor in the Twentieth-Century South,* edited by Robert Zieger. Knoxville: University of Tennessee Press, 1991. 183–222.

Strahan, Jerry E. *Andrew Jackson Higgins and the Boats That Won World War II.* Baton Rouge: Louisiana State University Press, 1994.

Strickland, Arvarh E. "Remembering Hattiesburg: Growing up Black in Wartime Mississippi." In *Remaking Dixie: The Impact of World War II on the American South,* edited by Neil McMillen. Jackson: University of Mississippi Press, 1997. 70–92.

Sullivan, Patricia. *Days of Hope: Race and Democracy in the New Deal Era.* Chapel Hill: University of North Carolina Press, 1996.

Takaki, Ronald. *Double Victory: A Multicultural History of America in World War II.* Boston: Little, Brown and Co., 2000.

Taylor, Quintard. "Blacks and Asians in a White City: Japanese Americans and African Americans in Seattle, 1890–1940." *Western Historical Quarterly* 22 (November 1991): 401–29.

———. *The Forging of a Black Community: Seattle's Central District from 1870 through the Civil Rights Era.* Seattle: University of Washington Press, 1994.

———. *In Search of the Racial Frontier: African Americans in the American West, 1528–1990.* New York: W. W. Norton, 1998.

Thomas, Mary Martha. "Rosie the Riveter." *Alabama Review* (July 1986): 196–212.

Tindall, George. *The Emergence of the New South, 1913–1945.* Baton Rouge: Louisiana State University Press, 1967.

Valdes, Dennis Nodin. *Al Norte: Agricultural Workers in the Great Lakes Region, 1917–1970.* Austin: University of Texas Press, 1991.

Vander Meulen, Jacob. "Warplanes, Labor, and the International Association of Machinists in Nashville, 1939–1945." In *Southern Labor in Transition, 1940–1995*, edited by Robert Zieger. Knoxville: University of Tennessee Press, 1997. 37–57.

Volanto, Keith. "Burying White Gold: The AAA Cotton Plow-up Campaign in Texas." *Southwestern Historical Quarterly* 103, no. 3 (January 2000): 327–55.

Weaver, Robert. *Negro Labor: A National Problem*. New York: Harcourt Brace and Company, 1946.

Weber, Devra. *Dark Sweat, White Gold: California Farm Workers, Cotton, and the New Deal*. Berkeley: University of California Press, 1994.

Weiss, Nancy. *The National Urban League, 1910–1940*. Oxford: Oxford University Press, 1974.

Wells, David Lee. "The ILWU in New Orleans: CIO Radicalism in the Crescent City, 1937–1957." Master's thesis, Baylor University, 1979.

Whayne, Jeannie. *New Plantation South: Land, Labor, and Federal Favor in Twentieth-Century Arkansas*. Charlottesville: University of Virginia Press, 1996.

White, Walter. "What Caused the Detroit Riots?" From *What Caused the Detroit Riots?* by Walter White and Thurgood Marshall. New York, 1943. In *Afro-American History: Primary Sources*, edited by Thomas Frazier. Belmont, Calif.: Wadsworth Publishing Co., 1988. 299–300.

Woodruff, Nan E. "Mississippi Delta Planters and Debates over Mechanization, Labor, and Civil Rights in the 1940s." *Journal of Southern History* 60 (May 1994): 263–84.

———. "Pick or Fight: The Emergency Farm Labor Program in the Arkansas and Mississippi Deltas during World War II." *Agricultural History* 64 (spring 1990): 74–85.

Wright, Gavin. *Old South, New South: Revolutions in the Southern Economy since the Civil War*. New York: Basic Books, 1986.

Wynne, Lewis N., and Carolyn Barnes. "Still They Sail: Shipbuilding in Tampa during World War II." *Maritime History of the Gulf Coast* 5 (spring 1990): 179–91.

Zamora, Emilio. "The Failed Promise of Wartime Opportunity for Mexicans in the Texas Oil Industry." *Southwestern Historical Quarterly* 45 (January 1992): 232–50.

———. *The World of the Mexican Worker in Texas*. College Station: Texas A&M University Press, 1993.

Zieger, Robert. *The CIO, 1935–1955*. Chapel Hill: University of North Carolina Press, 1995.

———, ed. *Organized Labor in the Twentieth-Century South*. Knoxville: University of Tennessee Press, 1997.

———, ed. *Southern Labor in Transition, 1940–1995*. Knoxville: University of Tennessee Press, 1997.

Index

Acosta, S. P., 223 (n. 16)

Aero Reclamation Company, 119

Agee, James, 2

Agricultural Adjustment Administration (AAA), 6, 23, 24

Alabama Department of Industrial Relations, 194

Alabama Dry Dock Shipbuilding (Addsco), 143, 156; implements segregated setup, 141, 144–45, 157; organized by IUMSWA, 55, 217–18 (n. 54); resists upgrading African American workers, 56

Alabama State Employment Service (ASES), 22–23, 26, 28–29, 33, 35

Alexander, Hursel, 109

Alexander, Kelly, 51

Alexander, Lester, 212 (n. 6)

Alexander, Will, 49, 56–57,

Alexandria, Louisiana, 21, 22, 24, 80, 226 (n. 42)

All American Canal, California, 49

Amalgamated Clothing Workers Association, 44; in New Orleans, 148, 151, 185

Amarillo, 20, 224 (n. 25)

American Council on Race Relations, 177

American Federation of Labor (AFL):
African American unions within, 44, 181, 196; in Atlanta, 45, 56; in Birmingham, 33; in Dallas, 49, 53; in Houston, 49; in Little Rock, 47; in Memphis, 52–53; in Mobile, 53, 56; mobilization and, 16–17, 49, 52–56; in New Orleans, 28, 33, 47, 49, 53, 56, 58, 60–62, 148, 178; in Pascagoula, 53; in Pensacola, 53; racial conservatism of, 52–56; in Richmond, 47; sharing common goals with CIO, 37; support of a Permanent FEPC, 180; use of African American organizers, 44, 148, 151, 178, 184–85; voter registration campaign, 150, 151–52, 184–85, 192; War Manpower Commission and, 32–33, 42, 212 (n. 6)

American Legion, 165

American Shipbuilding Corporation, 28

American Sugar Cane League, 23, 79

Anderson, C. F., 26

Anderson, James, 95

Armour (Meatpacking), 195

Arnall, Ellis, 81

Asebedo, Cabelo, 82

Ashe, B. F., 75

Atchison, Topeka and Santa Fe Railroad, 212 (n. 6)

Bratt, Charles, 161
Brazier, Wesley, 176–77
Bremerton, Washington Naval Yards, 110, 114
Bridges, Harry, 111, 118, 119, 140, 148–50, 243 (n. 63)
Brooks, Will, 94
Brotherhood of Railway Carmen of America, 151, 185
Brotherhood of Sleeping Car Porters, 44, 130, 143, 152, 178; Ladies Auxiliary, 130
Brown, George, 212 (n. 6)
Brown, "Sport," 94
Brown Shipbuilding Corporation, 63–64, 212 (n. 6)
Brown v. Board of Education, 200
Brownwood, Texas, 29
Brunswick, Georgia, 144
Bureau of Agricultural Economics (BAE), 74, 167, 168, 224 (n. 25)
Bureau of Employment Security (BES), 16–17, 20, 22, 25–26, 28, 30,
Buster and Dewitt Bean Farm, Florida, 80
Butane Equipment Company, 182
Byars, S. B., 63–65
Byrd, Daniel, 81, 178–79

Cade, E. V., 94
Caldwell, Orville, 106
California Shipbuilding (Cal-Ship), 65, 101, 110, 113, 116,
Camden Naval Ordnance Works, Arkansas, 94
Camp Beauregard, Louisiana, 17
Camp Blanding, Florida, 15, 17, 29, 32
Camp Bowie, Texas, 29
Camp Claiborne, Louisiana, 17
Camp Gordon, Georgia, 47
Camp Hitchcock, Texas, 29
Camp Hood, Texas, 20

Camp Picket, Virginia, 47
Camp Robinson, Arkansas, 47
Camp Shelby, Mississippi, 17, 29, 79
Campbell Soups, 85–86
Carrol, R. C., 140
Castaneda, Carlos, 139, 157, 179–80
Cedar Grove Ordnance, 21
Centenary Church (Memphis), 183
Chandler, L. L., 77
Chapital, Arthur, 179
Chapman, Arthur, 97–98, 115
Charleston, 17, 34–35, 192
Charleston Navy Yards, 143, 145
Charlestown, Indiana, 15
Charlotte (North Carolina) NAACP, 51
Chatman, Willie, 149
Chester, Bill, 117–18, 257 (n. 67)
Chicago Mill and Lumber Company, 91
Chicago NAACP, 88
Chicago Urban League, 131–32
Chickasaw Shipbuilding Company, 53–54
Childersburg, Alabama, 17, 21, 28–29
CIO-PAC. *See* Congress of Industrial Organizations–Political Action Committee
Citizens Committee on Services to Veterans (New Orleans), 165
Civilian Conservation Corps (CCC), 11, 227 (n. 48)
Civilian Works Administration, 11
Clerc, Everett, 132–33
Clewiston, Florida, 79
Clinton Engineer Works, 91–93, 95
Coates, Peter, Jr., 87
Cobb, James, 3
Coca-Cola, 212 (n. 6)
Colar, Arthur, 147
Colgate Ajax plant (Berkeley), 120
Colored Domestic and Allied Service Association (New Orleans), 213–14 (n. 19)

Del Rey Beach, Florida, 79–80

Delta Council, 169–70

Delta Pine and Land Company, 75, 212 (n. 6)

Delta Shipbuilding (shipyards), 52, 59; AFL and, 33, 55, 217 (n. 54); African American workers protest at, 145–47; closing of, 158–59, 192; failure to upgrade African American workers, 56, 61–62, 64; imports skilled workers, 28; upgrades African American workers, 141, 144–45, 156, 190

demobilization, 154–80, 244–45 (n. 3)

Democratic Party, 180; African American patronage and, 48–49; alliances with AFL, 144; CIO-PAC and, 150; gains political strength in the West through southern migration, 105

Detroit, 99, 102, 138, 143, 155, 257 (n. 67)

Devall, B. C., 172

Dickerson, Ernest, 50

Dining Car Employees (Union), 130

Dixon, Frank, 21, 28, 30, 57, 219 (n. 65)

Dixon, Paul, 40–41, 53, 55–56, 62, 64–66, 221 (n. 92)

Donnell, William, 56

Donulut and Williams Shipbuilding Company, 53

Dorsey, William (Willie), 148–50

Double V (Double Victory) slogan, 4–5, 61

Douglas, R. T., 174

Dow (Chemical Corporation), 18

Drake, Videll, 123–24

Draper, E. S., 19

Drolet, Father Jerome, 148–49

Dunjee, Roscoe, 250 (n. 75)

Du Pont Corporation, I. E., 15, 21, 28, 69, 91–93, 193, 230 (n. 79)

Durr, Robert, 195

Edmonds, Dr. Henry L., 195

Ellender, Allen, 172

Ellinger, Don, 140–41, 147, 156–58, 178

Emergency Farm Labor Program, 81, 84

Employment Act of 1946, 162

Employment Services. *See* State Employment Services; United States Employment Service

Engleman Gardens, 83

Equal Opportunity Employment Commission (EEOC), 200

Erringer, Orville, 137

Ethridge, Mark, 188

Evans, Walker, 2

Executive Order 8802, 48

Extension Service (USDA), 8

Fair Employment Practices Committee (FEPC), 5, 34, 41, 42, 48, 49, 107–8, 144, 146, 200; in Atlanta (Region VII headquarters) 133, 178; Birmingham Hearings, 50–52, 56, 59, 67; creation of Region XIII, 239 (n. 8), 246 (n. 14); in Dallas (Region X headquarters), 129, 132–33, 137, 163; demobilization and, 156–59, 160–61; dismantling of, 177–80; historical views of, 4–6, 212 (n. 4); Houston Hearings, 178; in New Orleans (Region XIII headquarters), 178; opposition to FEPC in the South, 57, 168, 171, 179–80; permanent FEPC campaign, 162, 166, 177–80, 184; reconstituted under Executive Order 9346, 133–34; in Region XII, 112–13; strategies for upgrading African American workers in defense industries, 56–57, 140–42; transfer to WMC, 59–60, 219 (n. 72); West Coast Aircraft Hearings, 50

Fair Labor Standards Act, 7, 30, 168, 231 (n. 99)

Farley, Grady, 132–33, 187, 190

Farm Bureau, 8, 78, 172

Los Angeles, 89–90, 100–106, 111, 115–28, 155, 234 (n. 30), 237 (n. 76); housing for migrants in, 103–6; USES office in, 112, 116, 123

Los Angeles NAACP, 112, 123, 128, 161

Los Angeles Urban League, 113, 121–22, 161

Louisiana Department of Labor, 28

Louisiana Federation of Labor, 58

Louisiana Ordnance, 21

Louisiana State Employment Service (LSES), 22, 23, 24, 26, 28, 33, 62, 192, 216 (n. 43)

Louisiana State Federation of Labor, 150

Loveman, Joseph and Loeb, 195

Lowe, Charles, 53

Lower Rio Grande Valley, Texas, 80–84, 88–89

Lynch, John W., 170

MacAvoy Shipbuilding Company (shipyards), 144–45

Macon, Georgia, 80, 186, 193

Macon (Georgia) Citizens Committee, 50–51

Manhattan Project, 91–93

March on Washington Movement, 46–47, 49, 143; decline of, 180

Mare Island Naval Shipyard, 65, 100, 110, 114, 236 (n. 63)

Margolis, Ben, 113–14, 127–28

Marinship (Shipyards), 110, 111; *James v. Marinship*, 111, 113–14

Marshall, Thurgood, 221 (n. 92)

Martin Aircraft Corporation, 34, 121

Maslow, Will, 141

McAllister, Rev. C. Lopez, 90

McCain, Johnny, 227 (n. 52)

McCollum, J., 56

McCray, George, 168, 180, 181–82,

McDonald, J. E., 226 (n. 45)

McFarland, W. B., 226 (nn. 45, 47)

McGee, Willie, 116

McGehee, Arkansas, 51

McLeod Bethune, Mary, 48, 134, 215 (n. 35)

McNary Lumber Company, 94

McNutt, Paul, 32, 40–41, 65–66, 144; appointed as Chairman of WMC, 30; comments on demobilization, 155; defends WMC's record on utilizing African American workers, 248 (n. 40); dismantling of WMC and, 164; promotes postwar federalization of USES, 163

McSherry, Frank, 67, 221 (n. 92)

McWilliams, Carey, 73–74, 89–90, 103–4, 223 (n. 16)

Meadow Valley Lumber Company, 94, 231 (n. 92)

Meat and Cannery Workers Union, 86

Memphis, 86–87, 138, 183, 194, 217 (n. 44)

Memphis Urban League, 52, 184, 216–17 (n. 44)

Mertz, Paul, 221 (n. 91)

Methodist Ministerial Alliance, 214 (n. 19)

Mexican American workers, 196, 211–12 (n. 4); excluded from western defense industries, 234 (n. 33); gain leverage with labor shortage, 77; as migrant cotton workers, 76–77, 79, 83–84; recruited for defense industries, 88–89, 100; recruited for Great Lakes sugar beet industry, 73–74, 88; recruited for Mississippi cotton industry, 74; recruited for western agriculture/lumber, 82–83, 102

Mexican workers: recruited by the WMC for western defense industries, 89, 102; working in Texas agriculture, 76, 83. *See also bracero* program

Meyer, Agnes, 1, 4, 18–19, 20, 36, 197

Miami Shipbuilding Company, 55

migrant workers, 9–14, 222–23 (n. 9); African American defense workers as, 63–68, 69–96, 97–128, 232 (n. 2), 257 (n. 67); in defense industries, 15–39; exploitation of, 224 (n. 25); in Texas, 204–5 (n. 18), 222–23 (n. 9). *See also* Mexican American workers

Miles, Katie Mae, 123

Miles, Sidney, 143

Millington, Tennessee, 17

Mine, Mill and Smelter Workers, International Union of (IUMMSW), 200

Mingledorf Shipbuilding Company (shipyards), 144–45

Mississippi Delta, 174–75; attempts to prevent outmigration from, 79, 169–70, 172; defense workers recruited from, 82, 86–88, 92–93; Mexican workers recruited to, 74; peonage in, 44–45

Mitchell, Clarence, 141, 156, 180

Mitchell, H. L., 86

Mitchell, Thomas, 131

Mobile, 17, 20, 35–39, 53–55, 81, 192, 196

Mobile NAACP, 53, 56, 81

mobility (economic and geographic): for African American defense workers in the Pacific West, 97–128; for African American defense workers in the South, 40–68, 141–42, 173–77, 198–99; mobilization chaos in the South and, 34–39; for southern workers historically, 9–12; War Manpower Commission interregional recruitment and, 63–68; for workers in the Cotton Belt, 69–96, 222 (n. 3)

mobilization: changes United States national identity, 13–14; expansion of federal state and, 20–21; jobs movement as a consequence of, 26, 40–68, 107–15, 131–41; leads to struggles over control of southern workers, 2–5, 20–25, 30–34, 69–96; provides mobility/leverage for

southern workers, 2–3, 13–14, 20–25, 59–68, 69–96, 97–128, 145–48; southern communities unwilling to plan for, 17–20

Mohawk Refinery, 100

Molinarro, Nate, 137

Monday, W. J., 175

Monroe, Louisiana, 69

Montgomery, Alabama, 31

Moore Dry Docks (shipyards), 65, 115–17

Morrison, "Chep," 190

Mount Pleasant Sugar Company, 223 (n. 16)

Mount Zion Baptist Church, Fort Worth, 130

Mount Zion Baptist Church, New Orleans, 183

Myrdal, Gunnar, 155

Nashville, Chattanooga and St. Louis Railroad, 212 (n. 6)

Nation, Otis, 86

National Association for the Advancement of Colored People (NAACP), 163, 199–201; in California, 128; supports the jobs movement, 42, 44, 46, 131, 143, 152, 212 (n. 4); supports veterans' rights, 164, 177; supports voting rights, 164; voter registration campaign, 182–86

National Association of Postal Employees (NAPE), 179

National Baptist Convention, 90, 171

National Cotton Council, 75, 78

National Industrial Recovery Act (NIRA), 6, 231 (n. 99)

National Labor Relations Act (Wagner Act), 7, 30

National Labor Relations Board (NLRB), 33

National Maritime Union (NMU), 139

National Negro Business League, 43

Norfolk Navy Yards, 145
North American Aviation Corporation
(NAA): in Dallas, 27, 49, 50, 56, 59,
121, 136–37, 139, 158–59, 179; in
Kansas City, 121; in Los Angeles,
119, 121, 123–26
Northrup, Herbert, 54

Oakland, 98, 111, 115, 117, 119–20, 252
(n. 5)
O'Connell, Charles, 212 (n. 6)
O'Daniel, W. Lee "Pappy," 179
Odum, Howard, 8, 219 (n. 65)
Office of Production Management
(OPM), 16–17, 28, 33, 34, 47, 48, 49,
50, 51, 53; Minority Groups Ser-
vices, 49; Negro Employment and
Training Division, 49; Plant Site
Board Committee, 25, 27
Office of War Information, 19
Oil Workers International Union
(OWIU), 139–40, 196
O'Kelly, W. H., 132
Okies, 36
Old Regulars, 151
Orange, Texas, 18, 29, 54
Oscar Krenz Copper and Brass Works,
100
Overton, John, 172
Owens-Illinois Glass, 193
Oxley, Lieutenant Lawrence, 48, 49,
161

Pace Amendment, 81
Pacific Bridge (shipyards), 65
Packinghouse Workers Organizing
Committee (PWOC), 127, 130, 195
Pascagoula, Mississippi, 20, 54
Pearl Harbor Naval Yard, 97–98, 110
Pennsylvania shipyards (Beaumont),
217 (n. 54)
Pensacola Naval Air Station, 53
People's Defense League, 46, 55, 56;

voter registration campaign, 150–52,
183, 185
People's Independent Church of Los
Angeles, 111
Pepper, Claude, 77
Perez, Leander, 255 (n. 37)
Perrault, A. J., 53, 55–56
Perry, L. E., 82
Pfeffer, Paula F., 257 (n. 69)
Philips Petroleum, 100
Phipps, C. T. and E. B., 94
Pieper, Fred, 140, 151, 185
Pirating of Labor, 69–70, 80–83, 85,
88–89, 91–93, 230 (n. 89)
Portland, Oregon, 41, 111, 233 (n. 24);
housing discrimination, 103; reac-
tion to black migrants in, 105, 110
Port Neches, Texas, 20
Powell, Adam Clayton, 174
Prairie View A&M University, 63, 221
(n. 92)
Price, Lillian, 120
Public Law, 45, 81, 84
Pueblo Del Rio, 234 (n. 30)

Radford, Virginia, 17
Railway Shop Workers (Union), 130
Randolph, A. Philip, 44, 46, 180, 257
(n. 69)
Rankin, John, 162
Raper, Arthur, 74
Rathborne, Marvyn, 113
Ray, Edgar "Ed," 143, 188, 190
Reagor, J. R., 234 (n. 33)
Reconstruction Finance Corporation, 159
Record, Cy, 134
Red River Ordnance, 17–18, 21–22, 29
Reed, Aaron, 145
Reed, Merl, 5, 211–12 (n. 4)
Reid, Ira De A., 52, 74, 186, 250 (n. 75)
Resettlement Administration (RA),
11–12,
Rice, C. W., 46
Richmond, California, 98, 106, 113

Townsend, Willard, 166
Transport Workers Union (TWU), 148–50, 178, 185
Trice, Lowell, 87
Trimble, Ernest, 58, 219 (n. 72)
Truman, Harry, 163
Tureaud, A. P., 46
Turner, Moses, 151, 185
Tuskegee Institute, 63
Twing, W. D., 92–93
Tydings Amendment, 79
Tyler, Texas, 124

Underground Railroad (of World War II), 85–96
Unemployment Compensation (UC), 11, 25–27, 30, 194, 255 (n. 49)
Union Bag and Paper, 193
United Auto Workers (UAW), 46; in California, 118–19, 124, 125; in Detroit, 138; in the South, 138–40, 159, 193, 195
United Cannery, Agricultural, Packing and Allied Workers of America (UCAPAWA), 77–78, 139, 198, 231 (n. 98); in California, 109; in Florida, 86; lobbies for protection of farmworkers, 24
United Garment Workers Association (UGWA), 46
United Labor Council (New Orleans), 151
United Mine Workers (UMW), 183
United Packinghouse Workers of America (UPWA), 139
United Retail, Wholesale, and Department Store Employees of America (URWDSEA), 149
United States Air Force, 159
United States Army Corps of Engineers, 44–45
United States Department of Agriculture (USDA), 8, 77, 82, 166–67, 204 (n. 14)

United States Department of Justice, 81
United State Department of Labor, 48
United States Employment Service (USES): in Arkansas, 174–75; clearance of lumber workers, 69, 84, 92; in California, 112, 116, 160; discriminatory placement of workers, 32–33, 34, 40–41, 45, 160, 164, 177; in Florida, 143, 225 (n. 38); formation of, 30; in Georgia, 135, 193–94; interregional recruitment program of, 40–41, 61–68, 86–96, 223–24 (n. 20); in Louisiana, 40–41, 62, 69, 92, 94, 232 (n. 9); in Mississippi, 82, 87, 92–93; Negro placement offices, 135, 137, 188, 193–94; postwar status of, 162, 163; in Texas, 91, 93, 175, 212 (n. 92). *See also* War Manpower Commission: Statement of Availability, defined
United States Housing Authority (USHA), 19, 215 (n. 35)
United State Immigration Service, 83
United States Maritime Commission (USMC), 32, 57–58, 60
United States Office of Education, 62, 136
United States Public Health Service, 20
United States Public Housing Administration, 20
United States War Department, 135
United Steel Workers of America (USWA), 196
United Transport Service Employees (UTSE), 166,

Vahlsing Gardens, 82–83
Valentine, William, 186, 191–92
Valtair, Jackson, 129
Vance, Robert, 58–59
Vance, Rupert, 8
Vasquez, Simon, 223 (n. 16)
Veterans Administration (VA), 194

Work or Fight Laws, 62, 80–81

Works Progress Administration (WPA), 72, 165; artists' view of migrant workers, 4, 10; defense industries vocational training programs, 62, 65; exclusion of African Americans from programs, 26, 51; removal of African Americans from relief rolls, 11

World War I, 3, 20, 30, 32, 45, 53–54, 62, 79–80, 107, 161, 165

Wright, Andrew, 100

Wright, Ernest J., 46, 52, 56, 61, 146, 151, 178, 182, 183, 185, 190

Wysinger, Virginia, 120

Xavier University, 63–74, 238 (n. 3)

Yearwood, Ruby, 190

Yea Vote Committee, 122–23, 128

Young, Coleman, 257 (n. 67)

Zamora, Emilio, 211–12 (n. 4)